# NEOTESTAMENTICA ET SEMITICA

# NEOTESTAMENTICA ET SEMITICA

## STUDIES IN HONOUR OF MATTHEW BLACK

EDITED BY

E. EARLE ELLIS
MAX WILCOX

EDINBURGH: T. & T. CLARK, 38 GEORGE STREET

PRINTED IN GREAT BRITAIN BY
MORRISON AND GIBB LIMITED
FOR
T. & T. CLARK, EDINBURGH

SBN 567 02305 2

FIRST PUBLISHED 1969

# PREFACE

As former students of Principal Black it is a great pleasure to share with others of his colleagues—from different confessions and of many nationalities—in this tribute of admiration and appreciation on his sixtieth birthday. All of us, contributors and congratulants, are justly grateful to him. Not only has he enriched our knowledge by his scholarly contributions to biblical research, he has also enriched our profession by selfless and sacrificial service to his colleagues and to their common enterprises. In a remarkable way also, as his publications and *vita* testify, he has combined a superior technical scholarship with a wholehearted commitment to the witness of the Church in the modern world.

It has been thought appropriate to structure this volume in accordance with Principal Black's own special interests: New Testament interpretation, textual criticism, and Semitic backgrounds of the New Testament. We hope, thereby, in some small measure to return to him his many gifts to us.

E. EARLE ELLIS
MAX WILCOX

# A *CURRICULUM VITAE* OF MATTHEW BLACK

*Background and Education*

Born 3rd September 1908 in Kilmarnock, Ayrshire, Scotland.

1930—M.A., University of Glasgow, First Class Honours in Classics ; Second Class Honours in Mental Philosophy, 1931 (Buchanan Prize ; Caird Scholar)

1934—B.D., University of Glasgow, with distinction in Old Testament (President, Glasgow Students' Evangelical Union ; President, Trinity College Theological Society)

1937—Dr. phil., Universität Bonn (Thesis : " *Rituale Melchitarum. A Christian Palestinian-Syriac Euchologion* ")

1944—D.Litt., University of Glasgow (Thesis : " An Aramaic Approach to the Gospels and Acts ")

*Honorary Degrees*

D.D., Glasgow, 1954 ; Cambridge, 1965 ; Queen's, Ontario, 1967
D.Theol., Münster, 1960

*Professional Activities and Honours*

1935–37—Assistant to the Professor of Hebrew, University of Glasgow

1937–39—Assistant Lecturer in Semitic Languages and Literatures, University of Manchester

1939–42—Lecturer in Hebrew and Biblical Criticism, University of Aberdeen

1942–47—Area Military Chaplain and Minister of Dunbarney, Church of Scotland

1947–52—Lecturer in New Testament Language and Literature, Leeds University

1952–54—Professor of Biblical Criticism and Biblical Antiquities, University of Edinburgh

1954– —Professor of Divinity and Biblical Criticism and Principal of St Mary's College, University of St Andrews

Bruce Lecturer, Trinity College, Glasgow, 1940
Morse Lecturer, Union Theological Seminary, New York, 1956
Russell Lecturer, Auburn Theological Seminary, New York, 1956
De Hoyt Lecturer, Union Theological Seminary, New York, 1963
Thomas Burns Lecturer, University of Otago, New Zealand, 1967
Treasurer, *Studiorum Novi Testamenti Societas*, 1947–54
Editor, *New Testament Studies*, 1954–
Fellow of the British Academy, 1955
Member, Göttingen Akademie der Wissenschaften, 1957

Member (h.c.), Society of Biblical Literature, 1958
British Academy Burkitt Medal for Biblical Studies, 1962
Director and Honorary Vice-President, National Bible Society of Scotland, 1962
Dean of the Faculty of Divinity, University of St Andrews, 1963–67
Life Member (h.c.), American Bible Society, 1966
President, Society for Old Testament Studies, 1968
Moderator, Presbytery of St Andrews, 1968–69
Chairman, Leiden Peshitta Project, 1968–

# A BIBLIOGRAPHY OF THE PUBLISHED WRITINGS OF MATTHEW BLACK


1937

*Rituale Melchitarum : A Christian Palestinian Euchologion*, Inaugural-Dissertation zur Erlangung der Doktorwürde genehmigt von der Philosophischen Fakultät der Universität-Bonn, pp. 36.

1938

*Rituale Melchitarum : A Christian Palestinian Euchologion*, edited and translated, *Bonner Orientalische Studien*, Heft 22, Stuttgart, 1938, pp. 104, 3 pl.

" The Syriac Inscription of the Nestorian Monument ", *Transactions of the Glasgow University Oriental Society* 8 (1936–37), 18–25. (Publ. 1938.)

1939

" The Palestinian Syriac Gospels and the Diatessaron ", *Oriens Christianus* 36 (1939), 1–11.

" A Palestinian Syriac Palimpsest Leaf of Acts xxi (14–26) ", *BJRL* 23 (1939), 201–214.

1941

" Does an Aramaic Tradition underlie John i. 16 ? ", *JTS* 42 (1941), 69–70.

" The Aramaic of τὸν ἄρτον ἡμῶν τὸν ἐπιούσιον: Matt. vi. 11 = Luke xi. 3 ", *JTS* 42 (1941), 186–189.

1945

" The ' Fulfilment ' in the Kingdom of God ", *ExpT* 57 (1945–46), 25–26.

" A Christian Palestinian Syriac Horologion ", in *Studia Semitica et Orientalia*, Vol. 2, *Presentation Volume to William Barron Stevenson*, Glasgow University Oriental Society, Glasgow (1945), 21–36.

1946

*An Aramaic Approach to the Gospels and Acts*, Clarendon Press, Oxford, 1946, pp. vii + 250.

" The Covenant of People ", *ExpT* 57 (1945–46), 277–278.

1947

" The Cup Metaphor in Mark xiv. 36 ", *ExpT* 59 (1947–48), 195.

" The Marcan Parable of the Child in the Midst ", *ExpT* 59 (1947–48), 14–16.

" Unsolved New Testament Problems : The Problem of the Aramaic Element in the Gospels ", *ExpT* 59 (1947–48), 171–176.

1948

" Aramaic Studies and the New Testament : The Unpublished Work of the Late A. J. Wensinck ", *JTS* 49 (1948), 157–165.

" Unsolved New Testament Problems : The ' Son of Man ' in the Old Biblical Literature ", *ExpT* 60 (1948–49), 11–15.

" Unsolved New Testament Problems : The ' Son of Man ' in the Teaching of Jesus ", *ExpT* 60 (1948–49), 32–36.

1949

" The Aramaic Liturgical Poetry of the Jews ", *JTS* 50 (1949), 179–182.

" The Messiah in the Testament of Levi xviii ", *ExpT* 60 (1948–49), 321–322.

" The Messiah in the Testament of Levi xviii ", *ExpT* 61 (1949–50), 157–158.

1950

" The Aramaic Spoken by Christ and Luke xiv. 5 ", *JTS* (n.s.) 1 (1950), 60–62.

" Isaac ", *A Theological Word Book of the Bible*, edited by Alan Richardson, SCM Press, London, 1950, pp. 114–115.

" Let the Dead Bury their Dead ", *ExpT* 61 (1949–50), 219–220.

" Ministerial Training and Vocational Needs ", *ExpT* 62 (1950–51), 100–103.

" The New Testament Peshitta and its Predecessors ", *Studiorum Novi Testamenti Societas Bulletin* 1 (1950), 51–62.

1951

" The Doctrine of the Ministry ", *ExpT* 63 (1951–52), 112–116.

*From Babylon to Bethlehem : The Story of the Jews for the last five centuries before Christ*, by L. E. Browne, revised and enlarged with the assistance of Matthew Black, Heffer, Cambridge, 1951, pp. viii+106.

" The Gospel Text of Jacob of Serug ", *JTS* (n.s.) 2 (1951), 57–63.

" Rabbula of Edessa and the Peshitta ", *BJRL* 33 (1950–51), 203–210.

" The Origin of the Name Metatron ", *VT* 1 (1951), 217–219.

1952

" The Eschatology of the Similitudes of Enoch ", *JTS* (n.s.) 3 (1952), 1–10.

" The Kingdom of God has Come ", *ExpT* 63 (1951–52), 289–290.

" The Origins of English Presbyterianism ", *University of Leeds Review*, 3 (1952), 68–71.

" Zur Geschichte des syrischen Evangelientextes ", *TLZ* 77 (1952), 705–710.

1953

" The Beatitudes ", *ExpT* 64 (1952–53), 125–126.

" Servant of the Lord and Son of Man ", *SJT* 6 (1953), 1–11. (Inaugural Lecture to the Chair of Biblical Criticism and Biblical Antiquities, University of Edinburgh, delivered in the Rainy Hall, New College, 9th October 1952).

" The Text of the Peshitta Tetraeuangelium ", *Studia Paulina* (*in honorem Johannis de Zwaan Septuagenarii*), De Erven F. Bohn, Haarlem, 1953, pp. 20–27.

" Theological Conceptions in the Dead Sea Scrolls ", *Svensk Exegetisk Årsbok*, 18–19 (1953–54), 72–97. (Two lectures delivered to the Uppsala Exegetiska Sällskap on 29th September 1953.)

1954

*A Christian Palestinian Syriac Horologion* (*Berlin MS. Or. Oct.* 1019), *TSt* (n.s.) 1, University Press, Cambridge, 1954, pp. x+485+4 pl.

*An Aramaic Approach to the Gospels and Acts*, Clarendon Press, Oxford, 1954, 2nd Edition, pp. viii+304.

" The Festival of Encaenia Ecclesiae in the Ancient Church with special reference to Palestine and Syria ", *Journal of Ecclesiastical History* 5 (1954), 78–85.

Foreword, to *NTS* 1 (1954–55), 1–4.

" Important and Influential Foreign Books: Ernst Percy's *Message and Mission of Jesus* (*Die Botschaft Jesu*) ", *ExpT* 66 (1954–55), 68–71.

" The Pauline Doctrine of the Second Adam ", *SJT* 7 (1954), 170–179.

1956

" The Account of the Essenes in Hippolytus and Josephus ", *The Background of the New Testament and its Eschatology* (Studies in Honour of C. H. Dodd), edited by W. D. Davies and David Daube, Cambridge University Press, Cambridge, 1956, pp. 172–175.

1957

" Messianic Doctrine in the Qumran Scrolls ", *Studia Patristica*, vol. XI, edited by Kurt Aland and F. L. Cross, *TU* 63 (1957), 441–459. (Papers presented to the Second International Conference on Patristic Studies held at Christ Church, Oxford, 1955, Part I).

" Die Erforschung der Muttersprache Jesu " (Otto Eissfeldt zum 70. Geburtstag), *TLZ* 82 (1957), 653–668.
" The Recovery of the Language of Jesus ", *NTS* 3 (1956–57), 305–313.
" Marriage and Divorce in the New Testament ", *Reports to the General Assembly of the Church of Scotland* (1957), 843–850.

1958
" The Greek New Testament Project of the American and Associated Bible Societies ", *NTS* 4 (1957–58), 344–345.
" Thomas Walter Manson, 1893–1958 ", *Proceedings of the British Academy* 44 (1958), 325–337.

1959
" The Arrest and Trial of Jesus and the Date of the Last Supper ", *New Testament Essays: Studies in Memory of Thomas Walter Manson, 1893–1958,* edited by A. J. B. Higgins, Manchester University Press, Manchester, 1959, pp. 19–33.
" The Gospels and the Scrolls ", *Studia Evangelica, TU* 73 (1959), 565–579. (Papers presented to the International Congress on " The Four Gospels in 1957 ", held at Christ Church, Oxford, 1957.)
" The Patristic Accounts of Jewish Sectarianism ", *BJRL* 41 (1958–59), 285–303.

1960
" The Parables as Allegory ", *BJRL* 42 (1959–1960), 273–287.

1961
*The Essene Problem,* Dr Williams's Trust, London, pp. 27. (Friends of Dr Williams's Library, Fourteenth Lecture.)
*The Scrolls and Christian Origins,* Scribner, New York, and Nelson, Edinburgh (1961), pp. x, 206, 16 pl.
Sections on J. B. Lightfoot, R. H. Lightfoot, Rabula (with R. Abramowski), and C. C. Torrey (with W. Michaelis), for *RGG*³, edited by K. Galling, J. C. B. Mohr (Paul Siebeck), Tübingen, 4, 376–377; 5, 760; 6, 952.

1962
" The Interpretation of Romans viii. 28 ", *Neotestamentica et Patristica.* (Eine Freundesgabe, Herrn Professor Dr Oscar Cullmann zu seinem 60. Geburtstag überreicht.) E. J. Brill, Leiden, 1963. *Suppl. to NovT* 6, pp. 166–172.
*Peake's Commentary on the Bible,* General Editor, New Testament Editor, and Contributor. Nelson, Edinburgh (1962); article, " The Development of Judaism in the Greek and Roman Periods (*c.* 196 B.C.–A.D. 135) ", pp. 693–698.

*Studies in the Gospels and Epistles,* by T. W. Manson ; editor. Manchester University Press, Manchester, 1962.

" Theologians of our Time : Joachim Jeremias ", *ExpT* 74 (1962–63), 115–119.

Walter Bauer : Editor's Note in *NTS* 9 (1962–63), 1.

" Marriage and Divorce in the New Testament ", in *Marriage Breakdown, Divorce, Remarriage : A Christian Understanding,* Board of Christian Education of the United Church of Canada, 1962, 60–68.

1963

" Hebraisms in the New Testament " and " The Original Language of the New Testament ", in *Enciclopedia de la Biblia,* Ediciones Garriga, Barcelona, 1963.

" The Inter-Testamental Literature ", *A Companion to the Bible,* by T. W. Manson, new edition edited by H. H. Rowley. T. and T. Clark, Edinburgh, 1963, pp. 71–89.

*On Paul and John,* by T. W. Manson : editor. SCM Press, London, 1963 (Studies in Biblical Theology 38).

" The Son of Man Problem in Recent Research and Debate ", *BJRL* 45 (1962–63), 305–318. (Manson Memorial Lecture, 1962.)

1964

" Critical and Exegetical Notes on Three New Testament Texts, Hebrews xi. 11, Jude 5, James i. 27 ", in *Apophoreta : Festschrift Ernst Haenchen* (Beiheft *ZNTW*), A. Töpelmann, Berlin, pp. 39–45.

" Joachim Jeremias ", *Judentum, Urchristentum, Kirche : Festschrift fur Joachim Jeremias* (Beiheft *ZNTW*), edited by W. Eltester, A. Töpelmann, Berlin, 1964, pp. IX–XVIII.

" Theologians of our Time : Thomas Walter Manson ", *ExpT* 75 (1963–64), 208–211.

1965

" Modern English Versions of the Scriptures ", *The New Testament in Historical and Contemporary Perspective : Essays in Memory of G. H. C. Macgregor,* edited by Hugh Anderson and William Barclay, Blackwell, Oxford, 1965, pp. 83–98.

" Paul Ernst Kahle, 1875–1965 ", *Proceedings of the British Academy* 51 (1965), 485–495.

" Second Thoughts IX : The Semitic Element in the New Testament ", *ExpT* 77 (1965–66), 20–23.

" The Tradition of Hasidaean-Essene Asceticism : Its Origins and Influence ", *Aspects du Judéo-Christianisme,* Travaux du Centre d'Etudes Supérieures Spécialisé d'Histoire des Religions de Strasbourg, 1965, pp. 19–33 (Bibliothèque des Centres d'Etudes Supérieures Spécialisés, Presses Universitaires de France).

*Society for New Testament Studies Monograph Series*, University Press, Cambridge, 1965– , General Editor.

1966

*The Dead Sea Scrolls and Christian Doctrine*, Athlone Press, London, 1966, pp. 24. (The Ethel M. Wood Lecture, delivered before the University of London on 8th February 1966.)

" The Dead Sea Scrolls and Christian Doctrine ", *Christian News from Israel* 17 (1966), 27–30.

*The Greek New Testament* (joint editor with Kurt Aland, Bruce M. Metzger, and Allen Wikgren), Joint Bible Societies, Stuttgart, 1966, pp. lv+920.

*The Judaean Scrolls*, by G. R. Driver. Review article in *NTS* 13 (1966–67), 81–89.

*The Century Bible Commentary Series*, Thomas Nelson & Sons, London, 1966– , New Testament Editor.

1967

*An Aramaic Approach to the Gospels and Acts*, Clarendon Press, Oxford (1967), 3rd edition, pp. x+359.

" From Schweitzer to Bultmann : The Modern Quest of the Historical Jesus ", *McCormick Quarterly* 20 (1967), 271–283.

" Palestinian Syriac ", *An Aramaic Handbook*, edited by Franz Rosenthal. O. Harrassowitz, Weisbaden, 1967, vol. 2, i, 9–18, and 2, ii, 13–28.

1968 : In the Press.

*Apocalypsis Henochi Graeca.* Brill, Leiden. (Etudes des pseudépigraphes grecs d'Ancien Testament.)

" Biblical Languages ", *Cambridge History of the Bible. From the Beginnings to Jerome*, edited by C. F. Evans and P. R. Ackroyd.

" The Development of Aramaic Studies since the Work of Kahle ", *In Memoriam Paul Kahle*, edited by Georg Fohrer and Matthew Black, appearing as *Beiheft* to *ZATW*.

*The Scrolls and Christianity : Historical and Theological Significance* (editor and contributor). S.P.C.K., London.

" A New Look at the Bible ", *Theological Review* 1968 (Dunedin, New Zealand), 5–7.

" The Son of Man in the Gospel Tradition ", *ZNTW* 60 (1969).

" *Εφφαθά* (Mk 7 : 34) and *Δίδραχμα* (Mt 17 : 24) ". *Hommage au Béda Rigaux*, Louvain, 1969.

*Forthcoming :*

*A Commentary on the Epistle to the Romans*, The Century Bible Series.

*A Commentary on the Gospel according to St. Matthew*, Macmillan Series.

*A History of the Jewish People in the time of Jesus Christ,* by E. Schürer. New edition. Joint Editor.

*The Book of Enoch.* New edition. Joint Editor.

" The Chi-Rho Sign—Christogram or Staurogram ? " in the F. F. Bruce *Festschrift.*

# CONTENTS

## III

# LISTS OF ABBREVIATIONS

(partially applicable to the essays in German and French)

*Old Testament*

Gn = Genesis
Ex = Exodus
Lv = Leviticus
Nu = Numbers
Dt = Deuteronomy
Jos = Joshua
Jg = Judges
Ru = Ruth
1 S, 2 S = 1 and 2 Samuel
1 K, 2 K = 1 and 2 Kings
1 Ch, 2 Ch = 1 and 2 Chronicles
Ezr = Ezra
Neh = Nehemiah
Est = Esther
Job
Ps = Psalms
Pr = Proverbs
Ec = Ecclesiastes
Ca = Canticles
Is = Isaiah
Jer = Jeremiah
La = Lamentations
Ezk = Ezekiel
Dn = Daniel
Hos = Hosea
Jl = Joel
Am = Amos
Ob = Obadiah
Jon = Jonah
Mic = Micah
Nah = Nahum
Hab = Habakkuk
Zeph = Zephaniah
Hag = Haggai
Zec = Zechariah
Mal = Malachi

*Apocrypha*

1 Es, 2 Es = 1 and 2 Esdras
Ad. Est = Additions to Esther
Wis = Wisdom
Sir = Sirach or Ecclesiasticus
Bar = Baruch
Ep. Jer = Letter of Jeremiah (Bar 6)
Three = Song of the Three Children
To = Tobit
Jth = Judith
Sus = Susanna
Bel = Bel and the Dragon
Pr. Man = Prayer of Manasses
1 Mac, 2 Mac = 1 and 2 Maccabees

*New Testament*

Mt = Matthew
Mk = Mark
Lk = Luke
Jn = John
Ac = Acts
Ro = Romans
1 Co, 2 Co = 1 and 2 Corinthians
Gal = Galatians
Eph = Ephesians
Ph = Philippians
Col = Colossians
1 Th, 2 Th = 1 and 2 Thessalonians
1 Ti, 2 Ti = 1 and 2 Timothy
Tit = Titus
Phn = Philemon
He = Hebrews
Ja = James
1 P, 2 P = 1 and 2 Peter
1 Jn, 2 Jn, 3 Jn = 1, 2, and 3 John
Jd = Jude
Rev = Revelation

### *Dead Sea Scrolls*

1QIs[a] = First Isaiah Scroll
1QpHab = Habakkuk Commentary
1QS = Rule of the Community
1QSa = Rule of the Congregation
1QH = Hymns of Thanksgiving
1QM = Rule of War
CD = Damascus Document
4QpPs37 = Ps 37 Commentary
4QpIsB = Isaiah Commentary (B)
4QpNah = Nahum Commentary
4Qflor = Florilegium
4Qtest = Messianic Testimonia

### *Babylonian Talmud Tractates*

Ab. = Aboth
Bab.M. = Baba Metzia
Ber. = Berakoth
Git. = Gittin
Hag. = Hagigah
Hor. = Horayoth
Hul. = Hullin
Ker. = Kerithoth
Ket. = Kethuboth
Kid. = Kiddushin
Meg. = Megillah
M.Kat. = Moed Katan
Pes. = Pesahim
R. Hash. = Rosh Hashanah
Sanh. = Sanhedrin
Shab. = Shabbath
Sheb. = Shebuoth
Sot. = Sotah
Taan. = Taanith
Yeb. = Yebamoth
Yoma = Yoma
Zeb. = Zebahim

### *Others*

*Ant. Bibl.* = *Biblical Antiquities*
*ATR* = *Anglican Thelogical Review*
*BJRL* = *Bulletin of the John Rylands Library*
*BASOR* = *Bulletin of the American Schools of Oriental Research*
*BC* = *Beginnings of Christianity,* 5 vols, ed. Foakes Jackson and K. Lake, London, 1920–32
*BR* = *Biblical Research*
CAP = R. H. Charles, *Apocrypha and Pseudepigrapha,* 2 vols., Oxford, 1913
*CBQ* = *Catholic Biblical Quarterly*
Dion. Hal. = Dionysius of Halicarnassus
DSS = Dead Sea Scrolls
ET = English Translation
*ExpT* = *The Expository Times*
Eus = Eusebius, *The Ecclesiastical History*
*HDB* = *Hasting's Dictionary of the Bible*
*HJP* = E. Schürer, *A History of the Jewish People,* 6 vols., Edinburgh, *c.* 1890
*HTR* = *Harvard Theological Review*
*Int.* = *Interpretation*
j = Jerusalem Talmud
*JBL* = *Journal of Biblical Literature*
Jos. *Ant.* = Josephus, *The Jewish Antiquities*
Jos. *Ap.* = Josephus, *Against Apion*
Jos. *B. J.* = Josephus, *The Wars of the Jews*
*JQR* = *Jewish Quarterly Review*
*JR* = *Journal of Religion*
*JSS* = *Journal of Semitic Studies*
*JTS* = *Journal of Theological Studies*
Jub = The Book of Jubilees

LXX =Septuagint
MPG =J. P. Migne, *Patrologiae Graecae*
MPL =J. P. Migne, *Patrologiae Latinae*
MT =Masoretic Text
*NKZ* =*Neue kirchliche Zeitung*
*NovT* =*Novum Testamentum*
NT =New Testament
*NTS* =*New Testament Studies*
par. =parallel
Ps-Clem. Rec. =Pseudo-Clementine Recognitions
R =Midrash Rabbah
*RB* =*Revue biblique*
*REJ* =*Revue des études juives*
*RGG* =*Religion in Geschichte und Gegenwart*, 6 vols., ed. K. Galling, Tübingen, [3]1957–62
*RHPR* =*Revue d'histoire et de philosophie religieuses*
*RQ* =*Revue de Qumran*
*RSR* =*Recherches de science religieuse*
SBK =H. L. Strack and P. Billerbeck, *Kommentar zum Neuen Testament aus Talmud und Midrasch*, 4 vols, München, 1922–28
*SJT* =*Scottish Journal of Theology*
*ST* =*Studia Theologica*
Test. =Testaments of the Twelve Patriarchs
*TLZ* =*Theologische Literaturzeitung*
Tos =Tosephta
TR =Textus Receptus
*TSt* =*Texts and Studies*
*TU* =*Texte und Untersuchungen*
*TWNT* =*Theologisches Wörterbuch zum Neuen Testament*
*TZ* =*Theologische Zeitschrift*
*VC* =*Vigiliae Christianae*
*VD* =*Verbum Domini*
*VDBS* =*Dictionnaire de la Bible Supplément*, ed. L. Pirot, vol. 5, Paris, 1957
*VT* =*Vetus Testamentum*
WH =B. F. Westcott and F. J. A. Hort, *The New Testament in Greek*, London, 1882
*ZATW* =*Zeitschrift für die alttestamentliche Wissenschaft*
*ZNTW* =*Zeitschrift für die neutestamentliche Wissenschaft*
*ZThK* =*Zeitschrift für Theologie und Kirche*

The transliteration of Semitic scripts follows the system given in H. H. Rowley, ed., *The Old Testament and Modern Study*, Oxford, 1951, p. 13.

# I

## TITUS

C. K. Barrett

THE literary and historical problems evoked by 2 Corinthians are too well known and too complicated to be enumerated here. It will suffice to mention three outstanding questions:

(1) Can ch. 10–13 belong to the same letter as ch. 1–9? If they form part of a different letter, is this to be dated before[1] or after ch. 1–9?

(2) Do ch. 8 and 9 belong together, or are they two separate notes dealing at different times with different aspects of the collection?

(3) Is 2:14–7:4 to be regarded as a misplaced insertion which divides up a single reference (2:13; 7:5) to Paul's encounter with Titus? [2]

The present essay will not provide answers to these questions, which are in fact wider open today than a generation ago, when a fair measure of agreement seemed to have been reached, at least on the proposition that 6:14–7:1 was originally part of the "previous letter", and ch. 10–13 part of the "severe letter".[3] In all probability, the questions never will be finally settled; and we are unlikely to make much advance towards their solution by surveying them as a whole and trying to think out a comprehensive hypothesis capable of explaining everything at once. If advance is to be made at all it will be made by the pursuit, and eventual integration, of a number of details. Among such details we may count the career of Titus. "Career" is

[1] It is often thought to be, or to be part of, the "severe letter" of 2 Co 2:4; 7:8.

[2] Within this section a special problem is raised by 6:14–7:1, which some think to be part of the "previous letter" (1 Co 5:9), and others believe not to have been written by Paul.

[3] Detailed bibliography would be out of place in this essay; see W. G. Kümmel, *Introduction to the New Testament*, London, 1966, p. 205.

indeed a somewhat grand word for one of whom we know so little, but it is precisely from 2 Corinthians that we learn most about this evidently trusted helper of Paul's, and a careful tracing of his probable movements can only serve to clarify the historical background of the epistle. It may also appear that there are some passages where commonly accepted exegesis needs to be revised.

It is surprising that Titus is not mentioned in Acts. W. M. Ramsay [4] suggested the explanation that Titus was Luke's relative, whom the author named as little as himself, and for similar reasons. Perhaps a more convincing explanation is that Titus was closely bound up with Paul's collection and with Corinth, and that Luke—no doubt for the good reason that both provided insights into the life of the early church that would not have proved edifying for the church of his own day [5]—gives abridged and edited versions of them.

There are however a few passages in Acts which, for various reasons, are worthy of brief consideration. At 13 : 1 there is evidence [6] for a Latin text that ran as follows:

Erant etiam in eclesia (*sic*) prophetae et doctores Barnabas et Saulus, quibus imposuerunt manus prophetae: Symeon qui appellatus est Niger, et Lucius Cirenensis, qui manet usque adhuc et Ticius conlactaneus, qui acceperant responsum ab Spiritum sanctum (*sic*), unde dixerunt, Segregate, etc.

Zahn [7] argued that this was a pure form of the Western text, that it contained a reference to Titus, and that it could claim to be original. The text is evidently corrupt,[8] it was probably based (if Titus was in mind at all) on his connection with Antioch (deduced from Gal 2 : 1), and (so far as I know) no one has followed Zahn's suggestion. A. C. Clark,[9] adopting the Ciceronian proverb, says that "Zahn has attempted *arcem facere ex cloaca*".

[4] *St Paul the Traveller and Roman Citizen*, London, [10]1908, p. 390. See also *BC* 5, p. 490.

[5] This does not imply falsification, but a practical, pastoral intent; and Luke's knowledge was probably limited.

[6] A ninth-century Latin manuscript, *Prophetiae ex omnibus libris collectae*, in the library at St Gall (Codex 133).

[7] Zahn's views are briefly and accessibly stated in *BC* 5, pp. 492 f.

[8] Zahn supposes that *Ticius* should be *Titus*, and that between *Ticius* and *conlactaneus* the words *Antiocensis, Manaenque Herodis tetrarchae* have fallen out.

[9] *The Acts of the Apostles*, Oxford, 1933, p. 350.

At Ac 15 : 2 there is no textual evidence, even the slightest, for including Titus's name, but in view of Gal 2 : 1 there is a strong case for supposing that Titus may have been among those described as accompanying Paul and Barnabas from Antioch. This however means interpreting Acts by Galatians, and adds nothing of consequence to what will be said below on Galatians.

It was a tortuous eccentricity of criticism that identified the Silas of Acts 15 : 22 with Titus,[10] and the " suspicion " that the account in 16 : 3 of the circumcision of Timothy " is a confused and perhaps erroneous memory of the story of Titus " [11] does not afford a convincing explanation of what is certainly a puzzling narrative. At 18 : 7 the reading Titius Justus should probably be accepted : " Titus Justus " may represent an attempt to get Titus into Acts, and " Justus " the easiest way of escaping a confusion. According to a popular view,[12] it was at 20 : 2 that Paul met Titus in Macedonia ; it is worth noting that Luke shows no awareness of any such event.

We leave Acts, therefore, having learnt nothing whatever about Titus, and turn to Gal 2, which, though it does provide explicit mention of Titus, raises more difficulties than can conveniently be handled here. Titus was taken by Paul (συμπαραλαβών) to Jerusalem about sixteen years [13] after Paul's conversion. Unfortunately however we can date Paul's conversion only by identifying the events of Gal 2, and then working back sixteen years ; and the visit to Jerusalem in Gal 2 is notoriously difficult to identify with any of the visits recorded in Acts. It cannot however be earlier than the so-called " famine visit " of Ac 11, 12, which may not unreasonably be placed in about A.D. 46.[14] It may well be [15] that the Council described in Ac 15 is a doublet of this visit. If so, we may conclude that Titus had already been not less than five years in the Pauline group of missionaries when

[10] For an account of this view, and of some other curiosities, see the article on Silas by P. W. Schmiedel in *Encyclopaedia Biblica*, London, 1914, cols. 4514–4521.

[11] *BC* 4, p. 184.

[12] See below, p. 8.

[13] By the inclusive reckoning of antiquity, the " three years " of Gal 1 : 18 means probably two and a fraction, the " fourteen years " of 2 : 1, thirteen and a fraction. Adding them together we reach fifteen or sixteen years. It is possible that the fourteen of 2 : 1 includes the three of 1 : 18.

[14] See *BC* 5, pp. 452–5, 468.

[15] See *BC* 5, pp. 201–4.

Paul first reached Corinth [16]; if not, the time may possibly but not necessarily be reduced by the duration of the so-called first missionary journey (Ac 13, 14).

Much more important than these dubious considerations (since there is in any case no doubt that Titus was a trusted assistant of Paul's by the time of the Corinthian episode) are the facts, and guesses at facts, provided or suggested by the narrative in Gal 2 itself.

Titus was a Greek (*Ἕλλην*), that is, in accordance with Paul's (and others') usage,[17] a Gentile. Why did Paul take him to Jerusalem? He may have been one of the deputation appointed (according to Ac 15 : 2) by the church at Antioch—possibly the Gentile member of it; Paul may have chosen him as a second colleague along with the Jew Barnabas; Paul may even have been acting provocatively, as Luther (quoted by Schlier [18]) suggests:

> Tunc (hunc ?) enim assumpsit, ut probaret gratiam equaliter gentibus et Iudeis tam in circumcisione quam sine circumcisione sufficere.

None of these suggestions is impossible; some can be combined; the first might account for the association between Paul and Titus, but is not needed as an explanation.

What happened to Titus? The question whether or not he was circumcised is warmly disputed, and by no means settled. It turns on (a) the text of Gal 2 : 4 f.; (b) the stress laid on *ἠναγκάσθη*; and (c) the view taken of the general probabilities of the situation.

As far as (a) is concerned the question appears to be[19] whether Paul is more likely to have offended copyists by affirming in anacolouthon (*οἷς οὐδέ*) that he did not yield to false brethren, or by admitting in correct Greek that he did. It seems to be probable that he wrote the offending Greek (it is not the only place where his syntax is at fault), that he refused to yield, and that copyists mended his Greek at the expense of the sense. If other considerations seem equal it is surely decisive that the

[16] Probably in A.D. 51.; see below, p. 7.

[17] Ro 1 : 16; 2 : 9, 10; 3 : 9; 10 : 12; 1 Co 1 : 22, 24; 10 : 32; 12 : 13; Gal 3 : 28. Ro 1 : 14 and Col 3 : 11 are not so clear. See also e.g. Mk 7 : 26; Ac 14 : 1; 16 : 1; 18 : 4; 19 : 17; 20 : 21.

[18] H. Schlier, *Der Brief an die Galater*, Göttingen, 1949, p. 34.

[19] Notwithstanding B. W. Bacon, "The reading *οἷς οὐδέ* in Gal 2 : 5", *JBL* 42 (1923), pp. 69–80.

persons in question, to whom Paul may or may not have yielded, are described as παρείσακτοι ψευδάδελφοι, who sneaked in (παρεισῆλθον) as spies. Compromise with those who were reputed to be pillars is conceivable, though v. 11 does not suggest that it was probable ; but " I gave in to the dirty spies, in the interests of truth " is not very convincing.

The same considerations probably settle questions (b) and (c). In any case, the stressed ἠναγκάσθη (" he was not actually *forced* to be circumcised, though in fact the operation took place ") involves an artificiality of style [20] that is not Pauline. One further fact, seldom, as far as I know, observed, lends some support to this view. We know little about Titus except that he was Paul's confidential agent in the gathering of the collection for poor Jews—the saints in Jerusalem. Now it is not impossible that Paul should have employed a born Jew or a proselyte for this purpose. But we know that he was sensitive about the arrangements he had made (1 Co 16 : 1–4 ; 2 Co 8 : 20 f. ; 12 : 17 f.), and if, being himself a Jew, he was careful to have a Gentile as his colleague, this would at least make very good sense. A far less convincing suggestion, though it could be true, is that Timothy and Titus were selected as the " recipients " of the Pastoral Letters as representing the circumcised and uncircumcised wings of the church respectively.

There is thus a strong probability that Titus emerged from the Jerusalem meeting the uncircumcised Gentile he had always been, and that he would retain from this gathering a keen awareness of the peril of legalistic Judaism and of the activities of false brothers ; also that he would be aware of the quite different (even if not wholly satisfactory) attitude of the main Jerusalem apostles.

Before leaving Galatians we ought to note the suggestion that in this epistle we have words from Titus's own pen. In *ExpT* 62 (1950–51), 380 D. Warner made the suggestion that Gal 2 : 3–8 should be regarded as an interpolation. The following grounds are adduced. (1) Vv. 3–8 break the continuity of vv. 1, 2, 9, 10. (2) They reveal a different estimation of the Jerusalem apostles ; in vv. 1, 2, 9, 10 these are οἱ δοκοῦντες, οἱ δοκοῦντες στῦλοι εἶναι, whereas the writer of v. 6 does not care who they are. (3) Vv. 3–8

[20] Unless A. D. Nock (*St Paul*, London, 1938, p. 109) was right in suggesting that Titus, to keep the peace, had himself circumcised without consulting Paul, and to Paul's embarrassment.

contain words not elsewhere used by Paul (ἀναγκάζειν, διαμένειν, εἴκειν, κατασκοπεῖν, παρείσακτος). (4) The writer of vv. 3–8 uses the name Πέτρος whereas Paul elsewhere has Κηφᾶς [21]. The conclusion is that vv. 3–8 are an interpolation; that they were written by a Paulinist whose views on the Jewish apostles were more extreme than Paul's; that they were written by a Greek. It is very tentatively that Mr Warner adds the suggestion that the Greek may have been Titus.

If Gal 2 : 3–8 is indeed an interpolation its author could as well have been Titus as any other; but there is no adequate reason for not ascribing the verses to Paul. Vv. 1, 2, 9, 10 are not in fact continuous; v. 9 may begin in the middle of a sentence. The *hapax legomena* are required in the description of circumstances which Paul did not have to describe elsewhere. The use of the Greek name Πέτρος is interesting, but not in itself convincing.[22] The gospels and Acts show that it was widely current. Titus was, we may think, a witness but not the recorder of one of the turning-points of Paul's career, which was at the same time one of the most important moments in the history of the church. Part of this event was the request that Paul and his colleagues should remember the poor—essentially the Jerusalem church (Ro 15 : 26): an obligation Paul himself was eager to fulfil. His word, ἐσπούδασα, could be rendered as an English pluperfect: I had (already) shown myself eager to do this. There would then be a reference back to the alms brought by Paul and Barnabas to Jerusalem (Ac 11 : 30; 12 : 25). In this case it might be correct to render μνημονεύωμεν (v. 10), "that we should go on remembering". But these suggestions do nothing to identify the visit to Jerusalem that Paul is describing, or to define further the role of Titus. We may simply take it that Paul records a request that was addressed to a group (μνημονεύωμεν), and his own reaction to it (ἐσπούδασα), though he may well have reflected at the same time that he had begun the work of charity without being asked. This leads us to 2 Corinthians.

It will be helpful first to recall the dates of Paul's own move-

[21] Wherever Κηφᾶς occurs in this epistle (1 : 18; 2 : 9, 11, 14) the Western text has Πέτρος.

[22] See Lietzmann and Schlier, *ad loc.*, with the reference to Holl's suggestion that, for Paul, Peter was the name of the missionary, Kephas that of the Jerusalem apostolic official. Moreover, though in vv. 3, 6, 7, 8 the references to Paul in the first person singular could come from a glossator they can hardly have stood in Titus's own account.

ments in relation to Corinth, in order that those of Titus, as mentioned in 2 Corinthians, may be fitted into them.[23] On a probable view, Paul reached Corinth in the spring (say, March) of A.D. 50, and stayed there for eighteen months, that is, till about September 51. At this point, according to Ac 18 : 18, he left for Syria, but the visit was a flying one, and he was probably back in Ephesus (which he had merely touched—Ac 18 : 19 ff.—in the journey east) in late summer 52. In Ephesus he stayed two years and three months (Ac 19 : 8, 10 ; cf. 20 : 31), and it is within this period that most of the Corinthian story, as it can be reconstructed from the epistles, must be accommodated. The Pentecost Paul was anxious to keep in Jerusalem (Ac 20 : 16) will have been that of 55, and the three months he spent in Greece (*Ἑλλάς*, Ac 20 : 2f.) will have been approximately January to March 55. This period can hardly have failed to include a visit to Corinth. The Pentecost of 1 Co 16 : 8 is likely to have been that of 54 (less probably, 53), so that 1 Corinthians was probably written early[24] in 54, or possibly late in 53. What happened next ? Certainly a great deal in a short time.

There is no reference to Titus in 1 Corinthians, nor anything to suggest that he had had any contact with Corinth. We have seen reason to think that he was already at this time one of Paul's trusted colleagues, and it is very probable that if he had already visited Corinth Paul would have spoken of him—either to send his greetings to the church or to remark on his absence. Before we leave 1 Corinthians it will be worth while to note the earliest reference to the collection, with which Titus was later to be closely connected, in 1 Co 16 : 1–4. It seems that the Corinthians had heard, not directly from Paul himself but perhaps from Galatia, that a collection was being made, and had inquired what steps they ought to take. It is to be noted that the plan Paul suggests—private savings, contributed to a common fund on Paul's arrival in Corinth—does not require or even leave room for the collaboration of Titus, or of any other of Paul's

[23] I have discussed these dates in *A Commentary on the Epistle to the Romans*, London, 1957, pp. 2–5 and *A Commentary on the First Epistle to the Corinthians*, London, 1968, pp. 3 ff., 22 f., and here state the results without giving the arguments.

[24] 1 Co 5 : 7 has led some to think that Paul was writing at Passover time. This is possible, but the reference to Christ as our Passover could have been made at any season.

agents. Paul himself and the Corinthians will see to it between them.

The first appearance of Titus in 2 Corinthians is a non-appearance. In 2 : 12 Paul states that he went to Troas, and there had an excellent opportunity for evangelism. He could not however bring himself to take advantage of it because he was so perturbed by the fact that he did not find Titus, whom presumably he had expected to meet in Troas. Instead he set out for Macedonia, on the other side of the Thracian Sea. It is often supposed that this journey is to be identified with that described in Ac 20 : 1, according to which Paul left Ephesus at the end of his long ministry there and set out for Macedonia. This journey (on the scheme given above) must have taken place towards the end of 54, immediately before Paul's final visit to Corinth in the spring of 55. It should be noticed however that Acts mentions neither Troas nor Titus, and the identification is far less certain than is often thought. If we confine our attention to 2 Corinthians it appears (a) that Paul had reason to expect that he would meet Titus in Troas; (b) that Paul went into Macedonia, not to evangelize that region, or to look after his churches there, or to reach some other mission field, but simply to find Titus as soon as possible; and (c) that Titus must therefore have been at work possibly in Macedonia, or in some other region beyond, but most probably in Corinth, with an agreed return route.

Unless the route had been agreed in detail Paul's departure from Troas was rash. The most natural way from Troas to Macedonia was by ship to Neapolis, thence by road, but there was also a land route, involving the crossing only of the Hellespont. Whichever way Paul went, he risked missing Titus. If he went by land, Titus might be on the sea; if he went by sea, Titus might be on land, or in a boat that never came in sight of Paul's. It is interesting, if no more, to conjecture that the two did miss each other, and that this is why Paul (a) breaks off the narrative here and does not return to it till 7 : 5, and (b) continued to be so upset when he reached Macedonia. Alternatively, it may still have been too early for sailing so that only the land route was open and Paul could safely take it, knowing that Titus, if on the way at all, would be found there.

At 2 : 13 Paul drops the story of his Macedonian journey in search of Titus. It is resumed at 7 : 5; for it is difficult to doubt that this verse takes up the same incident. The coincidence of wording as well as thought and narrative establishes this.

| | |
|---|---|
| ἐλθών | ἐλθόντων ἡμῶν[25] |
| εἰς τὴν Τρῳάδα | εἰς Μακεδονίαν |
| οὐκ ἔσχηκα ἄνεσιν τῷ πνεύματί μου | οὐδεμίαν ἔσχηκεν ἄνεσιν ἡ σάρξ ἡμῶν[26] |

When Titus at last appeared he brought good news from Corinth. He had himself been comforted by the Corinthians' passionate attachment to and longing for Paul, and Paul was comforted by Titus's satisfaction—comforted, and perhaps, as 7 : 7 may suggest, a little surprised. Paul had expected to find comfort in Titus's arrival and presence, but in addition to these there was the good news from Corinth. Paul had written a letter[27]; it had cost him many tears, and it grieved the Corinthians when they received it, but theirs had been the right kind of penitent grief, and it had borne splendid fruit.

Paul comes back in 7 : 13 to the theme of comfort: *παρακεκλήμεθα, ἐπὶ τῇ παρακλήσει*. These words surely link the new paragraph with vv. 6 f. (*παρεκάλεσεν ἡμᾶς ὁ θεός, ἐν τῇ παρακλήσει*)—a most important observation, in view of what follows in v. 14. Paul, it seems, had boasted to Titus about the Corinthians (*ὑπὲρ ὑμῶν κεκαύχημαι*), and his boasts had been proved true by the favourable response, the recollection of which still kindled Titus's affection for the Corinthian church (v. 15). This boasting of Paul's is to be noted, because it virtually rules out the commonly accepted view that Titus had been sent to Corinth to put down a rebellion, and as the bearer of 2 Co 10–13. How could Paul possibly have boasted to Titus about the Corinthians, and at the same time put in his hand a letter containing, for example, the words, " I am afraid lest, as the serpent by his guile deceived Eve, your thoughts may be seduced from single-minded and pure faithfulness to Christ " (11 : 3) ; " I am afraid lest, when I come,

[25] The change from first person singular to first person plural does not mean that a different event is being described, but it furnishes an argument against the view that 2 : 13 and 7 : 5 were originally continuous, 2 : 14–7 : 4 being an interpolation from another letter.

[26] *πνεῦμα* and *σάρξ* are here (though not usually) almost equivalent psychological terms ; cf. 7 : 1, where the similar parallel use is often, but wrongly, taken as proof that Paul was not the author of 6 : 14–7 : 1.

[27] References to this letter, like those to Titus, have the effect of binding chapters 2 and 7 together.

I may find you not such as I wish . . . lest, when I come again, my God should humble me before you, and I should mourn for many who sinned before and did not repent of the uncleanness and fornication and wantonness they committed" (12 : 20 f.)? In these circumstances he would have warned Titus of the Corinthians' vices, not boasted of their virtues.

We conclude, accordingly, that Titus had not, on this occasion, been sent to put down rebellion, and that he carried not 2 Co 10–13 but a letter which though less drastic had nonetheless been painful both to write and to read. It was presumably directed to the incident obscurely described in 2 : 5, in which it seems that Paul had been insulted; perhaps his apostleship had been questioned.[28] Had Titus any other task to perform on this occasion? To answer this question we must continue through the epistle.

The next reference to Titus is in 8 : 6, in relation to the collection. The chapter begins with mention of the Macedonian churches: in the matter of the collection they have set a good example, which Paul presumably observed at about the same time that he eventually met Titus and heard the good news from Corinth. In these circumstances it was natural to suggest that Titus should forthwith complete (ἐπιτελέσῃ) the task that he had already set in hand (προενήρξατο). This answers the question asked at the end of the last paragraph: when Titus conveyed the "severe letter" he was also charged with the task of initiating the collection—that is, the actual gathering together of the money, which Paul in 1 Co 16 : 1–4 had said he would himself carry out when he arrived in Corinth. This is a further indication that Titus had not been sent to quell rebellion: a collecting bag is not the most tactful of instruments for such a purpose. Some exhortation follows, and in vv. 10 ff. the verbs used above with reference to Titus are used of the Corinthians (προενήρξασθε, ἐπιτελέσατε). The latter has the same time reference in each case, for it is evident that though Titus and the native Corinthians did not have identical tasks, the task of giving and the task of collecting would finish at the same time. προενάρχεσθαι, however, must have different time references, for 1 Co 16 : 1–4 shows that the Corinthians had made a beginning of sorts before

[28] It had already been questioned (e.g. 1 Co 1 : 12; 3 : 4; 4 : 9–13, 15 : 9 : 1 f.; 15 : 8), and the theme continues to play a vital part in 2 Corinthians (1 : 17, 24; 3; 4; 6 : 1–10; 10–13 *passim*).

Titus appeared on the scene.[29] This point is important because it means that ἀπὸ πέρυσι (v. 10) does not apply to Titus's visit. It is true that " last year " is a most imprecise term (especially as we do not know which reckoning Paul employed and when he thought the year ended and began), and could be applied to quite recent events ; but if applied to Titus's first visit it would make the view of events suggested here if not impossible at least very improbable.

Vv. 16 f. refer back to v. 6 (παρακαλέσαι, παράκλησιν), and may suggest Paul's relief that what might have seemed a somewhat unreasonable request (that Titus should immediately retrace his steps and return to Corinth)[30] met with a warm welcome. Titus was equally keen (τὴν αὐτὴν σπουδήν), and needed no prompting (αὐθαίρετος). συνεπέμψαμεν in vv. 18 and 22 should be taken as an epistolary aorist—" we send herewith " ; Titus and his colleagues must have been the bearers of the letter which thus commended them.[31] The two colleagues are not named. The names may have dropped out, or have seemed unnecessary, since the men in question would have the letter in their hands. The different commendations in v. 23 should be noted. Two things are said of Titus that are not said of the brothers—he is on Paul's staff (κοινωνὸς ἐμός), and he has already had contact with Corinth (εἰς ὑμᾶς συνεργός). But all are thoroughly trustworthy.

Titus is not mentioned by name in 2 Co 9, but there are a few passages in this second collection chapter that should be noted. In v. 2 Paul is boasting (cf. his earlier boasting to Titus, 7 : 14) to the Macedonians that Achaea was ready ἀπὸ πέρυσι[32] :

[29] We may find here an explanation of the puzzling οὐ μόνον τὸ ποιῆσαι ἀλλὰ καὶ τὸ θέλειν (8 : 10). At first sight this seems inverted : " not only to will but also to do " would make better sense. But all is clear if, as seems reasonable, we can take the meaning to be, " You not only began (under the guidance of Titus) to make the collection ; you had already last year, and without prompting, formed the intention of joining in the collection ".

[30] To judge from 1 Co 16 : 1–4 the collector's task ought not to have been a big one, and Titus might have shown resentment at the interruption, and at being made to travel a long way back for a duty that could be very quickly discharged.

[31] Commendatory letters play a large part in the Corinthian correspondence (e.g. 2 Co 3 : 1 f.). It was the intrusion of credible (and, in some sense, accredited) outsiders that caused most of the trouble in this church.

[32] In 8 : 10 they had *begun* last year. This does not mean that ch. 9 was written a year or so later than ch. 8, but only that to the Macedonians Paul had enthusiastically overstated the case ; hence his embarrassment (9 : 4).

this puts ch. 9 at the same date (approximately at least) as ch. 8. The tense of ἔπεμψα in v. 3 corresponds to that of συνεπέμψαμεν in 8 : 18, 22. It is possible to take it as a simple aorist of past time, and to suppose that ch. 9 was written a little later than ch. 8, but there seems to be no good reason for this nor for the view that ch. 9 was addressed not to Corinth but to Achaea in general. Paul moreover asked (παρακαλέσαι, v. 5 ; cf. 8 : 6) the brothers to go on ahead and get things ready in advance of his own arrival (ἵνα προέλθωσιν . . . καὶ προκαταρτίσωσιν) ; that is, he will follow them southward from Macedonia to Achaea and Corinth. There is nothing to suggest that his visit will be long delayed.

There is only one more reference to Titus. In 2 Co 12 : 16 ff. Paul faces what must have been as hurtful an allegation as any made against him. He has pointed out that he (unlike others who could be named) has not made himself burdensome to the Corinthians by taking pay from them. No, his enemies reply, he has not been so honest ; he has tricked his converts, and defrauded them under cover of a collection for the poor. But the charge can be repudiated. So far he himself has taken no direct part in the collection, and he can trust the behaviour and reputation of his delegates. I asked (παρεκάλεσα ; cf. 8 : 6) Titus to do the work, and I sent with him (συναπέστειλα ; cf. the synonymous συμπέμπειν in 8 : 18, 22) the brother. Their record speaks for itself. The coincidence of language is such that the identity of this visit to Corinth with that described in ch. 8 is scarcely open to question. There is only one difference ; in ch. 8 Paul sends Titus and two brothers, in ch. 12 he sends Titus and " the brother ". But in ch. 8 one brother was particularly involved from Paul's side (ὃν ἐδοκιμάσαμεν ἐν πολλοῖς πολλάκις σπουδαῖον ὄντα, 8 : 22) ; the other was χειροτονηθεὶς ὑπὸ τῶν ἐκκλησιῶν, and therefore did not need Paul's defence. Thus in ch. 12 Paul is able to look back on the visit which in ch. 8 and 9 was still in prospect, and appeal to the honourable behaviour of his representatives. It is impossible not to conclude that ch. 12 was written later than ch. 8, 9, and it is probable that ch. 12 was written later than the whole of ch. 1–9, since we have seen some reasons, and there are others, for thinking that 1–7 belong to the same date as 8, 9.

After this point in the New Testament Titus disappears from view. The epistle that claims to have been directed to him conveys no serious information about him beyond the fact that towards the end of the first century his name was remembered, with Timothy's, as that of an outstanding younger member of the Pauline circle. It may be that he spent some time in Crete; Tit 1 : 5 need not be pure fiction, though it may reflect the provenance of the epistle rather than recollections of Titus's career.

It remains only to put together as briefly as may be an outline of Paul's dealings with the church at Corinth as these appear in our sketch of Titus's work, and to bring these into relation with the literary problems of 2 Corinthians.

(1) About the beginning of A.D. 54 Paul wrote 1 Corinthians, promising that he would come to Corinth quickly (4 : 19), but not too quickly, for he would stay in Ephesus till Pentecost (16 : 8). This would bring him into the season when the seas were open, and facilitate a voyage across the Aegean that would not take long.

(2) Paul made this journey, and was surprised and hurt to encounter a personal insult (2 Co 2 : 5). For this reason he forebore to make a third visit (1 : 23), even though the business of the collection still needed to be set in hand.

(3) There was no reason why Titus should not be sent to do this work; he was authorized to begin the collection, and also carried a letter of rebuke that cost Paul many tears in the writing. This letter has been lost. Its disappearance confirms the belief that it was essentially personal, and dealt mainly, or even exclusively, with one member of the church. Of the Corinthians in general Paul could boast to Titus (2 Co 7 : 14).

(4) Paul went to Troas to meet Titus. Because he did not find him there [33] he was troubled and went on into Macedonia, where the two met. It was a joy to meet Titus again, but especially to hear how enthusiastically the Corinthians had embraced his cause.

(5) Paul, happy on the personal issue and indeed anxious that the punishment proposed for the offender should be mitigated, but not, it seems, satisfied that the Corinthians understood fully the apostolic gospel and the nature of the apostolate, sent

[33] *τῷ μὴ εὑρεῖν με Τίτον τὸν ἀδελφόν μου* (2 : 13)—not because of anxiety about affairs in Corinth. Paul may well have been anxious about Titus. If the collection had (as Paul might have expected) been completed, Titus would have been carrying a considerable sum of money, and would have been a likely prey for robbers (cf. 2 Co 11 : 26).

Titus straight back to Corinth to finish the work on the collection (which he may have interrupted because he was so pleased with the Corinthian response—though this may have been a superficial judgment) and to convey 2 Co 1–9. This was partly a commendation of the collectors (who were only now about to convey money away from Corinth), but it also contained instruction in matters the Corinthians still understood none too well.[34]

(6) Titus came back, this time with the bad news that evoked 2 Co 10–13. It is easy to understand the difference between 1–9 and 10–13, even if Titus had not to some extent misjudged the earlier situation. The agony of 10–13 is due to the fact that false apostles have entered the Corinthian church (perhaps not for the first time) and swept the Corinthians off their feet. Who conveyed 2 Co 10–13 we do not know; in view of the fact that 12 : 18 is the only reference to him, presumably not Titus. In the course of this letter Paul threatens a third visit.

(7) This visit took place, and is referred to in Ac 20 : 1. Apparently it took three months (if we can accept the figure in Acts) to deal with the trouble.[35] Ro 15 : 26 shows that Achaea did produce a contribution for the collection, but we may infer from the absence of an Achaean name in Ac 20 : 4 that the sum was not large. It may have been the false apostles who infiltrated into Corinth who awakened Paul's fears regarding the way in which his gift might be received in Jerusalem (Ro 15 : 31); the narrative in Acts suggests that his fears were not groundless, and the discreet silence of Ac 20 : 2 f. about the church in Corinth, and the reference to a plot made by the Jews, may reflect the strife that preceded Paul's success in winning the church there to his side.

[34] See note 28. Their present vigorous support of Paul probably betrayed their mistaken notion that an apostle should be a figure of imposing and aggressive dignity.

[35] It was, however, Paul, not Titus, who dealt with it. This makes better sense than the common reconstruction of the Corinthian story, according to which Paul failed to control his own church, withdrew in disorder, and left it to his junior colleague to redeem his failure.

# THE ATONEMENT—AN ADEQUATE REWARD FOR THE AKEDAH? (Ro 8 : 32)

NILS ALSTRUP DAHL

BY the Atonement I here understand the death of Jesus interpreted as a divine act of redemption, regardless of the specific terminology used by various writers. The Akedah means what in Christian tradition is called the sacrifice and in Jewish tradition the binding of Isaac (*ʿaḳēdaṯ yiṣḥāḳ*), as interpreted in the Aggadah. Similarities between the Atonement and the Akedah have long been observed. Modern discussion of the relationship between the two traditions started when Isidore Lévi in 1912 argued for the independence and priority of the Jewish lore.[1] The immediate reaction was slight, but after World War II the theme was taken up by a number of scholars, including H. J. Schoeps,[2] H. Riesenfeld,[3] and E. R. Goodenough.[4] A brilliant analysis of Akedah traditions up to the twelfth century C.E. has been presented by S. Spiegel, originally published in Hebrew and recently translated into English by Judah Goldin, whose Introduction conveys important insights into the general nature of aggadic interpretation.[5] Later studies by G. Vermes[6] and R. Le Déaut[7] have concentrated upon early traditions, with special attention paid to the various versions of the Palestinian

[1] " Le sacrifice d'Isaac et la mort de Jésus." *REJ* 64 (1912), 161–85.

[2] *Paulus*, Tübingen, 1959, pp. 144–52. (ET, *Paul*, Philadelphia, 1961, pp. 141–49). Cf. *JBL* 65 (1946), 385–92.

[3] *Jésus transfiguré*, Copenhagen, 1947, pp. 86–96.

[4] *Jewish Symbols*, New York, 1954, 4, pp. 172–94; cf. 9, pp. 71–77; 12, pp. 68–71, etc.

[5] S. Spiegel, *The Last Trial*. Translated from the Hebrew, with an Introduction, by Judah Goldin, New York, 1967. The original essay appeared in *Alexander Marx Jubilee Volume*, New York, 1950.

[6] *Scripture and Tradition in Judaism*, Leiden, 1961, pp. 193–227.

[7] *La nuit pascale* (Analecta Biblica, 22), Rome, 1963, 133–208. " La présentation targumique du sacrifice d'Isaac et la soteriologie paulinienne." *Studiorum Paulinorum Congressus Internationalis Catholicus*, Rome, 1963, 2, pp. 563–74. Cf. *RSR* 49 (1961), 103–06. Cf. also F.-M. Braun, *Jean le Théologien*, 2, *Les grandes traditions d'Israel*, Paris, 1964, pp. 179–81, and R. A. Rosenberg, *JBL* 84 (1965), 374–80.

Targum. Even patristic and iconographic materials have been gathered.[8]

It may be assumed that the most relevant sources have been fairly well exhausted by these studies. Lévi's presentation has been supplemented and modified at a number of points, but his main thesis concerning the independence of the Jewish tradition has been confirmed. Reactions to the Christian doctrine of the Atonement may have stimulated the development of the Aggadah, but only as a secondary factor. Much more open is the other problem, namely, to what extent and in which ways the Akedah served as a model for early Christian understanding of the Atonement. The number of parallels would be hard to explain without the assumption of some kind of relationship, and yet the New Testament texts are elusive. The few explicit references to the sacrifice of Isaac do not deal with the Atonement,[9] and passages that deal with the Atonement may be more or less reminiscent of the Akedah but never make the allusion explicit.[10] This is the case even in Ro 8 : 32 where the formulation, " He who did not spare His own Son but gave him up for us all ", is obviously reminiscent of Gn 22, as has been recognized by exegetes from Origen onward.[11] Why did Paul use a phrase drawn from the story of Abraham's sacrifice of his son in order to speak about the death of Christ ? An answer to this question would illuminate the way in which the Atonement was first related to the Akedah. The results may remain conjectural, but an exploration is worth attempting.

In Ro 8 : 32 the allusion is unambiguous, but Paul in no way draws it to the attention of his readers. They might perfectly well understand what he had to say in this context without being aware of the biblical phraseology. In fact, a number of commentators pass it over in silence.[12] If the allusion is recognized, it may simply call for an emotional response : No gift can be greater than that of Abraham, who did not withhold his only son ! One can hardly object when C. K. Barrett notes

[8] Cf. D. Lerch, *Isaaks Opferung, christlich gedeutet,* Tübingen, 1950 ; I. Speyart van Woerden, " The Iconography of the Sacrifice of Isaac ", *VC* 15 (1961), 214–55 ; Spiegel, *Last Trial,* p. xi.

[9] Cf. Ja 2 : 21 f. ; He 11 : 17 f.; cf. 6 : 13 f.

[10] Cf. Ro 3 : 24 f. ; 4 : 25 (?) ; 8 : 32 ; 1 Co 5 : 7 (??) ; Gal 3 : 13–14 ; Eph 1 : 3+6 f. (??) ; Jn 1 : 29 ; 1 P 1 : 19 f. ; Rev 5 : 6 (??).

[11] Hom. 8, *MPG* 12, 208. Cf. Lerch and Speyart van Woerden, note 8 above.

[12] E.g., Jülicher, Lietzmann, Dodd, Schlatter, Nygren, Leenhardt.

the allusion but writes, " Paul makes no serious use of it ".[13] Adolf Jülicher even issued a warning : " The words of the poet do not provide materials for critical exercises ".[14] Yet, research starts with curiosity, and I wonder whether there might not be more behind the biblical phraseology than what is apparent in the context of Paul's letter.

The form of Ro 8 : 32 is that of a syllogism ; if the protasis is valid, the apodosis cannot but follow. Within its present context, the passage reminiscent of Abraham's sacrifice therefore functions as a warrant for the certitude of full salvation. As to its content, the passage runs parallel to Ro 5 : 8–9 and 5 : 10, where we have the more regular form for a conclusion *a fortiori*, with πολλῷ μᾶλλον.[15] The formulations are open to variation, but Paul can assume that there is agreement upon the protasis and, quite likely, that such formulations were familiar to Christians at Rome. The same holds true also for the famous *hilastērion*-passage in Ro 3 : 24–26, to which the other passages on the atonement refer back. In general, while Paul drew new and radical consequences, his basic affirmations concerning the person of Christ and the event of atonement conform to accepted statements of kerygma, creed, and liturgy.[16]

In his commentary on Romans O. Michel has argued that Ro 8 : 32a is based upon some fixed form of preaching.[17] He finds the use of first person plural to be typical for the style of confession and points to the creed-like relative clauses in v. 34 as well as to the analogous passages in Ro 4 : 25 and Jn 3 : 16. Even the linguistic form favours the assumption that Paul's formulation is based upon tradition. Whereas οὐκ ἐφείσατο corresponds to the Septuagint, τοῦ ἰδίου υἱοῦ does not, but is rather an independent rendering of the Hebrew text.[18] Paul is

[13] *A Commentary on The Epistle to the Romans*, London, 1956, p. 99, cf. p. 172.

[14] *Die Schriften des Neuen Testaments*, 2nd ed., Göttingen, 1908, 2, p. 280.

[15] On the parallelism between Ro 5 : 1–11 and Ro 8 cf. my " Two Notes on Romans 5 ", *ST* 5 (1951), 37–48. Today I would not argue so strongly that Ro 1–8 should be divided in 1–4+5–8 rather than into 1–5+6–8. The sections 5 : 1–11 and 5 : 12–21 function both as conclusions of what precedes and as introductions to what follows.

[16] Cf. e.g., R. Bultmann, *Theology of the New Testament*, New York, 1951, 1, pp. 78–86, 124–33, etc. A. M. Hunter, *Paul and his Predecessors*, 2nd ed., London, 1961.

[17] *Der Brief an die Römer* (Meyer, 10. ed.), Göttingen, 1955, p. 184.

[18] Gn 22 : 16 LXX, καὶ οὐκ ἐφείσω τοῦ υἱοῦ σου τοῦ ἀγαπητοῦ. Hebrew, *wᵉlō' ḥāśaḵtā 'eṯ binḵā 'eṯ yᵉḥiḏeḵā*

likely to have commented upon the traditional formula not only by appending the apodosis but also by adding πάντων to the current phrase ὑπὲρ ἡμῶν in the protasis. Thus he stresses a main theme of his letter, at the same time achieving a rhetorical correspondence between ὑπὲρ ἡμῶν πάντων and τὰ πάντα ἡμῖν. The latter phrase probably refers to nothing short of the eschatological inheritance promised to Abraham and his offspring.[19] Persons familiar with the Genesis texts and their early Christian interpretation may have realized that Paul's cryptic allusion indicated the possibility of scriptural backing for what he wrote.

If Paul's formulation in Ro 8 : 32a is not created *ad hoc*, it is no longer sufficient to assume a loose and not very serious use of biblical phraseology. In recent years a number of scholars, representing various schools, have proved that the New Testament use of Scripture presupposes much more conscientious exegetical work than we were formerly inclined to think.[20] The formulation in Ro 8 : 32a is likely to go back to some kind of midrashic interpretation. The exegetical pattern can hardly have been other than one of correspondence : as Abraham did not spare his son, so God did not spare His own Son. The question is how this correspondence was understood. According to a predominant, now somewhat fading, mood one would immediately think of the analogy between type and anti-type. And certainly it was possible to find a typological relationship between the " binding of Isaac " and the death of Christ.[21] But typology cannot be made the general principle of early Christian hermeneutics, and the statement in Ro 8 : 32a relates to the conduct of Abraham and not to the suffering of Isaac. It is unlikely that Abraham's act of obedience was ever considered a typological prefiguration of God's act of love.[22]

[19] τὰ πάντα is related to the cosmic outlook in Ro 8, esp. vv. 17–23 and 35–39. For the promises to Abraham, cf. Gn 12 : 7 ; 13 : 14–17 ; 22 : 17 f. ; 26 : 3–5; etc., and the interpretation implied in passages like Ro 4 : 13 ; Gal 3 : 16–18 and 4 : 7. Cf. esp. Zahn and Michel.

[20] It may here be sufficient to mention names like Dodd, Daniélou, Daube, Doeve, Stendahl, Lindars, Ellis, Vermes, Gerhardsson, and Borgen.

[21] Barnabas 7 : 3 : Melito, Paschal Homily 59 (431) ; 69 (499) ; fr. 9. Cf. J. Daniélou, *Sacramentum futuri*, Paris, 1950, pp. 97–111. Vermes, *op. cit.*, p. 220, finds that " the Akedah merely prefigures the redemption by Christ ", and Le Déaut, *Nuit Pascale*, p. 203, still tends to subsume all New Testament allusions to Gn 22 under " l'aggadah typologique propre à la perpective chrétienne ".

[22] Not even Jn 3 : 14 would be a real analogy.

The text of Gn 22 : 16–17 suggests a different type of correspondence, that of act and reward. "By myself I have sworn, says the LORD, because you have done this, and have not withheld your son, your only son, I will indeed bless you," etc. A homiletic exposition or paraphrase of this may well have been the original context of the passage now found in Ro 8 : 32a. God rewarded Abraham by a corresponding action, not sparing His own Son, but giving him up for us (i.e. the descendants of Abraham), and thus He indeed blessed Abraham and made all nations be blessed in his offspring. A homiletic interpretation of this type is not a pure construction. It is attested by Irenaeus: "For Abraham, according to his faith, followed the commandment of the Word of God, and with ready mind gave up his only and beloved son, as a sacrifice to God, in order that God might be pleased to offer His beloved and only Son for all his offspring, as a sacrifice for our salvation." [23] In the Armenian version the idea of reward is even more explicit; it speaks of Abraham as the one "who also through faith asked God that for the sake of humanity (=philanthropy?) He might reward him for his son." [24] The language used is not derived from Ro 8 : 32 and the reference to Abraham's offspring points to a Jewish-Christian origin of the paraphrase. Is it conceivable that Irenaeus cites a later version of the "Aggadah" from which already Ro 8 : 32a was drawn? [25]

The passage in Irenaeus does not provide more than late and therefore uncertain evidence in favour of a conjecture which I would have dared to venture even without it: the allusion to Gn 22 in Ro 8 : 32a is best explained on the assumption that it is derived from an exposition in which the Atonement was under-

[23] Adv. Haer. 4, 5, 4. A fragment of the Greek text is preserved: *προθύμως τὸν ἴδιον μονογενὴ καὶ ἀγαπητὸν* [+ *υἱὸν* ?] *παραχωρήσας θυσίαν τῷ θεῷ, ἵνα καὶ ὁ θεὸς εὐδοκήσῃ ὑπὲρ τοῦ σπέρματος αὐτοῦ παντὸς τὸν ἴδιον μονογενὴ καὶ ἀγαπητὸν υἱὸν θυσίαν παρασχεῖν εἰς λύτρωσιν ἡμετέραν.*

[24] "Qui et advocavit per fidem deum quoniam (*vel* ut) pro humanitate pro filio retribuit (*vel* retribueret) ipse." Latin translation by Mercier in *Irénée de Lyon, Contre les hérésies, livre IV*, ed. A. Rousseau, Paris, 1965.

[25] In fact, Irenaeus seems to draw upon old traditions. Thus, Isaac is seen as a prototype for Christians who are to carry their cross, rather than as a prefiguration of Christ. In the present context the "Word of God", whose commandment Abraham obeyed, is the pre-existent Logos, but originally it may have been God's *memra*. Elsewhere Irenaeus has certainly preserved interpretations of "presbyters" and even fragments of Hebrew-Christian midrash, cf. N. Brox, *Offenbarung, Gnosis, und gnostischer Mythos bei Irenaus von Lyon*, Salzburg/München, 1966, pp. 83, n. 103 and pp. 150–57, with literature.

stood as an " adequate reward " for the Akedah. Obviously, the adequacy should not be understood in terms of quantitative equivalence but as an exact correspondence of quality. In fact, this is how the rule " measure for measure " was applied both in Judaism and in early Christianity.[26] Some early Jewish adherent of the crucified Messiah may have taken Gn 22 to imply that God, who judges those who judge and shows mercy upon those who act with mercy, rewarded Abraham's sacrifice by offering up His own Son. If this view was actually held, it would provide a most satisfactory explanation for Paul's otherwise cryptic reference in Ro 8 : 32. Caution forbids us to postulate that Paul's statement may not be explained otherwise. The conjecture would, however, gain in probability if it can be proved: (1) that the understanding of the Atonement as a reward for the Akedah conforms to some trend in contemporary Aggadah, (2) that the hypothesis is supported rather than contradicted by other evidence in Paul's letters, and (3) that it would be in harmony with our general knowledge of pre-Pauline Jewish Christianity. In all three respects I regard the evidence as favourable to the conjecture.

## I

In Jewish traditions, Isaac was early regarded as a model for suffering martyrs,[27] but there is little, if any, evidence that he was ever seen as a prototype of the Messiah.[28] In several texts, however, God is said to remember the Akedah and therefore to rescue the descendants of Isaac on various occasions, from the Exodus to the resurrection of the dead.[29] Both the daily sacrifices in the temple and the blowing of the Shofar at Rosh

[26] Mt 7 : 1 f. ; Lk 6 : 37 f. ; Mishnah Sotah 1 : 7–9, etc. Cf., e.g., H. Ljungman, *Guds barmhärtighet och dom*, Lund, 1950, pp. 25–30.

[27] Cf. 4 Mac 7 : 14 ; 13 : 12 ; 16 : 20. Isaac's willingness is also stressed by Josephus, *Ant.* 1, 232, and Ps.-Philo, *Ant. Bibl.* 32 : 3 ; 40 : 2. Cf. Vermes, *op. cit.*, pp. 197–204. This emphasis does not diminish the role of Abraham, who is a model for the mother of the seven brothers in 4 Mac.

[28] Riesenfeld, *Jésus transfiguré*, pp. 86–96, argues to the contrary, on the basis of a very broad use of the term Messiah.

[29] The evidence is conveniently summarized by Vermes, *Scripture and Tradition*, pp. 206–08. Of special interest is an exegesis of Ps 79 : 11 (and 102 : 21) according to which the one in fetters (*'āsîr*) and close to death (*t^emûṭāh*, cf. Jastrow s.v.) is Isaac, whose children God will set free. This interpretation is presupposed already by R. Joshua (ca. 100 C.E.), who makes God speak to Isaac with the words of the psalm, Mekilta de-Rabbi Simeon on Ex 6 : 2 (ed. Hoffmann, p. 4). Cf. Pesikta 31 (or 32), ed. Buber, 200 b (in spite of Vermes, p. 207, n. 6).

ha-Shanah are said to make God recall the Akedah.[30] References in prayers offer features of special interest. The kernel of the tradition may be a simple prayer that God might remember the binding of Isaac to the benefit of Israel.[31] But in various ways this was spelt out in terms of an " adequate reward ". In the Palestinian Targums a prayer is attributed to Abraham, with the following conclusion : " I have done Thy word with joy and have effected Thy decree. And now, when his (Isaac's) children come into a time of distress (*ʿaḳtā*), remember the binding (*ʿaḳēḏāh*) of Isaac, their father, and listen to their prayer, and answer them and deliver them from all distress." [32] Here the point of correspondence is that God might listen to Israel's prayers, as Abraham listened to God's word.

A version of the Aggadah on the prayer of the Patriarch, attributed to Rabbi Johanan, includes a reference to Gn 21 : 12, " Through Isaac shall your descendants be named." When God, in spite of this promise, told Abraham to offer Isaac as a burnt offering, he could have made a retort. But he suppressed his impulse and asked God to act likewise : " Whenever Isaac's children enter into distress, and there is no one to act as their advocate, do Thou speak up as their advocate." [33] That is, as Abraham made no retort, so God should make no retort. Another variation of the motif is found in the Zikronoth, part of the additional prayer for Rosh ha-Shanah : " Consider (lit. may there appear before Thee) the binding with which Abraham our Father bound his son Isaac on the altar, suppressing his compassion in order to do Thy will. So let Thy compassion suppress Thine anger (and remove it) from us." [34] It is not necessary here to discuss the relationship between legends and liturgy or to mention all variants. What is important may best be summarized in Spiegel's statement : " It may be surmised that all these variations

[30] Vermes, *op. cit.*, pp. 208–14.

[31] Cf. Targums Lv 22 : 14; Le Déaut, *Nuit pascale*, pp. 171 f.

[32] Targum Neofiti, Gn 22 : 14. The other versions differ only on minor points; cf. Le Déaut, *op. cit.*, pp. 154, 163–69.

[33] j Taan 2 : 4, 65d, in the translation of J. Goldin, Spiegel, *Last Trial*, p. 90. Cf. the various texts treated by Spiegel on pp. 89–98. R. Johanan lived in the third century, but the contrast between Gn 21 : 12 and Gn 22 is already stressed in He 11 : 18.

[34] Text in e.g. *The Authorized Daily Prayer Book*, ed. J. H. Hertz, Rev. ed., New York, 5709/1948, p. 882. The additions in parenthesis are taken from Goldin's translation of Spiegel, *op. cit.*, p. 89. Cf. also GnR 56 : 10, translated by Goldin, p. 90.

originally had one feature in common: a parallelism between Abraham's conduct at the Akedah and the conduct expected in return from God." [35]

The parallelism is also attested outside the Akedah prayers. Already R. Benaiah, third generation Tannaite, said that at the Exodus the waters were cleft because Abraham cleaved the wood.[36] From later sources we hear similar comments: "As Abraham bound his son below, so the Holy One, blessed be He, tied the princes of the pagans above." [37] Due to Abraham's worship the descendants of Isaac were found worthy to worship at Mount Sinai and the exiles will be reassembled to worship in Jerusalem.[38] "On the third day" the dead will be raised up because of the "third day" of Father Abraham.[39] His ten trials were rewarded by the ten plagues in Egypt, and they may serve as a compensation when the ten commandments are broken.[40] The playfulness of such interpretations should not be overlooked, nor should the basic principle of "adequate reward". The same principle can also be applied to other chapters of Abraham's story, as in a homily on Gn 18 where it is explicity stated: "'And the LORD went before them by day' (Ex 13 : 21). This is to teach you that with what measure a man metes, it is meted out to him. Abraham accompanied the ministering angels . . . (Gn 18 : 16), and God accompanied his children in the wilderness. . . . (Ex 13 : 21)." A similar correspondence is found with regard to supply of water, bread, and meat, shelter, and attendance and protection.[41]

None of this material is older than Paul, but all of it illustrates a tendency, well established in the tannaitic period, to relate the history of Israel to the story of Abraham, including the Akedah, by application of the principle "measure for measure". Yet at the crucial point, Abraham's offering of his son, the principle

[35] Spiegel, *Last Trial*, p. 93.

[36] Gn 22 : 3–Ex 14 : 21. Mekilta be-Shallah 4, on Ex 14 : 15 (Lauterbach, 1, 218).

[37] R. Haninah, fourth generation Amoraim, GnR 56 : 5.

[38] Gn 22 : 5–Ex 24 : 1–Is 27 : 13. Lekah Tob, p. 98.

[39] GnR 56 : 1. Cf. Spiegel, *Last Trial*, pp. 109–16, re notes 36–39.

[40] ExR 15 : 17; 44 : 4.

[41] Mekilta Be-Shallah 1, on Ex 13 : 21 (Lauterbach 1, pp. 184 f.). The further references are to Gn 18 : 4; Nu 21 : 17; 18 : 5; Ex 16 : 4; 18 : 7; Nu 11 : 13; 18 : 4; Ps 105 : 39; 18 : 18; Ex 12 : 23. The text as a whole is inspired by Ps 105 : 39–42. For the principle of adequate retribution cf. already Wis 11 : 15 ff.; 15 : 18 ff., etc.

was not applied in non-Christian Judaism. Only an interpreter who believed the crucified Jesus to be Messiah and Son of God could dare to follow the trend consistently to its bitter end, saying that as Abraham offered up his son, so God offered up His own son for Isaac's children.

## II

Apart from Ro 8 : 32 the clearest Pauline allusion to Gn 22 is found in Gal 3 : 13–14. V. 14a, " That the blessing of Abraham might come upon the Gentiles," is a paraphrase of Gn 22 : 18, " And in your offspring shall all the nations of the earth be blessed." The expression " the blessing of Abraham " is taken from Gn 28 : 4, and " in Christ Jesus " has been substituted for " in your offspring ".[42] It is also likely that the notion of substitution in v. 13 is related to Gn 22. Here too there is a conscientious interpretation in the background. In Dt 21 : 23 it was stated that a hanged man was accursed. This might be taken to exclude faith in a crucified Messiah, but the passage could be turned into an argument in favour of the Christian faith if " a man hanging upon a tree " was combined with " a ram caught in a thicket " (Gn 22 : 13). Thus the crucified Jesus was understood to be the lamb of sacrifice provided by God. Here there is an element of typology ; but the ram, rather than Isaac, is seen as a type of Christ.

The allusions to Gn 22 in Gal 3 are all contained in vv. 13a–14. These verses must be a fragment of pre-Pauline tradition. By his comment in v. 14b Paul identifies the blessing of Abraham with the Spirit, given as a down-payment even to Gentile believers. Thus he makes the fragment bear upon the Galatian controversy, but blurs the distinction between " us ", the Israelites, and the Gentile nations. Moreover, Paul interprets redemption from the curse of the Law to imply freedom from the Law itself. But the phrase, " Christ redeemed us from the curse of the Law," by itself suggests no more than liberation from the curse inflicted by transgressions of the Law, in analogy with Dn 9 : 11. According to the pre-Pauline tradition the Messiah, through his substitutionary death upon the cross, redeemed the Israelites from the curse caused by their transgressions. As a

[42] Cf. Gal 3 : 16 and 19 ; Ac 3 : 25 f. I hope to be able to deal with Gal 3 in a forthcoming publication.

consequence of Israel 's redemption the blessing of Abraham would come upon the Gentiles in Abraham's offspring, the Messiah Jesus. The fragment must be of Jewish-Christian origin. Most likely it is derived from a " midrash " on Gn 22.

Without considering possible connections with the Akedah a number of scholars have argued that Paul makes use of traditional formulations in Ro 3 : 24–25.[43] Others have found that the passage alludes to Gn 22 : 8, " God will Himself provide the lamb for a burnt offering." [44] It is philologically possible to translate ὃν προέθετο ὁ θεὸς ἱλαστήριον as " whom God appointed (designed, purposed) to be an expiation ".[45] There is some difficulty in that we have no evidence προτίθεσθαι was ever used to render *yir'eh*, Gn 22 : 8, or the *y r'h* of 22 : 14.[46] But the twofold theory, that Paul cites a tradition of Jewish-Christian origin in which the Atonement was related to the Akedah, would help explain several features in the text of Ro 3 : 24–26. The use of the term ἱλαστήριον has its closest analogy in δία . . . τοῦ ἱλαστήριου [τοῦ] θανάτου αὐτῶν, 4 Mac 17 : 22, where the vicarious death of the Maccabean martyrs is seen as an imitation of Isaac. The blood of Isaac is mentioned in early traditions, and redemption, mostly the prototypical redemption from Egypt, is related to the Akedah.[47] The phrase ἐν Χριστῷ Ἰησοῦ may well be of pre-Pauline origin on the assumption that " in Christ Jesus " is a paraphrase of " in your offspring ", as in Gal 3 : 14a.[48]

Considerable problems have been caused by the phrase διὰ τὴν πάρεσιν τῶν προγεγονότων ἁμαρτημάτων. This has often been taken to mean God's tolerant " passing over " sins in the

[43] Cf. Bultmann, *Theology*, I, p. 46 ; E. Käsemann, *Exegetische Versuche und Besinnungen* I, Göttingen, 1960, pp. 96–100 = *ZNTW* 43 (1950/51), 150–54 ; J. Reumann, *Int.* 10 (1966), 432–52.

[44] Thus Schoeps, *Paul*, p. 146, following G. Klein, *Studien über Paulus*, Stockholm, 1918, p. 96. Cf. Le Déaut, " Présentation targumique ", 571 f.

[45] Cf. Ro 1 : 13 ; Eph 1 : 9. This interpretation has been defended quite apart from the question of allusion to Gn 22, cf. C. Bruston, *ZNTW* 7 (1906), 77. Cf. also W. H. Moulton and G. Milligan, *The Vocabulary of the Greek New Testament* London, ²1915, p. 554.

[46] But cf. the use of *'izdammen, yizdammen*, or *yibḥar*, in the Targums; Le Déaut, *Nuit Pascale*, pp. 157 f. and 171.

[47] Cf. Ps.-Philo, *Ant. Bibl.* 18 : 5, " Pro sanguine eius eligisti istos ". See also note 29 above.

[48] Thus a solution is provided for a problem felt by Reumann, *Int.* 20 (1966), 40–42. Is Gn 22 : 18 reflected also in ὁ εὐλογήσας ἡμας . . . ἐν Χριστῷ, Eph 1 : 3 (cf. 1 : 6 f.)? Cf. also the paraphrase in *Ant. Bibl.* 32 : 2, " In me adnuntiabuntur generationes ".

past, but a number of exegetes take πάρεσις as a synonym for ἄφεσις. They mostly assume that δία with accusative is in the sense of δία with genitive. Thus, the clause would state that God's righteousness was manifested through the forgiveness of past sins. The rare word πάρεσις is, however, attested to mean legal non-prosecution, dropping of a case.[49] There is no reason why it should not be used in the same sense in Ro 3 : 25. The sins were committed in the past, in the generations between Isaac and Christ. That the prosecution was dropped, however, is the negative counter-part of providing for expiation and does not refer to tolerance in the past. The following translation may be proposed : "Whom God designed to be an expiation . . . by his blood, in order to manifest His righteousness, because the prosecution of the sins committed in the past was dropped in the forebearance of God, so that His righteousness might be manifested in the present time." [50] This interpretation is favoured by the analogy with Ro 8 : 31 ff. There the allusion to the Akedah is followed by the question, "Who shall bring any charge against God's elect ? " As God, who did not spare His own Son, is the one who justifies, the case has been dropped, and there will be no prosecution. Somewhat analogous also are the Akedah prayers in which God is asked not to make any retort to the children of Isaac or not to listen to their accusers, but to speak up as their advocate.[51]

Along this line of interpretation also the meaning of the clause εἰς ἔνδειξιν τῆς δικαιοσύνης αὐτοῦ becomes clear. It does not refer to a justice that requires either punishment or expiation, or to righteousness as a gift of God, or simply to God's covenantal faithfulness.[52] The phrase is best understood in analogy with Ro 3 : 4 f, "That thou mayest be justified in Thy words," etc. Providing for an expiation, God manifested His righteousness,

[49] Dion. Hal. 7, 37. Cf. J. M. Creed, *JTS* 41 (1940), 28–30, and literature referred to in note 43 above.

[50] διὰ τὴν πάρεσιν could also be taken to indicate the *causa* finalis, "So that the prosecution . . . . could be dropped ". In the translation διὰ πίστεως has been left out as a Pauline comment. How far parts of v. 26 belonged to tradition may here remain an open question.

[51] Texts given by Spiegel, *Last Trial*, pp. 90–92, cf. n. 33 above. Cf. already Jub 18 : 12, " And the prince Mastema was put to shame ". According to *Ant. Bibl.* 32 : 1, 4 the mouths of envious angels were shut.

[52] The notion of the covenant is imported into the text of the fragment by Käsemann, *op. cit.*, n. 43 above. Cf. P. Stuhlmacher, *Gottes Gerechtigkeit bei Paulus*, Göttingen, 1965, p. 89. Apart from exegetical details, however, my results concur with Käsemann's.

i.e., He vindicated Himself as being righteous and doing what He had said.[53] This He did in spite of Israel's sins in the past, because in divine forbearance He dropped the charge against them. In the original context of the fragment it would have been clear that the manifestation of God's righteousness implied, quite especially, that He kept His oath to Abraham, Gn 22 : 16–18. Thus, the fragments of ancient tradition preserved in Ro 8 : 32, Gal 3 : 13–14, and Ro 3 : 25 f. concur not merely by using a phraseology vaguely reminiscent of the Akedah but also in interpreting the Atonement as the fulfilment of what God promised by a solemn oath to Abraham after the sacrifice of Isaac.[54]

In the Pauline Epistles all passages reminiscent of the Akedah seem to reproduce traditional phraseology.[55] Paul's own interest in the story of Abraham is focused at other points. The understanding of the Atonement as reward for the Akedah might even seem to run contrary to Paul's point of view, indeed to an extent that would exclude his incorporating fragments of a tradition that expressed this idea. Yet, on closer examination, the theory of dependence is confirmed rather than disproved. Stressing that the Atonement excludes the kauchema (of the Jews), Paul goes on to argue that not even Abraham had anything to boast of.[56] His reward was given *κατὰ χάριν* and not *κατὰ ὀφείλημα*. (It is not denied that he was rewarded!)[57] Concentrating upon interpretation of Gn 15 : 6, Paul avoids any direct reference to Gn 22, even where we might have expected one.[58] As it would not have been difficult to argue that the trial was a test of Abraham's faith, Paul may have avoided doing so for the sake of simplicity.

Paul's use of the ancient Jewish-Christian tradition implies a critical interpretation, sharply formulated in the statement,

[53] Cf. *εἰς τὸ εἶναι αὐτὸν δίκαιον* Ro 3 : 26; cf. Is 45 : 21, Neh 9 : 8; H. Ljungman, *Pistis*, Lund, 1964, pp. 37, 106, etc.

[54] Vermes, *Scripture and Tradition*, pp. 221 f., has seen that the Akedah motif was not introduced by Paul, but has not attempted to distinguish between Paul's interpretation and the inherited materials with which he worked.

[55] This would also apply to passages like Ro 4 : 25; 5 : 5–10; 1 Co 5 : 7; Eph 1 : 7; and Col 1 : 13 f. The question whether or not they contain any allusion may therefore be left open.

[56] Ro 3 : 27 (cf. 2 : 17 ff.); 4 : 1–5.

[57] Ro 4 : 4.

[58] Cf. esp. Ro 4 : 17, Abraham believed in God, " who makes the dead alive ". In Jewish tradition the second of the Eighteen Benedictions (" Who makes the dead alive ") was connected with the Akedah. Spiegel, *Last Trial*, 28–37. Cf. already He 11 : 19 and 4 Mac 7 : 19; 13 : 17; 15 : 3; 16 : 25.

"There is no distinction".[59] Yet Paul did not contradict the old tradition but incorporated it in a new context. He recognized "Jew first" to be a principle of divine economy and reckoned both "the oracles of God" and "the fathers" among the privileges granted to the Israelites.[60] Even when the order was reversed, Gentiles believing the Gospel and Jews rejecting it, Paul insisted that the Israelites were "beloved for the sake of the fathers".[61] At the end of his letter to the Romans Paul can summarize in words that fully conform to the Jewish-Christian interpretation we have been tracing, "Christ became a servant to the circumcised to show God's truthfulness, in order to confirm the promises given to the fathers, and in order that the Gentiles might glorify God for His mercy," etc.[62] Both directly and indirectly evidence from Paul's letters supports the conjecture that he was familiar with Jewish-Christian interpretation of the promises given to the fathers, especially in Gn 22 : 16–18.

## III

It has been surmised, and may today be generally accepted, that to the earliest churches in Judea the ministry, death and resurrection of Jesus were believed to bring redemption to Israel, according to the Scriptures. The effect upon the Gentile nations was considered a further consequence, an object of eschatological hope rather than of missionary efforts.[63] In this respect my tentative results simply add support to the scant evidence that this really was the case. If true, however, they would increase our knowledge at another point; there existed a specifically Jewish-Christian "doctrine of the Atonement", more explicit than has often been assumed on the basis of Acts. The death of Jesus upon the cross was interpreted as fulfilling what God had promised Abraham by oath: As Abraham had not withheld his son, so God did not spare His own Son, but gave him up for Isaac's descendants. As the sacrifice, provided by God, he expiated

[59] Ro 2 : 23, cf. vv. 29–30; 10 : 12; and also Gal 2 : 14b and the possible addition of *πάντων* in Ro 8 : 32.

[60] Ro 1 : 16; 3 : 2; 9 : 4 f.

[61] Ro 11 : 28.

[62] Ro 15 : 8 f. The phrase *ὑπὲρ ἀληθείας θεοῦ* is virtually synonymous with *εἰς ἔνδειξιν τῆς δικαιοσύνης αὐτοῦ*, as shown by 3 : 3–7.

[63] Cf., e.g., J. Munck, *Paul and the Salvation of Mankind*, Richmond, 1959 pp. 255–81; J. Jeremias, *Jesus' Promise to the Nations*, London and Naperville, 1958, pp. 55–73.

their former sins. Vicariously he was made a curse to redeem them from the curse caused by their transgressions of the Law, so that even the Gentile nations might be blessed in the offspring of Abraham, the crucified Messiah Jesus. That God in His great mercy rewarded Abraham by acting as the patriarch did at the Akedah would thus seem to be part of fairly coherent early Jewish Christian theology in which the crucifixion of Jesus was interpreted in the light of Gn 22.

The fragments surmised to be contained in Paul's letters to the Romans and the Galatians cannot belong to the very beginnings of Christian doctrine. The interpretation of Gn 22 presupposes that Jesus was not only identified as the Messiah but also predicated Son of God, in accordance with 2 S 7 : 14 and Ps 2 : 7. By way of analogy not only " offspring of David " but also " offspring " of Abraham was taken to refer to Jesus as the Messiah. Yet, the interpretation must be early, because it would seem to have been germinal to the phrase " God gave His Son," [64] and possibly to the designations of Jesus as " the only Son " and " the lamb of God ".[65]

The use of Gn 22, attested by the texts we have considered, presupposes some familiarity with aggadic traditions as well as with the biblical text.[66] But it is not possible to assume that current ideas about the vicarious suffering of Isaac were simply taken over and applied to the passion of Jesus.[67] Like the biblical story, the New Testament allusions emphasize the conduct of Abraham and the promise of God. If the motifs had been directly transferred from Isaac to Christ, one would have expected more emphasis upon the voluntary submission of the former, as in the Aggadah. In many respects it would seem better

[64] Ro 8 : 32 ; Jn 3 : 16. The phrase, " God sent His Son ", might be a variation of this ; cf. esp. Gal 4 : 3 f. Influence from Wisdom terminology is assumed by E. Schweizer, *ZNTW* 57 (1966), 194–210 ; *TWNT* 8, pp. 376 f.

[65] Cf. also " My beloved Son ", Mk 1 : 11, etc. Cf., e.g., Vermes, *Scripture and Tradition*, pp. 221–25. Due to the possibility of various connotations and biblical allusions it is hard to know the extent to which the New Testament use of terms like μονογενής, υἱὸς ἀγαπητός, and ἀμνός was originally derived from Gn 22. There is only scant evidence for the theory of Vermes, pp. 202 f., that Is 53 was related to the Akedah in pre-Christian Judaism.

[66] The fact that early traditions associate the Akedah with Passover, rather than with New Year, should be mentioned here. Cf. Spiegel, Vermes, and Le Déaut.

[67] Spiegel, *Last Trial*, pp. 81–86, 103 f., 113, etc., thinks that ancient pagan beliefs, suppressed in Judaism, continued and returned in Christianity from Paul onward.

to regard the early Christian interpretation of Gn 22 as an independent parallel rather than as derived from Jewish Akedah traditions. What the earliest Jewish Christian traditions presuppose is not so much any special features of the Aggadah as the general spiritual climate of Midrash. It cannot be characterized better than in the words of Judah Goldin: "That conviction lies at the heart of Midrash all the time: The Scriptures are not only a record of the past but a prophecy, a foreshadowing and foretelling, of what will come to pass. And if this is the case, text and personal experience are not two autonomous domains. On the contrary, they are reciprocally enlightening: even as the immediate event helps make the age-old text intelligible, so in turn the text reveals the fundamental significance of the recent event or experience." [68] Without alteration this statement might also be applied to early Christian use of Scriptures.

Early Christian use of Scriptures was not differentiated from contemporary Jewish midrash by some new hermeneutic. The methods of interpretation remained much the same, with variations in various branches both of the primitive Church and of Judaism. What caused a basic difference was new events and new experiences. For Judaism, the story of the binding of Isaac provided help in understanding that the God of the fathers allowed the sufferings and death of faithful Jews in the days of Antiochus Epiphanes and later. The same story helped followers of Jesus to overcome the scandal of the cross and to understand what had happened as an act of God's love and a manifestation of His righteousness. For centuries the interpretation of Gn 22 was a part of the controversy between Christians and Jews, and even the common use of scientific methods has not quite brought the controversy to an end. It is interesting, and may be important, to realize that the earliest Christian interpretation antedates the controversy. Not any competition, but the close correspondence between the Akedah and the Atonement was stressed, quite possibly to the extent that the redemption by Christ was seen as an adequate reward for the binding of Isaac.

[68] Spiegel, *Last Trial*, p. xvi.

# THE RELEVANCE OF THE MORAL TEACHING OF THE EARLY CHURCH *

W. D. Davies

In a study of " Ethics in the New Testament ",[1] I traced the context, centre of gravity, and dimensions of the moral teaching of the Early Church : its context in primitive Christian eschatology ; its centre of gravity in the life, death and Resurrection of Jesus of Nazareth, the Christ ; its dimensions both in its vertical concentration in Christ, the Risen Lord, and in its horizontal concern with the community. It might appear from that study that the moral teaching of the Early Church was somewhat in-grown, concerned with the Christian verities and experience and with the Christian community alone, unrelated to the larger world. Was the moral teaching of Christianity, at first, that of a ghetto, just as so much Protestant morality has historically been " ghetto morality " ? As we shall see later, the answer to this question is exceedingly difficult. In this essay, I shall address myself to the question whether the moral teaching of the Early Church was pertinent to the larger world of the first century and whether it remains relevant to that of the twentieth. It is a question which, despite his immersion in the minutiae of technical Biblical studies, has always concerned my friend, Matthew Black, and this treatment, inadequate as it is, may serve not only to indicate my debt and gratitude to him, but also to salute him, not so much as a scholar of a vast erudition—the other contributors will liberally do this—but as a concerned Christian and *pastor pastorum*.

But before I do so, it is well to recognize a familiar and not altogether irrelevant fact. In much of the New Testament and of the practice of the Early Church there is no clear indication of the relevance of the early Christian moral teaching to society

* This is one lecture in the series of *Haskell Lectures* which, along with Dean Krister Stendahl, I delivered at Oberlin College, Oberlin, Ohio in March, 1968. The first of my lectures, which is presupposed in the present one, was entitled, " The Moral Teaching of the Early Church ".

[1] See *The Interpreter's Dictionary of the Bible* (New York, 1962), E–J, pp. 167–176.

and to the world at large. It would be easy to gather from a reading of the New Testament that its moral teaching was primarily, if not entirely, designed to cultivate the garden of the Church. The fragrance of that garden was, indeed, to sweeten the wilderness of the surrounding world, and to attract men into the redeemed community, but only as an indirect consequence.[2] There is no suggestion in the New Testament that the Church should in any way instruct the world as to how to carry on its business. The secular magistrates and judges, the rulers of this world are not directly addressed as if the Church had either any right to do so or any superior wisdom to offer. There was, generally, a deep awareness of the cleavage between the Church and the world, and even of an antagonism, a necessary antagonism, between the two.[3] It was not the primary concern of the Church to influence society and culture but to be itself in its moral life, as in other respects, the People of God, in the world but not of it.

Must we then, in the light of this, give up any attempt at finding early Christian moral teaching relevant to our world? If I understand it aright, this is the thrust of some protests against the profound secularization of the Christian Faith which is now so prevalent. I may illustrate from a recent article by Paul Peachey entitled " New Ethical Possibility: The Task of Post-Christendom Ethics? "[4] According to him, the notion that Christians should make society as a whole Christian was the outcome or concomitant of a disastrous event in the history of the Church, the recognition of Christianity by Constantine as the established religion of the Empire. It was then that Christendom, as distinct from Christianity, was born. As Peachey puts it: " the ethical consequence of the Constantinian shift was the transfer of the framework of Christian ethical thought from the community of grace, the new people of God, to the larger domain of the natural performance which, paradoxically, she could not

[2] Jn 17 : 20 ff.

[3] Jn 14 : 17; 15 : 18; Ro 12 : 2; 1 Co 4 : 9 ff.; 1 Jn 2 : 15 ff.; 2 P 1 : 4. But this antagonism did not prevent Christians from participating fully in the world's work. Paul urges the Thessalonian Christians to carry on with their work, 2 Th 3 : 11 ff., etc. Erastus was the city treasurer (Ro 16 : 23). Similarly, and very significantly, the Emperor can be called God's *diakonos* and the officers of the State are *leitourgoi theou* (Ro 13 : 4, 6).

[4] See *New Theology No.* 3, edited by M. E. Marty and Dean G. Peerman, New York, 1966. The secularisation is best illustrated in Harvey Cox, *The Secular City*, New York, 1965; revised ed., 1966.

postulate for her own members . . . [the Churches after Constantine] while failing in their internal ethical discourse, enlisting the legislature and police power of civil government to demand of the whole society levels of performance not yet implicit in their own life." [5] Peachey pleads that the Church should give up the idea that it can create a Christendom, that is, a Christian civilization, as generations of Christians have understood such a phrase, and concentrate on the cultivation of its own garden. History has disowned the idea that world society can be made more Christian : let us abandon it. The task of the Church is itself to be the church before it seeks to direct the world. Before it can or should address the world let it be true to itself. Peachey quotes with approval the words of Walter Hobhouse :

> " the Church of the future is destined more and more to a condition of things somewhat like that which prevailed in the Ante-Nicene Church : that is to say, that instead of pretending to be co-extensive with the world, it will accept a position involving a more conscious antagonism with the world, and will, in return, regain to some measure its former coherence." [6]

Few who are familiar with certain pietistic and nonconformist traditions will find such a view strange. There have always been in the Church monastaries, conventicles, sects, groups. The most recent expression of this view in British life is that of T. S. Eliot in his well-known essay *The Idea of a Christian Society* (New York, 1940), in which he argues for what he calls a clerisy or Christian community. He writes : " We need therefore what I have called " the Community of Christians ", by which I mean, not local groups and not the Church in any of its senses, unless we call it ' the Church within the Church ' . . . These will be consciously and thoughtfully practising Christians especially those of intellectual and spiritual superiority." [7] And yet before we accept this view, attractive as at first sight it might seem, and while, indeed, we might not only agree but insist that the first call upon the Church is to be the Church, we must ask whether it does justice to what was implicit, if not made explicit, in the New Testament. Before we concede that the Early

[5] See pp. 112–13.

[6] p. iii. The quotation is from Walter Hobhouse, *The Church and the World in Idea and History*, London, 1910, pp. ix f.

[7] *op. cit.*, pp. 34, 43. Has Eliot merely substituted intellectual pride for the pietistic self-righteousness of so many sects?

Church was turned in upon itself and not directly concerned with the structures of this world, let us consider certain aspects of its thinking.

Two aspects of early Christian thought have been claimed to justify the view that the early Christian moral teaching had relevance to the world. They centre on two points, first, eschatology, and second, creation.

First, it has been claimed that the eschatological ideas of the Early Church have a direct bearing on the political realities of society as a whole. Two scholars in the Anglo-Saxon world have made this view familiar—the late G. H. C. Macgregor,[8] and Amos N. Wilder. In a now famous article in the *Festschrift in Honour of C. H. Dodd,*[9] Wilder made the attempt to find a basis for what he called " a kerygmatic social ethic and an aggressive social action " in Paul's view of the conflict between God, Christ, the Church and the evil, unseen forces, the demonic principalities and powers, the rulers of this world, about which we read in his epistles and also especially, in Colossians and Ephesians. These demonic powers are not simply mythological beings. For the Early Church they represented the structural elements of unregenerate society, the false authorities, or rather tyrannies, of culture and power. Early Christians spoke of principalities and powers just as Negroes today speak of the white-power structure, that is, as social and political realities to be opposed.

For the Early Church the might of these demonic powers had been confronted in a set-encounter with Christ. During his ministry of exorcism, and especially in his death, He had overcome them. The demonic in the world and in society had been subdued. But it had not been completely subdued. The struggle between Christ and the demonic goes on until the Parousia. In this struggle Christians are called to share. This it is that justifies social action : here is the sanction for the Social Gospel, for Christian involvement in politics. To participate in the defeat of the demonic means to be pitted against all the evil structures, customs and powers that exploit man.

This impressive attempt to find the relevance of the Christian way in its eschatology, that is, more particularly, in its under-

[8] See G. H. C. Macgregor, " The Concept of the Wrath of God in the New Testament ", *NTS* 7 (1961), 103 ff.

[9] The article has been re-printed in the Biblical Series of *Facet Books,* Fortress Press : Philadelphia, 1966, as " Kerygma, Eschatology and Social Ethics ".

standing of the victory of Christ over the demonic, breaks down in the quagmire of what is called de-mythologization. We must ask whether the demythologization of the principalities and powers proposed by MacGregor and Wilder is justified. Did the Early Church understand them to refer to political and social realities? It may be plausibly argued in the light of Jewish concepts of the relation between angels and the States [10] that the principalities and powers and such entities in the Pauline epistles may be mythological expressions of social, political and economic actualities. But it is exceedingly difficult to ascribe them this significance in the Gospels, which belong largely to the same milieu. In the Gospels the demons attack individuals, not society as a whole. The proposed justification of social action in terms of the vanquished demons of eschatology must be regarded as dubious.

But despite this, the appeal to the moral relevance of eschatology is not to be dismissed. It was the conviction of the Early Church that it was taken up " in Christ " into the purpose of God in a cosmic drama of redemption. Part of this drama was the defeat—incipient as it might be—of the world powers by Christ. In this defeat, by participation in the redemptive activity of God in Christ, the Christian shares. It is his to *discern* the activity of the divine purpose in Christ, to prove it and to throw in his lot in decision for it. The moral activity of the Christian consists of discerning the times and the purpose of God in the times: it is his to *decide* for that purpose, to recognize the things that are different.[11] In this sense the whole of the Christian moral life is eschatologically determined. Christian morality has a cosmic awareness. In this connection, it is exceedingly important to read the New Testament, which otherwise can seem to be, and has often been treated as, a very parochial document, against its total background in the large world of the Old Testament and Jewish eschatology.

[10] See, e.g., G. B. Caird, *Principalities and Powers*, Oxford, 1956; C. D. Morrison, *The Powers That Be*, London, 1960; also D. S. Russell, *The Method and Message of Jewish Apocalyptic*, Philadelphia, 1964, pp. 244 ff.

[11] It is Oscar Cullmann who has most made this clear. See his works, *Christ and Time* (ET, 1951, [2]1962) and *Salvation in History* (ET, 1967), the section in the latter on " Salvation History and Ethics ", pp. 328 ff., is particularly relevant: " The ' conscience ' finds its function in the δοκιμάζειν performed in the context of salvation history " (p. 333). But it is important to know that it is *agapē* that governs this ' discerning '. Here I agree with V. P. Furnish, *Theology and Ethics in Paul*, Nashville, 1968, p. 235.

And, finally, the moral life of the Early Church was even more strictly governed by eschatology. It was governed by a lively hope—the hope that at the end victory was assured, the kingdoms of this world were to become the kingdoms of our God and of His Christ. Christians were called to a hope which informed all their moral life. In this way, the eschatological determined the ethical, and by its very nature the former gave to the latter a social and cosmic dimension.[12]

More directly convincing perhaps is the second factor in early Christian thought to which we now refer. It cannot be sufficiently emphasized that the moral teaching of the Early Church was conceived of in intimate relation to creation. The Church took over for its own purposes non-Christian ethical forms and norms. It borrowed from Judaism and Hellenism codes which it readily applied, without any sense of incongruity, to its own life. The parainetic sections of the Pauline epistles bear eloquent testimony to this. The moral teaching of the Early Church was not severely cut off from non-Christian moral traditions. On the contrary, it was open to and appreciative of such traditions: it used them without compunction.

There was, therefore, a point of contact of some kind between Christian teaching and morality and the non-Christian. There

[12] It is the great service of Jürgen Moltmann in his excellent and seminal study *Theology of Hope* (ET, New York, 1967) to have brought this home to us. His words on pp. 334 f. deserve quotation:

" 'Creative discipleship' cannot consist in adaptation to, or preservation of, the existing social and judicial orders, still less can it supply religious backgrounds for a given or manufactured situation. It must consist in the theoretical and practical recognition of the structure of historic process and development inherent in the situation required to be ordered, and thus of the potentialities and the future of that situation. Luther, too, could claim this creative freedom for Christian faith: '*Habito enim Christo facile condemus leges, et omnia recte judicabimus, imo novos Decalogos faciemus, sicut Paulus facit per omnes Epistolas, et Petrus, maxime Christus in Euangelio*'. ('For when we have Christ we shall easily issue laws, and judge all things aright, and even make new decalogues, as Paul does in all his epistles, and Peter, and above all Christ in the Gospel.') 'Creative discipleship' of this kind in a love which institutes community, sets things right and puts them in order, becomes eschatologically possible through the Christian hope's prospects of the future of God's kingdom and of man. It alone constitutes here in our openended history the appropriate counterpart to that which is promised and is to come. 'Presentative eschatology' means nothing else but simply 'creative expectation', hope which sets about criticizing and transforming the present because it is open towards the universal future of the kingdom." It should not be overlooked, however, that in 2 P 3:5 ff. there is revealed an eschatology which seems to be unrelieved pessimism, the world is to be destroyed not redeemed.

was not a complete break between the moral teaching of the Church and that of the Graeco-Roman world: there was some affinity between them.[13] Where did this affinity lie? It lay in the relation of the morality demanded by the New Testament to the created order which both Christians and non-Christians shared. This relationship first appears in the teaching of Jesus as it is presented in the Gospels. For Jesus there was an inward affinity between the natural and the moral, a kind of "natural law" in the "spiritual world". He found natural human relationships, at one level, a clue to the will of God. Mt 7:11 reads:

"If you then, who are evil, know how to give good gifts to your children, how much more will your Father who is in heaven give good things to those who ask him?"

In Mt 5:43 ff. the created order is clearly made a paradigm for the moral order:

"You have heard that it was said, 'You shall love your neighbor and hate your enemy'. But I say to you, Love your enemies and pray for those who persecute you, so that you may be sons of your Father who is in heaven; for he makes his sun to rise on the evil and on the good and sends rain on the just and on the unjust.

For if you love those who love you, what reward have you? Do not even the tax collectors do the same? And if you salute only your brethren, what more are you doing than others? Do not even the Gentiles do the same?

You, therefore, must be perfect, as your heavenly Father is perfect."

Quite as clearly the natural order is a paradigm for the moral in the parables of Jesus. C. H. Dodd's words deserve quotation:[14]

"There is a reason for this realism of the parables of Jesus. It arises from a conviction that there is no mere analogy, but an inward affinity, between the natural order and the spiritual order; or as we might put it in the language of the parables themselves, the Kingdom of God is intrinsically *like* the processes of nature and of the daily life of men. Jesus therefore did not feel the need of making up artificial illustrations for the truths He wanted to teach. He found them ready made by the Maker of man and

---

[13] See C. H. Dodd, *Gospel and Law*, NewYork, 1951, pp. 22 ff. I deeply regret that G. W. H. Lampe's illuminating Study, "Secularization in the New Testament and the Early Church", *Theology*, ed. G. R. Dustan, London, April 1968, Vol. LXXI, No. 574, pp. 163–75, came into my hands too late for use in the above. He rightly emphasises the continuity between the "New Creation" in Christ and the old creation. But I ascribe more significance than does he to Eschatology and its moral connotations.

[14] *The Parables of the Kingdom*, London, 1935, pp. 21 f.

nature. That human life, including the religious life, is a part of nature is distinctly stated in the well-known passage beginning ' Consider the fowls of the air . . .' (Mt vi. 26–30 ; Lk xii. 24–8). This sense of the divineness of the natural order is the major premiss of all the parables. . . ."

The appeal to the created order is found not only in the strictly didactic portions of the Gospels, as in the Sermon on the Mount and the parables, but also in discussions between Jesus and his opponents on moral questions, as in Mk 10 : 2–9, where monogamy is grounded in the creation. " But from the beginning of creation, " God made them male and female ! " (10 : 6).

What we find in Jesus re-emerges in Paul. In teaching that Christ was the agent of creation Paul, too, we cannot doubt was seeking to express that to live after Christ is the natural life. Paul was essentially a townsman and hardly does he ever turn in Wordsworth fashion to nature's " old felicities " for parable or illustration,[15] but, strange as it may seem, his doctrine of the agency of Christ in creation really sets forth the truth to which we have already referred that Jesus always assumed in his parables—that there is an inward affinity between the natural order and the spiritual order. He can, therefore, refer to what nature itself teaches in order to derive a rule for worship, as in 1 Co 11 : 13 ff., which reads :

" Judge for yourselves ; is it proper for a woman to pray to God with her head uncovered ? Does not nature itself teach you (οὐδὲ ἡ φύσις αὐτὴ διδάσκει ὑμᾶς) that for a man to wear long hair is degrading to him, but if a woman has long hair it is her pride ? For her hair is given to her for a covering."

Paul here appeals to " nature " in order to decide an issue of custom. In the same way he uses the term—a Stoic one—" what is fitting " (τὰ καθήκοντα), as in Ro 1 : 28. By this he means what is truly natural or what nature itself teaches. There is a kind of conduct which is improper because it is unnatural. This appears particularly from Paul's references to sexual perversions. Again in Ro 1, 2 the Apostle makes appeal to a " law " written on the hearts of all men in virtue of their creation, a kind of natural law, if such a loose term be permitted. We read :

[15] But W. Sanday and A. C. Headlam, *The Epistle to the Romans* (*ICC*), Edinburgh, 1896, p. 212, find that in Ro 8 : 21 ff. Paul is Franciscan in his sensitivity to nature. " He is one of those (like St Francis of Assisi) to whom it is given to read as it were the thoughts of plants and animals."

"When the Gentiles who have not the law do by nature what the law requires, they are a law to themselves, even though they do not have the law. They show that what the law requires is written on their hearts, while their conscience also bears witness and their conflicting thoughts accuse or perhaps excuse them." (Ro 2 : 14–15.)

The use of the term "conscience", although not an important concept in Paul's thought,[16] points in the same direction as we have indicated. It is further possible to argue that the Apostolic Decree in Ac 15, in which it was agreed to write to the Gentiles that they should "abstain from the pollution of idols and from unchasity and from what is strangled and from blood"—that this decree rests on the Noachian commandments,[17] that is, laws which were considered as binding upon every living soul, which had been given to Noah, the father of mankind, before the revelation of Sinai.

But more important than all these details is what we first pointed out in Paul and was surely true for the Early Church generally—that Christ, the Redeemer, and revealer of God's moral purpose, is also the agent of creation (see Jn 1 : 1 ff.; Col 1 : 15 ff.; He 1 : 1 ff.). The Redeemer is the Creator. Thus the ethics of the New Testament, rooted as it is in the gospel, is not only of relevance to the Church but also to the world in so far as it affirms and confirms what is truly natural for all men in virtue of their creation. The created order and man as part of this order is of God. It is, therefore, to be expected that the ethical tradition of mankind should be of use to the Church and often be consonant with its moral teaching. Christ, Creation and the Church and the moral dimensions of that Church and of that Creation are not in opposition. The Christian moral life is the "natural" life and the teaching of the Church does not annul the virtues of the natural man: rather it confirms them and even depends on them. In this sense, the moral teaching of the Church is continuous with the morality of those outside even while it is a mirror of what that morality should be. That there are also elements of discontinuity or peculiar emphasis in the moral teaching of the Church is to be expected.

But, it will be noted, all the above does not take us very far.

[16] On conscience see my article 'Conscience", *The Interpreter's Dictionary of the Bible*, A–D, New York, 1962.

[17] See my *Paul and Rabbinic Judaism*[2], New York, 1956, pp. 114 ff. But see also C. K. Barrett, *The Epistle to the Romans*, New York, 1957, pp. 52, 99, 111; he finds no use of the concept of the Noachian commandments in Paul.

Granted that the moral teaching of the Early Church is a mirror in which the world can judge itself, can we go further? Can we claim that the Early Church provides an ethic directly relevant to our society? Has its moral teaching not merely a judgmental role in the world, but a regulative one? Can it supply society with positive, direct guidance?

Before we attempt to answer this question, it is important to recognize two salient facts about the Early Church. First, during the period of the New Testament the Church was an insignificant minority, numerically and otherwise, in the Graeco-Roman world. Its position was such that it was unlikely to indulge in any notions that it might wield any political or social influence or power. And, secondly, although there was evident in the Early Church a real Christianizing of personal relationships within the existing order, as for example in the life of Philemon, that order was expected to end at a not too distant future. Under the influence of this expectation, it was natural that the Church, at first at least, was not concerned to change social and political structures, evil as many of them were. For example, when Paul discovered that the term "Kingdom of God" had disturbing political implications, he was led to drop it from his vocabulary.[18] Stormy petrel though he was, Paul was anxious not to be a disturbance. It was not quite clear—though perhaps probable—that Paul would advise a slave who could do so to take advantage of a chance to be free.[19] Even in 1 Co 6 : 1–11, where Paul deals with legal procedures, he gives no rules for institutional reform, even in the Church, but merely demands that at each step Christians should be aware of their role as the People of God who, in the future, but not now, were to judge the world. This appears generally to be the case. Paul does not seem to be directly concerned with political panaceas of any kind. In Ro 12 he merely warns against being conformed to the world. But in Ro 13 : 1 ff. he explicitly enjoins obedience to the worldly powers.[20] At first at least, the expectation of the End seems to have turned Christians in upon themselves despite their vast missionary activity.[21] And we may well ask again whether this means that the Early Church was in any way concerned to sustain

[18] See *Paul and Rabbinic Judaism, ad rem.*

[19] See under Χράομαι on 1 Co 7 : 21 in W. Bauer, *A Greek-English Lexicon of the New Testament*, Chicago, 1957.

[20] On this see Barrett, *op. cit.*, pp. 244 ff.

a frontal attack on the evils of society. Was it not concentrated on its own communal life, as it awaited the End, despite its deep missionary urge?

The answer is both negative and positive. There was no direct road from the Early Church to social action and what would now be called "contemporary relevance". And yet the Early Church did speak to both the Jewish and Hellenistic worlds of its day by its very existence as the People of God with all the challenges that this set before the world. And it presents the same challenges *mutatis mutandis* to our world. These challenges may be conveniently presented as follows.

The Early Church confronted the world with a body of moral teaching, a Messianic law. Elements of this teaching were, although simple in their forms, stark in their demands, inescapable in their penetration, impossible of fulfilment. Other elements were prescriptive, catechetical or parainetical. Christians brought with them to any situation which they encountered a body of moral prescriptions and insights: they were not only open, as were all others, to the demands of the "context" in which they moved, but they confronted that "context" with demands under which they knew themselves to stand. The body of moral teaching which they cherished they thought of as directed primarily to themselves: the Messianic law was for the Messianic community. But, inevitably, even when the Church was unworthy of it, this teaching of necessity challenged the world also. This is still so.

At this point the distinction between the absolute aspect—what Stendahl has called the Messianic "licence"—of the moral teaching of early Christianity and its prescriptive, catechetical directions must be emphasized. The New Testament presents both absolute and parainetic demands.

Let us look at the latter first. The moral teaching of the Early Church contains specific rules for conduct in and through which that Church considered that it could manifest its true life. These rules express for it the structure of *agapē*; they are the ways in which "love" has worked itself out in daily traffic.[22]

[21] It will be clear that I cannot follow the thesis of S. G. F. Brandon, *Jesus and the Zealots*, Manchester, 1967, who finds Jewish-Christianity "politically" oriented. I cannot give the reasons for my rejection of his brilliant but—in my judgment—misleading study here.

[22] See Paul Ramsey, "Faith Effective through In-principled Love", *Christianity and Crisis*, New York, May 30th, 1960.

These principles, prescriptions, laws—however we choose to call the New Testament directives—are part of the moral experience of the Church as it ordered its life beyond the Resurrection and, after the Parousia had delayed, when it had to settle down to live in a cold world in the light of a common day. And as long as we are in the period before the Parousia, which is the period of the Church, he would be a bold man who would, without much circumspection, scrap the prescriptions for the ordering of its life which the Church preserved.[23] No one generation can lightly set itself above, condemn or reject the element of moral directive set forth by the Early Church. Without these, a single generation might perchance live, but the generations would starve.

This, most emphatically, does not mean that every generation is called upon to accept the body of the moral directives of the Early Church in the same way. The deposit of that tradition must remain: its interpretation must vary. As I have shown elsewhere, the Early Church itself engaged in the application of the moral demands under which it lived in a casuistic manner.[24] And there must be a Christian casuistry today. So, too, just as the Early Church borrowed from the surrounding culture in the formulation of its moral teaching, so all the resources available to us from the contemporary world—psychological, sociological, philosophical—should be exploited for the same purpose. It is

[23] It should be borne in mind that the prescriptions of the New Testament are not presented neat. They are " Christified " by the addition of the phrase " in Christ ". See *Paul and Rabbinic Judaism*, p. 136, where I refer to A. M. Hunter, *Paul and His Predecessors*, London, 1940, p. 64, and to M. Dibelius, *From Tradition to Gospel* (ET, London, 1934), p. 241. Paul Lehmann in his various works has been critical of any prescriptive element in Christian Ethics. For him ethics is an art. In this connection I am reminded of words in the Phaidon book *The Story of Art*, London, 1952, by E. H. Gombrich. He writes: " What an artist worries about as he plans his picture, makes his sketches, or wonders whether he has completed his canvas, is something much more difficult to put into words. Perhaps he would say he worries about whether he has got it ' right '. Now it is only when we understand what he means by that modest word ' right ' that we begin to understand what artists are really after. . . . Anybody who has ever tried to arrange a bunch of flowers, to shuffle and shift the colours, to add a little here and take away here, has experienced the strange sensation of balancing forms and colours without being able to tell exactly what kind of harmony it is he is trying to achieve . . . and suddenly [it] may seem to come ' right '. . ." (p. 14). Doubtless the centre of gravity of the moral teaching of the Early Church is grace and *agapē*. But the writers of the New Testament clearly thought that the ' art' of Christian living would not be quite ' right ' without a prescriptive element. The element, indeed, might be secondary, but to ignore it would have been to throw the picture of the moral life out of focus." (For Lehmann's work, see n. 40, below.)

[24] See *The Setting of the Sermon on the Mount*, Cambridge, 1964, pp. [illegible] ff.

impossible not to recognize in the Early Church a prescriptive, casuistic concern. And such a concern remains indispensable.

But once this is recognized, it has also to be noted that prescriptive casuistry was not very highly developed in the Early Church: it remained comparatively uncomplicated. Contrast with the very simple casuistry of the New Testament, the elaboration of casuistic materials in Judaism as exemplified in the Mishnah. The peculiar genius of Christian moral life does not lie with these moral directives with which we are now dealing.[25]

And this leads me to the other kind of moral teaching in the Early Church—the presentation of the absolutes of Jesus. Here is the peculiarity of Christian moral teaching: that it places us not in the presence of the normal moral virtues, but under the judgment of absolute demands. These remain to stir up what Stendahl has called " the eschatological itch ".[26]

All this means that the moral teaching of the Church in its two forms recognizes the necessity of two things which seem incompatable but must be kept in living tension. It recognizes the need for patient application of moral rules and duties to the ongoing life of the Church and the world in which the Parousia has not taken place, and also the need to stand always under the absolute demands of the New Sinai. In short, it allows for patience and impatience, the inevitability of gradualness and the inevitability of radical change.

So far I have dealt with the direct moral teaching of the Early Church, but this is only part and not the chief part of the challenge of the Church to the world. There is another challenge to which we now turn, which is really inextricable from the first. In the New Testament, along with the Christian legal tradition, there is also, in some documents especially, a tendency to subsume all the moral requirements of the Gospel under the demand

[25] Here I find myself in agreement with C. F. D. Moule in *The Birth of the New Testament*, New York, 1962, p. 212, a page enlarged upon in his article "Important Moral Issues: Prolegomena: The New Testament and Moral Decisions", *ExpT* 74 (1963), 370–73. I should, however, insist that, although, to quote Moule, " The genius of the New Testament is not legislation (p. 371) ", nevertheless the Holy Spirit is informed by the moral, prescriptive teaching ascribed by the Gospels to Jesus, and that any " ethical translation of the Gospel " must likewise be informed. The Spirit is not autonomous but governed by the revelation in Christ. See *Paul and Rabbinic Judaism*, p. 196. For a criticism of my emphasis see V. P. Furnish, *op. cit.*, pp. 51–65.

[26] See R. Niebuhr, *An Interpretation of Christian Ethics*, New York, 1935, and John Knox, *The Ethic of Jesus in the Teaching of the Church*, New York, 1961.

of *agapē*, " love ", and to see in the Cross of Jesus the supreme expression of *agapē*.[27] From the earliest days, there has, therefore, been a concern to let *agapē* rule in all moral activity, or, to put the same thing in other words, to make the self-giving exemplified in the Cross normative for all behaviour. All the demands of the new law of the Gospel are placed under the sign of *agapē* or of the Cross.[28] However seriously they are taken, all response to the demands of the Gospel, expressed in prescriptions, is to be informed by *agapē*, which is translatable as openness to suffering and moral sensitivity. The prescriptions are not annulled, but understood in the context of grace ; they are themselves to become the expression of grace. This can best be illustrated from the Sermon on the Mount itself, where the demands of the Messiah are placed after the Beatitudes, which are an expression of grace.

It follows that, along with a tradition of both parainetic and absolute moral prescriptions, the Early Church presented to the world the challenge of a way of life governed by the Cross, the sign of *agapē*, the ultimate demand of God. Under this Cross all human activity is finally to be judged. That this is relevant in a world where the Vietnam war is raging I need not argue.

But we have remained in the realm of moral generalities. Apart from the challenge of the moral tradition of the Early Church and of the Cross, can we go further to assert that that tradition offers positive guidance for the directions in which society should move ? I think it can. But we can best see the relevance of the Christian " way " today by looking at its relevance to the world of the first century.

[27] For the evidence, see *The Setting of the Sermon on the Mount*, pp. 401 ff. The pertinent references are Mt 7 : 12 ; Mk 12 : 28 ; Jn 15 : 9–13 ; 1 Jn 3 : 16 f. ; Ro 13 : 9 ; Gal 5 : 14 ; Col 3 : 14 ; Ja 1 : 25 ; 2 : 8 ; 1 Jn 4 : 7–12 ; 4 : 21.

[28] The effort to understand the " crucifix " form of all Christian living has best been exemplified by Joseph Sittler, *The Structure of Christian Ethics*, Baton Rouge, 1958. Christian ethics is for him : " a re-enactment from below on the part of man of the shape of the revelatory drama of God's holy will in Jesus Christ . . . Suffering, death, burial, resurrection, a new life—these are actualities that plot out the arc of God's self-giving deed in Christ's descent and death and ascension ; and precisely *this shape of grace* in its recapitulation within the life of the believer and the faithful community, is the nuclear matrix which grounds and unfolds as the Christian life " (p. 36). It is possible to urge that seldom, if ever, in the New Testament is the Cross directly referred to as a ground for moral action. Even in Ph 2 : 5 ff. it has been denied that the Cross has ethical implications ; see the discussion in R. P. Martin, *Carmen Christi, Philippians ii. 5–11*, Cambridge, 1967, pp. 68 ff., 84 ff. But it is difficult not to see in the Cross—the supreme act of obedience—an event which did have such implications.

At this point I must reiterate what was noted in the first footnote, that this treatment was originally inextricably connected with an essay on " The Moral Teaching of the Early Church ", in its theological dimensions, as its sequence. Our concentration on " relevance " in this the present essay endangers this connection because it isolates the moral teaching from its context in the total life of the Church and therefore distorts its character. Suffice it as a corrective here to recall that the morality of the Early Church was a communal morality, that of a community under the authority of a Living Lord, and the guidance of the Spirit, sustained by a great hope. Within the total life of that community the parainesis and absolute demands to which we have referred above played their part as we have seen. But more important was the Spirit that dwelt in the community and the quality of life which it was designed to embody and which both was informed by those demands and " interpreted " those demands. Our question, then, as to what positive guidance is provided by the moral tradition of the Early Church can best be answered by looking at the relevance of the " way " of the Christian community in the first century and thereby discovering, perhaps, its relevance for today.

First, let us consider how " the way " of the Church infringed upon society in the realm of allegience to the State. The attitude of Jesus himself and of the Early Church was ambiguous. Sometimes, as in Ro 13 : 1, submission to " the powers that be " was enjoined ; at others, as in Revelation, an abortive hatred that could only lead not to their redemption but to their destruction. Care is expressed to recognize the State as in 1 Peter.[29] We may sum up the matter by claiming that while the due rights of the State are acknowledged, so that, whenever possible, obedience to it is enjoined, in early Christianity, as in Judaism, any overweening rights claimed by the State are denied.[30] Early Christians, like Jews, could not worship the Emperor. But neither could they support the Zealots.[31] Jewish-Christians, in

[29] 1 P 2 : 13 ff. ; cf. 1 Ti 2 : 1 ff.

[30] I have here followed O. Cullmann, *The State in the New Testament*, New York, 1965. He writes : " Jesus' attitude is to be sought beyond any uncritical absolutizing of the Roman State, and at the same time beyond any thoroughgoing political resistance to it " (p. 23). This might well be applied to the Early Church also.

[31] It will again be clear that I cannot accept S. G. F. Brandon's reconstruction of early Church history in his books *The Fall of Jerusalem*, London, 1951, and

what numbers we do not know, refused to enlist in the war against Rome. The New Testament forbids us to give to the State rights that do not belong to it. I know of few things more relevant to our present situation than the demand urged upon us in the New Testament to honour the State but not to divinize or absolutize it. Nationalism, often defined as man's other religion, finds its proper evaluation in the Christian moral tradition.

The second way in which I find the " way " of the Early Church particularly relevant is in what I may call the realm of culture. I have to be brief to the point of distortion. The Christian community came to be understood as one in which there was to be neither Jew nor Greek, bond nor free, male nor female.[32] It was to transcend cultural, economic and sexual differences. On the cultural side it aimed at the reconciliation of Jew and Greek, between whom there was probably the deepest social, cultural and religious cleavage of the first century.[33] But the Church, as the community of the Messiah, conceived its very purpose to be to inaugurate the eschatological unity of which the initial unity of creation is the prototype, that is, to recreate the unity broken between man and man as well as between man and God.

The most impressive expression of this is found in the Epistle to the Ephesians, where Paul, or at least one of his followers, sets forth the purpose of the Church. C. H. Dodd[34] has summarized this as follows :

" In Ephesians the Church is regarded as the society which embodies in history the eternal purpose of God revealed in Christ. This purpose is the ultimate unity of all being in him. While in the universe at large there are still unreconciled powers affronting the sovereignty of God, the ultimate issue is certain. God has determined to ' sum up all things in Christ '. That might be pure speculation, but for the fact that history and experience witness to the reconciling power of Christ in the creation of that supernatural society in which warring sections of the human race are perfectly reconciled into a whole of harmoniously functioning parts—the Church. That Jews and Gentiles should have found their place in the unity of the

---

*Jesus and the Zealots*, Manchester, 1967. For a critique of the former work—in part—see *The Setting of the Sermon on the Mount*, pp. 317 ff.

[32] See Gal 3 : 28.

[33] See my article on " The Jewish State in the Hellenistic World " in *Peake's Commentary*, edd. M. Black and H. H. Rowley, London, 1962, pp. 686 ff.

[34] " Ephesians," *The Abingdon Bible Commentary*, Nashville, 1929, pp. 1222 f. See also Stig Hanson, *The Unity of the Church in the New Testament*, Uppsala, 1946.

Church seems to the writer the most signal manifestation of reconciling grace. The enmity of Jew and Gentile was one of the fiercest in the ancient world : and the unity of Jewish and Gentile Christians in the one church *a mystery and a miracle*. He saw that the reconciliation was not accomplished by any kind of compromise between the diverse parties, but by a divine act creating out of both one new humanity. This new humanity is mediated by Christ. He sums up in Himself the whole meaning of God, and communicates Himself to men so that humanity may come to realize and express that meaning. The Church is ' in Christ ' ; it is His body, and its members have " put on " the new humanity which is Christ in them (2 : 11–22). . . . In the great universe, too, there is a movement toward unity and completeness : Christ's work will not be done till the whole universe is one in Him, to the Glory of God. The living and growing unity of the Church is, so to speak, a sacrament of the ultimate unity of all things."

But not only in Ephesians does this become clear. The Pauline doctrine of Christ as the Second Adam is pertinent here. Paul accepted the traditional Rabbinic doctrine of the unity of mankind in Adam. That doctrine implied that the very constitution of the physical body of Adam and the method of its formation was symbolic of the real oneness of mankind. In the one body of Adam, east and west, north and south were brought together, male and female. Paul, when he thought of the new humanity being incorporated " in Christ ", conceived of it as the " body " of the Second Adam, where there was neither Jew nor Greek, male nor female, bond nor free. The difference between the body of the First Adam and that of the Second Adam was for Paul that whereas the former was animated by the principle of natural life, was *nephesh*, the latter was animated by the Spirit ; and the purpose of God in Christ is " in dispensation of the fullness of times " to " gather together in one all things in Christ " (Eph 1 : 10), i.e. the reconstitution of the essential oneness of mankind in Christ as a " spiritual " community, as it was one in Adam in a physical sense. Finally, we refer to the Farewell Discourses in the Fourth Gospel where the meaning of the Christian Ecclesia comes to full expression again. Christ prays not only for the Twelve but for Christians yet unborn. " Neither pray I for these alone, but for them also which shall believe on me through their word; that they all may be one ; as thou, Father, art in me and I in thee, that they also may be one in us : that the world may believe that thou hast sent me " (Jn 17 : 20–21).

This goal of the Christian community to achieve a truly universal society remains urgently relevant at a time when the division between East and West, rich and poor threatens the stability of the nations, and the tension between Black and White is rending the most powerful of them all.

The third area where the " way " of the Early Church is relevant is that of sex, where, although much in the New Testament seems to remain legislatively cold, a new spirit, that of *agapē* was shed abroad. The demand for radical *agapē,* which in the tradition of the Early Church is the true interpretation of God's will, indicates the quality and direction at which the life of sex as the life of all spheres is to aim. This, it must be emphasized, does not do away with casuistry in this realm but rather demands it.[35]

And, in the fourth place, the Pauline verse cited from Gal 3 : 28 indicates the quality at which economic relationships should aim. Economic distinctions are not fundamental and whenever they are such that they become a hindrance to the true equality of men " in Christ " they are to be combated. It requires no profound subtlety to recognize that the *agapē* under which those " in Christ " stand demands a realistic, earthly recognition of the economic rights of all at which all social legislation and political action should aim.[36] The " Social Gospel ", after all, in this sense, requires no other justification.

I have pointed out some areas where, it seems to me, the moral tradition of the Early Church provides us with what President John Bennett would, I think, call " middle axioms ",[37] although he would not derive them as directly as is here done from the New Testament—deference but not subservience to the State, racial equality, sexual responsibility and economic justice. They are derived, albeit indirectly, from the Christian " way " in the Early Church. They provide broad guide-lines in their respective areas for moral action. That they cannot, and must not, always be directly implemented in terms of the New

[35] The absolute principle not to divorce is enumerated by Jesus, but Paul found it necessary, in dealing with a specific problem of married life, to give his own judgment. He accepted the absolute principle ; but nevertheless, engaged in his own casuistry. See on this C. H. Dodd, " *'ΕΝΝΟΜΣ ΧΡΙΣΤΟΥ* ", *Studia Paulina, in hon. J. de Zwaan,* ed. J. N. Sevenster and W. C. van Unnik, Haarlem, 1953, pp. 96 ff., and contrast C. F. D. Moule, " Important Moral Issues ", *ExpT* 74 (1963), 371.

[36] I know of no more penetrating insistence on the " concreteness, almost crudity, in stating the moral requirements of religion [which] belongs to the genius of New Testament Christianity in general " than that presented by C. H. Dodd in his comment on 1 Jn 3 : 16–18. See *The Johannine Epistles, Moffatt Commentaries,* London, 1945, p. 86.

[37] J. C. Bennett, *Christian Ethics and Social Policy,* New York, 1946 ; " Principles and the Context ", *Storm over Ethics,* New York, 1967.

Testament suggests that, in other newer realms of moral perplexity about which early Christians could know nothing but which now confront mankind, it is the creative " way " and " the Spirit " of the Early Church that will guide us rather than rigid adherence to its prescriptions, however valuable these still are.

In conclusion, two things remain to be noted. The implementation of all the axioms, " crucifix " patterns, the *agapē*, and prescriptions, about which we have written, depends on the convictions which gave them birth : they are the implicates of the Christian Gospel, and it is from it that they draw their vitality. This essay must, therefore, be read in conjunction with its predecessor to which I have already referred.

And, finally, it is not superfluous to point out the relevance of all the above to the current ethical debate.[38] Those who favour a prescriptive ethic[39] are impatient with the contextualists who emphasize the free response of *agapē* in the "*Koinonia*".[40] In between these extremes are those who favour " middle axioms ". To a student of the New Testament—who may, probably, always be guilty of simplifying matters—the debate seems unreal or to use a term borrowed from Professor James M. Gustafson—" misplaced ".[41] Each " school " can find

[38] The most convenient survey of this was pointed out to me by my colleague, Professor Waldo Beach. It is by James M. Gustafson, entitled " Christian Ethics " in *Religion*, ed. Paul Ramsey, Englewood Cliffs, New Jersey, 1965, pp. 287 ff. The whole field is covered in its historical perspective in *A Survey of Christian Ethics* by E. L. Roy Long, Oxford, 1967.

[39] Represented most forcefully and convincingly by Paul Ramsey in various publications, e.g., " Faith Effective Through In-principled Love ", *Christianity and Crisis*, May 30, 1960 ; *Deeds and Rules in Christian Ethics*, Edinburgh, 1965, New York, ²1967 (enlarged edition) ; *War and the Christian Conscience*, Durham, North Carolina, 1961 ; Ramsey's position has changed since the publication of his first book, *Basic Christian Ethics*, New York, 1950.

[40] Best represented by Paul Lehmann, " The Foundation and Pattern of Christian Behaviour ", *Christian Faith and Social Action*, ed. John A. Hutchinson, New York, 1953, pp. 93–116 ; *Ethics in a Christian Context*, New York, 1963. R. Bultmann is usually included among contextualists. For a critique of his ethical interpretation, see C. W. Kegley, ed., *The Theology of Rudolf Bultmann*, New York, 1967, *ad rem*.

[41] See his excellent study ; " Context versus Principles : A Misplaced Debate in Christian Ethics ", *New Theology* No. 3, ed. M. E. Marty and Dean G. Pearman, New York, 1965, pp. 69 ff. There is a plentiful bibliographical guide in the footnotes on pp. 99 ff. In his recent book, already referred to in note 11 above, V. P. Furnish, writes as follows : " a survey of the various attempts to interpret Paul's ethic exposes as the central and decisive problem *the relation of concrete ethical materials to the apostle's preaching as a whole, especially to his basic theological presuppositions and convictions* " (p. 279, his italics). I should understand that relationship more in terms of the " new covenant " than does Furnish as is

support for its position in parts of the New Testament. But, what is more important, they can all find themselves reconciled there in the rich totality of the New Testament Church, where prescriptive morality, *agapē* and *Koinonia* morality, and, we might suggest, middle axioms, all co-exist in mutual inter-action. The relevance of the genius of the moral tradition of the Early Church is that it holds all these approaches in living tension, if not reconciliation.[42]

---

apparent from the first Haskell Lecture in this series and from *Paul and Rabbinic Judaism*, but his recognition of the " heart of the matter " is refreshing.

[42] Compare E. LeRoy Long in *Int.* 19 (1965), 149 ff., in an article on " The Use of the Bible in Christian Ethics ".

# MATTHIEU 18, 3 : *ἐὰν μὴ στραφῆτε καὶ γένησθε ὡς τὰ παιδία*

JACQUES DUPONT

POUR nous associer à l'hommage rendu au Professeur Matthew Black, nous avons cru ne pouvoir mieux faire que de reprendre un point particulier se rattachant à la question de l'arrière-fond sémitique des évangiles. Il s'agit de la manière dont s'exprime, en Mt 18, 3, la condition à remplir pour pouvoir entrer dans le Royaume : " Si vous ne vous retournez pas et ne devenez comme les petits enfants, vous n'entrerez pas dans le Royaume des Cieux."

Dans une note publiée en 1928,[1] P. Joüon soulignait la difficulté que soulève l'emploi du verbe *στραφῆτε* ; pour lui donner un sens intelligible, les traducteurs proposent " si vous ne changez pas ", " si vous ne vous convertissez pas ", lui attribuant ainsi une acception qui ne paraît pas lui convenir. Le plus simple serait de comprendre, comme quelques auteurs [2] : " si vous ne redevenez comme les enfants " ; on se trouverait en présence " de la manière hébraïque (*šûḇ*) et araméenne (*tûḇ*,[3] *h^e^pak*) d'exprimer l'idée de *re-* ". Le rôle de ce verbe correspondrait donc à celui d'un auxiliaire ; il indiquerait que l'action marquée par le verbe suivant est à faire " de nouveau ". Joüon conclut : " Il faut avouer que ce sémitisme est un peu gros, mais il ne semble pas possible de le nier ". Le même auteur reprend son hypothèse en 1930, dans sa traduction commentée des évangiles, où il explique : " *Στραφῆτε καὶ γένεσθε* est la manière hébraïque et araméenne d'exprimer notre idée complexe de *re*devenir ".[4]

[1] P. Joüon, *Notes philologiques sur les évangiles, RSR* 18 (1928), 345–59 (347s.).

[2] Joüon ne fournit pas d'indication sur ses devanciers. Notons que, dans leurs rétroversions hébraïques du N.T., F. Delitzsch et D. Ginsburg rendent ainsi l'expression qui nous occupe : *'im lo' tâšûḇû lihyôṯ kayelâdîm.* Au lieu de coordonner les deux verbes, ils subordonnent le second au premier en l'introduisant par la particule *le* et en le mettant à l'infinitif. Ici également, le sens est naturellement celui de la répétition : " si vous ne revenez pas pour être comme des enfants" signifiant en réalité : " si vous ne redevenez pas comme des enfants ".

[3] Joüon cite l'exemple de *Megillat Ta'nit*, 8 : *tâḇaṯ sulletâ lemissaḳ 'al maḏbeḥâ*, " la fine farine revint à monter sur l'autel ", c'est-à-dire " fut de nouveau offerte sur l'autel ".

[4] P. Joüon, *L'Evangile de Notre-Seigneur Jésus-Christ. Traduction et commentaire du texte original grec, compte tenu du substrat sémitique* (Verbum salutis, V), Paris, 1930, p. 112.

Adoptée en 1935 par D. Buzy, dans son commentaire de Matthieu,[5] cette interprétation a été reprise par P. Benoit dans sa traduction de la " Bible de Jérusalem " (1950) : " si vous ne retournez à l'état des enfants " [6] ; elle se trouve ainsi largement diffusée chez les lecteurs français.[7] Du côté allemand, J. Jeremias s'en est fait le champion convaincu.[8] Elle semble avoir moins de succès aupres des exégètes de langue anglaise, où M. Black la signale dans la 2e édition de son *Aramaic Approach*,[9] avec une réserve qui semble significative ; il cite l'explication de Joüon, mais sans prendre parti et en ne lui faisant pas affirmer plus qu'une possibilité.

L'hypothèse a provoqué des critiques. C'est ainsi que W. G. Kümmel,[10] avec d'autres,[11] lui reproche de ne pas tenir compte du vocabulaire de la LXX, où στρέφομαι peut fort bien prendre le sens de " se convertir ". I. de la Potterie [12] lui reproche de négliger le témoignage des anciens : celui des versions syriaques et latines, et celui d'abord de l'évangéliste grec lui-même.

Il ne paraît donc pas inutile de revenir sur la question.[13] La réponse à lui donner dépend de plusieurs considérations : celles

[5] D. Buzy, *Evangile selon saint Matthieu* (La Sainte Bible . . . L. Pirot, T. IX), Paris, 1935, p. 235.

[6] P. Benoit, *L'Evangile selon saint Matthieu* (La Sainte Bible . . . de Jérusalem), Paris, 1950, p. 109=3e éd., 1961, p. 116.

[7] Elle est reprise, en particulier, par A. Descamps, *Du discours de Marc, IX, 33–50 aux paroles de Jésus*, dans *La Formation des Evangiles. Problème synoptique et Formgeschichte* (Recherches Bibliques, II), Bruges, 1957, pp. 152–77 (165) ; X. Léon-Dufour, *Les évangiles et l'histoire de Jésus* (Parole de Dieu), Paris, 1963, pp. 403s.

[8] J. Jeremias, *Die Gleichnisse Jesu* (ATANT 11), Zurich, 1947, p. 97, n. 255= 6e éd., Goettingue, 1962, p. 189, n. 2 ; *Hat die Urkirche die Kindertaufe geübt?* 2e éd., Goettingue, 1949, pp. 43s. ; *Die Kindertaufe in den ersten vier Jahrhunderten*, Goettingue, 1958, pp. 63–65 ; *Das Vater-Unser im Lichte der neueren Forschung* (Calwer Hefte, 50), Stuttgart, 1962, p. 19. Voir aussi M. Zerwick, *Analysis philologica Novi Testamenti graeci*, Rome, 1953, pp. 44s. ; W. Grundmann, *Die νήπιοι in der urchristlichen Paränese*, *NTS* 5 (1958–59), 188–205 (203).

[9] M. Black, *An Aramaic Approach to the Gospels and Acts*, 2e éd., Oxford, 1954, p. 253.

[10] W. G. Kümmel, *Verheissung und Erfüllung. Untersuchungen zur eschatologischen Verkündigung Jesu* (ATANT 6), 3e éd., Zurich, 1956, p. 118, n. 77.

[11] Cf. E. Percy, *Die Botschaft Jesu. Eine traditionskritische und exegetische Untersuchung* (Lunds Univ. Aorsskrift, N.F. Avd. 1. Bd 49. Nr 5), Lund, 1953, p. 36, n. 5 ; W. Trilling, *Das wahre Israel. Studien zur Theologie des Matthäus-Evangeliums*, 3e éd. (SANT 10), Munich, 1964, p. 108.

[12] I. de la Potterie, " *Naître de l'eau et naître de l'Esprit* ". *Le texte baptismal de Jn 3, 5*, dans *Sciences Ecclésiastiques* 14 (1962), 417–44 (p. 436, n. 61).

[13] Nous l'avons déjà touchée dans l'ouvrage *Mariage et Divorce dans l'Evangile: Matthieu 19, 3–12 et parallèles*, Bruges, 1959, pp. 202–4.

qui relèvent de la lexicographie, celles aussi de la critique littéraire qui s'applique à déterminer ce que le logion de Mt 18, 3 doit au rédacteur évangélique et ce qui est attribuable à une tradition plus ancienne.

## I

Il n'y a aucune difficulté à donner raison à Joüon sur le fait que le verbe *šûḇ* (aram. *tûḇ*), " revenir ", peut avoir simplement valeur itérative ; au verbe qui le suit et lui est rattaché par la conjonction *we*, il ajoute l'idée que l'action exprimée par ce verbe se fait " de nouveau ".[14] La Bible fournit bon nombre d'exemples de ce sémitisme. Ainsi Gn 26, 18 ; Dt 23, 14 ; Jg 19, 7 ; 2 R 1, 11. 13 ; 21, 3 ; 24, 1 ; Is 6, 10 ; Jer 12, 15 ; 18, 4 ; Os 2, 11 ; Mal 3, 18. Il convient d'observer cependant :

1. Que ce sens ne s'impose pas partout où l'on rencontre la construction en cause. Il arrive souvent aussi que *šûḇ* conserve sa valeur propre, même quand il est suivi d'un verbe coordonné.[15] C'est le cas, par exemple, en Dt 1, 45 ; Jos 7, 3 ; 8, 21 ; Jer 22, 10.

2. La nuance particulière du sémitisme a plus d'une fois échappé aux traducteurs grecs. Il est clair alors qu'on ne saurait, sans lui faire violence, ramener la signification de la version grecque à celle de l'original sémitique. Ainsi Is 6, 10, " de peur qu'il ne revienne et ne guérisse ", signifie sans doute : " de peur qu'il ne retrouve la santé " ; mais ce n'est évidemment pas le sens de la LXX : μήποτε . . . ἐπιστρέψωσιν καὶ ἰάσομαι αὐτούς.

3. Joüon assimile le cas de *hap̄ak* (*hâp̄ék*, *'ap̄ak*) à celui de *tûḇ*. Cette affirmation est discutable. Nous ne connaissons en tout cas pas d'exemple clair où ce verbe ait simplement valeur itérative.

## II

Le sémitisme qu'on soupçonne en Mt 18, 3 se dissimulerait dans l'emploi de στραφῆτε. Il n'est pas sans intérêt d'interroger la LXX sur l'usage qu'elle fait de ce verbe.

[14] Pour *šûḇ*, voir W. Gesenius-F. Buhl, *Hebräisches und aramäisches Handwörterbuch über das Alte Testament*, 17e éd., Leipzig, 1921, p. 811 A ; explications plus détaillées et références plus nombreuses, mais qui demandent à être contrôlées, dans F. Zorell, *Lexicon Hebraicum et Aramaicum Veteris Testamenti*, Rome, 1964, p. 825 B. Voir également M. Jastrow, *A Dictionary of the Targumim, the Talmud Babli and Yerushalmi, and the Midrashic Literature*, New York, 1950, *II*, 1528 B. Pour *tûḇ*, *ibid.*, p. 1650 A.

[15] Cf. Zorell, *op. cit.*, p. 826 A.

1. On constate d'abord qu'elle ne l'emploie jamais pour rendre le verbe *šûḇ*.[16] C'est dans l'évangile de Jean (12, 40) qu'on trouve une citation d'Is 6, 10 où στραφῶσιν se substitue à ἐπιστρέψωσιν. Compte tenu du grec biblique, il n'est donc pas très indiqué de faire appel au verbe *šûḇ*, ou *tûḇ*, pour rendre compte de Mt 18, 3.

2. στρέφω (στρέφομαι) correspond le plus souvent à *hâpak*: c'est le cas 22 fois sur les 33 emplois de la LXX qui se basent sur le texte hébraïque [17] ; on peut y ajouter Sir 6, 28, ainsi que Dn 10, 16 TH. Il est question du bâton de Moïse " changé " en serpent (Ex 7, 15 ; cf. 4, 17 LXX), d'un rocher " changé " en étang (Ps 114, 7), de malédiction " changée " en bénédiction (Neh 13, 2), de lamentation " changée " en joie (Ps 30, 11 ; cf. Est 9, 22 ; Jer 31, 13 ; La 5, 15 ; Sir 6, 28). En 1 S 10, 6, Samuel prédit à Saül qu'il rencontrera une bande de prophètes : " L'Esprit du Seigneur fondra sur toi, tu feras le prophète avec eux et *tu seras changé* en un autre homme ". Dans le grec biblique, le " retournement " signifié par στρέφομαι s'applique à un changement résultant d'une transformation profonde.

Après *hâpak* on peut mentionner *sâḇaḇ*, qui est rendu 5 fois par στρέφω : à l'arrivée des Israélites, le Jourdain " retourna " en arrière (Ps 114, 3.5) ; Dieu fait " retourner " en arrière le coeur de son peuple, lorsqu'il le ramène à lui en manifestant sa puissance (1 R 18, 37).[18]

3. L'examen des textes ne favorise pas l'opinion de W. G. Kümmel,[19] pour qui στραφῆτε, en Mt 18, 3, relève de la langue de la LXX et de la manière dont elle exprime l'idée de " se convertir ". " Conversion " paraît trop précis pour correspondre au sens plus général de στρέφομαι. A la lumière du vocabulaire de la Bible grecque, le texte de Matthieu pourrait se traduire :

[16] στρέφω s'est introduit à la place de ἐπιστρέφω dans des variantes secondaires en Soph 3, 20 et Jer 34 (41), 15 ; à la place de ἀποστρέφω en Is 38, 8 (hiph). Cf. G. Bertram, art. στρέφω, *TWNT* VII (1964), pp. 714s. (714, n. 4).

[17] Bertram arrive à un total de 37 ; c'est sans doute en comptant les variantes secondaires de Dt 3, 1 ; Soph 3, 20 ; Is 38, 8 ; Jer 34 (41), 15. Nous considérons également comme secondaire la présence de στρέφω en Sir 31, 20 et 1 Macc 2, 63. Il reste ainsi 7 emplois propres à la Bible grecque : Ex 4, 17 ; Esth 4, 8. 17ab ; Sir 33, 5 ; 1 Macc 1, 39. 40.

[18] Voir encore 1 R 2, 15 et Prov 26, 14. στρέφω correspond 3 fois à *pânâh* : 1 S 14, 17 ; Jer 2, 27 ; 31 (48), 39, et est encore employé 3 fois pour trois verbes différents.

[19] W. G. Kümmel, *Verheissung und Erfüllung*, p. 118, n. 77. Cf. E. Percy, *Die Botschaft Jesu*, p. 36, n. 5.

" Si vous ne changez pas et ne devenez comme les petits enfants ", ou encore : " Si vous ne vous transformez pas..." Assurément, l'idée de conversion est toute proche ; mais elle n'est pas explicitée, comme elle le serait par l'emploi du verbe composé *ἐπιστρέφω*. En rendant *στρέφω* par " changer ", nous obtenons un sens qui, de toute évidence, est parfaitement satisfaisant.

## III

Dans la tradition synoptique, le logion qui nous occupe fait partie de la péricope de Mt 18, 1–5, dont le parallèle se trouve en Mc 9, 33–37. La confrontation des textes est instructive.

1. Mc 9, 33–37 —et l'on pourrait aller jusqu'au v. 50— est le plus bel exemple de ce que M. Black appelle les " stromates " de Marc [20] : sa manière de coudre ensemble les pièces dont il fait une sorte de tapisserie. Malgré leur manque d'homogénéité, les vv. 33–35 constituent une unité : le v. 33 sert d'introduction,[21] mais la déclaration de Jésus, au v. 35, est pourvue de son introduction propre.[22] Aux disciples qui discutaient pour savoir qui est le plus grand, Jésus enseigne : " Si quelqu'un veut être le premier, il devra être le dernier de tous et le serviteur de tous." Ce fragment donne l'impression d'être la version brève de l'incident rapporté en Mc 10, 35–44. Il est suivi, sans aucune transition, par l'épisode du petit enfant placé au milieu des disciples ; le serrant dans ses bras, Jésus déclare : " Quiconque accueille en mon nom un de ces petits enfants comme ceux-là, c'est moi qu'il accueille " (9, 36–37a). Le rapprochement s'impose avec l'autre

[20] M. Black, *An Aramaic Approach*, p. 264. Sur la composition de Mc 9, 33–50, voir L. Vaganay, *Le schématisme du discours communautaire à la lumière de la critique des sources*, *RB* 60 (1953), 203–44 ; *Le Problème synoptique. Une hypothèse de travail* (Bibl. de Théol., III, 1), Tournai, 1954, pp. 361–404 ; R. Schnackenburg, *Mk 9, 33–50*, dans *Synoptische Studien A. Wikenhauser*, Munich, 1954, pp. 184–206 ; A. Descamps, *Du discours de Marc IX, 33–50 aux paroles de Jésus*, dans *La Formation des Evangiles. Problème synoptique et Formgeschichte* (Recherches Bibliques, II), Bruges, 1957, pp. 152–77 ; F. Neirynck, *La Tradition des paroles de Jésus et Marc 9, 33–50*, *Concilium*, No. 20 (1966), pp. 57–66. Sur 9, 33–37 : M. Black, *The Markan Parable of the Child in the Midst*, ET 59 (1947–48), 14–16 (cf. *An Aramaic Approach*, pp. 264–68) ; E. L. Wenger, *The Marcan Parable of the Child in the Midst*, ET 59 (1947–48), 166s. ; G. Lindeskog, *Logia-Studien*, *ST* 4 (1950), 129–89 (171ss.). Et, naturellement, les commentaires : par exemple, V. Taylor, *The Gospel according to St. Mark*, Londres, 1952, pp. 403s.

[21] La scène se passe " à la maison ", comme au v. 28 ; mais entretemps on a traversé la Galilée.

[22] " S'étant assis, il appela les Douze et leur dit." Cet " appel " des Douze semble ne pas tenir compte du fait que Jésus était en train de leur parler. Le trait se comprend mieux dans le parallèle de 10, 42.

scène où il est question de petits enfants, Mc 10, 13–16. Enfin 9, 37b ajoute : " Quiconque m'accueille, ce n'est pas moi qu'il accueille, mais celui qui m'a envoyé " ; ces mots font écho à une sentence qui nous est transmise dans le discours de mission, où elle semble en meilleure situation (Mt 10, 40 ; cf. Lc 10, 16 ; Jn 13, 20).

2. La péricope de Mt 18, 1–5 témoigne d'un effort d'unification qui, tout en restant limité dans son résultat, répond sans doute à un état plus récent de la tradition. Le point de départ n'est plus une discussion de préséance, mais la question proprement théologique : " Qui donc est le plus grand dans le Royaume des Cieux ? " (v. 1).[23] L'épisode du petit enfant placé au milieu des disciples sert d'introduction à la réponse de Jésus (v. 2).[24] C'est le v. 4 qui fournit cette réponse [25] : " Celui-là qui s'abaissera lui-même comme ce petit enfant, c'est celui qui sera le plus grand dans le Royaume des Cieux." On a l'impression d'une adaptation de la sentence " Celui qui s'élèvera sera abaissé, et celui qui s'abaisse lui-même sera élevé " (Mt 23, 12 ; Lc 14, 11 ; 18, 14), comme Mc 9, 35 était l'application d'une sentence qui se retrouve ailleurs (Mc 10, 43s. ; Mt 20, 26s. ; 23, 11 ; Lc 22, 26), mais qui était moins bien adaptée à l'exemple du petit enfant. Le changement de Mt 18, 4 par rapport à Mc 9, 35 est évidemment lié au fait que, chez Matthieu, l'enfant est proposé en exemple aux disciples.

Si les vv. 1, 2 et 4 forment une unité solide dans le récit de Matthieu, le v. 5, sur l'accueil à faire aux petits enfants, n'est

[23] La mention de l'arrivée à Capharnaüm, par laquelle commence la péricope de Mc 9, 35, se trouve, chez Matthieu, au début de la péricope précédente (17, 24) ; il commence donc 18, 1 par la soudure rédactionnelle " A cette heure même " (cf. 11, 25 ; 12, 1 ; 13, 1 ; 14, 1 ; 22, 23 ; 26, 55). Matthieu continue : " les disciples s'avancèrent vers Jésus " ; il faut attribuer au rédacteur évangélique l'emploi du verbe προσέρχομαι (cf. J. C. Hawkins, *Horae Synopticae*, 2e éd., Oxford, 1909, p. 7), ainsi que l'explicitation du sujet et du complément de ce verbe. Comme souvent, l'interrogation directe remplace chez Matthieu l'interrogation indirecte chez Marc (cf. L. Vaganay, *Le Problème synoptique*, p. 369) ; la question est explicitée par l'adjonction de ἄρα (cf. Mt 19, 25. 27), du verbe ἐστίν et du complément " dans le Royaume des Cieux ", qui transpose le problème.

[24] Jésus ne " prend " pas l'enfant (Mc), il " l'appelle à lui ". Il est clair que Matthieu ne saurait se résoudre à montrer Jésus serrant un petit enfant dans ses bras!

[25] Matthieu se plaît à établir une correspondance exacte entre la question et la réponse : autre exemple en Mt 12, 10. 12. Cf. H. J. Held, *Matthäus als Interpret der Wundergeschichten*, dans G. Bornkamm, G. Barth, H. J. Held, *Ueberlieferung und Auslegung im Matthäus-Evangelium* (WMANT 1), Neukirchen, 1960, pp. 155–287 (223s.).

plus qu'un appendice, sans lien réel avec la péricope.[26] Quant au v. 3, celui qui nous intéresse plus particulièrement, il fait manifestement figure de pièce rapportée, interrompant la suite normale du développement [27] : il concerne, non plus la question de savoir qui est le plus grand dans le Royaume, mais celle de savoir qui pourra y entrer.

3. Mt 18, 3 doit être comparé avec Mc 10, 15 :

| Matthieu | Marc |
|---|---|
| En vérité je vous le dis, | En vérité je vous le dis, |
| si vous ne changez pas et ne devenez | quiconque n'accueille pas |
| | le Royaume de Dieu |
| comme les petits enfants | comme un petit enfant, |
| vous n'entrerez pas | n'y entrera pas. |
| dans le Royaume des Cieux. | |

Il est assez facile de se rendre compte que, dans l'épisode des petits enfants repoussés par les disciples (Mc 10, 13–16), le v. 15 constitue un élément étranger.[28] Il interrompt la suite naturelle entre le v. 14 et le v. 16 [29] ; il nuit à l'unité de la péricope, mieux conservée en Mt 19, 13–15, qui n'a pas le logion à cet endroit. Il semble donc que nous avons affaire à un logion indépendant, que Matthieu et Marc ont introduit dans deux contextes différents.

Mais s'agit-il bien d'un même logion ? Les exégètes s'accordent à le penser,[30] et leur opinion nous paraît fondée. Cela

[26] Matthieu n'a pas le supplément adventice de Mc 9, 37b ; en cela, son texte représente un état de la tradition antérieur à celui du texte de Marc. Cf. B. C. Butler, *M. Vaganay and the " Community Discourse "*, *NTS* 1 (1954–55), 283–290 (289).

[27] C'est l'avis général des exégètes.

[28] Ici encore, nous nous trouvons d'accord avec l'immense majorité des auteurs ; nous n'avons relevé que peu de voix discordantes : F. C. Grant, S. E. Johnson, J. Schniewind, V. Taylor, dans leurs commentaires ; E. Percy, *Die Botschaft Jesu*, p. 35 ; L. Vaganay, *Le Problème synoptique*, p. 376 ; J. Blinzler, *Kind und Königreich Gottes nach Markus* 10, 14. 15, dans *Haec loquere et exhortare* = *Klerusblatt*, 38 (1934), 90–96 ; voir aussi F. A. Schilling, " What Means the Saying about Receiving the Kingdom of God as a Little Child (τὴν βασιλείαν τοῦ θεοῦ ὡς παιδίον) ? Mk x. 15 ; Lk xviii. 17 ", *ExpT* 77 (1965–66), 56–58.

[29] Noter, en particulier, que les vv. 14 et 16 parlent des petits enfants au pluriel, tandis que le v. 15 emploie le singulier. Cf. B. C. Butler, " The Synoptic Problem Again ", *Downside Rev.*, 73 (1955), 24–46 (39–41).

[30] Ainsi L. Vaganay, peu suspect de partialité en faveur de Marc : " Les divergences légères (de Matthieu) constituent une amélioration du texte de Marc . . ." (*Le Problème synoptique*, p. 376). Cf. T. W. Manson, *The Sayings of Jesus*, Londres, 1949, p. 207 : " Verse 3 is Mt.'s interpretation of Mk 10, 15 . . . , a free rewriting of Mk 10, 15 ". Voir E. Percy, *Die Botschaft Jesu*, p. 36, n. 5 ; W. G. Kümmel, *Verheissung und Erfüllung*, p. 118, n. 77 ; W. Trilling, *Das wahre Israel*, p. 108.

suppose qu'il est possible de rendre compte des divergences qui séparent les deux versions. On le fait généralement en expliquant le texte de Matthieu comme une forme révisée de celui de Marc. Il y a cependant des voix discordantes, faisant valoir soit le caractère plus sémitisant de la rédaction de Matthieu,[31] soit la résonance plus chrétienne de l'expression de Marc : " accueillir le Royaume ".[32] Il ne paraît pas nécessaire de s'engager ici dans cette discussion ; nous pouvons laisser ouverte la question de savoir si la version de Matthieu repose sur un texte identique à celui de Mc 10, 15 ou sur une forme plus ancienne qui ne nous a pas été conservée. Ce qui nous importe est de déterminer la pensée de Matthieu quand il rapporte ce v. 3 et le place dans le contexte où nous le lisons.

## IV

1. Pour entendre le v. 3 dans le sens que l'évangéliste lui prête, il est essentiel de tenir compte du lien étroit qui l'unit au

[31] Cf. J. Jeremias, *Die Kindertaufe in den ersten vier Jahrhunderten*, p. 64, n. 4. Cet auteur croit reconnaître quatre sémitismes en Mt 18, 3 : (1) στραφῆτε employé pour *tûḇ* au sens itératif. Nous avons vu dans la deuxième partie de cet article que cette explication ne s'impose pas. (2) Emploi de ὡς suivi d'un substantif pour remplacer un adjectif. E. Percy (*loc. cit.*) répond qu'on voudrait bien savoir quel adjectif aurait pu être employé ici en grec ; il serait peut-être plus simple de faire remarquer que la même construction se trouve également en Mc 10, 15. (3) Emploi de τὰ παιδία avec l'article, bien que le mot ait un sens indéterminé. Réponse : l'emploi de l'article défini est normal avec le pluriel ; il s'agit de la catégorie des petits enfants prise dans son ensemble. Cf. A. T. Robertson, *A Grammar of the Greek New Testament in the Light of Historical Research*, 3e éd., New York, 1919, p. 757. (4) τῶν οὐρανῶν, périphrase pour désigner Dieu. Mais cette périphrase est en même temps un matthéisme caractérisé.

[32] Cf. E. Lohmeyer, *Das Evangelium des Markus* (KEK 1/2, 11e éd.), Goettingue, 1951, pp. 204s. ; J. Jeremias, *Mc 10, 13–16 Parr. und die Uebung der Kindertaufe in der Urkirche*, *ZNTW* 40 (1941), 243–45 (244s.) ; W. G. Kümmel, *Verheissung und Erfüllung*, p. 118, n. 77 ; J. Schmid, *Das Evangelium nach Markus* (RNT 2), 4e éd., Ratisbonne, 1958, p. 189 ; W. E. Bundy, *Jesus and the First Three Gospels*, Cambridge, Mass., 1955, p. 398 ; R. Schnackenburg, *Règne et Royaume de Dieu. Essai de théologie biblique* (Etudes théol., 2), Paris, 1965, pp. 119s. ; I. de la Potterie, " *Naître de l'eau et naître de l'Esprit* ", p. 436, n. 62. Pour attribuer une origine chrétienne à l'expression " accueillir le Royaume de Dieu ", on l'entend au sens de : "accueillir le (message du) Royaume de Dieu ". Mais une autre interprétation a été mise en honneur par G. Dalman (*Die Worte Jesu*, I, Leipzig, 1898, pp. 101s.), et elle conserve beaucoup de partisans: " accueillir " traduirait *ḳibbēl*, et l'expression de Marc signifierait pratiquement " prendre sur loi le (joug du) Royaume ", c'est-à-dire reconnaître la souveraineté de Dieu en se soumettant à elle. Dans ce cas, il n'y aurait pas lieu de faire appel à un vocabulaire spécifiquement chrétien.

v. 4, lien que souligne le οὖν placé au début du v. 4.[33] Le v. 3 se présente ainsi comme l'énoncé du principe général dont le v. 4 fait l'application en fonction de la question posée. Celui-là sera grand dans le Royaume qui " se sera abaissé lui-même comme ce petit enfant " (ταπεινώσει ἑαυτὸν ὡς τὸ παιδίον τοῦτο), en vertu de la règle suivant laquelle on ne saurait entrer dans le Royaume sans " changer et devenir comme les petits enfants " (ἐὰν μὴ στραφῆτε καὶ γένησθε ὡς τὰ παιδία). L'invitation à " changer et devenir comme les petits enfants " semble donc n'être qu'une forme plus générale de l'appel à " s'abaisser soi-même ", en se faisant petit comme un enfant.[34]

2. Le ton du v. 3 est celui, non d'un énoncé théorique, mais d'un pressant avertissement. L'emploi du verbe γένησθε est significatif à cet égard. Les adultes auxquels la sentence s'adresse ne sont plus des enfants ou pareils à des enfants ; mais ils ont à le " devenir ", à se rendre tels, en modifiant dans ce but leurs dispositions et leur conduite.[35] L'attention se porte sur la condition à remplir,[36] sur l'attitude à prendre, sur un redressement à réaliser, au prix sans doute d'un certain effort.[37] En rapportant l'appel de Jésus à aimer ses ennemis, Matthieu ajoute : " afin que vous deveniez (ὅπως γένησθε) les fils de votre Père " (5, 45 ; cf. Lc 6, 35 : " vous serez alors les fils du Très-Haut "). Le logion transmis par Luc sous cette forme : " Tout disciple accompli sera pareil à (ἔσται ὡς) son maître " (Lc 6, 40 ; cf. Jn 13, 16 ; 15, 20), est rapporté de cette manière par Matthieu : " Il suffit

[33] Sur l'emploi de οὖν chez Matthieu, voir J. Dupont, *Les Béatitudes*, 2e éd., T. I, Bruges-Louvain, 1958, p. 148, n. 1.

[34] L'appel à " s'abaisser soi-même " revient en 23, 12, servant de conclusion à un développement qui met en garde contre la vanité des scribes et des Pharisiens: " Toutes leurs actions, ils les font pour se donner en spectacle aux hommes " (v. 5) ; par contraste avec leur recherche des titres honorifiques, les disciples de Jésus ne se feront pas appeler Maître, Père, Docteur (vv. 7–11). Ce passage est fort éclairant pour pour saisir l'esprit dans lequel Matthieu a rédigé 18, 1–4.

[35] Cf. W. Bauer, W. F. Arndt, F. W. Gingrich, *A Greek-English Lexicon of the N.T.*, Cambridge-Chicago, 1957, p. 158 (sub 4a) ; J. Blinzler, *Kind und Königreich Gottes*, p. 96, n. 11.

[36] Mt 18, 3 doit être rapproché de deux autres sentences du premier évangile qui définissent également une condition d'accès au Royaume : 5, 20 et 7, 21. Ces sentences caractérisent la manière de l'évangéliste et sa préoccupation catéchétique. Voir à ce sujet H. Windisch, *Die Sprüche vom Eingehen in das Reich Gottes*, *ZNTW* 27 (1928), 163–92.

[37] " L'usage même de ce verbe ' devenir ' suggère que ce changement ne se fait pas en une fois ; Jésus nous demande de nous transformer progressivement " (I. de la Potterie, " *Naître de l'eau et naître de l'Esprit* ", p. 437) : cette exégèse ne tient pas compte du fait que le verbe est à l'aoriste.

au disciple de devenir pareil à (γένηται ὡς) son maître " (10, 25). A la déclaration : " Je vous envoie comme des brebis au milieu des loups " (Mt 10, 16 ; Lc 10, 3), Matthieu ajoute : " Devenez (γίνεσθε) donc prudents comme les serpents et simples comme les colombes ".[38] Le γένησθε de 18, 3 traduit si bien le point de vue catéchétique de l'évangéliste Matthieu qu'on hésiterait à le faire remonter à sa source, indépendamment même du témoignage de Mc 10, 15.

3. A propos de στραφῆτε, il faudrait observer d'abord que Matthieu emploie facilement ce verbe : s'il peut remonter à la source en Mt 5, 39 (contre Lc 6, 29) et 7, 6 (propre), c'est à la rédaction qu'il faut l'attribuer en 9, 22 (contre Mc 5, 34) et en 27, 3 (propre), ainsi qu'en 16, 23, où il se substitue à ἐπιστρέφω (Mc 8, 33).[39] Pour déterminer la nuance particulière qu'il prend en 18, 3, où le parallèle de Marc permet de douter de sa présence dans la source, il est de bonne méthode de chercher à l'éclairer par la préoccupation dont témoigne le contexte immédiat. Au v. 4, Matthieu ne se contente pas de dire que, pour être le plus grand, il faut " être le dernier de tous et le serviteur de tous " (Mc 9, 35) ; il tient à souligner la nécessité de " s'abaisser soi-même ". Il voit là une application concrète de l'obligation qu'on a de " devenir comme les petits enfants ". Il se montre soucieux de mettre en valeur la conduite que les disciples sont appelés à suivre pour répondre aux exigences du Sauveur. On n'a pas de peine à comprendre que, dans cet esprit, il ait tenu à préciser que l'humilité requise des chrétiens suppose ce " changement ", cette " transformation ", que le verbe στρέφομαι exprime fort bien dans le grec biblique. Si, comme la précision γένησθε, le verbe στραφῆτε s'explique naturellement au niveau du travail rédactionnel que l'évangéliste grec fait sur ses sources grecques, cette interprétation semble préférable à celle qui fait appel à l'hypothèse d'un sémitisme que le P. Joüon lui-même avoue " un peu gros ".

Malgré son caractère forcément sommaire, notre étude d'une expression évangélique permet de toucher du doigt la nécessité de faire appel, dans la question du substrat sémitique des évangiles,

[38] Voir encore Mt 6, 16 (propre à Mt) ; 24, 44 (=Lc 12, 40), et la retouche analogue pratiquée par Luc en Lc 22, 26 (contre Mc 9, 35 ; 10, 43–44).

[39] Matthieu n'emploie que 4 fois ἐπιστρέφω, et toujours en suivant une source : en 13, 15, il cite Is 6, 10 ; en 24, 18, il suit Mc 13, 16 (Lc change) ; en 10, 13 et 12, 44, il est en désaccord avec Lc 10, 6 et 11, 24, mais c'est parce que Luc a cherché un verbe plus exact.

non seulement à des considérations philologiques, mais aussi à celles qui relèvent de la critique littéraire, qu'il s'agisse de la condition synoptique des matériaux qui nous sont transmis ou du point de vue personnel des évangélistes qui nous les transmettent.

# MIDRASH, TARGUM AND NEW TESTAMENT QUOTATIONS

E. Earle Ellis

Several years ago Principal Black graciously supervised my doctoral dissertation on *Paul's Use of the Old Testament.* In writing an anniversary essay in his honour it seemed appropriate to return to an aspect of that theme. Recent advances in midrashic and targumic studies have had important implications for the nature of Old Testament quotations in the New Testament. The inquiry below seeks to discern, in the light of these studies, a pattern of development in the use of the Old Testament by the early Christian community.

## I

Since mid-century increased attention has been given to the investigation and classification of midrash.[1] In part this has been stimulated by the interest in biblical literary genres and in biblical hermeneutics generally, in part by the manuscript discoveries at Qumran. More importantly, it has been marked by a shift away from the rabbinical Midrashim as the standard by which the genre is to be defined or measured. A. Robert (cf. *VDBS* 5, 1957, 411–21) had noted in the Old Testament a " procédé anthologique " in which Old Testament writers contemporized or reapplied to the present situation the phraseology and/or ideas of prior Scriptures.[2] Building upon these observations Miss R. Bloch [3] identified such contemporization (and reference to Scripture) as the essence of the midrashic procedure. She saw it not only in the use of prior Scriptures by the Old Testament (and later) writers but also in the interpretive glossing in the LXX,

[1] Cf. especially J. W. Doeve, *Jewish Hermeneutics in the Synoptic Gospels and Acts*, Assen, 1954 ; R. Bloch, " Midrash ", *VDBS* 5 (1957), 1263–81 ; G. Vermes, *Scripture and Tradition in Judaism*, Leiden, 1961 ; A. G. Wright, *The Literary Genre Midrash*, New York, 1967=*CBQ* 28 (1966), 105–38, 417–57.

[2] Cf. Jer 32 : 18 with Ex 20 : 5 f. ; Dn 11 : 30 with Nu 24 : 24 ; Jer 7 : 21 f. with Am 5 : 25 f. ; Jer 48 : 45 with Nu 21 : 28 ; 24 : 17.

[3] Bloch, *op. cit.*, p. 1266 ; cf. Vermes, *op. cit.*, pp. 7 f. ; Doeve, *op. cit.*, p. 116.

the Targums, and the successive redactions of the Hebrew text.[4] Her broad definition of midrash has not found complete acceptance,[5] but it does accord with the use of the term in intertestamental Judaism as an activity of biblical interpretation.[6] It may be helpful, however, to distinguish such implicit midrash,[7] i.e., interpretive paraphrase of the Old Testament text, from explicit midrash, i.e., the lemma (a cited Old Testament text) plus its commentary. Both forms appear at Qumran.

In the Qumran literature the explanation of an Old Testament text often is preceded by the phrase, " the interpretation (*pēšer*=*pesher*) ", or " its interpretation concerns ". The literary structure of the *pesher* texts has formal parallels with some rabbinic midrash,[8] and the *pesher* is identified as midrash at 4Qflor 1 : 14, 19. It appears in anthology (4Qflor), in consecutively interpreted Old Testament texts (e.g., 1QpHab), and in single Old Testament quotations (CD 4 : 14). Probably to be defined as a form of haggadic, i.e., non-legal midrash, the distinctiveness of Qumran *pesher* is not in its structure nor in its specific subject matter[9] but in its technique and, specifically, its eschatological perspective. In these passages the Old Testament text-form undergoes interpretive alterations,[10] in order to fit it to a present-

[4] So, also, Vermes, *op. cit.*, p. 176. Thus in Is 9 : 11(12) " Aramaeans and Philistines " become in the LXX the contemporary " Syrians and Greeks " ; in Ex 4 : 24 ff. " Lord " becomes in the LXX and *Targum Onkelos* " angel of the Lord ", and " the blood " is given explicit sacrificial merit. Vermes, *op. cit.*, pp. 178–92, in agreement with Bloch, characterises the LXX and Targums as a " re-writing of the Bible " in which contemporary interpretations are woven into the text (p. 179).

[5] A. G. Wright (*op. cit.*) apparently prefers to use the term of a literary genre in which the primary intention is to illumine a prior biblical text.

[6] It designates both an activity and a genre, a way of expounding Scripture and the resultant exposition. Cf. Sir 51 : 23 ; CD 20 : 6 (=9 : 33 CAP) ; 4Qflor 1 : 14 ; W. Bacher, *Die exegetische Terminologie der jüdischen Traditionsliteratur*, Darmstadt, 1965 (1899), 1, p. 103 ; Doeve, *op. cit.*, p. 55.

[7] I am dependent here on M. Gertner (*JSS* 7, 1962, 268) who uses in a similar way the terms, covert and overt midrash.

[8] E.g., EcclR 12 : 1 ; cf. L. H. Silberman, *RQ 3* (1961–62), 28. It also has affinities with the gnostic *Pistis Sophia*, e.g., 120a ; cf. J. Carmignac, *RQ* 4 (1963–64), 497–522.

[9] I.e., the interpretation of Scripture. Cf. O. Betz, *Offenbarung und Schriftforschung*, Tübingen, 1960, pp. 40–54, 80 ff. Silberman (*op. cit.*), following K. Elliger (*Studien zum Habakkukkommentar zum Toten Meer*, Tübingen, 1953, p. 157), identifies *pesher*, in accordance with the use of term in Daniel, with the explanation of dreams and visions. But see 1Q22Moses 1 : 3 f. ; Nu 12 : 6 ff.

[10] Cf. W. H. Brownlee, *The Meaning of the Qumran Scrolls for the Bible*, New York, 1964, p. 64 ; K. Stendahl, *The School of St. Matthew*, Uppsala, 1954, pp.

time eschatological fulfilment.[11] Strictly speaking, the cited Old Testament text is followed by exposition in which words from the text are repeated[12] and its " mystery " therewith " interpreted ". Qumran *pesher* reflects an eschatological perspective similar to the New Testament and unlike that in rabbinic midrash, and it combines characteristics of the implicit and explicit midrash mentioned above.

The so-called *Genesis Apocryphon* or *Genesis midrash* and *The Book of Jubilees* (1Q17, 18 ; 2Q 19, 20 ; 4Q) offer examples at Qumran of a kind of " implicit midrash ". The former, in particular, illustrates the difficulty of specialists in this area in finding a satisfactory definition of targum and midrash in their relationship to one another. It was identified by some initially as a targum and then as a midrash.[13] The latter classification seems to be followed by most writers on the subject.[14] However, M. R. Lehmann (*RQ* 1, 1958–59, 249–63) suggests that it represents " the oldest prototype of both ", and J. A. Fitzmyer, apparently following the rabbinic models of Targum and Midrash, declines to classify it as either.[15]

The problem is not new : on the similar *Book of Jubilees* (London, 1902, p. xiii) R. H. Charles commented that as the " most advanced pre-Christian representative of the midrashic tendency, which had already been at work in the Old Testament Chronicles, . . . [it] " constitutes an enlarged Targum . . . in which difficulties . . . are solved . . . and the spirit of later Judaism infused . . ." [16] This does not appear far removed from Miss Bloch's (*VDBS* 5, pp. 1271, 1278 f.) conclusions about Chronicles, Jubilees, and the Palestinian Targum. The last is " nearer

---

183–202. The changes most often are word-play alterations of letters. Cf. B. Gärtner, *ST* 8 (1964), 1–15 ; F. F. Bruce, *Biblical Exegesis in the Qumran Scrolls*, Grand Rapids, 1959, pp. 32 f.

[11] I.e., to the " last generation ". CD 1 : 12 ; 1QpHab 2 : 7 ; 7 : 2 ; Mk 13 : 30 ; cf. Mt 4 : 14–17 ; Lk 16 : 16 ; Ac 2 : 17 ; 3 : 24 ; 1 Co 10 : 11 ; 1 Jn 2 : 18.

[12] B. Gärtner, *ST* 8 (1954), 13 f.

[13] Cf. M. Black, *The Scrolls and Christian Origins*, London, 1961, pp. 192–98 with *An Aramaic Approach to the Gospels and Acts*, Oxford, [3]1967, p. 40 ; cf. Brownlee, *op. cit.*, p. 81n : except for the use of the first person, " the *Genesis Apocryphon* might be described as a sort of Targum ".

[14] See the annotated bibliography in J. A. Fitzmyer, *The Genesis Apocryphon of Qumran Cave 1*, Rome, 1966, pp. 8 f.

[15] *Ibid.*

[16] Similarly, M. R. James (*The Biblical Antiquities of Philo*, London, 1917, p. 33) viewed Chronicles as the " chief model " of the *Biblical Antiquities*.

midrash than version" (p. 1279), and each in its own way is representative of the midrashic development of older Scriptures. Following Miss Bloch's broad definition of midrash, there are at Qumran at least three kinds, the *pesher*, the highly elaborated paraphrase of the *Genesis midrash* and *Jubilees*, and the (unpublished) more literal targums of Job and (fragments of) Leviticus.[17] According to P. Kahle, followed by others, the elaborated paraphrase of the Palestinian Targum represents an earlier stage of development than the more literal official rabbinic Targum Onkelos.[18] The presence of both literary forms at Qumran cautions against positing this (or its opposite) as a general law of development.[19] Nevertheless, it may represent one way in which the midrashic practice proceeded. Further, Kahle (*Geniza*,[2] p. 202) contends that the so-called Fragment Targum largely represents midrashic commentary culled from the older Palestinian Targum[20]; *Targum Pseudo-Jonathan* apparently reflects a similar process, Scripture + commentary→detached commentary, after which the older midrash or commentary is grafted into a later biblical paraphrase (? Onkelos).

To one who is dependent on the specialists the above developments raise a number of questions. What are the guidelines to distinguish midrash as a literary genre and midrash as an activity? Or is this distinction a later refinement that has no place in pre-Christian or pre-rabbinic usage?[21] How much and what kind

[17] Cf. Brownlee, *op. cit.*, pp. 64 f., 81. He believes that the interpretations of 1QpHab are influenced by the Targum to the Prophets and that the *pesher* form, text + commentary, derives from the synagogue practice of Scripture reading + targum. G. Vermes (*RHPR* 35, 1955, 99–103) also found affinities between the Qumran *pesher* and the Targum.

[18] P. Kahle, *The Cairo Geniza*, London, [1]1947, pp. 125 f.; Oxford, [2]1959, pp. 200 ff.; cf. A. Wikgren, *JR* 24 (1944), 91 f.; contrast Fitzmyer, *op. cit.*, pp. 32–35. Kahle is apparently supported by Neofiti I, a recently discovered Palestinian Targum to the Pentateuch. Cf. Black, *Approach*,[3] p. 42; Vermes, *Scripture*, p. 6 R. Bloch (*VDBS* 5, p. 1279) suggested that originally the Palestinian Targum was "une sorte de midrash homilétique, ou simplement le canevas d'une suite d'homélies sur l'Ecriture, faites à la synagogue après la lecture publique de la Torah". Cf. M. McNamara, *The New Testament and the Palestinian Targum to the Pentateuch*, Rome, 1966, pp. 31 f., 64; A. Diez-Macho in *Melanges E. Tisserant*, Citta del Vaticano, 1964, 1, pp. 184 f.

[19] Cf. McNamara, *op. cit.*, p. 25n.

[20] Cf. J. Z. Lauterbach, "Midrash and Mishnah", *JQR* 5 (1914–15), 504–13. He sees a development in halachic literature from wholly midrash (Scripture + commentary) to the Mishnah form (independent halacha).

[21] W. Bacher (*op. cit.*, pp. 103 ff.) notes the difference in rabbinic (tannaitic) usage. A. G. Wright's (*op. cit.*) restricted definition of the genre seems to reflect more a practical than an historical distinction.

of paraphrastic elaboration is required before a " targum " becomes a " midrash " (or " midrash-targum ") ? As yet there seem to be no clear answers to these questions of definition and classification. In spite of this the New Testament student can only be grateful for the progress achieved and seek to apply it judiciously to problems within his own discipline.

The inquiry below addresses an issue raised by the presence of midrashic techniques in certain New Testament quotations. Specifically, is there discernable a development or transition from an earlier midrash form ? What do the techniques signify for the use of the Old Testament in the primitive Christian community ?

## II

A number of Old Testament texts appear in the New Testament both in an explicit midrash and as an independent citation. Among them are Hab 2 : 3–4 ; Ps 8 : 6 ; 110 : 1 ; 118 : 22 f. ; 2 S 7 : 12–14. J. W. Doeve has contended that words lifted from their Scriptural context can never be a *testimonium* to the Jewish mind. What was required was a midrash, an exposition of that text in the context of other Scriptures. The *testimonia*, then, were a secondary phenomenon for non-Jewish Christians growing out of, and extracted from Christian midrash.[22] The presence of *testimonia* at Qumran shows that such collections were used previously in Judaism. But it still may be correct that their value depended upon a preceding midrash.

A New Testament example that may illustrate this kind of development is Paul's use of Hab 2 : 4 in Gal 3 : 11 and, later, in Ro 1 : 17. Gal 3 includes the citation in a midrash on Gn 15 : 6, whose literary form is found also in the Rabbis and Philo.[23] Hab 2 : 4 appears in Ro 1 : 17 as an independent citation. The foundation of Paul's teaching of " righteousness through faith " is the story of Abraham ; Hab 2 : 4 is only an apposite expression of it.[24] Therefore, Ro 1 : 17 presupposes the midrash of Gal 3 or something like it. But Paul does not presuppose that his

[22] Doeve, *op. cit.*, p. 116. B. Lindars in his closely argued *New Testament Apologetic*, London, 1961, pp. 186, 251–59, sought to trace the development topically, e.g., in the consecutive application of the Old Testament to the resurrection, the passion, and the birth of Jesus.

[23] This has been shown in the recent investigation of P. Borgen, *Bread from Heaven*, Leiden, 1965, pp. 51 f.

[24] Cf. E. E. Ellis, *Paul's Use of the Old Testament*, Edinburgh, 1957, p. 120.

readers knew this since in Ro 4 he presents a virtually identical midrash on Gn 15 : 6, but without introducing the citation from Hab 2 : 4.[25] Therefore, unless Ro 1 : 17 (καθὼς γέγραπται !) is only rhetorical or is not intended for Jewish Christians, the instructional force of a *testimonium* did not depend upon its previous establishment in the context of midrash.[26] Nevertheless, it may still be correct that the early Christian use of Scripture did in fact develop from midrash to *testimonia* in many instances and that the *apologetic* effectiveness of the latter depended in some measure upon a midrashic undergirding.

Hab 2 : 3 f. is cited again, independently of Paul,[27] in He 10 : 37 ff. There, also, it appears to be the concluding text of a homiletic midrash (? He 10 : 5–38).[28] In view of its affinities with 1QpHab, however, He 10 : 37 ff. could also well illustrate a Christian *pesher*-type midrash.[29]

The use of Ps 8 : 6 (7) and Ps 110 : 1 presents similar phenomena. With midrashic techniques He 2 : 6–9 establishes (for the believer in Jesus' resurrection) that Ps 8 finds its fulfilment not in " man in general " (8) but in Jesus (9). In 1 Co 15 : 27 this understanding of Ps 8 (and Ps 110) is assumed, and the exposition is restricted to the meaning of the " all things " that are subjected to Jesus. The allusions to Ps 8 and Ps 110 in Eph 1 : 20, 22 apply the texts to Jesus as though the interpretation were self-evident.

Ac 2 : 16–36, perhaps in the form of a homiletic midrash and certainly using midrashic methods,[30] includes a citation of Ps 110 : 1 in which a traditional interpretation is disallowed and an application to Jesus is established. Thereby the pregnant question posed earlier by Jesus (Lk 20 : 42 ff.) finds its exegetical answer. This answer is presupposed in the frequent use of the verse elsewhere, including a catena of *testimonia* in He 1, the

[25] Cf. Borgen, *op. cit.*, pp. 47–52 ; J. W. Bowker, *NTS* 14 (1967-68), 110.

[26] This may be the case also in 4Qtest ; however, one of its citations (Jos 6 : 26) is midrashically elaborated.

[27] Cf. C. H. Dodd, *According to the Scriptures*, London, 1953, pp. 49 ff.

[28] A number of catchwords join He 10 : 5 ff. (= Ps 40 : 7–9) to the subsequent citations and exposition: θυσίαν (8, 26), προσφοράν (8, 10, 14, 18), περὶ ἁμαρτίας (8, 18, 26), ἥκω (9, 37). Note also the (? created) variants εὐδόκησας (6), necessary for a verbal tally with Hab 2 : 4 (38), and ὁ ἐρχόμενος (37), important for an explicit connection with Dt 32 : 35 ; Ps 135 : 14 (30). There is a shift in theme, however, and commentators usually make a major division at He 10 : 18.

[29] Note the tendentious alterations of the Old Testament text and the repetition of the text in the exposition (39), fitting it to a present-time eschatological fulfilment (ἡμεῖς).

[30] Doeve, *op. cit.*, pp. 171 f. ; Bowker, *op. cit.*, pp. 105 ff.

exposition in He 10, and the allusion to this text at the trial of Jesus.[31]

In Mt 21 : 33–44 and parallels an allegory built on Is 5 : 1 ff. is applied to Jesus and concluded with a citation from Ps 118 : 22 f. and an allusion to Dn 2 : 34 f., 44 f. Although the matter is disputed, it appears probable that the allegory originated in the pre-resurrection mission.[32] The introductory formula ἀνέγνωτε (42) suggests that the Psalm citation also goes back to Jesus.[33] The coupling catchwords, οἰκοδομέω (33, 42) and λίθος (42, 44) favour the supposition of an originally unified midrash of some kind.[34] Differently understood, Ps 118 : 22 is introduced as a testimony in Ac 4 : 11, much in the manner of the ἵνα πληρωθῇ quotations in Matthew.[35] There the application to Jesus is not so much explained as it is asserted. The same is true in 1 P 2 : 7, where the text appears in a mosaic of *testimonia* with their *pesher*-

[31] Mk 14 : 62. N. Perrin (*NTS* 12, 1965–66, 150–55) argues that the verse represents the " historicizing " of Christian *pesher* traditions on Ps 110 and other Old Testament texts. For a similar approach to Mt 4 : 1–11 cf. B. Gerhardsson, *The Testing of God's Son*, Lund, 1966. If the texts were culled from some form of Christian midrash, they may still only summarize (and thus not " historicize " in the radical sense) Jesus' actual trial response, in biblical words whose exegesis was understood in the Christian community. But the opposite is equally possible : Jesus' application to himself, then and earlier, of such passages pointed his disciples to them. On this reading their altered, i.e., contemporized, post-resurrection interpretation was only an extension of Jesus' usage. Cf. Doeve, *op. cit.*, pp. 153 f.

[32] Cf. E. E. Ellis, *The Gospel of Luke*, London, 1966, p. 232 ; in *Hommage B. Rigaux*, forthcoming 1969.

[33] It is found in the New Testament only on the lips of Jesus, usually in midrashic exposition (cf. Doeve, *op. cit.*, pp. 105 f., 163 ff. on Mt 12 : 3, 5 ; 22 : 29, 31). It may reflect a well-known rabbinic distinction between reading and knowing Scripture. Cf. D. Daube, *The New Testament and Rabbinic Judaism*, London, 1956, pp. 422–36 ; Ac 8 : 30 ; 13 : 27 ; 2 Co 3 : 14 f.

[34] In Hebrew/Aramaic there may have been a word-play on " to stone " (35) and " to clear stones " (*sḳl* ; Is 5 : 2 ; cf. 62 : 10) and, with a change of synonym, an additional word tally with Ps 118 and Dn 2 (*'bn*). Cf. Is 62 : 10 Targum. Cf. also B. Gerhardsson, *NTS* 14 (1967–68), 165–93, on Mk 4 : 1–20.

[35] I.e., the tendentious rendering (ὑμῶν), the present-time eschatological application (οὗτός ἐστιν), and the sequence, Current Event→Scripture (cf. Mt 3 : 3 ; 11 : 10 ; Ac 2 : 16 ; 1QpHab 3 : 2 ; 4QpIsB 2 : 7). The sequence is opposite to that of the New Testament midrash considered thus far, i.e., Scripture →Current Event. (I am indebted to Professor R. N. Longenecker for calling this distinction to my attention.) Cf. Jn 6 : 31, 50 ; Ro 9 : 7 f. ; 10 : 6, 8 ; He 13 : 15 ; 1QpHab 12 : 3 ff., 7–9 ; 4QpIsB 2 : 6 f., 10 ; 4QpNah 1 : 11 ; 4 Qpatr 2 ; 4Qflor 1 : 2 f. ; CD 6 : 4, 7. As the references indicate, the latter sequence is more frequent in the Qumran *pesher*. The formula, " this is ", or its equivalent is found in the Old Testament, Qumran, and the rabbinical writings. Cf. Is 9 : 14 f. ; Ezk 5 : 5 ; Dn 4 : 24 (21) ; 5 : 25. In Dn and the DSS it is used in conjunction with or as an equivalent of *pesher*. Cf. McNamara, *op. cit.*, p. 72.

type elaboration. The allusion to Ps 118 in Eph 2 : 20 ff. simply takes the Christian reference for granted.

2 S 7 : 6–16 offers a clearer example. Ac 13 : 16–41 alludes to it (22 f.), probably as the haphtarah text of a synagogue homily.[36] Its application to Jesus is confirmed by other Scriptures and by the events of Jesus' Davidic descent and his resurrection. The messianic use of 2 S 7 is pre-Christian [37]; what is interesting is that the early Church was not content simply to appropriate it but established its interpretation by means of midrash. Such exegesis may undergird the *testimonia* use of 2 S 7 in 2 Co 6 : 18 and He 1 : 5, where the Christian reference of the text is assumed.

## III

In these and similar contexts, some closer in structure to homiletic midrash and some closer to the Qumran *pesher*, the text of the Old Testament citation is sometimes shaped to fit the contiguous exposition.[38] *Testimonia* in the New Testament also are characteristically tendentious in their text-form, but they often lack any accompanying exposition or elaboration.[39] In the light of the above discussion such independent citations may represent lemma texts that have been excerpted from midrash. Some quotations that combine texts from the Law and the Prophets (and the Writings) [40] or that merge an Old Testament text with a

[36] The midrash form of the passage has been demonstrated, to a fair degree of probability, by J. W. Bowker (*NTS* 14, 1967–68, 101–4) and J. W. Doeve (*op. cit.*, cf. pp. 172–76). They take 2 S 7 to be the underlying haphtarah text. Regarding the allusion to 2 S 7 cf. Egypt (17), judges (20), Saul (21), David (22), raise up (22) my son (33). The verbal tallies between texts and exposition also reflect a midrashic procedure : Δαυὶδ (22, 34 ff.), ἐγείρω (22, 23D, 30, 37) and perhaps ὑψόω (17) = ἀνίστημι (33 f.) in an underlying Semitic text-form.

[37] Cf. 4Qflor 1 : 7–11 ; 4Q Son of God.

[38] Cf. σημεῖα, Ac 2 : 19, 22 ; καθίζω, Ac 2 : 30, cf. 34 ; δίδωμι, Ac 13 : 34, 35 (cf. Bowker, *op. cit.*, p. 104 ; Dt 4 : 38) ; προσκυνεῖν, βαβυλῶνος, Ac 7 : 43 ; ἐλευθέρας, Gal 4 : 30 f., 22 f. ; σοφῶν, 1 Co 3 : 20, 19 ; παιδεύει, He 12 : 6, 7–10. Further, see my article, " Quotations ", *International Standard Bible Encyclopedia*, Revised ed., ed. G. W. Bromiley, Grand Rapids, forthcoming 1969. The New Testament appears to be more radically creative in reshaping the text than is the Qumran midrash. Interpretive variants in 1QpHab depend largely on word-play ; but cf. 4Qtest 22, 29 f. which makes a significant omission of Jericho.

[39] E.g., some of the ἵνα πληρωθῇ citations in Mt. The lack of elaboration occasioned B. Gärtner's (*ST* 8, 1954, 12 f.) criticism of the identification of them as *pesher* midrash *contra* K. Stendahl (*op. cit.*, pp. 194–202).

[40] Cf. Ellis, *Testament*, pp. 49 f., 186 ; Stendahl, *op. cit.*, p. 216.

snippet of another[41] may have a similar background. However, the Targums and, as W. H. Brownlee has pointed out, the Isaiah text at Qumran (1QIs[a]) also have assimilated related Old Testament passages. Whether behind a merged citation in the New Testament lies such a targumizing "implicit" midrash, an explicit midrash, an *ad hoc* assimilation by the New Testament writer, or some other explanation is not easy to determine. For example, behind Ro 9 : 33 ; 10 : 11 ; 1 P 2 : 6 ff. (Is 28 : 16 ; 8 : 14) there may have been a *testimonium*[42] or, on the other hand, an earlier midrash similarly re-employed in Romans and 1 Peter.

If some New Testament quotations represent the lemma texts of an explicit midrash, it is equally possible that the midrashic commentary, with or without its Old Testament allusions, also was detached and used. Taking this approach, M. Gertner (*JSS* 7, 1962, 267–92) and others identified as midrashic commentary a number of New Testament passages, including parables of and stories about Jesus.[43] It is true that in some Gospel narratives there is a tendency for Old Testament allusions to fade in transmission.[44] But in the absence of a clear allusion or an explicit quotation it is, in the nature of the case, difficult to establish a midrashic background for a New Testament passage.

In conclusion, the presence of different types of midrash—targum, *pesher*, synagogue homily—is most likely reflected in the use of the Old Testament in the New. Also, some New Testament writers used midrash to establish a Christian interpretation of Old Testament texts, an interpretation that is assumed in the *testimonia* use of the same texts. The results of the above study are not as conclusive as one might wish. But they do underscore the plausibility if not probability that some independent New Testament quotations have been extracted from an earlier context of Christian midrash.

[41] Cf. Ro 11 : 26 f. (Is 59 : 20 f. + 27 : 9) ; He 10 : 37 ff. (Is 26 : 20 + Hab 2 : 3 f.) ; Mt 2 : 6 (Mic 5 : 2(1) + 2 S 5 : 2) ; Lk 19 : 38a (Ps 118 : 26 + ? Zec 9 : 9) with Jn 12 : 13, 15 ; Mt 21 : 5 (Zec 9 : 9 + Is 62 : 11) with Jn 12 : 15 (Zec 9 : 9 + ? Zeph 3 : 14, 16). Mt 21 : 13 (Is 56 : 7 + Jer 7 : 11) and Mt 21 : 42 ff. (Ps 118 : 22 f. + Dn 2 : 34 f., 44 f.) are somewhat different.

[42] Dodd, *op. cit.*, p. 43 ; Ellis, *Testament*, p. 89 ; B. Lindars, *ExpT* 75 (1963–1964), 173.

[43] Mk 4 : 1–22 (on Jer 4 : 3) ; 7 : 31–37 (on Is 35 : 5) ; Jn 10 (on Ezk 34), 15 (on Ezk 19 : 10–14) ; 2 Co 3 (on Ex 34) ; Ja (on Ps 12).

[44] Cf. Lk 20 : 9 ; 21 : 20 ; (12 : 53) with the Markan parallels.

# IS THE SON OF MAN PROBLEM INSOLUBLE?

A. J. B. Higgins

Whether or not Jesus spoke of the Son of man and, if so, in what sense; or, if he did not use the expression, why it appears so often in the Gospels—these are questions of paramount importance for the understanding both of his ministry and of the growth of christology. But agreement seems to be as far off as ever.

This study was suggested by the almost simultaneous publication in 1967 of two books, Dr Morna D. Hooker's *The Son of Man in Mark* and Professor Norman Perrin's *Rediscovering the Teaching of Jesus*. No two writers could differ more from one another in their treatment of the Son of man in the Gospels. Moreover, in 1965 Professor R. H. Fuller, in *The Foundations of New Testament Christology*, announced a radical change of view from that presented in his *The Mission and Achievement of Jesus* in 1954. Fuller's conclusions also differ widely from those of both Hooker and Perrin. In the following pages I shall enquire whether any one of these three recent investigations represents a real advance, or whether, taken together, they tend to confirm the suspicions of those who regard the problem as likely to remain insoluble.

## I

Let us begin with Fuller. As he points out, there are two main issues. The first is the derivation of the term Son of man in the Gospels. Fuller regards Dn 7:13 f. as from an earlier source, in which the Son of man was an individual eschatological figure. In adapting it to his own composition, the apocalyptic writer does not abandon this conception, but expands it so that the figure is also the representative of the saints of the Most High over whom he rules. Referring to doubts about the pre-Christian origin of the Similitudes of Enoch, Fuller maintains that the Son of man figure here, and also in the later 2 Esdras, can hardly belong to supposed Christian interpolations, since it lacks " the distinctively Christian differentia " of identification with Jesus of Nazareth. He concludes " that despite the well-founded doubts of British scholars about the Similitudes, there is good reason to believe with the majority of scholars outside Britain, both in continental Europe and in America, that the figure of the Son of man was established in pre-Christian Jewish apocalyptic as the eschatological agent of redemption ".[1]

The second question is whether or not Jesus used the term Son of man as a self-designation. Although Fuller has now abandoned the position he defended in *The Mission and Achievement of Jesus,* it is important to notice that in neither work does he treat the Son of man as a direct self-designation of Jesus. In his earlier book he wrote that Jesus in his ministry is not to be identified " *tout court* with the coming Son of Man ", although he is closely associated with him.[2] The relation between Jesus and the Son of man corresponds to that between the earthly ministry and the coming kingdom of God. In the ministry the kingdom, although not yet having arrived, is operative proleptically in Jesus' words and healings. Jesus is not yet the glorified Son of man, but suffers as one destined to be the Son of man. Thus Fuller rightly rejected any idea of a fusion of the Servant and Son of man concepts into the entity: suffering Servant-Son of man. Jesus distinguished between two periods. " First, there is the period of earthly obedience and suffering, which he conceives in the language of the Servant, and the future period, in which the kingdom will have come, and which he expresses in terms of the Son of man. The dividing point between them is the cross, which is as decisive for his person as it is for the kingdom." [3] So when Jesus speaks of the Son of man, he is not using the term as a present self-designation. But neither, when Fuller says that Jesus acts as the Son of man designate, does he apparently mean that Jesus thought that he would be equated or identified in some way with an objective figure. It is rather that Jesus applied to himself and his ministry the *imagery* of the mission and destiny of Israel described in Dn 7. In so doing, he individualized the corporate metaphor for the saints of the Most High, transforming it into " a title for the glorified, supernatural bringer of salvation ".[4] As we have seen, however, Fuller in his more recent book maintains that the figure of the Son of man as

[1] *Foundations,* p. 38.
[2] *Mission,* p. 103.
[3] *Ibid.,* p. 107.
[4] *Ibid.,* p. 102.

the eschatological agent of redemption was already established in pre-Christian Jewish apocalyptic.

I turn to Fuller's radical reconstruction in *The Foundations of New Testament Christology*. In his earlier book he wrote that Jesus' thought about himself as performing proleptically the functions of the eschatological Son of man, while not a christology, " does involve a ' Messianic consciousness ' or a ' Messianic claim ' ".[5] Now, however, Jesus' " self-understanding " is completely divorced from messianic categories, and his ministry is described in terms of " eschatological prophecy ". In the basic and authentic saying in Lk 12 : 8 f., " the Son of man is brought in simply to reinforce the decisiveness of his present offer. The Son of man merely acts as a kind of rubber stamp at the End for the salvation which is already being imparted in Jesus ".[6] In place of his former interpretation, that Jesus' fulfilment of his mission in terms of the suffering Servant would lead to his vindication *as* Son of man, Fuller now maintains that ' Jesus understood his mission in terms of eschatological prophecy and was confident of its vindication *by* the Son of man at the End." [7] In other words, Jesus thought it necessary to appeal to a supposed Jewish apocalyptic figure, independent of and distinct from himself, as a sort of court of appeal on his ministry.

There are two main reasons why, in my opinion, Fuller's new solution of the problem is unsatisfactory. In the first place, he appears to rely on the idea of the Son of man as Jesus' vindicator, as a somewhat desperate expedient at all costs to assign *some* role to that figure. Despite all that has been said recently to the contrary,[8] I agree with Fuller that there is no compelling reason for abandoning the view that in pre-Christian Jewish apocalyptic there did exist a belief in an eschatological Son of man. On the other hand, I do not believe that an individual, supernatural Son of man " was part of the mental furniture *of Jesus himself* " (C. F. D. Moule's expression, italics mine), however it may have been with some of his contemporaries. The authority inherent in Jesus' reported words and actions does not suggest that he would have appealed to any other than God himself as, to him, Father

[5] *Mission*, p. 108 ; but cf. p. 116 for the term " pre-Messianic ", rather than " Messianic " (in the usual sense) as a description of Jesus' life.

[6] *Foundations*, p. 123.

[7] *Ibid.*, p. 130 (italics mine).

[8] Cf., e.g., C. F. D. Moule, *The Phenomenon of the New Testament*, London, 1967, p. 34, n. 21.

(Abba) in a special and unique sense. A " functional " re-interpretation by Jesus of the Son of man concept as applicable to himself has more in its favour.[9]

Secondly, Fuller's abandonment of his former view that Jesus understood his earthly mission in terms of the Servant in favour of the concept of eschatological prophecy is, I feel, a retrograde step. Is this " working concept " really deep enough to have led the early church to find in it the seeds of christology ? As Fuller agrees,[10] Jesus was certainly crucified not simply as a messianic prophet, but as a messianic pretender. So in spite of his remarks on the basic datum of christology being the nature of Jesus' own preaching and activity, rather than the mere concept of Jesus as eschatological prophet,[11] the probability is that he identified his own person more closely and directly with the kingdom he proclaimed than can be accounted for by the concept of eschatological prophecy.

## II

In the introduction to her book Dr Hooker expresses dissatisfaction with the form-critical and traditio-historical methods. " The same principles and methods ", she complains, " lead one scholar to trace the title ' Son of man ' to Jesus, another to attribute it to the Church, and a third to trace the term itself to Jesus, but its use as a christological title to the community." [12] Therefore, she implies, such methods had better be given up. One might just as well suggest that literary criticism of the Gospels should be abandoned, and that efforts to solve the synoptic problem are fruitless, because there is disagreement about Q, Proto-Luke, and even the priority of Mark.[13] However, she is not content merely to cling to the traditional belief that Jesus did refer to himself as the Son of man. Neither is her object once again to analyse the groups and sources, " but to study the problem of the Son of man from another angle ", " to

[9] As suggested in my book, *Jesus and the Son of Man*, London, 1964, pp. 197, 202 ff. My use of the title Son of God in this connection has been misunderstood by some as narrowly " traditional " ; but in fact it is intended as the obverse of Abba (p. 208).

[10] *Foundations*, p. 110.

[11] *Ibid.*, pp. 130 f.

[12] *The Son of Man in Mark*, p. 5.

[13] W. R. Farmer, *The Synoptic Problem*, New York, 1964.

study the impact which the ' Son of man ' sayings make when we look at one Gospel—St Mark's ".[14] She undertakes to discover whether the Markan sayings form a consistent pattern and, if so, although the pattern in the first place would reflect the evangelist's own interpretation, whether it also sheds light on Jesus' own use of the term. Because, as she claims, many recent writers have ignored the Jewish background material, she devotes Part I of her book (pp. 11–74) to a survey of it. We are told that the error committed by recent writers has been to assume, on the basis of 1 Enoch, " that during the first half of the first century A.D., the " one like a Son of man " in Dn 7 was universally interpreted by the Jews as an individual eschatological and glorious judge ".[15]

The theme of Dn 7, as expounded by Hooker, is the rejection by the other nations of the God-given rule belonging to the righteous remnant in Israel, symbolized by the figure " like a son of man ", their sufferings, and their ultimate vindication. She argues that the common idea that the Son of man here does not suffer, " rests upon a false understanding of his relationship with those he represents ",[16] for although the Son of man is only mentioned when he is presented before the Ancient of Days and receives everlasting dominion, the righteous in Israel who are first at this point symbolically represented, certainly did, as a fact of history, endure suffering and persecution. Therefore their vindication is more than a pious hope. Although not yet acknowledged as such on earth, Israel is already the Son of man, the true heir of Adam, to whom dominion rightfully belongs. But on the other hand, there is no getting away from the fact that the author of Dn 7 does not use the Son of man concept (" one like a son of man ") in referring to the sufferings of the saints of Israel. Why is this ? Scholarly opinion continues to be divided on the answer to this question. But I cannot see that Hooker's answer is the correct one. She contends that in Dn 7 the apocalyptic element is much less important and less central than the theme of rejection, suffering, and vindication. But the other view is the more cogent, that in this passage we have an adaptation, in a corporate sense, of an already familiar belief in an individual eschatological Son of man, associated with judgment and deliverance, but quite unconnected with suffering.

At this point I venture to quote Hooker again. Referring

[14] *The Son of Man in Mark*, p. 7. [15] *Ibid.*, p. 48. [16] *Ibid.*, p. 28.

back to her investigation, in Part I, of other Jewish works, she writes:

"This same theme of Israel's divine right to rule the earth, a right usurped by other nations, was found in much of the intertestamental literature, expressed sometimes in terms of Adam, though the phrase 'Son of man' is not used. In 1 Enoch, in spite of the fact that the Son of man has become an individual of supernatural character, he is still closely associated with the themes of election and obedience. Both he and the community which is so closely linked with him are defined as the 'elect' and 'righteous'."[17]

Whatever may be said of Dn 7, the Son of man (or the Elect One) in 1 Enoch is himself nowhere subjected to humiliation and suffering. In 1 En 46:3, for example, the angel says to Enoch, "This is the Son of man who hath righteousness, with whom dwelleth righteousness"; and he will overthrow the mighty and the sinners. These enemies of the Lord of Spirits "persecute the houses of His congregations, and the faithful who hang upon the name of the Lord of Spirits" (v. 8). In 48:4 the Son of man is called "a staff to the righteous", and in vv. 8–10 the fate of the wicked enemies of "the holy and righteous ones" (v. 7) is described. Nowhere does the Son of man actually share in the tribulations of the righteous. His function is to reward them, and to punish the wicked. It is true that this individual Son of man is "closely associated with the community of the righteous of which he is the head", and that he is the Righteous One and the Elect One, as the members of the community are "the righteous ones" and "the elect ones".[18] But he does not suffer, as they do. Hooker maintains that this is because the Danielic figure (associated with suffering) is the older conception, and that a separation of the Son of man from the idea of humiliation and suffering was a consequence of individualization of the concept and more exclusive emphasis on the future glory.[19] But it is much more likely that 1 Enoch provides a close approximation to an original apocalyptic Son of man figure, not associated with suffering, of which the Danielic figure is an adaptation. Moreover, the so-called evidence for the attachment of the idea of suffering to the Danielic figure in Jewish exegesis, and therefore for a

[17] *Ibid.*, pp. 189 f., cf. p. 71. How far can we suppose that the primary significance of Dn 7 really is its representation, in terms of the Son of man, of the idea of Israel as the true descendant of Adam and the heir of Adam's lost rule?

[18] *Ibid.*, p. 46.

[19] *Ibid.*, p. 30.

suffering Son of man, is extremely tenuous.[20] And if there is substance in the view that, quite apart from 1 Enoch, there is little or nothing to support the idea of a suffering Son of man in Dn 7, a very important element in the Markan pattern according to Hooker, is absent from the most relevant Jewish background material.

In Dn 7 vindication is promised to the faithful in Israel, who are destined to inherit the rule once given to Adam. Their present sufferings are the result of the rejection of their authority by other nations. According to Hooker, it is precisely this pattern that unifies the three types of Son of man sayings in Mark. The dominant feature, transcending the customary three-fold classification of the sayings, is that of authority. Each group of sayings, she contends, implies the other two.

" The sayings in ch. 2 do not in themselves involve the others, but because they are rejected by the Jewish leaders they are inevitably followed by the sayings about suffering and final vindication. These two themes of suffering and vindication are also linked together. It is sometimes maintained that the two groups of sayings are entirely separate and are never combined. Here, however, we see one of the dangers of dividing the sayings into groups, for this statement is an over-simplication which conceals the truth. It is true that nowhere in Mark is there a saying which holds together the necessity for suffering with the imagery of coming in glory. But the belief in the ultimate vindication of the Son of man is contained in every one of the Marcan passion predictions, expressed in terms of the resurrection." [21]

Moreover, Hooker continues, the future sayings (8 : 38 ; 13 : 26 ; 14 : 62) belong to contexts concerned with the sufferings, either of Jesus himself or of his followers, and with subsequent vindication. Taken together, therefore, the three groups of sayings offer " three aspects of the Son of man's authority—an authority which is in turn proclaimed, denied and vindicated ", and the Markan pattern is revealed " as a logical and coherent whole ".[22] The question is then asked, whether this pattern is the evangelist's own construction, or whether it is traceable to earlier tradition, and even to Jesus himself. It is generally agreed

[20] All that needs to be said on this is to be found in S. Mowinckel, *He That Cometh*, Oxford, 1956, pp. 410–15.

[21] *Ibid.*, pp. 180 f.

[22] *Ibid.*, pp. 181 f.

that the Markan sayings came to the evangelist from the tradition with which he was familiar. But it by no means follows that the presumed Markan pattern is also pre-Markan.

Even in the Gospel of Mark itself, as it stands, the pattern is far from being as self-evident as is maintained in this book. As we have seen in the quotation above, while it is correctly stated that the two sayings about authority in Mk 2 : 10 and 2 : 28 do not in themselves involve the other kinds of sayings about suffering and vindication, they are yet " inevitably " followed by them, because the Jewish leaders reject Jesus' claims to authority expressed in those two utterances. Surely this is to infer a connection on very tenuous grounds. Why does the evangelist not use the term Son of man again until the first passion prediction in 8 : 31, if this, and the others that follow, are so closely connected thematically with the sayings in ch. 2? Moreover, these passion predictions allude not to the parousia or exaltation, but to the resurrection of the Son of man; and this is why they have been thought to have a different origin from the parousia sayings. In none of the latter is there a word about suffering. Hooker, however, says that all three (8 : 38; 13 : 26; 14 : 62) are found in contexts concerned with suffering, and that we must concentrate on the context. Certainly the evangelist's own understanding of a saying can only be gathered from the context. But the context of Mk 8 : 38, as well as that of the superior Q, form of the saying (Lk 12 : 8 f.), is secondary.[23] Of both this *logion* and Mk 13 : 26 we are told that the coming of the Son of man " represents the vindication of those who have suffered for Jesus' sake, and the shame of those who have not been prepared to share in his suffering "; while in 14 : 62 " it signifies the vindication of Jesus himself, now standing before the high priest, about to bear the sufferings which he has foretold for the Son of man ".[24] Certainly in this way we may say that the Son of man's triumph is not isolated from the idea of suffering. But as usual, it is Dn 7 which is the basis of this strained exegesis.[25]

Even if it were conceded that the three groups of Markan Son of man sayings in themselves do actually fall into a logical and coherent pattern, there are formidable difficulties in the way of tracing such a pattern back to earlier tradition, and still more to

[23] Cf. *Jesus and the Son of Man*, p. 60.
[24] *The Son of Man in Mark*, p. 181.
[25] *Ibid.*, p. 181, n. 2.

Jesus himself. Hooker thinks that these sayings present a consistent interpretation " which would make sense within the life of Jesus ", and that it probably corresponds to Jesus' own use and understanding of the term as a self-designation.[26] But the study of Mark alone can give but a one-sided picture, which needs to be corrected by consideration of non-Markan traditions. For the presumed Markan pattern to be attributable to Jesus himself, it is not enough to rely on Mark alone, because what we find there could be nothing more than one interpretation of the Son of man, coming, if not from the evangelist himself, from the form of the tradition utilized by him. It is significant that, as Hooker admits, the pattern is much less clear in the other Gospels. She mentions " traces " of it in other sources, including the Fourth Gospel.[27] If the pattern really is pre-Markan, and ultimately derived from Jesus' teaching, it is strange that only vestiges of it can be discovered in the other Gospel sources.

In a very real sense, of course, the New Testament message as a whole is characterized by the theme of Jesus' rejection, despite his claims to God-given authority, followed by his final vindication by God in raising him from the dead, exalting him, and giving him " the name which is above every name ".[28] What is in question is whether in Mark this theme or pattern is deliberately and consciously drawn up in terms of the Son of man, whether it is all based on Dn 7,[29] and whether it stems from Jesus' own understanding of his mission and destiny as the Son of man. Although Hooker has made a valuable contribution

[26] *Ibid.*, p. 191.

[27] *Ibid.*, pp. 194–97.

[28] Ph 2 : 9.

[29] *The Son of Man in Mark*, p. 192 : " The authority, necessity for suffering, and confidence in final vindication, which are expressed in the Marcan sayings, can all be traced to Dan. 7 ". Hooker (pp. 187 f.) rightly rejects the still popular notion that Jesus preferred the term Son of man to Messiah as less political, and then reinterpreted it in terms of the suffering Servant. In *Jesus and the Servant* (London, 1959), arguing that Jesus did not regard himself as the suffering Servant at all, she transferred the idea of suffering to the Son of man, a thesis fully worked out in her present book. This view, however, is not radically different from the one she rejects. In both, the Son of man is a figure of suffering, only now he is not a suffering Servant-Son of man, but still a suffering Son of man. It is possible to be influenced too much (perhaps unconsciously) by the fact that Jesus allegedly used the *title* Son of man, whereas he never used the title of Servant. As Cullmann points out, Jesus' allusions to Is 53 are always obscure. " From the standpoint of form criticism this fact confirms rather than refutes the notion that Jesus thought of himself as the *ebed Yahweh* ' (*Salvation in History*, London, 1967, p. 227, n. 3).

to the debate, I am not convinced that she has proved these points, or has succeeded in overthrowing the results of traditio-historical study, according to which the only authentic sayings are to be found among those referring to the eschatological functions of the Son of man, while the other two categories originated in the early church's identification of Jesus with the figure to whom he seemed to be pointing.

## III

In 1963 Professor Norman Perrin published his serviceable book *The Kingdom of God in the Teaching of Jesus*. His recent work, *Rediscovering the Teaching of Jesus*, contains considerable changes of view to which he has been led in the short intervening period of four years. A strict application of form-critical methods has brought him to a more negative attitude to much of the traditional material. As he himself claims, the most important change of view concerns the Son of man sayings. Despite radical differences between him and Dr Hooker, there is at the same time a certain resemblance which is worth noting. To the latter the apocalyptic features of Dn 7 are less important than the pattern of Israel's rejection, suffering, and vindication. It is mainly a matter of imagery. What Jesus did was to apply this pattern and imagery to himself. It was in this sense that he used the term Son of man as a self-designation, and not by way of self-identification with an objective figure. To think that he made such an identification is to fall into the error of assigning too much importance to the Son of man in 1 Enoch, as if the figure in Dn 7 was *always* interpreted by the Jews as an individual eschatological judge and deliverer. Perrin, too, sees only imagery in Dn 7, 1 Enoch, etc. But he goes much further than Hooker. He tries to show that in Judaism there was no Son of man concept at all, but rather various uses of Son of man imagery. The similarity of view between these two scholars ends with this emphasis on imagery. In the first place, while Hooker argues for the basic thematic unity of the three types of Son of man sayings, Perrin confines himself to the apocalyptic sayings as quite distinct from the two other types. Secondly, he suggests that the Son of man in the Gospels, so far from being Jesus' self-designation, is the result of early Christian scriptural interpretation. He thus joins the ranks (but for different reasons) of those who maintain that Jesus did not use Son of man as a title at all.[30]

Perrin sets out to discuss the following "core" passages: Mk 8 : 38 ; 13 : 26 ; 14 : 62 ; Lk 12 : 8 f. par. ; 11 : 30 ; 17 : 24 par. ; 17 : 26 f. par.[31] He makes three main points.

1. The widespread assumption, shared by a number of scholars who differ on other aspects of the problem, of the existence in Judaism of a definite and consistent concept of an apocalyptic Son of man who would act as judge and deliverer at the end, is called in question. Neither of the two cycles of tradition represented by 1 En 37–71 and 2 Es 13 "introduce Son of man as an independent conception with a title which is in itself a sufficient designation; rather, each cycle begins afresh with clear and careful references to Dan. 7." [32] But the only features common to both the later writings are the references to Dn 7 : 13, and the ascription of pre-existence to the Son of man in 1 Enoch and to the man from the sea in 2 Es 13. The relationship between these figures is insufficient for the supposition that they reflect a common conception. It is rather a matter of independent use of the imagery of Dn 7 : 13. This imagery is derived from ancient Canaanite mythology, concerning the passing of power from one god to a younger god (in Dn 7 the Ancient of Days and the Son of man respectively).[33]

2. Just as, in the Similitudes, Enoch becomes Son of man on the basis of the interpretation of his translation in terms of Ezk 1 and Dn 7, so in the Christian tradition, and quite independently, Jesus becomes Son of man on the basis of the

[30] P. Vielhauer, "Gottesreich und Menschensohn in der Verkündigung Jesu", *Festschrift für Günther Dehn*, ed. W. Schneemelcher, Neukirchen, 1957, pp. 51–79; "Jesus und der Menschensohn: zur Diskussion mit Heinz Eduard Tödt und Eduard Schweizer", *ZThK* 60 (1963), 133–77; H. Conzelmann, *ZThK* 54 (1957), 277 ff., and *RGG*³ 3 (1959), 630 f.; E. Käsemann, *Essays on New Testament Themes*, London, 1964, pp. 43 f.; H. M. Teeple, "The Origin of the Son of Man Christology", *JBL* 84 (1965), 213–50; further literature in Perrin, *Rediscovering*, pp. 259 f. Perrin's own discussion is on pp. 164 ff.; most of his article, "The Son of Man in Ancient Judaism and Primitive Christianity: A Suggestion", *BR* 11 (1966), 17–28, corresponds to pp. 164–72 of this discussion; cf. also "Mark XIV. 62: The End Product of a Christian Pesher Tradition?" *NTS* 12 (1965–66), 150–55, and "New Beginnings in Christology: A Review Article" [of Fuller, *Foundations*], *JR* 46 (1966), 491–96, especially 495.

[31] *Rediscovering*, pp. 164–99.

[32] *Ibid.*, p. 165.

[33] *Ibid.*, p. 166. For a summary of the use of Dn 7 : 13 in midrashic literature in regard to the Messiah, see pp. 171 f.

interpretation of his resurrection in terms of Ps 110 : 1 and Dn 7 : 13.[34]

3. Since no concept of an eschatological Son of man existed in Judaism, Jesus could not have spoken of the coming Son of man, either meaning himself or some other figure. All the apocalyptic sayings are products of the early church.[35]

Perrin suggests three exegetical traditions using Dn 7 : 13. The first of these is combined with Ps 110 : 1, in order to interpret the resurrection-ascension-exaltation of Jesus. The second, in connection with early passion apologetic, uses Dn 7 : 13 in association with Zec 12 : 10 ff., which is interpreted as referring to the crucifixion (cf. Jn 19 : 37). Of special importance is Rev 1 : 7 which, in introducing the idea that the Son of man who has ascended to God will return, to the consternation of the crucifiers, represents the earliest parousia use of Dn 7 : 13. The third exegetical tradition is the fully developed parousia one as we see it in Mk 13 : 26. Here the tendency is to move away from the original tradition in the direction of a purely apocalyptic expectation of the " second coming " of Jesus as Son of man.

In view of its central importance, I turn to Mk 14 : 62. In his *NTS* article Perrin follows suggestions, with special reference to Fr Barnabas Lindars,[36] that there was an early Christian type of Old Testament interpretation which, because of its similarities to that of the Qumran community, can conveniently be termed a *pesher* tradition. If we adopt the explanations offered either by Lindars or by Perrin, the familiar difficulty of the order of events in Mk 14 : 62—the Son of man *first* sits at the right hand of Power and *then* comes with the clouds—simply disappears.[37]

Lindars [38] speaks of the second part of the text (" and coming with the clouds of heaven ") as a pre-Markan addition, from Dn 7 : 13, to the original form of the saying. This (Mk 14 : 62a) expressed the idea of Jesus' exaltation as the Son of man by conflating two texts, Ps 110 : 1 and Dn 7 : 13, understood as

[34] *Ibid.*, pp. 172 f., 198. C. K. Barrett, however (*Jesus and the Gospel Tradition*, London, 1967, p. 94), maintains that " the Enochic and the gospel developments of the Son of man theme " are not likely to be unrelated, and even that the story of Enoch as an eschatological prophet exalted to heaven to be the Son of man, could have been relevant to Jesus' own thought about himself, and to his use of the title.

[35] *Ibid.*, p. 198.

[36] *New Testament Apologetic*, London, 1961.

[37] For a discussion, see *Jesus and the Son of Man*, pp. 66–74.

[38] *Op. cit.*, pp. 48 f.

equivalent in meaning. The addition, made under the increasing influence of the parousia idea, thus introduced a fresh meaning, quite foreign to the original saying.

Perrin goes further. According to him Mk 14 : 62 is a conflation of two *pesher* traditions, namely, the interpretation of the resurrection and exaltation of Jesus in terms of both Ps 110 : 1 and Dn 7 : 13, and the interpretation of the crucifixion and the parousia in terms of Zec 12 : 10 ff. and Dn 7 : 13. Finally, this dual *pesher* has been "historicized" and transformed into an utterance of Jesus himself.

The following considerations need to be borne in mind in evaluating Perrin's suggestions.

1. We cannot be certain that various uses of the Son of man imagery of Dn 7 are a sufficient explanation of the phenomena, and that these phenomena cannot be satisfactorily accounted for as various applications and adaptations of a Son of man *concept*, although it may be conceded that this concept, if it existed, may not have been as unified and consistent as has been thought.

2. The idea of a Christian *pesher* type of interpretation of Old Testament passages, closely resembling that in the Qumran texts, is certainly correct. Like other Jews, the men of Qumran expected a Davidic Messiah, and interpreted a number of scriptural passages in reference to him.[39] This figure was also known to this community as the Messiah of Aaron and Israel,[40] because of its priestly and lay membership. But because of this dual constitution, and because its superior was a priest, the community, as the true Israel, also expected another anointed figure, a legitimate high priest as its leader, to whom even the Messiah, when he came, would be subordinate. Appeal was, indeed, made to the scriptures in support of this belief,[41] but what needs

[39] Gn 49 : 10 ; Nu 24 : 17 ; Is 11 : 1 ff. ; Am 9 : 11 ; 2 S 2 : 11 ; 7 : 13 f. ; Ps 2 : 1 f. ; see F. Hahn, *Christologische Hoheitstitel*, Göttingen, 1963, p. 147, n. 5.

[40] For this view see my art., "The Priestly Messiah", *NTS* 13, 1966–67, 215–19.

[41] Nu 24 : 17 in CD 7 : 17–19 : the star is the interpreter of the Law (cf. 4Qflor 1 : 11), with Dt 33 : 8–11 in 4Qtest 14–20 : Moses' blessing of Levi, and now, perhaps, most significant, 4QpPs 37 3 : 15 : verses 23 f. of the psalm refer to "the priest, the Teacher of Righteousness (or Rightful Teacher)". On "sacerdotal messianism" at Qumran see the illuminating discussion by Professor Black, *The Dead Sea Scrolls and Christian Doctrine*, London, 1966, pp. 4–11, who, however, relates the terms "the priest, the Rightful Teacher" to the Messiah of Aaron and Israel understood as a *priestly* Messiah, "who will exercise the same priestly functions as lawgiver as the priestly founder of the Community" [the original Rightful Teacher].

to be emphasized is that the expectation of this figure was not *based* on scriptural interpretation. It arose from the concrete facts that the community had been founded by a priest,[42] and that it had a priest as its head.

There is a possible, if incomplete, analogy between the origin of the Qumran expectation of the high priest, and the origin of the Son of man in the Gospels. The Qumran belief was anchored in a datum of experience—the priestly leader. Perrin suggests that the Son of man in the Gospels originated in early Christian interpretation of scripture, in the application of Dn 7 : 13 to Jesus' resurrection and exaltation. With the Qumran analogy in mind, however, it is just as legitimate to conclude that the Son of man belief was also anchored in a datum of experience, the knowledge that Jesus himself had used the title. Other considerations appear to point in the same direction.

3. The origin of the Son of man christology cannot be isolated from that of other christologies. The principle that the main christological beliefs developed from ideas implicitly present in the ministry is, I believe, a sound one, but naturally does not exclude the influence of scriptural interpretation.[43]

The designation of Jesus as Lord goes back to the Aramaic-speaking church (*marana tha*, 1 Co 16 : 22 ; cf. Didache 10 : 6). Among Greek-speaking Christians this became κύριος, which in the Septuagint often stands both for Yahweh and for Hebrew *'āḏōn*. The clearest example is Ps 110 : 1, " The Lord says to my lord : Sit at my right hand, till I make your enemies your footstool." The remarkable thing is that the early church was prepared to go so far as to apply to Jesus the term κύριος in the *former* sense.[44] But, as Professor F. F. Bruce has finely written, " it was not primarily this linguistic accident [κύριος = Yahweh] that made those early Christian writers apply to Jesus Old Testament passages which plainly referred to Israel's God. What moved them to do so was the impact which Jesus himself made on their lives—an impact so unparalleled that it made men who had been brought up as faithful monotheistic Jews give Jesus, inevitably and spontaneously, the glory which belonged

[42] Cf. Black, *op. cit.*, p. 10.

[43] Cf. my art., " The Old Testament and Some Aspects of New Testament Christology ", *Promise and Fulfilment : essays presented to Professor S. H. Hooke*, ed. F. F. Bruce, Edinburgh, 1963, pp. 128–41.

[44] E.g., Ro 10 : 13 (Jl 2 : 32) ; He 1 : 10 (Ps 102 : 25).

to the one God ".[45] In other words, the invocation of the risen Jesus as Lord already before Paul wrote to the Corinthians, expressed the conviction that the authority of the words and actions of Jesus had been of a supra-human order, a conviction independent of the use and the interpretation of scripture.

In the development of the Son of God christology Ps 2 : 7, " You are my son, today I have begotten you ", played a significant part.[46] In the synoptics Jesus never uses the title Son of God.[47] Yet the christology stems not from Christian application of the psalm, but from Jesus' consciousness of standing in a special filial relationship to God as Father (Abba). The early church expressed directly what was suggested by implication by Jesus himself.

In both these instances the source of the christological traditions, while it flowed into ever widening channels of interpretation, was what may be termed a datum of experience, the impact of Jesus' authoritative ministry in word and deed.

The problem of the Son of man christology is complicated by disagreement as to whether Jesus himself employed the title, as the Gospels claim. The fact that in the synoptics the Son of man is the only title Jesus is represented as using, is just as important as the other fact, to which more attention is usually given, that according to the Gospels no one but Jesus uses it. No attempted solution of the question is satisfactory which does not try to explain these two related facts. If Jesus alone used the title, and if this was the sole one he did use, there would be, as with " Lord " and " Son of God ", a datum of the church's experience to account for the genesis of the christology. This is, perhaps, after all, the most likely explanation.

Perrin himself admits that Jesus could have used the imagery of Dn 7 : 13 " to express the concept of a future vindication of his ministry and of men's proper response to it ".[48] He sees this as a possibility in regard to Lk 12 : 8, " Every one who acknowledges me before men, the Son of man will acknowledge before

[45] *Promise and Fulfilment*, pp. 49 f.

[46] Mk 1 : 11, parr. Mt 3 : 17, Lk 3 : 22 ; Mk 9 : 7, parr. Mt 17 : 5, Lk 9 : 35 ; Ac 13 : 33 ; He 1 : 5 ; 5 : 5.

[47] Nor " the Son ". Mk 13 : 32 either reflects the Son christology characteristic of the Fourth Gospel, or the words οὐδὲ ὁ υἱός are possibly an addition (J. Jeremias, *Abba*, Göttingen, 1966, pp. 40, 54 ; ET in *The Prayers of Jesus*, London, 1967, pp. 37, 52). On Mt 11 : 27, par. Lk 10 : 22, see now Jeremias, *Abba*, pp. 47–54 (*The Prayers of Jesus*, pp. 45–52).

[48] *Rediscovering*, p. 198 ; cf. pp. 191, 203.

the angels of God", where "the reference is only a general one" to the vindication imagery of Dn 7:13.[49] This, however, is an admission with implications apparently unwelcome to Perrin. He suggests that the oldest form of the second part of this *logion* was "will be acknowledged before the angels of God", the passive being the Aramaic circumlocution for the activity of God; and that this form, without any mention of the Son of man, could go back to Jesus.[50] The suggestion that the Son of man is not an original element in the saying is a hypothesis which cannot be proved, and need not be pressed. But the very admission that Jesus could have used the imagery of Dn 7:13 at all, opens the door to the recognition of the possibility that his use of this imagery included the actual expression Son of man.[51]

## IV

There is a fresh piece of evidence that the Son of man concept was probably familiar in Judaism in the time of Jesus. This is the recently published Melchizedek fragment from Qumran, 11QMelch.[52] In line 10 of the fragment Ps 82:1 is quoted.

> "God (*'ᵉlōhîm*) stands in the congregation of God (*'ēl*);
> He judges among the gods (*'ᵉlōhîm*)".

The quotation is introduced by the words "as it is written concerning him [i.e., Melchizedek, named in line 9] in the hymns of David who says". The first *'ᵉlōhîm* is accordingly Melchizedek, while the second probably means the evil angels. This is made clearer in the translation in the *NTS* article cited in the last

[49] *Ibid.*, p. 191.

[50] *Ibid.*, pp. 189–91.

[51] In that case Ac 7:56 would not (along with Mk 14:62a) merely represent an exegetical tradition interpreting the resurrection in terms of Ps 110:1 and Dn 7:13, but would testify to a Son of man christology identifying Jesus with the Son of man, and derived from Mk 14:62a as a saying of Jesus. For a recent defence of the authenticity of the whole of Mk 14:62, see O. Cullmann, *Salvation in History*, London, 1967, pp. 225 f. It is possible, of course, to exaggerate the importance of Dn 7:13 itself, and consequently both to over-emphasise the role of early Christian exegesis in regard to the Son of man problem, and to under-estimate the Son of man as a concept.

[52] A. S. van der Woude, "Melchisedek als himmlische Erlösergestalt in den neugefundenen eschatologischen Midraschim aus Qumran Höhle XI", *Oudtestamentische Studiën* xiv (1965), 354–73; A. S. van der Woude and M. de Jonge, "11Q Melchizedek and the New Testament", *NTS* 12 (1965–66), 301–26; D. Flusser, "Melchizedek and the Son of Man", *Christian News from Israel* 17. 1 (April 1966), 23–29; J. A. Fitzmyer, "Further Light on Melchizedek from Qumran Cave 11", *JBL* 86 (1967), 25–41; cf. also J. A. Emerton in *JTS*, n. s. 17 (1966), 399–401.

footnote; it reads, "The heavenly one standeth in the congregation of God; among the heavenly ones he judgeth". In line 13 Melchizedek executes the judgments of God upon Belial "and all the spirits of his lot" (the evil angels), and in this task he is assisted by "all the heavenly ones on high" (line 14), the good angels. It is unnecessary to go into further detail, except to note that over against the lot of Belial there are "the sons of light and the men of the lot of Melchizedek" (line 8). We are justified in seeing in this fragment the idea of Melchizedek as an eschatological figure, the champion of the righteous and the judge of the wicked in the last judgment in heaven.

It is possible, although incapable of proof, that the author of the epistle to the Hebrews was familiar with this kind of late Jewish representation of Melchizedek as an angelic being active in the presence of God. Such familiarity would help to explain why Melchizedek, although resembling (Christ) the Son of God (He 7 : 3), is yet inferior to him. While also a heavenly being, like the exalted Christ, he is only an angel.

Elsewhere I have suggested that there is some connection between the high priest christology in Hebrews and the Son of man concept, and that this christology originated in the understanding of Jesus' heavenly intercession as Son of man as a specifically priestly function.[53] More recently D. Flusser has pointed to similarities between Melchizedek in the new Qumran fragment and the Son of man in the Similitudes of Enoch and in the New Testament (especially Mt 25 : 31–46), and regards it as a plausible hypothesis that the Son of man influenced this portrayal of Melchizedek as the eschatological judge.[54] Melchizedek does not seem to be a priest, while in Hebrews Christ, as a high priest "after the order of Melchizedek", is an intercessor rather than a judge. Therefore Melchizedek himself, as a prefiguration of Christ, is understood differently from Melchizedek in the sectarian document. This means that, even if the author of Hebrews was acquainted with the concept as presented in 11QMelch, he has handled it differently with a different purpose in mind.

In 11QMelch the nature of the scriptural exegesis [55] implies

[53] "The Old Testament and Some Aspects of New Testament Christology" (see n. 43 above), p. 141.

[54] *Op. cit.*

[55] In Is 52 : 7 "thy God" (lines 16, 24, 25) is again interpreted as meaning Melchizedek; cf. van der Woude and de Jonge, *op. cit.*, p. 305.

that there was already in existence a concept of Melchizedek as an angelic being, which is thus being read into the texts.[56] Despite its incompleteness, the fragment preserves enough for us to see quite clearly that Melchizedek is portrayed in much the same way as the Son of man. It may be suggested that the Son of man concept could also have existed in late Judaism independently of scriptural interpretation (of Dn 7 : 13), and that therefore, as has been widely assumed, it could have been known to Jesus and the early church. This possibility is increased on Flusser's hypothesis that behind Melchizedek as the judge at the end, there lies the concept of the Son of man in a similar role. The fact that in the Gospels the title Son of man is found only on the lips of Jesus, is most probably due to his alone having employed it. But the view that he used it directly as a self-designation, is faced by the difficulty that such a use would be contrary to his avoidance of explicit application to himself of other Jewish titles. His use of this particular one may have been by way of adaptation of the idea of judgment inherent in the concept, to the allied thought primarily of witness, in indirect allusions to the Son of man as if to another figure.[57]

The three studies discussed in this paper attempt to solve the problem in three different ways. In the nature of the case, the first two are assured of their respective supporters. It is Perrin's suggestions that really break new ground; and perhaps, despite the reservations I have indicated, they may turn out to be an advance towards a solution, if not of the Son of man problem as a whole, at least of the difficulties of some of the crucial texts. To conclude at this stage that the problem is insoluble would be premature. It may well be, however, that agreement will never be reached, even if the correct solution is found in the future or, for all we know, already exists among the widely divergent ones familiar to workers in this field. But this would not be an occurrence unique in the world of biblical research.

[56] Cf. J. A. Fitzmyer, *op. cit.*, p. 31: "What is preserved is a midrashic development which is independent of the classic OT loci" (Gn 14 : 18–20 and Ps 110 : 4).

[57] For suggestions along the lines of a "functional" use of the title, see *Jesus and the Son of Man*, especially p. 202. There, as here, I have assumed that Son of man is indeed a title. Since the completion of this paper, Dr. G. Vermes has tried to show that the Aramaic *bar nāš(ā')* is nothing more than a surrogate for the first person pronoun (Appendix E in M. Black, *An Aramaic Approach to the Gospels and Acts*[3], Oxford, 1967). But this cannot account for the theological features of "Son of man" in the Gospel sayings.

# PAULUS ALS HILLELIT

JOACHIM JEREMIAS

## I

DIE Paulusbriefe zeigen, daß ihr Verfasser nicht nur in seiner Bibel lebte, sondern auch das volle zeitgenössische Rüstzeug für ihre Interpretation besaß. Er kennt den Midrasch, so die Vorstellungen von der Verfolgung Isaaks durch Ismael (Gal 4 : 29), von der Taufe der Wüstengeneration (1 Co 10 : 1 f., s. dazu u.S. 91), von der Mitwirkung der Engel bei der Gesetzgebung am Sinai (Gal 3 : 19), vom mitwandernden Felsen (1 Co 10 : 4), von der Verführung der Eva durch die Schlange (2 Co 11 : 3). Seine Auslegung alttestamentlicher Schriftstellen läßt erkennen, wie souverän er die exegetische Methodik der damaligen jüdischen Theologie zu handhaben versteht : er verwendet den Stichwortzusammenhang (Ro 9 : 25 f. *οὐ λαός μου* ; 9 : 32 f. *λίθος* ; 11 : 8–10 *ὀφθαλμοὺς τοῦ μὴ βλέπειν* ; 1 Co 1 : 19 f. *σοφίαν/σοφός* ; 3 : 19 f. *σοφοί* ; 15 : 54 f. *θάνατος* ; 2 Co 6 : 16–18 *ἔσομαι κτλ.* ; Gal 3 : 10, 13 *ἐπικατάρατος* ; 3 : 11 f. *ζήσεται*), gelegentlich zur Perlenschnur erweitert (Ro 15 : 9–12 *ἔθνη*), und die Kettenerklärung (Ro 10, 6–9) ; er liebt es, wie die Rabbinen, eine Torastelle mit einer Stelle aus den Propheten oder den K$^e$thubim zu verbinden (Ro 4 : 1 ff. ; 9 : 12 f. ; 10 : 6 ff., 19–21 ; 11 : 8 ; 12 : 19 f. ; 15 : 9–12 ; 2 Co 6 : 16–18) [1] ; er deutet den Numerus aus (Gal 3 : 16) [2] ; er benutzt wiederholt das argumentum e contrario (Ro 3 : 4 ; 1 Co 14 : 22 ; 15 : 44 f.) [3], ferner das argumentum e silentio (Ro 4 : 6 : *χωρὶς ἔργων*) [4] ; er gibt dem Text einen Tiefsinn (*ḥōmer* : 1 Co 9 : 9 f. ; 10 : 4b ; 2 Co 3 : 17a ; Gal 4 : 24–27). Dabei greift seine Kenntnis jüdischer Hermeneutik über den palästinisch-rabbinischen Bereich hinaus. 1 Co

[1] E. von Dobschütz, *Zum paulinischen Schriftbeweis*, *ZNTW* 24 (1925) 30 ; O. Michel, *Paulus und seine Bibel*, Gütersloh, 1929, p. 83 ; E. E. Ellis, *Paul's Use of the Old Testament*, Edinburgh-London, 1957, p. 186 (App. III).

[2] D. Daube, *The New Testament and Rabbinic Judaism*, London, 1956, pp. 438–44 : " The Interpretation of a Generic Singular ".

[3] O. Michel, a.a.O., p. 96. Vgl. auch 1 Co 6 : 16 f.

[4] Ebd., pp. 94 f.

9 : 9 f. ist er der hellenistischen Allegorese verpflichtet, die sich von der palästinischen dadurch unterschied, daß sie den Wortlaut der Schriftaussage zugunsten des Tiefsinnes zurückstellte [5]; seine geistige Heimat ist jedoch die palästinische Exegese, wie seine Bevorzugung der Typologie, die in Ereignissen der Heilsgeschichte Voraus-Darstellungen der eschatologischen Vorgänge sah (1 Co 10 : 1 ff.; Gal 4 : 21–31; Ro 9 : 13),[6] gegenüber der Allegorese zeigt und wie vor allem seine Inspirationslehre erkennen läßt. In neutestamentlicher Zeit hatte nämlich das hellenistische und das palästinische Judentum eine unterschiedliche Vorstellung von der Inspiration der Schrift. Während die griechisch redende Diaspora einer überaus strengen Auffassung huldigte, derzufolge die biblischen Autoren nur Griffel des heiligen Geistes waren (Philo, vgl. He 3 : 7), vertrat man in Palästina eine mildere Inspirationslehre, die die Persönlichkeit und Individualität der biblischen Autoren in Rechnung setzte; daß Paulus auf die palästinische Seite gehört, ist evident (vgl. Ro 9 : 27; 10 : 20).[7]

## II

Wir können nun aber die theologische Heimat des Apostels im Raum der zeitgenössischen jüdischen Theologie noch genauer fixieren. Zahlreiche Einzelbeobachtungen lassen erkennen, *dass Paulus Hillelit war.* Zunächst ist es die Theologie des Apostels, die in ihren Ansätzen Berührungen mit derjenigen Hillels und seiner Schule aufweist.

Es war einer der kühnsten theologischen Gedanken Hillels gewesen, daß er lehrte, die ganze Tora lasse sich in einem einzigen Satz zusammenfassen, zu dem alles andere lediglich Kommentar sei. Als diesen zusammenfassenden Satz nannte Hillel die goldene Regel in ihrer negativen Fassung.[8] Diese Vorstellung von einem Kerngesetz darf nicht verwechselt werden mit derjenigen von einem größten Gebot.[9] Das größte Gebot nennt das erste Glied einer

[5] SBK 3, pp. 382–400.

[6] L. Goppelt, *Typos. Die typologische Deutung des Alten Testaments im Neuen*, Gütersloh, 1939 (Nachdruck: Darmstadt, 1966); H. Müller, *Die Auslegung alttestamentlichen Geschichtsstoffs bei Paulus*, Diss. Halle, 1960, Selbstreferat in *TLZ* 86 (1961), 789; J. Daniélou, *Sacramentum futuri*, Paris, 1950, p. 4: Die Typologie zeigt " dans les événements passés la figure d'événements à venir ".

[7] Vgl. O. Michel, a.a.O., p. 69.

[8] Bab. Shab. 31a.

[9] Mk 12 : 28–34 par.; Mt 22 : 34–40; Ja 2 : 8.

an Wichtigkeit abnehmenden Reihe, das Kerngesetz einen Obersatz, von dem alle andern Sätze ableitbar sind; die Frage nach dem größten Gebot ist jüdisch, die Frage nach dem Kerngesetz dagegen wendet eine stoische Vorstellung auf die Tora an, nämlich die Vorstellung vom *ἄγραφος νόμος*. Die Überlieferung, daß die geradezu revolutionäre Lehre vom Kerngesetz auf Hillel zurückgehe, erhält eine starke Stütze durch die synoptische Überlieferung, die nicht nur die Vorstellung vom Kerngesetz kennt, sondern als dieses Kerngesetz—wie Hillel—die goldene Regel (allerdings positiv gefaßt) bezeichnet (Mt 7 : 12, ohne den Nachsatz Lk 6 : 31); außerdem werden wir bei der Besprechung der sieben Middoth Hillels bestätigt finden, daß Hillel hellenistische hermeneutische Prinzipien auf die Tora übertragen hat. Für unsern Zusammenhang ist das Bedeutsame, daß auch Paulus die hillelitische Lehre kennt, daß die Tora auf ein Kerngesetz zurückführbar sei (Gal 5 : 14; Ro 13 : 8 f.); als dessen Inhalt bezeichnet er an beiden Stellen die Nächstenliebe.

Als Pharisäer lehrten die Hilleliten im Gegensatz zu den Sadduzäern die Auferstehung der Toten und lehnten sie die sadduzäische Lehre von der uneingeschränkten Willensfreiheit des Menschen ab.[10] Im Unterschied zu den Schammaiten waren sie, wie schon Hillel selbst,[11] offen für den Anschluß der Heiden an das Gottesvolk; sie betrachteten den Übertritt zum Judentum als einen Übergang vom Tod zum Leben.[12] Mit ihrer Missionsoffenheit hängt es zusammen, wenn sie (wiederum in Auseinandersetzung mit den Schülern Schammai's) im Tauchbad des übertretenden Heiden den eigentlichen Konversionsakt sahen und ihm besondere Bedeutung zumaßen.[13] Es ist deutlich, daß alle diese Lehranschauungen in der paulinischen Theologie ihre Entsprechung haben.

Im Zusammenhang mit einer Taufaussage des Apostels begegnen wir über das Gesagte hinaus bei ihm einem spezifisch hillelitischen Lehrsatz. Es muß vorausgeschickt werden, daß das Tauchbad des Proselyten, ebenso wie seine erste Opferdarbringung, ursprünglich ein Nebenakt beim Übertritt war; der eigentliche Initiationsritus war die Beschneidung. Wenn die Hilleliten, im Gegensatz zu den Schammaiten, die an den alten

[10] SBK 4, p. 344.

[11] Bab. Shab. 31a; vgl. Ab. 1 : 12.

[12] "Wer sich von seiner Vorhaut trennt, trennt sich gleichsam von seinem Grabe" (Pes. 8 : 8).

[13] SBK 1, pp. 104 f.

Traditionen festhielten, das Tauchbad zum entscheidenden Akt erhoben, so geschah das vermutlich mit Rücksicht auf die Frauen, die das Hauptkontingent der Übertretenden stellten. Nun erhob sich aber die Schwierigkeit, daß die Proselytentaufe im AT nicht erwähnt wird; die Hilleliten mußten daher versuchen, auf indirektem Wege einen Schriftbeweis für die Proselytentaufe beizubringen. Sie gingen aus von Nu 15:14 "Er (der *ger* d.h. nach rabbinischer Exegese der Proselyt) soll ebenso verfahren wie ihr es tut" und folgerten aus dieser Schriftstelle, daß die Aufnahme der Väter in den Sinaibund das Vorbild für die Aufnahme der Proselyten bilde.[14] Die Hilleliten mußten also bemüht sein nachzuweisen, daß sich die Wüstengeneration vor dem Bundesschluß am Sinai einem Tauchbad unterzogen hatte. Sie suchten diesen Nachweis teils mit Hilfe von Ex 19:10 (Waschen der Kleider, was ein Tauchbad impliziere),[15] teils mit Hilfe von Ex 24:8 (Besprengung des Volkes mit Blut, was ebenfalls ein vorangegangenes Tauchbad voraussetze)[16] zu führen. Es kann kein Zweifel sein, daß die seltsame Anschauung, daß der Wüstengeneration beim Durchzug durch das Rote Meer ein Tauchbad widerfuhr, die wir 1 Co 10, 1 f. lesen, in die Reihe dieser Versuche der Hilleliten gehört, der Proselytentaufe durch den Nachweis, daß die Väter getauft waren, die fehlende Schriftgrundlage zu verschaffen. Wir stoßen also 1 Co 10:1 f. bei Paulus auf eine spezifisch hillelitische Anschauung, die Paulus auch als Christ beibehalten hat und die er benutzt hat, um vor einem magischen Mißverständnis der Taufe zu warnen (1 Co 10:1–13). Vielleicht ist es kein Zufall, daß auch die Warnung vor der Securitas, mit der der Abschnitt schließt (V. 12), den Geist Hillels atmet: "Verlaß dich nicht auf dich selbst bis zum Tage deines Todes" pflegte der große Theologe seine Schüler zu ermahnen.[17]

Ebenfalls in den Bereich der Paränese gehört eine letzte Gemeinsamkeit des Paulus mit Hillel. Die Mahnung Hillels: "Zeige dich nicht lachend (unter Weinenden) und zeige dich nicht weinend (unter Lachenden)"[18] hat ein (positiv formuliertes) Echo bei Paulus gefunden: χαίρειν μετὰ χαιρόντων, κλαίειν μετὰ κλαιόντων (Ro 12:15).

[14] Bab. Ker. 9a=81a.
[15] Bab. Yeb. 46a (Baraitha).
[16] Bab. Ker. 9a=81a; Bab. Yeb. 46a (Baraitha).
[17] Ab. 2:4.
[18] Tos. Ber. 2:21 (ed. E. Lohse—G. Schlichting, Stuttgart, 1956, p. 32).

## III

Noch eindrucksvoller als durch diese theologischen Berührungen erweist sich die hillelitische Schulung des Apostels an seiner glänzenden *Beherrschung der exegetischen Methodik Hillels.* Dieser hatte, anknüpfend an Prinzipien der hellenistischen Hermeneutik, für das exegetische Beweisverfahren sieben Regeln aufgestellt, die berühmten nach ihm benannten sieben Middoth.[19] Mit Hilfe der beiden ersten dieser Regeln hat Hillel die für die kultische Praxis überaus wichtige Frage positiv beantwortet, ob die Tausende von Passaopfern auch am Sabbath geschlachtet werden dürften,[20] eine Entscheidung, die seinen ruhmvollen Aufstieg einleitete. Sie bedeutete einen Bruch mit der Überlieferung, wie man daraus ersehen kann, daß die Samaritaner bis auf den heutigen Tag die Schlachtung der Passalämmer auf die Zeit nach Sonnenuntergang verschieben, wenn der 14. Nisan auf einen Sabbath fällt. Wieder bestätigt das Neue Testament die talmudische Chronologie, in diesem Fall sogar zweifach. Einerseits erhalten wir ein Datum für die sieben Middoth mit Hilfe der Feststellung, daß der Schluß a minori ad maius dem Alten Testament unbekannt, dagegen dem Neuen Testament geläufig ist, andrerseits mit Hilfe der Beobachtung, daß die Regeln in ihrer Gesamtheit Paulus bekannt gewesen sind. Nicht weniger als fünf der Middoth Hillels lassen sich bei ihm nachweisen. Die *erste* Regel *ḳal wāḥōmer*, Schluß a minori ad maius, wendet Paulus oft an (Ro 5 : 15, 17 ; 11 : 12 ; 2 Co 3 : 7 f., 9, 11). Nun hatte Hillel aber unter diese erste Regel nicht nur den Schluß a minori ad maius, sondern auch den umgekehrten a maiori ad minus subsumiert, und auch diesen Schluß finden wir bei Paulus wieder. Seine Argumentation Ro 5 : 6–9, 10 ; 8 : 32 ; 11 : 24 ; 1 Co 6 : 2, 3 wird erst verständlich, wenn man sich klar macht, daß Paulus an diesen Stellen nicht a minori ad maius, sondern umgekehrt a maiori ad minus folgert.—Die *zweite* Regel Hillels war die *geᵉzērāh šāwāh*, der Analogieschluß auf grund gleichlautender Worte. Wiederum ist kennzeichnend, daß Paulus nicht nur die Regel kennt, sondern daß er sie in einer besonders kunstvollen Weise

[19] W. Bacher, *Die exegetische Terminologie der jüdischen Traditionsliteratur*, I. *Die bibelexegetische Terminologie der Tannaiten*, Leipzig, 1899 (Nachdruck: Darmstadt, 1965), jeweils s.v. ; H. L. Strack, *Einleitung in Talmud und Midraš*, München, ⁵1921, pp. 96–99.

[20] j. Pes. 6 (33a oben).

anwendet.[21] Ro 4 : 1–12 finden wir nämlich einen zweifachen mit Hilfe des Wortes λογίζεσθαι erzielten Analogieschluß. Zunächst wird Ro 4 : 3 der Schriftvers Gn 15 : 6 zitiert (ἐλογίσθη αὐτῷ εἰς δικαιοσύνην). Die aus der Vokabel ἐλογίσθη gezogene Folgerung, daß Gott dem Abraham die Gerechtigkeit nicht auf grund von Verdiensten, sondern aus Gnaden zusprach (v. 4 f.), findet ihre Bestätigung aus der Schrift durch Ps 32 : 2 f., wo die Vokabel λογίζεσθαι wiederkehrt (μακάριος ἀνὴρ οὗ οὐ μὴ λογίσηται κύριος ἁμαρτίαν) und zwar zur Umschreibung der Vergebung der Sünde. Gn 15 : 3 wird also auf Grund eines Analogieschlusses mit Hilfe von Ps 32 : 2 erklärt. Nun aber fragt Paulus weiter, ob sich der Makarismus Ps 32 : 1 f. nur auf die Juden oder auch auf die Heiden beziehe (v. 9). Wieder gibt ein mit Hilfe der Vokabel λογίζεσθαι erzielter Analogieschluß die Antwort ; jetzt wird jedoch, und darin zeigt sich die exegetische Kunst des Apostels, umgekehrt das λογίζεσθαι in Ps 32 : 2 mit Hilfe des λογίζεσθαι in Gn 15 : 6 erklärt. Abraham, so argumentiert Paulus, war noch Heide, als ihm die Anrechnung des Glaubens widerfuhr (Ro 4 : 10–11a). Also gilt die Verheißung, daß die Sünden nicht angerechnet werden sollten (Ps 32 : 2), auch den Heiden (Ro 4 : 11b–12).—Die *fünfte* Regel, *k*ᵉ*lāl ûp̄*ᵉ*rāṭ*, Generelles und Spezielles, unterscheidet zwischen umfassenden und speziellen Geboten und läßt sie sich gegenseitig bestimmen. Paulus kennt diese Unterscheidung und wendet sie, ebenso wie die hillelitische Schule,[22] auf das Gebot der Nächstenliebe als alle anderen Gebote umfassend an (Ro 13 : 9 ; Gal 5 : 14).—Die *sechste* Regel Hillels *k*ᵉ*yôṣē' bô b*ᵉ*māḳôm 'aḥēr*, Näherbestimmung einer Bibelstelle mit Hilfe einer verwandten Stelle, wird von Paulus Gal 3 : 16 angewendet. Er hatte in 3 : 8 die dem Abraham Gn 12 : 3 gegebene Verheißung ἐνευλογηθήσονται ἐν σοὶ πᾶσαι αἱ φυλαὶ τῆς γῆς zitiert [23] und dabei zunächst das ἐν σοί textgemäß auf Abraham bezogen. Nun kehrt aber die Abrahamsverheißung in Gn 22 : 18 nochmals wieder und hier heißt es : ἐνευλογηθήσονται ἐν τῷ σπέρματί σου πάντα τὰ ἔθνη τῆς γῆς. Dieser Weschsel von ἐν σοί (LXX Gn 12 : 3) zu ἐν τῷ σπέρματί σου (LXX Gn 22 : 18)

[21] J. Jeremias, *Zur Gedankenführung in den paulinischen Briefen*, in : *Studia Paulina in honorem J. de Zwaan*, Haarlem, 1953, pp. 146–54, hier pp. 149–51 = *Abba*, Göttingen, 1966, pp. 269–76, hier pp. 271 f.

[22] W. Bacher, a.a.O., pp. 81 f. ; ders., *Die Agada der Tannaiten* I, Straßburg, ²1903, p. 4.

[23] Das Zitat ist nicht ganz wörtlich. Paulus sagt πάντα τὰ ἔθνη, vgl. LXX Gn 18 : 18.

an zwei inhaltlich engstens miteinander verwandten Stellen gibt Paulus die Handhabe, das ἐν σοί in Gal 3 : 16 auf den (Sing. !) Nachkommen Abrahams, nämlich Christus, zu deuten.—Die *siebente* Regel endlich *dāḇār halāmēḏ mē'inyānô*, die Folgerung aus der Stellung im Kontext, wird von Paulus Ro 4 : 10–11a angewendet, wo er seine Beweisführung darauf aufbaut, daß Abraham die Verheißung Gn 15 : 6 *vor* seiner Beschneidung (17 : 10 f.) erhielt. Auch Gal 3 : 17 (das Gesetz wurde nach Ex 12 : 40 430 Jahre später gegeben als die Verheißung) liegt Anwendung der siebenten Regel vor.

Wir haben nicht allzuoft die Möglichkeit, Angaben der Apostelgeschichte exakt auf ihre Zuverlässigkeit nachzuprüfen. Hier ist ein solcher Fall. Die Apostelgeschichte behauptet, Paulus sei Theologe und zwar Schüler des Hilleliten Rabban Gamli'el I. gewesen (Ac 22 : 3). Die Nachprüfung ergibt : der Verfasser der Paulusbriefe verfügte in der Tat über die theologische Bildung seiner Zeit und gehörte der hillelitischen Schule an.

# MARK 4 : 1–20 YET ONCE MORE

C. F. D. Moule

This essay sets out to attack a deeply entrenched exegesis. In self-defence, therefore, I should like to preface it by two remarks. First, I am not entirely convinced of the wrongness of what I am attacking—still less of the rightness of what I offer in its place. What I am convinced of is that many of the arguments used in the defence of what I am attacking are fallacious, and that it is high time they were re-examined. If the fortress itself is completely unmoved by the blast of my pop-gun, it will be something if I have managed to blow off bits of its façade here and there. Secondly, since my own tentative conclusions are decidedly " conservative ", I owe it to myself to state that I hold no brief at all for an uncritical " biblicism ", neither am I concerned to oppose the principles of *Formgeschichte.* I believe that traditions about Jesus were modified and reshaped in transmission ; and I know that one must reckon with the possibility (though I am not so clear about the probability) that incidents and sayings were actually " created " and added to the early tradition, perhaps by Christian prophets speaking, with genuine conviction, in the name of the risen Lord. I do not wish in any way to question the necessity for being fully alive to the influence of the interests and needs of the early church on the form and contents of tradition. But I do believe that each section of the Gospels needs to be examined on its own merits ; and all that this essay attempts to do is to re-examine and question the assumptions habitually applied in the exegesis of one particular passage.

The passage in question is Mk 4 : 1–20, especially vv. 10–13. This is a much-debated section, but my conviction is that it is not debated enough. Despite the elaborate critical techniques again and again brought to bear on it, there are certain assumptions, that are uncritically accepted by critic after critic ; and the exceptional critics who have begged to differ have tended to be given scant attention. I suspect that Adolf Jülicher was the scholar who first fastened these assumptions on New Testament scholarship. At all events they are evident in his classic discussion of the passage.[1]

To put the matter more specifically, I want to show that there is an unnoticed assumption in Jülicher's exegesis which led him to a conclusion which, in its turn, has become the unexamined assumption from which subsequent exegesis has set out. But, before I come to this, it may make for clarity if I start from my own proposal. This may also save the reader time; for he can stop reading at once, if I show him the worst at an early stage. It is only fair to add that a view similar, in several respects, to mine was elaborately defended long ago by C. E. B. Cranfield in a double article, "St Mark 4:1–34", *SJT* 4 (1951), 398 ff.; 5 (1952), 49 ff. While he would not wish to be associated with all my points, I must here gratefully acknowedge the light that he brings. He is one of the critics I have already mentioned, whose deviationist views have received little attention, although he has reiterated them briefly in his well-known commentary on Mark.[2] It remains to be seen what response B. Gerhardsson's approach[3] will evoke.

My own exegesis, then, starts by assuming that, not only for Jesus but also for the early Church, it was a commonplace (as it is today) that true learning is possible only when the learner is stimulated to think for himself. The idea that learning consists in the creative union of two minds—the teacher's and the learner's—co-operating and together reaching something new, is psychologically so sound and so fundamental to even the most elementary forms of genuine education, that it is reasonable to start by assuming that it was evident also at the time of Jesus and of the early Church. And if it was, then parable would undoubtedly be recognized as an extremely good tool for precisely such an operation. A parable is like a modern political cartoon. A good cartoon presents an interpretative analogy, and it is for the viewer to work out its meaning, first by understanding it, then by reacting to it critically and, finally, by taking action accordingly. If the viewer is half-witted or stupid or so shallow as to be virtually incapable of being educated, no doubt he will see nothing but the mere picture, and he will not get further

[1] *Die Gleichnisreden Jesu*, 2 vols., Tübingen, ²1899.

[2] *The Gospel according to St Mark*, in the *Cambridge Greek Testament Commentary*, Cambridge, ²1963.

[3] "The Parable of the Sower and its Interpretation", *NTS* 14 (1968), 165 ff.

than saying that he likes it or dislikes it. But anybody with a grain of intelligence will respond in one way or another. He will say, " Yes, of course that is exactly what is happening. I hadn't seen it so clearly before, but now I know that I mustn't vote Conservative [or whatever it may be] again ". Or perhaps he will say, " Yes, I see what the cartoonist is getting at, but I don't think his interpretation is fair. He is being cruel to X, who isn't really doing what the hog in the picture is doing." The moment the viewer is responding in one way or another, he and the cartoonist have entered into a partnership in creating something ; education is proceeding.[4]

Now, not only do we know today, retrospectively, that that is exactly how hearers of Jesus' parables might have unconsciously responded to them. We know also that the ancient world was consciously aware of the process. Ezekiel complained that his hearers regarded him as they might one who sang love-songs with a beautiful voice and played well on an instrument, but that they took no action in response (Ezk 33 : 32). The Epistle of James knows all about the man who glances in a mirror but goes off and forgets the lesson (Ja 1 : 23 f.). And what of all the rabbinic parables that are always quoted in profusion by commentators ? I know of no sign that they were used otherwise than for an educative purpose[5] ; and we need very strong evidence if we are to believe that the writers of the Gospels did not recognize this as the way in which parables worked. Therefore, with great respect, I cannot help questioning whether D. E. Nineham is justified when he writes, in his *Saint Mark, Pelican Gospel Commentaries*, London, 1963, p. 137 : " Some scholars have suggested that Our Lord's habit was to utter a dark saying and then to wait, ready to explain it further to any who, by coming to ask questions, showed that they had taken seriously

[4] American and English readers may be reminded of a popular book with a facetious title but a serious intention—R. Short's *The Gospel according to Peanuts*, London, 1966. This is a study of C. M. Schulz's cartoons as a medium for preaching. But these cartoons depend for their message on the words given to the characters in the pictures. The type of cartoon that I have in mind, as the closest parallel to the genuinely dominical parable, is the type that presents a pictorial analogy to the contemporary situation—not the type that satirises psychological features in words and sentences.

[5] Indeed, there is positive evidence of the rabbinic estimate of their worth. See *SBK* 1, 654 ; and the excellent section of E. Linnemann's *Gleichnisse Jesu*, Göttingen, (unverändert) [2]1962, pp. 27 ff., headed : " Das Gleichnis als Weise der Unterredung ".

what had already been said. But this is a modern approach, and hardly agrees with St Mark's view, which is much more in line with the Old Testament ideas of predestination and the remnant. The circle to whom the explanations are given are a determinate number, *his own disciples* (v. 34) predestined to be 'given' the mystery of the Kingdom of God". It must be pointed out, however, that the phrase in v. 10 is not *his own disciples* (as in v. 34) but *those who were about him with the twelve.* It is not a closed group but a chance gathering. Moreover, it is a circular argument to assume that Mark's view is predestinarian and then to exclude from consideration any approach which is not predestinarian; and certainly predestinarianism and "the remnant" are very far from being all that the Old Testament contemplates. C. E. B. Cranfield is more to the point, when he says (*Mark*, p. 159): "... *mašal/matlâ* can mean a dark, perplexing saying *that is meant to stimulate hard thinking*" (my italics). If that is correct for the Hebrew-Jewish mind, I can find no evidence that the Evangelists thought otherwise. They actually represent Jesus as one who not only told parables but frequently met a question with a counter-question. If there is anything that the Evangelists themselves underline in their portrait of Jesus, it is his refusal to be content with spoon-feeding, and his determination to make people think for themselves. The Evangelists' picture in general, therefore, seems to invite us to understand the parables neither as a *disciplina arcani* designed to conceal a secret, nor yet, on the other hand, as merely illustrative, but as provocative and dynamic and creative—a *Sprachereignis* or a *Sprachgeschehen* [6] by all means! There is no compelling reason, as far as I can see, to interpret Mk 4:34 otherwise; and the καθὼς ἠδύναντο ἀκούειν of the preceding verse (v. 33) certainly does not point to a conception of parable as an excluding agent.[7]

Now, if it be granted that this is how we should expect not only Jesus himself but also the Evangelists to understand parable, it is going to make a difference to the construction

[6] If I may borrow this much from E. Fuchs and G. Ebeling. Cf. E. Linnemann, *Gleichnisse*, pp. 38 ff.

[7] The epigram ὅστις ἔχει, δοθήσεται αὐτῷ ..., which is in line with the educational principle in question, occurs in the parables-collections of all three Synoptists, and Matthew (13:12) brings it into the context of the saying about those who do and those who do not receive the mysteries. Cf. also the νήπιοι of the "Jubelruf" of Mt 11:25, Lk 10:21, with S. Légane, "La Révélation aux νήπιοι", *RB* 67 (1960), 321 ff.

which is placed on Mk 4 : 11. It will at least dispose us not to see the giving of the μυστήριον and the hearing of parable as mutually exclusive alternatives ; and it will release us from the dogma that those who are addressed (ὑμῖν) and οἱ ἔξω are two irrevocably distinct groups. There is nothing in the context to suggest that the Evangelist intends the former group (the ὑμεῖς) to be understood as those who were elected to the privilege of direct revelation, whereas those outside were the permanently under-privileged, condemned to be baffled and kept at arm's length by deliberately obscure parables. Indeed, so little are the two kept in watertight compartments by Mark himself that (as Jülicher himself noticed, without drawing the conclusion [8]) one only has to wait until Mk 8 : 17, 21 to find Jesus applying to the Twelve terms borrowed from Is 6 similar to those which are here applied to those outside. In short, there is nothing to prevent our regarding the two positions—namely, " inside " (as we may, by implication, call it) and " outside " (as it is explicitly called)—as descriptions merely of the result of ways of responding to parables on a given occasion. On another occasion, those who before had responded and came inside were obtuse ; while, conversely, it may be that those who are now unresponsive will, next time, respond. I see no necessity for interpreting otherwise the τοῖς ἰδίοις μαθηταῖς of Mk 4 : 34.

Or, if we do not accept so fluctuating a conception of " inside " and " outside ", at most it indicates a *character* rather than a fixed *class*. This is essentially T. W. Manson's view in *The Teaching of Jesus*, Cambridge, 1935, p. 76 : "It is the man himself who places himself in one category or another, and that simply by the response which he makes to the parables." So (*ibid.*, pp. 79 f.) : " The quotation from Isaiah is not introduced by Jesus to explain the purpose of teaching in parables, but to illustrate what is meant by οἱ ἔξω : it is in fact a definition of the sort of character which prevents a man from becoming one of those to whom the secret of the kingdom is given."

This, then, is the major assumption in the exegesis which I offer ; and, so far as I can see, it is not merely permissible but plausible. A second assumption is, in part, anticipated by T. W. Manson's words just quoted. It is that Is 6 is here and in Mk 4 : 12 quoted, whether by Jesus himself or by the Evangelist, in a reasonable and intelligent way, and not with a pitiful literalism.

[8] *Op. cit.*, 1, 125 f.

It is difficult to believe that, in its original context in Is 6, it was intended as an instruction to the prophet to make sure that his message was unintelligible. Of course these are final clauses, as far as the grammar and syntax of the Hebrew go. But who seriously believes that such literalism was intended? It is only reasonable to take the final clauses as, at most, a vigorous way of stating the inevitable, as though by a very forceful indicative clause. And, as for the Evangelist's use of a Greek version, T. W. Manson observes, with characteristic common sense, that, if it was really the Evangelist's purpose to cite Isaiah in a predestinarian sense, he has missed a golden opportunity; for he omits precisely the part of the quotation which would most pointedly have met his requirements—the words " Make the heart of this people fat and make their ears heavy, and shut their eyes . . ." (*loc. cit.*, p. 78).[9]

Manson himself is among those who believe that, as a matter of fact, the Evangelists were using a targumic form which mitigated the paradox and eliminated the final construction (T. W. Manson, *loc. cit.*, p. 77; cf. J. Jeremias *Die Gleichnisse Jesu*, Göttingen, [6]1962, pp. 11 f.); and Matthew it is well known substitutes a ὅτι for Mark's ἵνα. But it is not really the precise form of the quotation that is decisive. Even Matthew, despite his ὅτι, reverts in the end to a (final) μήποτε.[10] What is decisive is whether the passage, both in Is 6 and in this New Testament context, is understood as quite literally describing the purpose of a ministry or as a vigorous and hyperbolic description of its conditions. And it is the latter which seems eminently the more reasonable. Those who remain outside are, by definition, such as go on looking without seeing, and hearing without comprehending; otherwise, they might change and enter into a right relation with God! And, if so, the burden of proof rests on those who want to make Mark's use of Is 6 part of a violently paradoxical interpretation of parables as instruments of obscuration.

My two assumptions, then, add up to the view that Jesus is not here portrayed by the Evangelist as contrasting a class of privileged persons, to whom the " mystery " is directly given, with an underprivileged class who are kept out by the intentional

[9] Even Matthew, who does include this clause (13 : 15), makes it indicative, not imperative.

[10] Despite the familiar possibilities in 2 Ti 2 : 25, it is too much to hope that, *in the present context*, that could mean " perhaps . . ."

obscurity of parables. Rather, he contrasts the group who have responded positively to the parables and have come inside for elucidation with those who stay outside because the parables have rolled over and off them like water off a duck's back—those, in other words, who are at present impervious to education because, so far, at least, they are too shallow to think and resolve for themselves.

This brings us to closer grips with verbal details. The passage, Mk 4 : 1–20, is almost universally treated by modern scholarship as a patchwork of incompatibles.[11] I want to ask whether there is really evidence for this, unless one starts from a different set of assumptions. On my assumptions the verbal details drop into place harmoniously. Or so it seems to me.

Mk 4 : 2–9 presents the parable of the sower as a specific example of how Jesus taught. It ends, significantly, with a challenge to response : ὃς ἔχει ὦτα ἀκούειν ἀκουέτω. Then follows (vv. 10–12) what, I suggest, is intended as a description of what frequently happened, not merely after this telling of the parable of the sower in particular, but generally whenever Jesus had been teaching in parables : " And when he was alone, those who were round him, together with the Twelve, would ask him about the parables. And [on such occasions] he would say : ' To you the mystery of the kingdom of God has been given. But those who [stay] outside never get any further than the parables themselves, in order that [as the prophet said sarcastically :] they may look without seeing, and hear without understanding—otherwise they might turn to God and be forgiven ! ' ".

The tenses in this section deserve notice. Not that Mark's use of tenses is not notoriously imprecise ; but, for what it is worth, the two imperfects, ἠρώτων and ἔλεγεν, may well be treated as genuine, iterative imperfects.[12] It is true that there is no evidence in Mark's usage that ὅτε ἐγένετο could mean " *Whenever* he was . . ." : all the evidence points to its meaning, quite properly, " *As soon as* he was . . .". But I see no reason why " As soon as he was alone " may not be combined with true imperfects, " they used to ask . . ., he used to say . . .", so as to make intelligibly, if illegitimately, a clause of which the total

[11] See, however, G. H. Boobyer, " The Redaction of Mark iv. 1–34 ", *NTS* 8 (1961–62), 59 ff.

[12] Paradoxically, the Vulgate renders *interrogaverunt* and *dicebat*.

effect would be iterative.[13] ἐρωτᾶν occurs again in Mark only at 7 : 26 and 8 : 5. Both times it is in the imperfect tense ; and in the latter case, if not the former, it is aoristically used ; but the occurrences are too few to generalize from, and there is no reason (so far as I can see) why it should not be taken as a true imperfect at 4 : 10. As for καὶ ἔλεγεν, this form certainly can do duty, in Marcan narrative, for an aorist (in this very chapter there are instances at vv. 2, 21, 24, 26, 30). But it seems also to represent a true imperfect (see, perhaps, 5 : 8, 6 : 15),[14] whereas the historic present, λέγει, never, I think, carries anything other than an aoristic force. Thus, however much caution should be exercised in deducing much from Marcan tenses, the ἠρώτων and ἔλεγεν of vv. 10 f., followed by the aoristic καὶ λέγει of v. 13, make my iterative interpretation of vv. 10–12 not unreasonable. Nobody, I think, would hesitate to treat vv. 33 f. as frequentative, giving full value to the imperfects :

*καὶ τοιαύταις παραβολαῖς πολλαῖς ἐλάλει αὐτοῖς τὸν λόγον, καθὼς ἠδύναντο ἀκούειν· χωρὶς δὲ παραβολῆς οὐκ ἐλάλει αὐτοῖς, κατ' ἰδίαν δὲ τοῖς ἰδίοις μαθηταῖς ἐπέλυεν πάντα.*

But, if so, is there anything to prevent our taking vv. 10–12 as a similar generalizing statement ? And if both these sections are so treated, the well-known difficulty that Jesus is in the boat at v. 1 and v. 36 but not at v. 10 disappears. So does also the alleged discrepancy between ἠρώτων αὐτὸν . . . τὰς παραβολάς (plural, v. 10) and Οὐκ οἴδατε τὴν παραβολὴν ταύτην (singular, v. 13) ; for now vv. 13 ff. become a particular example of the practice about which a frequentative and generalizing account has been given in vv. 10–12. With perfect logic, the narrator first gives the story of the sower, as a specimen of parabolic teaching (vv. 1–9) ; then he says that as soon as Jesus was alone, some used to ask him about the parables, and he used to say that because they had asked for explanation they would be rewarded ; and then he proceeds to give a specific example of one such occasion by harking back to the parable of the sower and recounting what Jesus said when they asked him about that. It is both natural and artistic.

[13] The admittedly bad grammar is no worse than that in 7 : 11, where ὃ ἐὰν ἐξ ἐμοῦ ὠφεληθῇς has to be treated as a conditional clause.

[14] W. G. Essame, "καὶ ἔλεγεν in Mark iv. 21, 24, 26, 30", *ExpT* 77 (1966), 121, suggests, even of those other occurrences, that they may correspond to an iterative formula of Pirke Aboth.

But now we must return to the question of how to interpret v. 11. I see no reason to assume that ἠρώτων . . . τὰς παραβολάς means [15] that the interrogators had no notion of what the parables meant, and were simply asking for the key to a riddle which, till then, would be wholly dark. Why should it not mean that they had begun to work out their significance, but wanted to ask questions about them ? And if it means this, why should not Jesus' reply mean that the " reward " for this positive response was that they became possessed of the divine design, the secret that was meant to be divulged to those who responded ? And, finally, why should not ἐκείνοις δὲ τοῖς ἔξω ἐν παραβολαῖς τὰ πάντα γίνεται mean " for those who are [still] outside, everything is parable from start to finish "—they have not got beyond mere parable ? τὰ πάντα γίνεται is an odd phrase [16] ; but it seems easier to render it thus than (with Jeremias [17] and others) to assume that someone was so stupid as to render by ἐν παραβολαῖς a phrase which, in an Aramaic floating saying, meant " enigmatically " [18] ; and then that the Evangelist placed this mistranslated Greek fragment here because it contained the word " parable " and suited his obscurantist theory of parable. Possibly one might compare Mt 5 : 18, ἕως ἂν πάντα γένηται, for the meaning " all [without remainder] is accomplished ". For those who stand outside, the process is finished at the level of [mere] parable. They do not probe beneath the surface.

The Matthaean version of the passage (13 : 10) makes the disciples ask " Why do you speak to them in parables ? " But even this—though quite likely a mere adaptation by the Evangelist or his " school "—does not necessarily imply a contrast between obscuring parables and plain revelation. It need only introduce, once again, the Lord's statement that for those who refuse to come further, nothing but the initial stage is possible.

But now we must retrace our steps and look at the interpretation which is most widely current. This, so far as I know, was imposed on scholarship by Jülicher's classic study and seems to have had as blinding an effect on subsequent exegesis as the

[15] There is an acute discussion of its possible meanings by Jülicher, *op. cit.*, 1, 121.

[16] See V. Taylor, *The Gospel according to St Mark*, London, ²1966, p. 256[a], and the ms. variants to which he calls attention.

[17] *Gleichnisse*, p. 12.

[18] Cf. J. W. Hunkin, " The Synoptic Parables ", *JTS* 16 (1915), 372 ff. (see p. 374).

parables, according to the theory which he attributed to Mark, had on their recipients.

That Jesus himself did not intend the parables to make the message difficult or impossible to receive is held by Jülicher and, I suppose, by almost all commentators. It is not to Jesus but to the Evangelist, and, no doubt, his contemporaries, that this perverse notion is attributed by Jülicher, who seems to have been driven to it reluctantly by his understanding of the passage under discussion. " Dass diese Theorie " (he confesses, *op. cit.*, I, 127) " in unlösbarem Widerspruch zu aller geschichtlichen Möglichkeit steht, räume ich gern ein ; aber ich darf einen Knoten nicht lösen, den Mc geschürzt hat und an dem sein religiöses Empfinden, seine Theologie Genüge findet ".

But what is it in Jülicher's understanding of the passage that drives him to this conclusion ? It is what I have already referred to as an unnoticed and unexamined assumption—the assumption, namely, that teaching in parables (if " teaching " is not too violent a misnomer on this showing !) is the exclusive *alternative* to the direct, unconcealed communication of " the mystery of the kingdom of God ". The privileged, thinks Jülicher, receive the " mystery " explicitly. Even if (vv. 13 ff.) they still fail to understand the parables, they suffer no loss, for they are given direct information superior to that. If the parables are, in fact, interpreted for them, that is something thrown in as a kind of bonus. Those who are outside, by contrast, get nothing but parables, which are positively obscuring and preclude understanding : " Denen draussen kommt das Gesamte, was Christus ihnen sagt, ἐν παραβολαῖς zu, *das heisst nicht* : *in Parabeln ohne hinzugefügte Erklärung*, sondern : in Parabeln ; den ὑμεῖς kommt es nicht auf diese Weise zu ; ihnen ist das, was für alle andern ein Geheimnis ist betreffs des Gottesreiches, bereits geschenkt worden ; *man wirft das* δέδοται *um, wenn man einschiebt* : *mittelst Erklarung der Parabeln* " (*op. cit.*, I, 124, my italics). But why cannot ἐν παραβολαῖς mean " in parables *without interpretation* " ? I cannot see why, in the context, this should not be precisely what it does mean—especially when, as we have seen, this is what happens in real life. When someone hears a story or looks at a cartoon without going any further, then the parable remains for him nothing but a parable ; for him ἐν παραβολαῖς τὰ πάντα γίνεται—parable is the beginning and end of the matter. And why should one be accused of turning the δέδοται upside down if one interprets the " giving of the mystery " to mean what happens to the responsible hearer, who recognizes the parable as a challenge to investigation and who asks the teacher for more light, and is *thereby and therewith* " given " the very heart of the matter? If Jülicher's trouble was the perfect tense, δέδοται, there is no more difficulty in that than in any of the other New Testament pronouncements which, while quasi-predestinarian in form, reckon, at the same time, with the fact of free-will and responsibility. To say that those who, by their own free choice, respond are the " elect " is no more than the basic paradox of personal relationships.

Perhaps this is the right point at which to observe that there seems to be no trace, elsewhere in the New Testament, of a theory that the effect of preaching the Gospel is to harden all hearers except the elect. There is plenty of evidence that the actual hardening of the opposition, especially unbelieving Jews, was a perplexity to Christians (cf. Joachim Gnilka's important study, *Die Verstockung Israels*, München, 1961); but nothing, so far as I can see, to suggest that it was explained by this particular theory—that the preaching itself positively hardened and blinded the non-elect. It was explained in terms of a qualified pre-destinarianism, or of God's inscrutable purposes; but where (unless one insists on finding it in Mk 4 : 11) is it ascribed to the preaching itself? Even Ro 9, the most extreme " predestinarian " passage, to which allusion is usually made in this connection (see references in V. Taylor, *Mark*, p. 257[b]), only makes the point that God can raise up a rebel Pharaoh *in order to* demonstrate his irresistible power. Even here, there is no hint that it is the preaching of the message that creates obscurity and hardness. If, therefore, we insist on so interpreting the Marcan passage, we have no right to explain it as a reflection of a current theory in the Church of the New Testament. Rather, we must treat it as a strange and unparalleled aberration, so far as New Testament thinking goes, and explain it by a pitifully literal reading of Is 6—which, however, I have already rejected as improbable.[19]

But commentators go their way regardless. A. E. J. Rawlinson, *The Gospel according to St Mark*, London, ³1936, p. 48, writing of allegorical interpretations as secondary, goes on: " It seems

[19] Incidentally, Jn 16 : 25 ff. exhibits a quite different idea, namely, that, even to the disciples, Jesus does not (or cannot ?) speak otherwise than enigmatically until the coming of the new era.

probable that these more or less allegorical interpretations do not, as a matter of actual history, go back to our Lord Himself, but are examples of early Christian exegesis. They were put forth, more or less authoritatively, as *the* explanation of what the parables meant, and the belief arose that the Lord had so explained them privately to the disciples. (Of course it is *possible* that in one or two cases the disciples were puzzled by something in a parable and asked our Lord to explain it, but it is equally possible that the whole conception of the parables as being difficult is of later growth.) In Mk 4 : 10–12, 33–34 this theory is developed further and applied to the parables of our Lord in general. They conveyed *the ' mystery ' of the Kingdom of God* . . . which only the initiated were intended to understand. The general mass of the people was not *intended* to repent ". Or again, Klostermann, *Das Markus-Evangelium*, Tübingen, [3]1936, *in loc.*, writes : " den nicht berufenen ἔξω (rabb. *ḥyswnym* Billerbeck [*SBK*] II 7) dagegen soll es [sc. das Geheimnis] nur in einer Form vorgetragen werden, die ihnen *das Verständnis unmöglich macht* " (my italics). And Jeremias (*Gleichnisse*, p. 12) draws the same sharp contrast between the two mutual incompatibles—the receiving of the mystery by the privileged (i.e. the recognition of the present irruption of the Kingdom of God) and nothing but riddling obscurity for those who are outside (ἐν παραβολαῖς being, as we have seen, taken by Jeremias as reflecting a mistranslation of *mšl* or *mtl'* where it really meant " riddle " [20]). This is in keeping with Jülicher's characterisation of the parables as " nicht zu Gunsten der Jünger . . . sondern allein zu Ungunsten des ὄχλος " (*op. cit.*, I, 126) ; or again : " durch diese Dunkelreden die Verstockung der Massen zu vollenden " (*op. cit.*, I, 128).

But I ask, once more, Why this assumption ? And I can find no adequate answer. If it be once allowed that parable is the initial medium—the form used by the good teacher to avoid " spoon-feeding " and to elicit response—and that intelligent and serious response to parable leads on—as it does in any observable educational process—to a further stage in understanding, which might very properly be described as " the giving of the mystery ", then the basic problem vanishes.

But it is now time to look at vv. 13 ff. Of course, nothing is

[20] Cf. Hunkin, *loc. cit.*, who renders the phrase : " the whole thing comes to be parabolic (i.e., cryptic) " (p. 374).

simpler than to say that this represents an allegorizing, by the post-resurrection Church, of an original dominical parable which is represented, more or less faithfully, in vv. 3–9. And I must repeat, lest I be misunderstood, that I am entirely ready to recognize the probability that such allegorizing did take place. I only question whether this is the right conclusion in this particular case. C. H. Dodd and J. Jeremias, among many others, believe that the message of the original parable, as told by Jesus himself, was no more than that, despite all hindrances and hazards, the crop is remarkably good. Dodd's words are: "In spite of all, the harvest is plentiful: it is only the labourers who are lacking" (*The Parables of the Kingdom*, London, revised ed., 1961, p. 147). Jeremias' formulation is: "In spite of every failure and opposition, from hopeless beginnings, God brings forth the triumphant end which he had promised" (*Gleichnisse*, ET, ²1963, p. 150[21]). Jeremias adds, in a footnote, that even Justin Martyr and the Pseudo-Clementine Recognitions, despite the then current tendency to allegorize, treat the parable not as a challenge to self-examination but as an encouragement to the Christian preacher not to be faint-hearted in his labours.[22] Similarly, G. E. Ladd, *Jesus and the Kingdom*, New York, 1964, p. 216: "The number of soils is unimportant. The one central truth is this: the word of the Kingdom is sown; sometimes it bears fruit, sometimes it does not." It is relevant at this point to recall that it is probably a mistake to imagine that the crop yielded by the good ground is fantastically exaggerated, and from this to draw further support for an interpretation which concentrates only on the success of the harvest (see, e.g., Jeremias, p. 150). K. D. White shows in "The Parable of the Sower", *JTS* n.s. 15 (1964), 300 ff., that a more natural interpretation of the multiples, "a hundredfold", etc., is "a hundred (etc.) grains from a single plant"—which is not impossibly excessive.[23] An example of circularity in argument is that a commentator, having decided (wrongly, as I believe) that the amazing harvest

[21] So, substantially, C. W. F. Smith, *The Jesus of the Parables*, Philadelphia, 1948, p. 64.

[22] He appeals here to M. F. Wiles, "Early Exegesis of the Parables", *SJT* 11 (1958), 287 ff.; but Wiles (p. 293) had himself cited Justin and the Recognitions only as examples of interpretations of this parable which show that the explanation given in the Gospels did not exert a compelling influence on later exegesis.

[23] So, too, E. Linnemann, *Gleichnisse*, p. 123. But see Jeremias' reply, *NTS* 13 (1966–67), 48 ff.

is the point of the parable, can then urge, among the counts against the originality of the interpretation in vv. 13 ff., " the loss of perception that, despite failures, the amazing harvest is the supreme lesson " (V. Taylor, *Mark*, p. 258).

Now, there is admittedly independent evidence that Jesus did remark on the richness of the harvest. There is the saying in Mt 9 : 37 f., Lk 10 : 2 : ὁ μὲν θερισμὸς πολύς, οἱ δὲ ἐργάται ὀλίγοι. But in this saying, the point is not the richness of the harvest, but the contrast between the quantity of the harvest and the inadequacy of the reapers. Again, in the comparable saying in Jn 4 : 35 ff. (λευκαὶ πρὸς θερισμόν), yet another point is made—that sower and reaper are different persons, and yet can share together the joy of the harvest. Why should it be assumed that the parable of the sower, in which there is no mention of either of these points, should be making a point which, even in these sayings, is only a subsidiary one ? C. H. Dodd, in the passage just quoted, brings in the point about the paucity of labourers (and goes on to quote : " Pray ye the Lord of the harvest . . .") ; but this is an arbitrary collocation of two passages which, in the traditions, are distinct. Besides, the very circumstantial description of the various types of soil in the parable of the sower is difficult to justify unless it is intended to serve some purpose.[24] This is a point well made by I. H. Marshall, in his important *Eschatology and the Parables*, London, 1963, p. 31. A little-heeded plea for a reconsideration of the matter by L. E. Browne should also be noted : *The Parables of the Gospels in the Light of Modern Criticism*, Cambridge, 1913.[25]

Surely, then, the most natural and least arbitrary assumption is that the structure and the details of the parable in vv. 3–9 are intended to signify something ; and why should they not signify that seed, however good, meets with all sorts of different receptions, and that it depends on the soil whether a good crop is yielded ? [26] And if this really is a parable about parables—a parable about how parables are received—it gives point to v. 13, which (as Jülicher rightly saw) must mean " If you do not understand this

[24] Contrast the brevity of the parable in 2 Es 8 : 41, where the point is that not all the seed sown prospers.

[25] G. V. Jones, in his excellent book, *The Art and Truth of the Parables*, London, 1964, devotes a separate note to the matter, but chiefly with a view to minimising its importance.

[26] See a good survey of various interpretations in C. E. B. Cranfield, *Mark*, 150 f., reaching the conclusion : " It is a parable about hearing the Word of God ".

parable, how are you going to understand any?" If, that is, this is a parable about response, how will the hearers respond to any parable if they do not respond to this one? On my assumption, admittedly, they have *begun* to respond. But need we take this rhetorical question too rigorously in this respect?

Now, that this is a parable about response is exactly what the so-called allegorical interpretation in vv. 13 ff. says. I say "so-called allegorical" because, if this is allegory,[27] it is of an extremely natural and unstrained kind. It is nearer the truth to say that the story of the sower is, by its very nature, a *multiple* parable.[28] It is a natural unforced description of a farmer's activity. Nothing is artificially introduced into the account for the sake of pointing a moral. It is certainly not, in that sense, an allegory; for it describes the natural hazards of the farmer's seed. But it does, in fact, present such a good analogy to a plurality of different receptions given to Jesus' teaching that it turns out to be a multiple parable. Any one of the descriptions of the different sorts of soil, had it been found in the traditions as an isolated *pericope*, would have been recognized by critical scholarship as belonging to the genuine parable-type. Thus, it is not strictly correct to describe vv. 13 ff. as an allegorizing application: they only make explicit what the multiple parable has already suggested.

Not that I entertain the dogma that Jesus cannot himself have used allegory. This is another legacy from Jülicher[29] which is too often accepted uncritically.[30] It is even said, from time to time, that the Old Testament itself makes it antecedently probable that Jesus would have avoided allegory in favour of parable alone. But a moment's reflection will produce a fair number of Old Testament allegories and strangely few parables.

[27] Jülicher (*op. cit.*, 2, 532) calls it allegory: "... die Deutung der Synoptiker behandelt die Parabelerzählung wie eine Allegorie ..."; C. H. Dodd (*Parables*, p. 145) calls it "an elaborate interpretation on allegorical lines".

[28] Volkmar, quoted by Jülicher, *op. cit.*, 1, 121, attempts thus to explain the plural, *παραβολαί*, in *v.* 10. I agree with Jülicher in dismissing this as a mere artifice (*Kunstgriff*); but it bears witness to my point about the multiplicity of the parable. See, however, G. H. Boobyer, as in n. 11 above.

[29] See *op. cit.*, 1, 49 f., and the phrase (p. 50): "... der Kampf gegen die *allegorisierende* Auslegung von Jesu-Parabeln" (the italics are his own). But Jülicher defines allegory more precisely than some of his successors.

[30] Contrast C. E. B. Cranfield, *Mark*, p. 159; and R. E. Brown, "Parables and Allegory Reconsidered", *NovT* 5 (1962), 36 ff. (reprinted in *New Testament Essays*, Milwaukee, 1965, pp. 254 ff.).

Nathan's story in 2 S 12 is an obvious parable. Perhaps Jeremiah's potter (Jer 18) began as a parable—but it was quickly marred in the prophet's hand, for the application does not really fit the image. Ezekiel's wicked shepherds (Ezk 34) make a parable. But a great deal else in Ezekiel is clearly and extravagantly allegorical (e.g. Ezk 15, 16, 17). Isaiah's vineyard (Is 5) is an allegory; and further examples could be found. However, whether we allow allegory to Jesus or not, in this instance, at least, if we have to do with allegory, it is allegory with a difference; it is better classified as multiple parable.

At this point it is appropriate to refer to a new development in exposition from Scandinavia. Recently, B. Gerhardsson, formerly of Uppsala, now of Lund, has put forward the view [31] that much of the New Testament, including, possibly, the original teaching of Jesus, follows patterns dictated by the use of Deuteronomy after the manner of later rabbinic techniques.[32] Applying rabbinic exegesis of the *Shema'* to our parable, he suggests that a rabbinic interpretation of the phrase "you shall love JHWH your God with your whole heart and with your whole soul and with your whole might" is discernible in the descriptions of the various sorts of soil in the Matthean version. In the cases where the sowing is unsuccessful, it is because the word has not been heard with the whole *heart* (cf. Mt 13 : 19), or not with the whole *soul* (the stony ground), or not with the whole *might* (i.e., property and possessions—the thorns represent possessiveness, Mt 13 : 22). Successful sowing means the sort of hearing that is also doing. Along these lines, Gerhardsson argues that the interpretation of the parable in Matthew, so far from being an alien allegorization, fits the parable like a glove; that the sorts of ground have been selected precisely so as to fit the standard exegesis of the *Shema'* (the hazard of too little rain, for instance, though a real hazard, is not alluded to, because it happens not to be appropriate to this scheme); and that, in so far as Luke and Mark do not fit this pattern quite so neatly, it is because these Evangelists failed to grasp the point of the selection.

It remains to be proved that such a technique was in use as early as the time of Jesus, or, if it was, that he would have been likely to adopt it. But Gerhardsson at least lends support to my

[31] "The Parable of the Sower and its Interpretation", *NTS* 14 (1968), 165 ff.

[32] See also his *The Testing of God's Son* (*Matt* 4 : 1–11 *and Par.*), *Coniectanea Biblica* 2, fasc. 1, Lund, 1966.

contention that the interpretation and the parable originally belonged together, and that the parable is not about the success of the harvest but about the different sorts of reception.

Further, he endorses my plea for the recognition of a common-sense principle of education, when he appeals to the Jewish wisdom tradition and to the rabbis for the rule that " he who *hears* is the one who *hears more*; he who *is wise* will *become wiser* . . ." (p. 174). And, finally, I welcome his observation that those who have become disciples of the kingdom of heaven and have been taught its secrets " are not referred to as any particular historical group, as 'the church' over against 'the synagogue' or anything similar . . . ; those included have to qualify for it by being *understanding hearers* and *genuine doers* of the word " (p. 179).

But what about the vocabulary of this section? It has been widely regarded as, in itself, a clear index of the secondary nature of the section.[33] I have already shown that the sudden change from the plural, παραβολαί, of v. 10, to the singular, παραβολή, of v. 13, need not be the sign of a " suture ", provided that vv. 10–12 are treated as a generalizing statement, and v. 13 seen as introducing a specific example. But there is the further fact that there are several words which arouse suspicion. C. H. Dodd, *Parables*, p. 3, n. 1, summarizes: " Μυστήριον, οἱ ἔξω, πρόσκαιρος, ἀπάτη are not found in the Synoptics outside this passage; ἐπιθυμία is found elsewhere only in Lk. xxii, 15, in a different sense; διωγμός and θλῖψις are found only in Mk. x, 30, and in the Synoptic Apocalypse (Mk. xiii), passages which are for other reasons suspected of being secondary ". True; but in judging whether a section is essentially dominical or essentially the creation of the Evangelist or his predecessors, it is important to ask not only where else a word occurs, but also whether or not it is, by its very nature, out of keeping with the *Sitz im Leben* of the ministry of Jesus himself. If one applies this test, there is not one word that could not quite easily be rendered in Aramaic or Hebrew; nor one that represents an idea anachronous (so far as can be judged) with the time of Jesus. That these words appear nowhere—or almost nowhere—else in the Synoptists can be explained as easily by the fact that this happens to be the only context in the Synoptic story in which

[33] It is described by Jeremias (*Gleichnisse*, pp. 75 f.) as " decisive " against its originality.

they are appropriate, as by postulating a post-resurrection setting. " Mystery ", " outsiders ", " time-servers ", " deceit ", " lust ", " persecution ", " distress "—not one of these has at any period been alien to the people of God, whether of the Old or New Dispensation.

Of the words enumerated by Dodd, the only ones that, in the LXX, do not represent Hebrew words are *ἀπάτη* and *πρόσκαιρος* But both occur in the Greek books of the LXX ; the verb *ἀπατᾶν* is common enough in the Hebrew-based books ; and the Peshitta, at any rate, has no difficulty in representing *πρόσκαιρος* by *dzbn'*, " temporary ".[34]

As for the argument that the confusion between the seed and the soils indicates the secondary character of the interpretation, this is an argument that is liable to recoil. There certainly is imprecision in the phrases *ὁ σπείρων τὸν λόγον σπείρει* (v. 14) and *οἱ ἐπὶ τὰ πετρώδη σπειρόμενοι* (v. 16). First it is " the word " that is the object of *σπείρειν*, then it is the persons who receive the word. But, as a matter of fact, the analogy is not itself clouded. It is easy enough for the reader to see that *σπείρειν* is used in the two senses of " throwing " the seed itself and " implanting " the soil. In English idiom similarly we can say that seed is sown, but also that ground is sown with seed.[35] Besides, whatever imprecision there may be might as easily be a mark of originality as not. It is the usual question, whether *difficilior lectio* is *potior* or *corruptior*. Of the Synoptists, Matthew leaves the " imprecision " virtually where it is in Mark. But Luke tidies it up a good deal ; and few will doubt that the tidying is not original, but is due to Luke's literary sense. So far as chronology goes, we have a document earlier, in all probability, than any of the Synoptists, namely Col 1, where exactly the same " imprecision " appears in much the same metaphor. The metaphor of growing and bearing fruit is applied, in Col 1 : 6 to the Gospel, in 1 : 10 to believers—that is, first to the seed sown and then to the ground sown with the seed.

All in all, then, it seems to me that a case can be made—not, as I say, for all interpretations of parables in the Gospels being dominical, for I am far from holding such a view—but for

[34] For further criticism of the drawing of rash deductions from these words, see Cranfield, *Mark*, pp. 161 ff.

[35] A query is placed against this idea by Gerhardsson (*loc. cit.*, p. 175, n. 3), but not, I think, decisively.

this particular one being at least plausibly attributed to Jesus himself, so far as its substance goes.

And if my attempt to explain vv. 10–12 as a generalizing section is allowed, then the whole section, vv. 1–20, becomes an intelligible whole, composed by the Evangelist but with a historically sensitive use of genuinely traditional material.

Since little attention seems to have been paid, not only to my own scattered references to this point of view, but to much more weighty treatments of the theme such as Cranfield's, and, before him, L. E. Browne's, I am the more grateful for the hospitality of a *Festschrift* for the reformulation of it ; and I offer this essay with respect and affection to the scholar in whose honour it is presented.

# ESCHATOLOGY IN MARK'S GOSPEL

EDUARD SCHWEIZER

THE problem of eschatology and apocalypticism has been greatly elucidated by M. Black, primarily within the realm of the inter-testamental Jewish thinking.[1] I wish therefore to treat this topic with regard to our earliest Gospel in the hope of contributing to this volume, as a cordial birthday greeting, a brief essay which would please him. The main problem with which we have to deal is the relation of the parousia of the Son of man to his suffering. Which one of these is, in Mark's understanding, the real centre of his book? Or are they both of equal importance, and if so, how are they related to each other?

W. Marxsen, in his very stimulating work on Mark,[2] opted definitely for the parousia as the focus of the whole Gospel. Written in a time of highest eschatological expectations, it urges the church to emigrate to Galilee in order to meet the coming Son of man and to share his triumph in his parousia there. This is, according to Marxsen, the meaning of the commandment of the angel in 16 : 7 and of the abrupt ending in 16 : 8.[3] Is this view really defensible?

H. Conzelmann [4] has pointed to a number of things which show that the apocalyptic discourse in Mk 13 did not expect the parousia in a very near future. First, there is the double warning in vv. 7 f.: " this, however, is not yet the end ", and " this is

[1] Cf. especially M. Black, *The Dead Sea Scrolls and Christian Doctrine*, London, 1966, pp. 18–22 (parallelism between Qumranian and Christian eschatology); " The Eschatology of the Similitudes of Enoch ", *JTS* n.s. 3 (1952), 1–10; " The Son of Man Problem in Recent Research and Debate ", *BJRL* 45 (1963), 305–18.

[2] *Der Evangelist Markus*, Göttingen, 1956, especially pp. 73–77 and 112–28.

[3] Cf. the work of E. Trocmé, *La formation de l'évangile selon Marc*, Paris, 1963, which is full of new and helpful suggestions. Quite a number of them deserve serious discussion. His main thesis is that the original Gospel, as it was known to Luke, had ended with ch. 13 and was written in Galilee around A.D. 50, whereas Matthew used the edition of a redactor in Rome (around A.D. 85), who had added ch. 14–16.

[4] " Geschichte und Eschaton nach Mc 13 ", *ZNTW* 50 (1959), 210–21. Cf. also M. Brunec, *VD* 30–31 (1952–53).

(only) the beginning of the sufferings". Also, there occurs a strong polemic against an identification of historical persons and events with apocalyptic manifestations of the approaching end (vv. 3–8). Additional elements are the central importance of a period of mission between the present time and the end-time (v. 10), the emphasis on the difference between a last period within the earthly history (vv. 14–23) and the supernatural phenomena of the parousia which will come suddenly, but only "after that tribulation" (v. 24). Finally the traditional position of an eschatological section at the end of a collection of sayings (Q, M), a catechism (He 6 : 1 f.), a sermon (Ac 17 : 22 ff.) or a document (Didache) is parallel to the position of ch. 13 in Mark's Gospel.[5]

By investigating the structure of the whole Gospel we may add a number of arguments pointing in the same direction:

(1) Eschatological or even apocalyptic passages are remarkably scarce in our Gospel. There is only one other passage: 8 : 38 f. This reveals clearly the way in which eschatology is important to Mark. The reference to the parousia of the Son of man stresses the absolute validity of Jesus' call to follow him.[6] The Son of man will judge everybody according to his or her obedience to this call. Therefore, the parousia of the Son of man is certainly of great importance for Mark, but only because it is a final confirmation of Jesus' call to discipleship. Discipleship constitutes the main theme of the whole section 8 : 27–10 : 52. The days in Jerusalem reveal the deep gulf which lies between those who try only to entrap him (12 : 13) and are like a withered fig tree (11 : 12–14, 20 f.) and those who are not far from the kingdom of God (12 : 34) and give all that they have to God like the poor widow (12 : 41–44). Thus Mk 13, coming after the portrayal of this gulf and immediately before the passion, speaks of the last judgment when the Son of man will gather from the ends of the earth those who have followed him and will recompense them for their sufferings.

(2) On the other hand Mark refers time and time again to the resurrection of Jesus: 8 : 31; 9 : 9; 9 : 31; 10 : 34. All these references combine the coming sufferings of Jesus with his

[5] We may also compare the "eschatological" outlook of a patriarch shortly before his death (Gn 49, etc.); cf. D. E. Nineham, *Saint Mark*, The Pelican Gospel Commentary, London, 1963, p. 340.

[6] Cf. similarly R. Pesch, *Naherwartung, Tradition und Redaktion in Mk 13*, Düsseldorf, 1968, pp. 235 ff., especially p. 242.

resurrection. The first one is accentuated by an explicit comment: Mark points out that this is the first word of Jesus which is no longer parabolic speech, but plain revelation of God's plan.[7] According to Marxsen the commandment of the angel in 16 : 7 does not refer to a vision of the risen Christ which would be granted to Peter and the disciples. He supposes that it refers rather to the parousia which the church should see in Galilee within a very short period after the publication of the Gospel. However, is it possible to assume that the readers would expect anything else at the end of the Gospel than the fulfilment of the three or four predictions of Jesus, that is, the narration of his resurrection after that of his sufferings?

(3) This is the more evident since the verb "to see" is very often used with reference to seeing the risen Lord, certainly much more frequently than with reference to the parousia.[8] Usually, of course, it is in a past tense, since when the New Testament was written the Easter appearances lay in the past.

(4) It is inconceivable that, in A.D. 65 (or 85), any Christian church existed which would not have heard that the risen Lord had appeared to his disciples.[9] If this is so, who could have read the story of the empty tomb without understanding the word of the angel as a reference to these appearances?

(5) On the one hand Mk 13 urges the church to emigrate, not now, but in a future time when "the sacrilege will be where it ought not to be" (v. 14). And they are not to go to Galilee but to the mountains of Judea (as many would have done at the beginning of the Jewish-Roman war). On the other hand the Christian church of Jerusalem did, as far as we know, not flee to Galilee but to Pella in Transjordan.[10]

[7] Mk 8 : 32a; cf. the same phrase "he spoke the word" in 2 : 2 and especially in 4 : 33.

[8] Mt 28 : 10; Jn 20 : 18, 25, 29; Ac 22 : 14 f.; 1 Co 9 : 1; cf. Lk 9 : 36 and the frequent use of the passive voice Lk 24 : 34, etc.; over against Mk 13 : 26 and par.; Rev 1 : 7.

[9] 1 Co 15 : 5–8 shows a chain of tradition which reaches at least from the church of Antioch to the churches in Greece, etc. And it refers to those who saw the risen Lord as still being alive and partially known to Paul and the churches founded by him. Moreover, Lk 24 : 34 contains a brief formula about the first appearance to Peter which must have been handed down as a primitive tradition; for Luke obviously knows no more than the mere fact mentioned in the formula.

[10] Eus 3, 5, 3. The view of W. Marxsen would be impossible if Mk 13 : 14 proved a composition of the Gospel after A.D. 70, as N. Walter thinks ("Tempelzerstörung und synoptische Apokalypse", *ZNTW* 57, 1966, 43–45). But why should the more general wording of this verse (over against Daniel), which omits a

(6) Would Mark, believing that the parousia would take place within some months, write a whole Gospel and include pericopes like that on the problem of matrimony and divorce (10 : 1–12) ?

(7) Finally, Mark himself seems to disclose his own position at the end of ch. 13. In vv. 34–37 we find the traditional similitude of the doorkeeper watching for the return of his master, not knowing the hour of the night when he will turn up (cf. Lk 12 : 35–38). This is a call to expect the imminent parousia ; it describes a watch lasting one night, in which the coming of the Lord may happen any hour between the fall of darkness and dawn. Mark, or perhaps the church before him, has changed the message of this parable in a remarkable way. No longer is the lord a man going to a supper and coming back in the same night, a bit earlier or a bit later. He becomes a traveller going abroad, putting all his servants in charge during his absence, each with his work (cf. Mt 24 : 45–51 ; 25 : 13–15 ; Lk 12 : 41–46 ; 19 : 12 f.). He would certainly not return by night, since the gates of the town would be closed then. And nobody would, in Palestine, travel at night outside of the walls of the town except in extreme need. Therefore v. 35 belongs to the old stratum : " watch therefore, for you do not know when the master of the house will come, in the evening, or at midnight, or at cockcrow, or in the morning ". It still betrays the original point of the story, the nearness of the parousia. The situation of the lord on a journey, having charged his servants with the maintenance of his household, as depicted in v. 34a, would actually require a conclusion like Mt 24 : 42 : " watch therefore, for you do not know on what *day* your Lord is coming ". For in the time of Mark the " watching ", to which the final v. 37 returns, has lost its apocalyptic meaning. The introduction of the servants in charge (v. 34) proves this. Even if it may still be connected with the idea of the coming judgment, it is actually understood in a merely ethical way, as in Ac 20 : 31 or 1 P 5 : 8. In an earlier time even 1 Th 5 : 6, despite its proximity to the apocalyptic passage 4 : 13–18, shows the transition to a merely ethical understanding. More important is that Mk 14 : 38 (where, as in 13 : 36 f., the

---

clear reference to the temple, not be equally possible before the event of A.D. 70 ? Cf. also M. Goguel, *HTR* 26 (1933), 1–55, esp. 28–55 : our text of Mk 13 : 14 dates from A.D. 80–85, whereas a first edition of A.D. 70–75 contained a text similar to Lk 21 : 20 (24) ; L. Hartman, *Prophecy Interpreted*, Lund, 1966, pp. 230 ff., 239 ff.

contrast to "sleeping" (v. 37) is involved) also is an ethical maxim dealing with the battle between spirit and flesh.

This means that the original expectation of a very near parousia has vanished. One cannot maintain over decades the fervid expectation of the Christ who will come in a week or a month. Therefore, the emphasis which lay first on the watching itself, on the being ready any day or any night, was shifted to the responsibility of the servants of the Lord for their work in the meantime. This is exactly the situation in which Mark finds himself and the church to which he addresses his Gospel.

The conclusion seems to be evident. The parousia of the Son of man, probably expected within some decades, is certainly important for Mark. For it will bring the final union of the disciples with their Lord and, therefore, the recompense for all the sufferings which they have shared with the master whom they have followed. However, the centre of this Gospel is not the parousia. It is the *suffering* of the Son of man which enables his disciples to follow him; to find, in this way, God as their Lord, no longer far away, but revealed to them in following the way of His son; and finally to receive the eternal life of the age to come (10 : 30).[11]

[11] Cf. my commentary on Mark (Göttingen, 1967), to be published in English by John Knox Press; also my article "Mark's contribution to the Quest of the Historical Jesus", *NTS* 10 (1963-64), 421–32.

# JESCHU BEN MIRJAM

## Kontroversgeschichtliche Anmerkungen zu Mk 6 : 3

Ethelbert Stauffer

### I

Von Hermann Gunkel haben wir gelernt, dass die Frage nach dem " Sitz im Leben " das A und Ω aller Gattungsforschung ist.[1] Martin Dibelius hat die fundamentale Bedeutung der Predigt und der Katechese für die Gestaltung der synoptischen Jesustradition aufgezeigt.[2] Viele Autoren aus vielen Ländern haben den Einfluss der christlichen Liturgie studiert. Dagegen hat ein anderer Sitz im Leben bisher nur geringe Beachtung gefunden: die Kontroverse. Erstaunlich genug. Denn wir besitzen eine Menge Nachrichten, die uns bezeugen, dass die Streitgespräche mit Andersgläubigen im Leben der frühen Christengemeinde eine entscheidende Rolle spielten,[3] und die Rückwirkung dieser Kontroversen auf die Formation, Deformation und Transformation der Jesusüberlieferung ist vielfach mit Händen zu greifen.[4] Die Entstehungsgeschichte des kanonischen Jesusbildes ist doch wohl ein wenig dramatischer verlaufen, als es in den mehr oder minder kontemplativen Betrachtungen zur Entwicklung des Kerygmas, der Paränese, der Liturgie, zur Tradition und Redaktion des christlichen Erbauungsstoffes den Anschein hat. Das mag hier an einem kleinen Beispiel illustriert werden.

[1] H. Gunkel, *Die Sagen der Genesis*, Göttingen, 1901 = *The Legends of Genesis*, New York, 1964 (1901); japanisch 1903.

[2] M. Dibelius, *Die Formgeschichte des Evangeliums*, Tübingen, 1919, pp. 4 ff., 36, 66 ff.

[3] Über Kontroversen mit Juden v., e.g., Lk 2 : 34; Mt 27 : 64; 28 : 15; Ac 2 : 22 ff.; 5 : 28 ff.; 6 : 9; 9 : 29; 10 : 37 ff.; 13 : 45; 17 : 2; 28 : 22 ff.; Tit 1 : 9 f.; 3 : 9; Hegesipp bei Euseb 2 : 23; Justin Dialogus passim. Mit Heiden, e.g., 1 Co 1 : 23; Ac 17 : 18 ff. Mit Täuferjüngern, e.g., Ac 13 : 24 f.; 18 : 25 ff.; 19 : 4; Ps-Clem Rec 1, 60, 1 ff. Mit christlichen Sondergruppen v. 1 Co 1 : 12; Gal 1 : 6 ff.; Ph 3 : 2 ff.; Ac 15 : 1 ff. u.a.m.

[4] Man denke, e.g., an den Einfluss, den die Auseinandersetzung mit den Täuferjüngern auf die Entstehung und Gestaltung von Lk 1 : 5–2 : 52 oder Jn 1 : 1–4 : 3 ausgeübt hat.

## II

In Mk 6 : 3 liest Nestle-Aland *ὁ τέκτων, ὁ υἱὸς τῆς Μαρίας*. Ebenso schon die Editoren Bengel, Lachmann, Tischendorf Westcott-Hort, Bernhard Weiss, Hermann von Soden, Weizsäcker, Huck-Lietzmann u.a. Ebenso die Exegeten Hugo Grotius, Heinrich Julius Holtzmann, Julius Wellhausen, Johannes Weiss, Lagrange, Schlatter, Gould, Lohmeyer, Josef Schmid, Blinzler u.a.[5] Ebenso die Vulgata (Sixto-Clementina ed. Hetzenauer, Ratisbonae, 1929), die neugriechische Bibel (Athenai, 1960), die Stuttgarter Lutherbibeln von 1912 und 1965 ; die Zürcher Bibel von 1955 ; die New English Bible von 1961. Ebenso die Greek-English Diglot (London Bible Society, 1961) und Alands Synopsis von 1964. Ebenso jetzt auch *The Greek New Testament* von 1966 (ed. Aland, Black, Metzger, Wikgren) das diese Lesart ausdrücklich mit der Note A versieht : " virtually certain". *Τί ἔτι χρείαν ἔχομεν μαρτύρων* ?

Aber Stimmenzählung genügt nicht. Rab Joseph bar Hijja unterbricht uns und fragt *rbwt' lmḥšb gbry h'* : " Ist es etwa eine Leistung, Autoritäten herzuzählen ? ! " (Jeb 45a). Das letzte Wort haben immer die inneren Gründe, und das entscheidende Kriterium lautet nach Johann Albrecht Bengel : Proclivi praestat ardua, Die anstössigste Textgestalt ist die beste. Das gilt nicht nur von der Textkritik, sondern auch von der Literar- und Traditionskritik.

Jeschu ben Mirjam.[6] Offenbar hat die kirchliche Jesustradition an dieser Metronymik ganz erheblich Anstoss genommen. Denn man hat die metronyme Namensform schon früh modifiziert und bald genug völlig eliminiert. In Mt 13 : 55 fragen die Leute von Nazareth : *οὐχ οὗτός ἐστιν ὁ τοῦ τέκτονος υἱός ; οὐχ ἡ μήτηρ αὐτοῦ λέγεται Μαριάμ. . .* ; In Lk 4 : 22 lautet ihre Frage : *οὐχὶ υἱός ἐστιν Ἰωσὴφ οὗτος* ; In Jn 6 : 42 murren die Leute von Kapernaum : *οὐχ οὗτός ἐστιν Ἰησοῦς ὁ υἱὸς Ἰωσήφ, οὗ ἡμεῖς οἴδαμεν τὸν πατέρα καὶ τὴν μητέρα* ; Schliesslich wirken diese Abänderungstendenzen auch auf die Markusüberlieferung selber zurück. Der Chester-Beatty-Papyrus (45) liest in Mk 6 : 3

[5] Anders A. Merx ; E. Klostermann ; F. C. Grant (*ATR 20, 1938, 116*) ; W. Grundmann ; G. Bornkamm (*Jesus, 1959, p. 181*) u.a.m. Zur Antikritik s. jetzt J. Blinzler, *Die Brüder und Schwestern Jesu*, Stuttgart, 1967, pp. 28–30.

[6] Zur Schreibeweise des Jesusnamens v. Sanh 43a im Codex Monacensis *yšw hnwṣry*.

ὁ τοῦ τέκτον]ος ὁ υ[ἱὸς τῆς Μαρίας. Origenes zitiert unsern Vers in ähnlichem Wortlaut und gleichem Sinn: ὁ τοῦ τέκτονος υἱὸς καὶ τῆς Μαρίας.[7]

Warum hat man an der Namensform ὁ υἱὸς τῆς Μαρίας Anstoss genommen? Der Anstoss wäre unverständlich, wenn diese Formel nur besagen wollte, dass Jesus der Sohn einer Witwe war.[8] Aber die metronyme Benennung Jesu will etwas ganz anderes sagen. Sie will sagen *'yn 'b̲ lw*: Er hat keinen Vater.[9] Jesus ist der Sohn Marias, nicht Josephs (s. unten pp. 122 ff.). Sobald man das begreift, wird der Text und Kontext von Mk 6 : 2ff. verständlich. Eine amtliche Delegation aus Jerusalem hat in Kapernaum die offizielle Damnatio über Jesus ausgesprochen (Mk 3 : 22). Von diesem Augenblick an darf und soll man alles Negative offen zur Sprache bringen, was man über den Zaubermeister weiss oder zu wissen meint. Das tun die Leute von Nazareth. Sie nehmen Anstoss an dem Vollmachtsanspruch Jesu (Mk 6 : 2 ἐξεπλήσσοντο; 6 : 3 ἐσκανδαλίζοντο) und erklären: Dieser Mann ist ein illegitimes Kind der Maria.[10] Damit ist der Geltungsanspruch Jesu erledigt und seine Wundertätigkeit im

[7] Origenes, contra Celsum, 6 : 36: οὐδαμοῦ τῶν ἐν ταῖς ἐκκλησίαις φερομένων εὐαγγελίων τέκτων αὐτὸς ὁ Ἰησοῦς ἀναγέγραπται. Diese Fehlanzeige des grossen Gelehrten ist einigermassen verwunderlich, sollte aber niemanden zu falschen Schlüssen verleiten. Denn schon Justin kennt Mk 6 : 3 in der Form ὁ τέκτων, ὁ υἱὸς τῆς Μαρίας. v. Justin Dialogus 88 : 8 (ἐλθόντος τοῦ Ἰησοῦ . . . τέκτονος νομιζομένου). Und nur wenige Jahre später (um 177/180) spottet Celsus über den Zimmermann Jesus, v. Origenes, *loc. cit.*

[8] So zuletzt Blinzler (*op. cit.*, p. 72) unter Berufung auf Renan u.a.m. Blinzler sieht das Skandalon von Mk 6 : 3 in dem Zimmermannsberuf Jesu: "Der Grund, warum Matthäus den Mk-Text abwandelt, scheint das Bestreben zu sein, Jesus nicht als niedrigen Handarbeiter erscheinen zu lassen" (*op. cit.*, p. 29). Aber die Schriftgelehrten in der Zeit und Heimat des Evangelisten Matthäus waren zum grossen Teil Handwerker, und niemand fand das peinlich. Im Gegenteil, man war stolz auf ihre ehrliche Handarbeit und wirtschaftliche Unabhängigkeit. Cf. Ac 18 : 3; 1 Co 4 : 12; 9 : 6 ff.; J. Jeremias, *Jerusalem zur Zeit Jesu*, Berlin, 1963, pp. 1 ff.

[9] v. E. Stauffer, *Jerusalem und Rom*, Bern, 1957, pp. 117 f.; *Jesus*, Bern, 1957, pp. 22 ff.; J. Delorme, "À propos des Évangiles de l'enfance", *Ami du Clergé*, 1961, p. 762: Cette façon de désigner (le fils de Marie) peut indiquer que le père est inconnue et constitue dans ce cas une insulte. Cf. A. Winandy, "La Prophétie de Symeon", *RB* 72 (1965), 347.

[10] Wenn ein Jude die Thora bricht, so forsche man nach den Umständen seiner Geburt und man wird in den allermeisten Fällen entdecken, dass ihm ein Geburtsmakel anhaftet, v. Kalla 41d. Nach dieser Logik gehen die Rabbinen auch bei der Exegese von Lv 24 : 10 f. vor. Der Angeklagte ist der Sohn der Israelitin Sulamith bath Dibri. Sein Vater ist Ägypter und bleibt ungenannt. Der Sohn der Sulamith lästert Gott. Ergo ist Sulamith eine Buhlerin, v. LvR 24 : 10; Raschi zu Lv 24 : 10 f.

Sinne von Dt 13 : 3 und Mk 3 : 22 diskreditiert. Die Atimie im Sinne von Dt 13: 7–10 und Mk 6:4 ist perfekt,[11] und die Steinigung im Stile von Lv 24 : 14 ; Dt 13 : 11 f. und Lk 4 : 28 f. wird zur religions-gesetzlichen Ehrenpflicht für alle thoratreuen Juden.

An dem jüdischen Ursprung des Kampfwortes Jeschu ben Mirjam kann doch wohl kein Zweifel sein. Denn das sicherste Kennzeichen für die historische Glaubwürdigkeit eines Jesuszeugnisses ist seine Anstössigkeit. Der Schimpfname Jeschu ben Mirjam aber war der Urkirche so unerträglich, dass nur Markus den Mut gehabt hat, ihn zu wiederholen. Alle anderen Evangelisten haben ihn unterdrückt.

## III

Die Urchristenheit hat dieses Kampfwort planmässig aus der kirchlichen Jesusüberlieferung eliminiert. Aber sie konnte es nicht aus der Welt schaffen. Die Behauptung, Jesus sei ein uneheliches Kind gewesen, ist vom ersten bis zum achtzehnten Jahrhundert ein Lieblingsthema der jüdischen Polemik. Wir zählen die wichtigsten Belege in chronologischer Reihenfolge auf.

Jebamoth 4 : 13 : Rabbi Simeon ben Azzai hat gesagt : Ich habe in Jerusalem ein Geschlechterbuch (*mglṯ ywḥsyn*) gefunden, darin stand geschrieben : NN ist ein Bastard (*mmzr*) von einer Ehefrau.

Tos. Hullin 2 : 24 : Rabbi Eliezer ben Hyrkanos spricht von Jesus ben Pantiri (*yšwʿ bn pnṭyry*). Die gleiche Bezeichnung ist (mit belanglosen Abweichungen) bezeugt in Tos. Hullin 2 : 22, 23 ; j Aboda Zara 40d ; j Sabbath 14d ; Koheleth Rabba zu 1 : 8.

Anderwärts spricht Eliezer ben Hyrkanos von einem jüdischen Apostaten mit Namen Ben Stada, der in Ägypten die Kunst der Schwarzen Magie gelernt hat (j Sabbath 12 : 4 ; Tos. Sabbath 11 : 15 ; b Sabbath 104b). Nach b Sabb 104a ist Ben Stada identisch mit Ben Pandera, seine Mutter hiess Mirjam und war eine Ehebrecherin. Nach b Sanh 67a ist Ben Stada am Rüsttag des Passahfestes gekreuzigt worden. Nach einer Baraitha in Sanh 43a ist Jesus von Nazareth am Rüsttag des Passahfestes gekreuzigt worden, weil er gezaubert und verführt und Israel zum Abfall verleitet hat.

Alle diese mehr oder minder verschlüsselten Nachrichten

[11] Der Begriff ἄτιμος in Mk 6 : 4 ist ein religionsgesetzlicher terminus technicus ; cf. Jn 8 : 49 und Origenes *Contra Celsum* 2 : 8 (ἀτιμάζειν) ; 2 : 31 (ἄτιμος).

finden wir zu einem parodistischen Jesusroman vereinigt beim Juden des Celsus. Maria war eine armselige Lohnspinnerin aus Galiläa, mit Joseph verheiratet, wurde aber von einem στρατιώτης namens Pantheras verführt und von Joseph mit Schimpf und Schande aus dem Hause gejagt. So musste sie ihren Sohn in aller Heimlichkeit zur Welt bringen (Origenes, *contra Celsum* 1 : 28, 32 f., 69). Jesus floh nach Ägypten und lernte dort die Zauberkunststücke, mit denen er später seine göttliche Würde beweisen und das Volk verführen wollte, aber sich selber das Grab grub (1 : 28 ; 2 : 5, 8 f., 31).

Die jüdischen Polemiker, die Tertullian in seinem *Libellus de Spectaculis* (30) zitert, diffamieren Jesus als den filius quaestuariae, den Sohn der Lohndirne. Cf. *Evangelium Thomas* 105.

In Pesikta Rabbathi 100b/101a nennt Rabbi Hijja bar Abba, der um 220 in Tiberias wirkte, Jesus zweimal den Sohn der Hure (*br' dznyt'*).

Euseb von Caesarea bezeugt wiederum die jüdische Kampftradition von Panther, dem illegitimen Vater Jesu (*Eclogae Propheticae* 3 : 10).

Den gleichen Namen (Pandera) und die gleiche Kampfthese kennt auch Amolo, der Erzbischof von Lyon (*Contra Judaeos* § 40, MPL 116, p. 141 ff.).

Im übrigen aber erbaut man sich in den Ghettos des Mittelalters vor allem an den Tholedoth Jeschu, die in phantasievoller Breite von der Verführung der jungen Mirjam erzählen[12]).

## IV

In Kidd 70b und anderwärts finden wir mehrfach die tannaitische Faustregel zitiert : " Ein Mensch, der einem anderen einen Familienmakel vorhält, trägt selber einen Geburtsmakel an sich." Das bedeutet praktisch, dass man jeden Angriff auf die eigene Familienehre mit einem Gegenangriff auf die Familienehre des Gegners erwidern konnte und durfte. Der Traktat Kidduschin erzählt in grosser Ausführlichkeit ein Musterbeispiel dieser Kampfesweise (Kidd 70a/b). Ein anderes Paradigma begegnet uns in Ruth Rabba 8 : Die Feinde Davids sprechen :

[12] J. Chr. Wagenseil, *Tela ignea Satanae*, Altdorf, 1681 ; J. J. Huldricus, *sp̣r twldwṭ yšw' hnwṣry*, *Historia Jeschuae Nazareni a Judaeis blaspheme corrupta*, Lugd. Batav., 1705 ; J. A. Eisenmenger, *Entdecktes Judentum* I – II, Königsberg, 1711 ; S. Krauss, *Das Leben Jesu nach jüdischen Quellen*, Berlin, 1902 ; H. J. Schonfield, *According to the Hebrews*, London, 1937.

Es hängt ein Familienmakel an ihm, denn er stammt von der Moabiterin Ruth (cf. Gn 19 : 37!). Aber David bleibt ihnen die Antwort nicht schuldig: "Stammt ihr denn nicht von zwei Schwestern ab?! (Jakob hätte nach der Vorschrift von Lv 18 : 18 mit den beiden Schwestern Lea und Rahel nicht gleichzeitig verheiratet sein dürfen). Und Thamar, zu der euer Ahnherr Juda einging, gehörte sie nicht zu denen, die mit einem Familienmakel befleckt waren? Seht, aus welcher Wurzel ihr herkommt, und schweigt!"

Genau so reagiert der Matthäuskreis auf die jüdischen Angriffe gegen die Mutter Jesu. Die Juden haben ein Geschlechterbuch über die *γένεσις Ἰησοῦ* fabriziert. Der Matthäuskreis antwortet mit einer Gegenschrift unter dem Titel *Βίβλος γενέσεως Ἰησοῦ Χριστοῦ*, keine poesievolle Legendensammlung zur Erbauung der frommen Gemeinde, sondern eine leidenschaftliche Kampfschrift gegen die jüdischen Greuelmärchen (Mk 6 : 3) und Greueltexte.[13] Die Juden haben Maria als Ehebrecherin diffamiert (Jeb 4 : 13). Mt bietet einen Stammbaum Salomos, in dem zwischen vielen Männern auch vier Frauen erscheinen, und mit all diesen Frauen hat es eine besondere Bewandtnis: Thamar, Rahab, Ruth, Bathseba (Mt 1 : 1–6). "Seht auf eure Wurzel und schweigt!"

## V

Aber das Geschlechterbuch Jesu macht der jüdischen Marienpolemik keine kleinlauten Zugeständnisse. Mag man über Thamar, Rahab, Ruth oder Bathseba denken, wie man wolle—bei Maria liegen die Dinge anders, ganz anders. So konstatiert der Matthäuskreis in Mt 1 : 18–25.

Die Geburtsgeschichte beginnt mit einer militanten Richtigstellung: *Τοῦ δὲ Ἰησοῦ Χριστοῦ ἡ γένεσις οὕτως ἦν* (*οὕτως, οὐκ ἄλλως*!). Das Jesuskind stammt nicht von einem unbekannten Vater, sondern *ἐκ πνεύματος ἁγίου* (Mt 1 : 18, 20).

Hier führt der Autor anscheinend gewisse Denkmotive des

[13] Wir brauchen das hier nur anzudeuten. Denn schon vor 65 Jahren hat Theodor von Zahn auf Jebamoth 4 : 13 und die späteren Tholedoth Jeschu hingewiesen und den Kampfcharakter von Mt 1 : 1 ff. energisch herausgearbeitet Scharfe apologetische und polemische Zuspitzung mit unverkennbarer Rücksicht auf die sehr bestimmten und den Lesern seines Buches wohlbekannten jüdischen Verleumdungen (Zahn, *Matthäus*, Leipzig, 1903, pp. 40, 45, 61, 63–65). Nur der Zusammenhang mit Mk 6 : 3 ist Zahn entgangen.

alexandrinischen Judentums weiter. Stets aber beschränkt er sich auf die theologische Deutung historischer Tatsachen. Er ist ein nüchterner Realist, gleichermassen allergisch gegen pseudohistorische Phantasien wie gegen haggadische Fabeleien. Das Jesuskind, das so wunderbar erzeugt und angekündigt wird, ist dennoch kein Wunderkind wie Noah, Melchisedek, Abraham oder Moses in der jüdischen Legendentradition.[14] Mt 1 : 25 sagt kein Wort von schmerzloser Geburt, von Lichtwundern im Geburtshaus, von Ansprachen des Säuglings oder dienstbaren Engeln.

Der Autor dieses Geschlechterbuchs ist viel mehr Jurist als Poet.[15] Ihm liegt vor allem die Klarstellung der familienrechtlichen Verhältnisse am Herzen. Joseph nimmt die schwangere Braut in sein Haus und legitimiert ihren Sohn, indem er selber ihm den Namen gibt (Mt 1 : 20 f., 24 f.). So ist Jesus per adoptionem in den Familienverband der Davididen aufgenommen, genau so wie etwa sein römischer Zeitgenosse Oktavian durch Adoption in die gens Julia rezipiert worden ist. Das bringt schon der Stammbaum so präzis und prägnant wie möglich zum Ausdruck mit der Schlussformel *τὸν Ἰωσὴφ τὸν ἄνδρα Μαρίας, ἐξ ἧς ἐγεννήθη Ἰησοῦς ὁ λεγόμενος χριστός* (Mt 1 : 16). Von irgendeinem Widerspruch zwischen Stammbaum und Geburtsgeschichte kann demnach keine Rede sein.

Es wäre nun ausserordentlich instruktiv, könnten wir hier den dramatischen Fortgang der Marienkontroverse zwischen Christen, Juden und Täuferjüngern weiterverfolgen über Lukas, Joh., Justin, das Protevangelium Jacobi, die Pseudoclementinen, Tertullian und Origenes bis zur Rabbinenschule von Caesarea Maritima und weiterhin. Aber das würde den Rahmen unseres kleinen Beitrags sprengen. Wir begnügen uns an dieser Stelle mit einem kurzen Ausblick auf den Gebrauch der Namensform Jeschu ben Mirjam in den samaritanischen, syrischen, mandäischen und islamischen Kontroversen.

## VI

Im semitischen Sprachgebrauch hat sich das Metronymikon Jeschu ben Mirjam vielfach bis heute erhalten, und überall hat diese Namensform den gleichen Bedeutungsgehalt : Jesus war

[14] v. L. Ginzberg, *Legends of the Jews* I–VII, Philadelphia, 1946 ff.

[15] Anders Dibelius, *loc. cit.*, p. 97 ; R. Bultmann, *Geschichte der synoptischen Tradition*, Göttingen, 1957, pp. 316 f. Hier und anderwärts erscheint die " Kindheitsgeschichte " des Mt lediglich als Sammelbecken lyrischer Traditionsstoffe.

der Sohn Marias, nicht Josephs. Die Samaritaner gebrauchen diese Bezeichnung im polemischen, die Syrer im doxologischen Sinn.[16]

Ganz aggressiv sind die Mandäer. Im Rechten Ginza lesen wir: Nach vierhundert Jahren "wurde Jesus, Sohn der Mirjam, geboren".[17] Im Buch des Herrn der Grösse wird die Geburt Jesu ausführlich besprochen: "Für neun Monate tritt Nbu-Christus in den Leib seiner Mutter, der Jungfrau, ein und hält sich da verborgen. Alsdann tritt er als Körper, Blut und Niddafluss heraus und wächst auf ihrem Schoss heran . . . Dann tritt er in das Volkshaus der Juden ein, eignet sich seine ganze Weisheit an, verdreht die Thora und verändert ihre Lehre und alle Werke. Er nimmt etliche unter den Juden durch Zauberei und Täuschung gefangen und zeigt ihnen Wunderwerke und Erscheinungen . . . Ferner wird in jenen Zeiten ein Kind geboren werden, dessen Name Johana genannt wird, der Sohn des greisen Vaters Zakhria . . . Seine Mutter, das Weib Enisbai, ward mit ihm schwanger . . . Wenn Johana in jenem Zeitalter die Taufe vollzieht, kommt Jesus Christus, geht in Demut einher, empfängt die Taufe des Johana und wird durch die Weisheit des Johana weise. Dann aber verdreht er die Rede des Johana . . . und predigt Frevel und Trug in der Welt."[18]

Man beachte die durchgehende Antithetik zwischen Jesus und Johannes, die in der Kontrapunktik zwischen Metronymikon und Patronymikon ihre äusserste Zuspitzung erfährt: Jesus, Sohn der Mirjam—Johana, Sohn des Zakhria. Das sind zwei festgelegte Namensformen, die mit der Frage, wann der Vater gestorben ist, gewiss nichts zu tun haben. Im übrigen wird man mühelos erkennen, wie in der mandäischen Jesusvita pervertierte Elemente aus den Evangelien mit traditionellen Kampfthesen aus der jüdischen Jesuspolemik zu einem mythologischen Zerrbild verschmolzen sind.

Im Koran ist die metronyme Benennung Jesu fester Sprachgebrauch. So, e.g., Sure 23 : 52 (Sohn der Maria), Sure 3 : 40 (Messias Jesus, Sohn der Maria). Viermal begegnet in Sure 5 die Namensform "Messias, Sohn der Maria" (19a; 19b; 76; 79). Sechzehnmal verwendet der Koran das dreigliedrige Metrony-

[16] v. E. N. Adler and M. Seligsohn, *Une nouvelle Chronique Samaritaine*, Paris, 1903, pp. 41 ff.; E. Bratke, "Religionsgespräch", *TU* 19 (1899), 36 (παῖς Μαρίας).

[17] Ginza, Rechter Teil, Buch 18 (388 : 11) = M. Lidzbarski, *Ginza, Der Schatz*, Göttingen, 1925, pp. 410 : 31 f.

[18] Ginza, R., 2 : 1 : 146-152 = Lidzbarski, *op. cit.*, pp. 50–51.

mikon " Jesus, Sohn der Maria ".[19] Auch hier ist der Sinn dieser Namensform immer derselbe : Jesus ist der Sohn Marias, nicht Josephs. Aber jeder polemische Ton ist verschwunden. Jesus ist der Sohn der unberührten Jungfrau, seine Geburt ist ein Wunder Gottes (Sure 3 : 37 ff. ; 19 : 16 ff.).

Der gleiche Geist und Sprachgebrauch herrscht in der nachkanonischen Überlieferung. Hier beschäftigt man sich ebenso ausgiebig wie liebevoll mit dem Mysterium der Parthenogenesis.[20] Das Ergebnis ist ein buntes Gemisch aus christlichen Jesustraditionen (aus Markus, Matth., Lukas, Joh., Protevangelium Jacobi u.a.m.) und jüdischen Legendenmotiven.[21]

In den 233 *Logia et Agrapha*, die Michael Asin y Palacios aus der nachkanonischen Tradition gesammelt hat,[22] findet sich etwa 46 mal die Namensform " Jesus, der Sohn der Maria ",[23] einmal (im Munde Gottes !) die Anrede " Sohn der Maria ",[24] dreimal die Formel " der Messias, der Sohn der Maria ",[25] einmal die Doppelformel " der Messias Jesus, der Sohn der Maria " [26] und einmal die plerophorische Formulierung " Der Sohn der unbefleckten Jungfrau, Jesus, der Sohn der Maria ".[27] Patronymische Formeln kommen in Verbindung mit dem Namen Jesus in diesen Logien m.W. nirgends vor, obgleich Joseph in der nachkanonischen Tradition oft erwähnt wird.

Das Gegenbeispiel bietet Johannes der Täufer, der niemals metronymisch benannt wird, dagegen mindestens siebenmal als " Johannes, der Sohn des Zacharias " erscheint.[28]

In einem Agraphon aus dem zehnten Jahrhundert (Logion 121) werden die beiden Männer ganz korrekt und pedantisch nebeneinander genannt, Jesus mit dem Metronym, Johannes mit dem Patronym : " Ferner wird in einer Schrift berichtet, wie Jesus,

[19] v. S. M. Zwemer, *Die Christologie des Islam*, deutsch von E. Frick, Stuttgart, 1921, pp. 15–17.

[20] Zwemer, *loc. cit.*, pp. 37–40.

[21] v.e.g. Zwemer, p. 37 (Maria mit dem Wasserkrug) ; p. 41 (Maria die Wollspinnerin).

[22] M. Asin y Palacios, *Logia et Agrapha Domini Jesu apud Moslemicos . . . usitata*, Paris, I 1919, II 1926 (=Patr. Or. 13, 3 und 19, 4).

[23] Dieselbe Namensform bei Zwemer, p. 42.

[24] Logion 7. Cf. die Anrede " Jesus, Sohn der Maria " (im Munde der Jünger !) bei Zwemer, p. 57.

[25] Logion 32 ; 77 ; 159.

[26] Logion 187.

[27] Logion 139. Den besten Kommentar dazu liefert die ausführliche Apologie der Parthenogenesis in Logion 187.

[28] Logion 114 ; 121 ; 143, 1 ; 143, 2 ; 149 ; 182 ; 195.

der Sohn der Maria, Johannes, den Sohn des Zacharaias, traf . . ." Man sieht, auch in den islamischen Texten haben diese Namensformen mit der Frage, ob oder wann der Vater gestorben ist, nicht das geringste zu tun.

Jesus war der Sohn Marias, nicht Josephs. Das ist das historische Faktum. Die jüdische Marienpolemik hat diesen Sachverhalt pornographisch interpretiert. Die christliche Kirche hat ihn im Sinne der Parthenogenesis gedeutet. " Ein Rätsel ist Reinentsprungenes " (Friedrich Hölderlin). Alle mysteria Christi sind paradoxe Tatbestände, die eine dialektische Deutung hervorrufen, positiv oder negativ, doxologisch oder polemisch. Das gilt von der Geburt Jesu genau so wie vom Faktum des Leeren Grabes, von seiner Wundertätigkeit genau so wie von seinem Selbstzeugnis. Darum entfaltet sich die christliche Jesusbotschaft a principio in der Kontroverse.

# THE CRITIQUE OF PAGANISM IN I PETER I: 18

W. C. VAN UNNIK

## I

THE First Epistle of Peter sets forth in glowing words the great change its readers had experienced in becoming Christians, and the new moral attitude to which they are called, even amidst all sorts of social pressure from their surroundings, because these new ethics are inseperably linked up with their new faith, are its natural form. The theme of this change is so much in the centre of the author's exposition that the letter has often been described as a baptismal sermon. This view may be accepted as correct if it is only borne in mind that it is not so much the ceremony of baptism as such which is central, but mainly that transition from one state to the other in which baptism is the outward mark of the dividing line.

Among the various descriptions of the situation out of which the Christians have come the most interesting, because of its uniqueness, is that in I P I : 18 *ἐλυτρώθητε ἐκ τῆς ματαίας ὑμῶν ἀναστροφῆς πατροπαραδότου.* Since scholarly opinion, as reflected in the modern Introductions to the New Testament, in general holds that the letter is addressed to former pagans, it would be superfluous to deal at length with that subject. The statement in 4 : 3 is decisive evidence. Other descriptions of the former state of the readers like I : 14 " the passions of your former ignorance ", 2 : 9 " darkness ", 2 : 10 " no people " and the list of sins in the pre-Christian existence can be paralleled from other books in the New Testament. However, the characteristic given in I: 18 stands all by itself and this fact may be sufficient to pay some special attention to this peculiarity.

The leading idea in this description is *ἀναστροφή*,[1] a word very dear to the author, for he uses it six times altogether. It is the " way of life ". In the other texts it is always used of the Christian manner of conduct, very definitely in 3 : 16, " your good

[1] *TWNT* 7, pp. 715–17 (G. Bertram). In the whole of the rest of the New Testament there are only 6 more instances.

behaviour in Christ ", and 1 : 15, " but as he who called you is holy, be holy yourselves in all your behaviour ". Cf. also 2 : 12 and 3 : 1, 2.[2] Here, however, it is a way of life from which the readers have been set free ; so it is an expression denoting here the state before they turned to Christianity, their pagan behaviour.

That particular Gentile way of life is specified by two features expressed by the adjectives μάταιος and πατροπαράδοτος. These two adjectives are not linked together by " and " ; so they do not stand exactly on the same line. The latter is more closely connected with the noun, while the former is separated from it by ὑμῶν. So we must take ἀναστροφὴ πατροπαράδοτος together and this unit is further qualified by μάταιος.

The question now is this : what did the writer and his readers understand by the words, " a way of life πατροπαράδοτος ", more specifically by the last word ? In the present time in which traditions of all kinds—ecclesiastical, national, political—and in all fields of human behaviour in individual and social relations are under heavy fire, a translation given by A. M. Hunter may appeal to the reader. In the widely used *Interpreter's Bible* he renders the adjective with the words : " utterly traditional and conventional, destitute of moral initiative or originality ".[3] But we who so easily combine " traditional " and " outworn " and other negative words must ask ourselves very seriously whether the same was true for the early Greek Christians. It may be that we are the victims of an optical illusion and that the standards of these men from the ancient world were different from our own. It is always the first and foremost task of exegesis, before we can proceed to hermeneutics, to confront us with this question.

The adjective πατροπαράδοτος has not been discussed in Kittel-Friedrich's great *Theologisches Wörterbuch zum Neuen Testament*. This is easily understood if one realizes that the word is a *hapax legomenon* in the New Testament and is not found in the Septuagint either. But it is not only to fill this little gap that made it worthwhile to devote some attention to this word. It is unique in the New Testament, but it is used in 1 Peter in a very significant connection, *viz.*, the redemption wrought by Jesus Christ. What He through His " precious blood " has done, is to set the readers free from that state of life they were in and that

[2] See also the verb in 1 : 17 " conduct yourselves with fear throughout the time of your exile ", i.e., their future life on earth.

[3] A. M. Hunter, in *The Interpreter's Bible*, Nashville, 1957, 12, p. 102.

was clearly stamped by that word πατροπαράδοτος.

This contribution, devoted to clearing up the meaning of this adjective, is also a kind of *retractatio*. Walter Bauer[4] in his treatment of the word referred to a study of mine on this passage from 1942; [5] but readers who would follow this lead should be warned of disappointment, for unfortunately at that time I had nothing more to say about the word than what was found in the commentaries. In the meantime the material has increased, although not to a very considerable extent.[6] Nevertheless, it may be useful to consider the word in the various contexts in which it is met since the meaning of the word is determined by its surroundings.

What was the meaning the word conveyed? According to E. G. Selwyn it meant "inherited", "traditional" and hence "the author has in mind readers who had been brought up in the varied and longstanding tradition of gentile paganism".[7] F. J. A. Hort's comments were that Peter "is not here challenging the authority of the heathen ἀναστροφή, but rather pointing out one of the sources of its tremendous retaining power"; the yoke that had to be broken was not just personal inclination, but "that which was built up and sanctioned by the accumulated instincts and habits of past centuries of ancestors".[8] J. H. A. Hart saw in it an indication of the "sources of the influence, which their old way of life—*patrius mos*—*patrii ritus*—still exercised over them", because the ancient religion had a strength "which often baffled both Jewish and Christian missionaries".[9] Knopf spoke of a way of life, "wie ihn Lehre, Erziehung und Sitte von Geschlecht zu Geschlecht weitergibt", especially religious rites, which both in Judaism and paganism were carried back to the ancestors.[10]

In contrast to the interpretation, "traditional", "ancestral", Wohlenberg, basing himself on the composition of the word,

[4] W. Bauer, *Griechisch-deutsches Wörterbuch zu den Schriften des Neuen Testaments und der übrigen urchristlichen Literatur*, Berlin, [5]1958, Sp. 1263.

[5] W. C. van Unnik, *De Verlossing* 1 *Petrus* 1 : 18–19 *en het probleem van den eersten Petrusbrief*, Amsterdam, 1942 (Mededeelingen der Nederlandsche Akademie van Wetenschappen, afdeling Letterkinde, N.R. V 1).

[6] G. W. H. Lampe (ed.), *A Patristic Greek Lexicon*, Oxford, p. 1053 gives a number of examples from Christian sources that have not been taken into consideration before.

[7] E. G. Selwyn, *The First Epistle of St. Peter*, London, 1946, p. 145.

[8] F. J. A. Hort, *The First Epistle of St. Peter* 1 : 1–2 : 17, London, 1898, p. 76.

[9] J. H. A. Hart, in: *The Expositor's Greek Testament*, 5, p. 50, referring to Clemens Alex., Protrepticus 10, 89, 1, ἀλλ' ἐκ πατέρων, φάτε, παραδεδομένον ἡμῖν ἔθος ἀνατρέπειν οὐκ εὔλογον.

[10] R. Knopf, *Die Briefe Petri und Juda*, Göttingen, 1912, S. 72.

compared it with other compounds with " father ". He concluded that it pointed to one's own father : " Er möchte ihnen ehrwürdig erscheinen, weil sie darin gleichsam ein väterliches Vermächtnis erblicken dürften ". That leads the author to a little psychological novel : " vielleicht erinnerte sich mancher Leser einer ihm unter Tränen vom Vater ans Herz gelegte Mahnung ", not to change the venerable religion for a crucified Jew.[11] We may end this conspectus of opinions by referring to a recent French commentary by C. Spicq. He says that the word corresponds to a Jewish mentality, expressed by Josephus in speaking of the " *patrioi nomoi* ", " désignant les préceptes ou contenues transmis par les ancêtres, et ayant de ce chef une double force impérative pour les descendants : les lois ancestrales sont des lois nationales ". He then continues : " Pierre oppose à ces moeurs très pures d'Israel, celles des Gentiles " ; the combination with μάταιος brings in an ironical note : the heritage was nothing but wind, and at the same time there is a sign of goodness because the readers themselves are not responsible for what they inherited.[12]

## II

The earliest text known to us using the word πατροπαράδοτος is a rather famous inscription. It is a letter of King Attalus III, written in 135–134 B.C., to the people of Pergamum. In it he informs his subjects that his mother Stratonike at her marriage had brought with her τὸν Δία τὸν Σαβάζιον πατροπαράδοτον. She came from Cappadocia and introduced this god into her new homeland.[13] In this inscription there is no indication whatever that the word was newly coined or that it would not have been understood by the readers ; no, everything points to the fact that it was a current word. We have here the case of a woman very much attached to the god of her fatherland, whom she

[11] G. Wohlenberg, *Der erste und zweite Petrusbrief und der Judasbrief*³, Leipzig-Erlangen, 1923, S. 37.

[12] C. Spicq, *Les Epîtres de Saint Pierre*, Paris, 1966, p. 67 ; K. H. Schelke, *Die Petrusbriefe. Der Judasbrief*, Freiburg-Basel-Wien, 1961, S. 49 : " dieser Wandel ist von den Vätern überliefert, da Religion und Kultus seit der mythischen Religionsbegründung von Geschlecht zu Geschlecht weitergegeben wurde ".

[13] The text is in C. Bradford Welles, *Royal Correspondence in the Hellenistic Period*, New Haven, 1934, p. 267 ; cf. p. 270 : " Whether πατροπαράδοτος means ' from the father ', or by an extension ' from the ancestors ', it is in any case ' from the father's side ' of the family. Sabasius was an Anatolian deity, worshipped in Phrygia and eastward in Cappadocia."

brought with her. Is it here more or less an excuse, why she did not find the gods of Pergamum sufficient? It is certainly not a god which she particularly received from her own father, but this Zeus Sabazios is presented here as the traditional god of that country and hence not to be rejected. The fact that he was *πατροπαράδοτος* shows that he was not a "new" god with all the ill-feelings that word could rouse in Greek minds, as may be clearly seen from Socrates' trial. One more final remark: it is curious that this first attestation of the word is found in the same geographical area to which I Peter was addressed though more than two centuries separate one text from the other.

In Dionysius Hal., *Antiq. Rom.* 5, 48, 2, the word is used in a strictly private sphere. It is the possession someone owns, because it belonged to the family and he has inherited it from his father. Speaking about Publius Valerius Publicola, a very important man who had had every opportunity to enrich himself by avarice the writer says: *ἐπὶ τῇ μικρᾷ καὶ πατροπαραδότῳ διέμεινεν οὐσίᾳ σώφρονα καὶ αὐτάρκη καὶ πάσης ἐπιθυμίας κρείττονα βίον ζῶν.* The fact that Publicola remained on the small family possession is a sign of his great virtue.

At various occasions the word is used by Diodorus Siculus, *Historiae.* In 17, 4, 1 he tells, how Alexander the Great persuaded the Thessalians to grant him *τὴν πατροπαράδοτον ἡγεμονίαν* of Greece; here it is of course the leadership which his father possessed and left to him, though it had to be accepted as such by the other party. In the same story of the early part of Alexander's career, when he had to maintain himself and had to make every effort, not to lose what his father had built up and bequeathed to him, Alexander makes an appeal to the Greeks *τηρεῖν πρὸς αὐτὸν τὴν πατροπαράδοτον εὔνοιαν* (17, 2, 2). The same expression is used by Diodorus, when he tells us, how in Syracuse Dionysius the younger takes over the tyranny of his father and appeals to the assembly with friendly words to keep their good will towards him (15, 74, 5).[14] This seems to have been a more or less standardized combination, for there is an inscription (middle first century, B.C.) which says: *πατροπαράδοτον παρειληφὼς τὴν πρὸς τὸν δῆμον ἡμῶν εὔνοιαν.*[15] But here it is the other side of the medal: in Diodorus the ruler is asking for that goodwill, here

[14] The text was as follows: *παρεκάλεσε τοῖς οἰκείοις λόγοις τηρεῖν τὴν πατροπαράδοτον πρὸς αὐτὸν εὔνοιαν.*

[15] C. Michel, *Recueil d'inscriptions grecques*, Bruxelles, 1900, no. 394.

the ruler on his side shows the favour. It is clear from these instances that this favourable inclination towards the other party did exist in the time of the father of the speaker. But by the change of government this relation has also changed and the goodwill had to be reaffirmed by the other side.

Dionysius and Alexander appeal to the goodwill which was shown to their fathers and hope it will be maintained in the new situation. It existed in the time of their fathers; it may continue for the sons who take the place of the fathers. To what is πατροπαράδοτον one can appeal, but it has to be taken up by a new generation. A very striking example of this usage is offered by Diodorus Sic., *Hist.* 4, 8, 5 in a passage dealing with the great exploits of Heracles; at this point Diodorus does not simply relate some facts, but suddenly adds a more general consideration. At great length he argues in this chapter that people of his own day do not believe that the works of the hero were real, because they sound so paradoxical. Hence it is necessary either to leave out the greatest of his works and take away something of the glory of the god or to tell everything and make the story incredible (8, 2). Then he calls it unnatural that the ancestors conferred immortality upon Heracles because of the excessive greatness of his virtue (ἀρετή), acknowledged by all, but "that we did not preserve even the traditional piety towards the god" (ἄτοπον . . . ἡμᾶς δὲ πρὸς τὸν θεὸν μηδὲ τὴν πατροπαράδοτον εὐσεβείαν διαφυλάττειν). This clause stands parallel to the preceding part of the sentence, in which it is said that the people during Heracles' lifetime did not praise his beneficent deeds as was due. The context shows that Diodorus is speaking here of human ungratefulness: instead of praising the magnificent works the hero did on behalf of humanity, the contemporaries of Diodorus are criticizing the stories about them. It is clear that the πατροπαράδοτος piety is here a minimum that might be expected with regard to a man whom the forefathers had immortalized. In the eyes of our writer it would have been far better if people had given all laud and honour to such a benefactor. This is expressed by "glory", "praise" and "honour", that is, personal expressions of gratitude and personal piety = right relation to the deity; the "πατροπαράδοτος piety" must, then, be conformity to and performance of the cult as it was instituted by the forbears. But even that is destroyed by this criticism of the myths.

Walter Bauer referred to a text in a magical papyrus from the third century A.D., in which a god introduces himself by saying : " I am the πατροπαράδοτος God ".[16] The fragmentary state of this papyrus makes it impossible to draw precise conclusions, but at any rate it is clear that the god uses this epithet to induce another being, called ἀκάματος, to bring about a healing. It may be that he appeals to the other power because he is the family-god of the sick person and had a right or obligation to do so.

In all these texts πατροπαράδοτος has a favourable meaning. What is called so, recommends itself thereby. Is this character maintained in the Christian usage ?

The first Christian author after the New Testament who may have used it is the apologist Aristides. The Greek text of this passage has not come to light yet ; so one has to rely on the Syriac version which uses more or less the same terminology as the Peshitta of 1 P 1 : 18.[17] In a description of the Jewish religion it is said in *Apology* 14 : 3 : " They imitate God by reason of the love which they have for man ; for they have compassion on the poor and ransom the captive and bury the dead,[18] and do things of a similar nature to these . . . *things which they have received from their fathers of old* ". This is the credit-side of the Jewish religion and is clearly " traditional " ; the negative counterpart is mentioned in the next paragraph but without any indication, as one might expect, of its recent introduction. This humane character of the Jewish religion is not a temporary whim but is an agelong element ; this traditional aspect is its recommendation. It is interesting to see a Christian apologist using this argument which is derived from the arsenal of Jewish apologetics (cf. Josephus, *c. Apionem* 2, 211).[19] Πατροπαράδοτος is not an expression of criticism, but of recommendation in the eyes of the (Greek and Roman) public.

In connection with the Christian religion the adjective is used by Dionysius of Corinth in his famous letter to the Church of Rome (*aptus* Eusebius, *Hist. Eccl.* 4, 23, 10). He praises the

[16] Pap. 33 in : K. Preisendanz, *Papyri Graecae Magicae*, Leipzig-Berlin, 2, 1931, S. 159.

[17] Text of Aristides in : *The Apology of Aristides*, ed. J. Rendel Harris, Cambridge, 1893, p. 212 (syr. t.) : *hlyn dḳblw mn 'bhyhwn ḳdmy'* ; and text of the Peshitta 1 P 1 : 18 : *hnwn dḳbltwn mn 'bhykwn.*

[18] Cf. *SBK* 4, 1928, S. 559 ff. : " Die altjüdische Liebeswerke ".

[19] The rabbinic texts given by Billerbeck (*SBK* 3, S. 763) are from the second half of the 3rd cent. ; in them the pagans are more or less excused for their idolatry because they stick to the customs of their fathers. The judgment of the Christians, as we shall see, was rather different.

Christians in the capital, because from the beginning it was their custom to help their brethren and fellow-churches. This is called πατροπαράδοτον ἔθος Ῥωμαίων which the Romans have kept and even extended.[20] The combination with " custom " is significant, and the parallelism with ἐξ ἀρχῆς is revealing. It is clear that the adjective cannot be taken in a literal sense, as Wohlenberg defined it, but means " traditional " in that one generation follows the other since the beginning of the Roman church in this benevolent and praiseworthy action. Is it pure accident that this word was used in connection with the practice of people living in Rome? It is certainly important to notice that it applied not to Christian faith and order, but to life and work. It has a favourable tone.

By the apologist Theophilus the word is used in an attack on pagan idolatry where images instead of the Creator are adored by people who are πειθόμενοι δόγμασιν ματαίοις διὰ πλάνης πατροπαραδότου γνώμης ἀσυνέτου (*ad Autolycum* 2 : 39 (or 34)). It is not immediately evident in which way the adjectives are combined with the nouns since it is possible to take πατροπαραδότου both with πλάνης and γνώμης. In view of what we shall find later in Eusebius who stands in the line of apologetic tradition (see below, pp. 138 ff.) I am inclined to connect it with the former, the more so as γνώμη goes better with ἀσύνετος, γνώμη being an opinion based on certain insights that are senseless in this case. Bardy [21] gave a reference to 1 P 1 : 18 which in itself is interesting, though the present text is not a direct quotation and cannot be considered as directly dependent on 1 Peter. The relation is, I think, more indirect : both texts reflect the views of early Christianity towards paganism. But whereas Peter speaks of behaviour in general, Theophilus attacks image-worship. One of the main and most striking differences between " paganism " and Christianity in that time was found, as is well-known, in the use or rejection of images of the gods; the Christians were called " atheists " because they had no images in their churches.[22] The adjective defines the pagan practice not as the mistaken idea of some individual, but as an hereditary, agelong error.

To these texts from the last quarter of the second century we

[20] The text runs as follows : ἐξ ἀρχῆς γὰρ ὑμῖν ἔθος ἐστὶ τοῦτο. πάντας μὲν ἀδελφοὺς ποικίλως εὐεργετεῖν . . . πατροπαράδοτον ἔθος Ῥωμαίων Ῥωμαῖοι διαφυλάττοντες.

[21] G. Bardy, in : *Théophile d'Antioche, Trois livres à Autolycus*, ed. G. Bardy–J. Sander, Paris, 1948, p. 187.

[22] W. Nestle, " Atheismus ", in : Th. Klauser (ed.), *Reallexikon für Antike und Christentum*, Stuttgart, 1, 1950, Sp. 869 f.

may add one, presumably from the same time,[23] of which only a Latin translation has been preserved. It is a very interesting sermon to recent converts, put into the mouth of Paul, in *Act. Petri Verc.* 2. The apostle addresses those " who have now begun to believe in Christ " in the following manner : " Si non permanseritis in pristinis operibus vestris et *paternae traditionis* et abstinueritis vos ab omni dolo et iracundia et sevitia et moechia et conquinamento, et a superbia et zelo, fastidio et inimicitia, dimittet vobis Jesus Christus vivus quae ignorantes egistis ". This is followed by a list of virtues with which the Christians must arm themselves. These lists show great similarity, though not direct identity, with the lists in the New Testament like Gal 5 : 19 ff. and Eph 4 : 17 ff. This is the answer to the question of the neophytes, whether God will forgive the former sins ; it is affirmative because they have been committed in the time of ignorance. This reminds us of 1 P 1 : 14 (cf. also Ac 17 : 30 and 3 : 17).[24] These vices not only have been their personal guilt, but they are works " paternae traditionis " (which is certainly the translation of πατροπαράδοτος) in which they have been brought up. For our investigation it is interesting to see that this text of the Act. Petr., although not a direct quotation from 1 Peter, moves in the same world of ideas. We may suspect that it is Christian missionary terminology. The pre-Christian time is both that of ignorance and of home-tradition which completely changes when Christ Jesus becomes their guide.

Two further testimonies of completely unknown date show a related, though somewhat different context. The first is found in one manuscript, the Vaticanus, of the apocryphal *Acta Johannis* 3. It is reported to the emperor that John, a Jew by birth, belonging to the religion of the Galileans, has confounded all the people of Asia and even of Ephesus καὶ ἀνέτρεψεν ἐκ τῆς πατροπαραδότου θρησκείας, ἕλκων πάντας ὀπίσω αὐτοῦ, ὥστε γενέσθαι ξένον ὄνομα καὶ ἔθνος ἕτερον.[25] Whatever may be the origin of this text,[26] it is at any rate an interesting and significant description of the

[23] E. Hennecke–W. Schneemelcher (edd.), *Neutestamentliche Apokryphen*, Tübingen, 2, ³1964, S. 187 (ET : 2, p. 275).

[24] I may refer here to the forthcoming thesis of one of my pupils, the Rev C. G. Baart, on the theme of " ignorance ".

[25] The text of the other manuscripts in this introductory part of the " Acts of John ", as printed in the edition of Lipius-Bonnet, is completely different.

[26] See K. Schäferdiek, in : Hennecke–Schneemelcher, *op. cit.*, S. 130 f. This introductory part does not belong to the ancient Acts.

religious change brought about by Christian preaching in antiquity. It is particularly so because of the underlying idea of a change in a political sense: to become a Christian means to become part of another "nation".[27] The pagan religion is characterized as the πατροπαράδοτος θρησκεία. We know how strongly the Ephesians were attached to the worship of their city-goddess.[28] πατροπαράδοτος is here not merely "traditional" but is at the same time "national"; he who abandons it steps out of the community, has another loyalty.

The second text is found in *Vita Prophetarum Jeremiah* 8.[29] It is told there that in Egypt they venerate a nursing virgin with a babe in a cradle and that when king Ptolemy inquired after the reason for it, he got the following answer: πατροπαράδοτόν ἐστι μυστήριον ὑπὸ ὁσίου προφήτου τοῖς πατράσιν ἡμῶν παραδοθέν. This prophet was Jeremiah who had foretold it long ago. The fact that the passage has every appearance of a Christian interpolation [30] does not affect our present investigation. The text as it stands is somewhat repetitious, but offers a good definition of the adjective. It shows that πατροπαράδοτος does not need to have the restricted sense Wohlenberg gave it (see above, pp. 131 f.), for the "fathers" lived many centuries before the speaker. This sacred tradition in the mystery—not only handed over by the fathers but entrusted to the fathers by the prophet—was *eo ipso* venerable. The strange usage was hallowed by this traditional character, its being πατροπαράδοτος forming its recommendation. If this sentence has been added by a Christian, it would show that the adjective in itself had no negative overtones, such as it has elsewhere in Christian literature. It stands in relation to a pagan practice which, however, went back to a Hebrew prophet.

Definitely unfavourable is the usage in Eusebius. This Church father calls the Christians apostates of the πατροπαραδότου δεισιδαιμονίας (*Praep. Ev.* 4, 4, 2) and says that the mystery of the evangelical economy consists in the fact that all people every-

[27] Still important in this connection is the masterly treatment by A. von Harnack, *Die Mission und Ausbreitung des Christentums in den ersten drei Jahrhunderten*, Leipzig, I, [4]1924, S. 259–89; particularly important are Celsus' complaints.

[28] Cf. Ac 19: 21 ff. and the commentaries, *in loc.*

[29] Cf. M. Philonenko, "Prophetenleben", in: L. Rost–B. Reicke (edd.), *Biblisch-Historisches Handwörterbuch*, 3, Göttingen, 1966, Sp. 1512 f.; he remarks (Sp. 1513): "Das Leben des Propheten Jr stellt indessen ein besonderes Problem".

[30] C. C. Torrey, *The Lives of the Prophets*, Philadelphia, 1946, pp. 9–10, 22.

where come out of the πατροπαραδότου πλάνης of the oppression by the demons (*Praep. Ev.* 4, 4, 1). This very same view on paganism is eloquently expressed in his description of the change brought about by the Sign of the Cross which " has thrown the fictions of all false religion from the beginning in the deepest shade, has buried superstitious terror in darkness and oblivion, and has revealed to all that spiritual light which enlightens the souls of men, even the knowledge of the only true God. Hence the universal change for the better which leads men to spurn their lifeless idols, to trample under foot the lawless rites of their demon deities and laugh to scorn the time-honoured follies of their fathers " (καὶ παλαιᾶς ἀπάτης πατροπαραδότου καταγελᾶν, *Laus Constantini* 10 : 1–2). A parallel expression is found in the panegyric which Eusebius included in his *Hist. Eccl.* 10, 4, 16 : " now, as has never happened before, the supreme rulers, conscious of the honour which they have received from Him, spit upon the faces of dead idols, trample upon the unhallowed rites of demons, make sport of the ancient delusion handed down from their fathers, and acknowledge only one God " (παλαιᾶς ἀπάτης πατροπαραδότου καταγελᾶν).

For Eusebius this was a standing expression. The former religion was traditional but, as such, was for him not venerable but deceitful.[31] The Christians had been delivered and broken away from this religion in which they had been brought up at home.[32] But it was more than the domestic religion, as is seen from the whole context. This " ancestral " religion with which Eusebius deals in the fourth book of his *Praeparatio*, is the " religion of the Lawgivers ",[33] the state-religion that was so essential in the Roman Empire and the stakes in the controversy between pagans and Christians in the fourth century. It is very likely that Eusebius, the apologist, took an expression current

[31] Lucianus Mart. (in : M. J. Routh, *Reliquiae Sacrae*, Oxford, 1814–18, 3, p. 285) : " Nec indiscussa, ut alii, *parentum traditione* decipimus ".

[32] Cf. Eusebius, *Praep. Ev.*, 4, 2, 13 where Eusebius admires the Cynics and Epicureans who rejected the oracles in spite of their pagan education : ἐν τοῖς Ἑλλήνων ἤθεσι τραφέντες ἐξέτι τε σπαργάνων παῖς παρὰ πατρὸς θεοὺς εἶναι τοὺς δηλουμένους παρειληφότες and *Praep. Ev.* 1, 6, 2 : παῖς παρὰ πατρὸς διαδεξάμενοι καὶ φυλάξαντες. . . . Very important is the testimony of Eusebius, *Praep. Ev.*, 1, 2, 1–2 : τί οὖν ἂν γένοιτο τὸ καθ' ἡμᾶς ξένον, καὶ τί ὁ νεωτερισμὸς τοῦ βίου; πῶς δ' οὐ πανταχόθεν δυσσεβεῖς ἂν εἶεν καὶ ἄθεοι οἱ τῶν πατρῴων θεῶν ἀποστάντες δι' ὧν πᾶν ἔθνος καὶ πᾶσα πόλις συνέστηκεν.

[33] J. Pépin, *Mythe et Allégorie, les origines grecques et les contestations judéo-chrétiennes*, Paris, 1958, pp. 276 ff.

among the adherents of the " old " religion, dear to them because it was that of the fathers, and twisted it round in the opposite direction in the light of the new faith in Jesus Christ.

## III

From the above texts the following conclusions may be drawn with regard to this adjective πατροπαράδοτος:

(a) It can mean " handed over to them by the fathers "; hence " traditional " and as such " venerable " and " recommendable ".

(b) The " fathers " may be ancient forbears or the direct parents, there being no difference between the two because the ancestral line was continued in the parental home.[34]

(c) It never contains the note of something outworn, decaying; on the contrary, it is a very living reality.

(d) This " traditional ", " ancestral " character was specifically connected with the way of life, strongly stamped by religious rites.

(e) By Christian authors this word is mostly used in a disparaging way; the adjective is connected with the (religious) life they had abandoned.

Within the limits of this paper we cannot give a full treatment of the high value that was placed by the Ancients on this " ancestral " character of life. Suffice it to recall the fundamental meaning the " mos maiorum " had in Roman national thought, both for the state and the individual.[35] A few texts chosen at random from a long array may illustrate the importance attached to the institutions of the " Fathers ": Isocrates, *Paneg.* 31 " the Pythia often ordered ποιεῖν πρὸς τὴν πόλιν τὴν ἡμετέραν τὰ πάτρια "; Inscription from Philadelphia in Lydia (first century B.C., Dittenberger, *Syll.*[3] 3 : 985) " Zeus gave instructions to do cleansings and sacrifices κατά τε τὰ πάτρια καὶ ὡς νῦν [εἴθισται]; " Epictetus, *Ench.* 31 " σπένδειν δὲ καὶ θύειν καὶ ἀπάρχεσθαι κατὰ τὰ πάτρια ἑκάστοις προσήκει "; Porphyrius, *Ad Marcellam* 18 " οὗτος γὰρ μέγιστος καρπὸς εὐσεβείας τιμᾶν τὸ θεῖον κατὰ

[34] Cf. W. C. van Unnik, *Tarsus or Jerusalem, the city of Paul's youth*, London, 1962, pp. 61 ff.

[35] Cf. J. Schmitt, *Ethos, Beiträge zum antiken Wertempfinden*, Borna-Leipzig, 1941, S. 35 ff.; see also my article, " Christendom en nationalisme in de eerste eeuwen der kerkgeschiedenis ", *Christendom en Nationalisme*, 's-Gravenhage, 1955, pp. 38–54.

τὰ πάτρια ". Very instructive is the speech which Eusebius puts into the mouth of Licinius as an introduction to a sacrifice: " πάτριοι μὲν οἵδε θεοί, οὓς ἐκ προγόνων τῶν ἀνέκαθεν παρειληφότες σέβειν τιμῶμεν, ὁ δὲ τῆς ἐναντίας ἡμῖν ἐξάρχων παρατάξεως τὰ πάτρια παρασπονδήσας τὴν ἄθεον εἵλατο δόξαν" (*Vita Const.* 2, 5). Performing the religious rites according to the ancestral customs was a safeguard for the life of the nation. To break away from these rites would mean to unsettle the whole of life, revolution. And as it was felt by the ancients, see the quotation from Clement of Alexandria, above, p. 131 n. 9.

The writer of I Peter was, as far as we know at present, the first Christian who applied this characteristic epithet to the religious way of life from which the Christians had been set free. The note of high esteem which the Ancients attached to πατροπαράδοτος is turned into its opposite by combining it with μάταιος, which is not only " idle " and " vain " but also in the LXX typically connected with idolatry.[36] Without vehement, abusive words and in a sentence whose force is its brevity the writer gives here a criticism of paganism that cuts at its very roots, at its glory in the eyes of its devotees. The source of the pagan way of life (πατροπαράδοτος) is worth nothing at all. This former life not only is a state of ignorance (I : 14) and debauchery (4 : 2 f.) but even its greatness, in which they had rejoiced, is null and void.

The ancient tradition of home and nation is broken, not for the sake of opposition but because of the work of Jesus Christ who had set them free. In this case the Christians did not take over, as far as we can see, the criticism of Jewish apologetics; but they struck a blow of their own. Transition from paganism to Judaism meant a transition from one system of ancestral traditions to another. Here it proclaimed a completely new life in Christ.

It is only in passing that the author pronounces this verdict. The heavy weight of these words is only discovered if we read a text like this with the eyes of an ancient reader and hear the ring of these words for him. Then words that at first sight are not very conspicuous become very powerful and small data yield interesting insights.

The work in the New Testament field of our generation has opened new vistas by such careful attention to what for the super-

[36] *TWNT* 4, pp. 525 ff.

ficial reader might seem insignificant details. Areas long neglected like the ancient versions of the Old Testament together with new discoveries are disclosing their secrets under the microscope of philological and historical study of the documents. Much work is still to be done also in the area of the hellenistic background of the New Testament to which the present contribution was devoted.

It is offered to you, my dear friend, as a token of gratitude for all the spadework you did in connection with the Aramaic background of the New Testament, for all the services you rendered to New Testament scholarship in general by your editorial work, above all for our personal friendship ever since our first meeting in Oxford in 1951. May our Lord grant you many years for the works of scholarship and the joy of friendship !

# THE COMPOSITION OF JOHN 13 : 21–30

MAX WILCOX

ALL four Gospels tell us that at the Last Supper Jesus disclosed that he knew the identity of his betrayer.[1] There are, however, significant differences between the accounts. Thus, in Mark and Luke, the disciples are depicted as wondering who it is that will betray him. In Matthew, in what looks rather like a secondary—perhaps " legendary "[2]—accretion, the villain is permitted to identify himself (Mt 26 : 25). By contrast, the Fourth Gospel not only names him, but purports to give the " inside story " of what actually took place on that momentous occasion. As a result, the passage in question—Jn 13 : 21–30—provides us with some interesting material for examining the possible relationship of the Fourth Gospel to the other three.

To be more precise, the section in John has affinities with more than one Synoptic evangelist, as C. H. Dodd noted in his study *Historical Tradition in the Fourth Gospel*:[3] it reflects Mark at one point, Luke at another, and the question naturally arises, whether we have here a case of a secondary composition based upon a conflation of these two written sources, or a third form of oral tradition.[4] Bultmann and Dodd would seem to incline towards the latter view.[5] Again, the presence of several Semitisms not found in the Synoptic material is a further factor which must be evaluated,[6] while the role of the author has also been quite considerable.

It is the aim of this study to examine the structure, and the literary and other affinities of Jn 13 : 21–30, with a view to discovering its mode of composition, and thus to take one step further towards an understanding of the relationship between the four Gospels.

[1] Mk 14 : 17–21 ; Mt 26 : 20–25 ; Lk 22 : 14, 21–23 ; Jn 13 : 21–30, 18.

[2] V. Taylor, *The Gospel according to St. Mark*, London, 1959, p. 539.

[3] Cambridge, 1963, p. 54.

[4] *Ibid.*

[5] R. Bultmann, *Das Evangelium des Johannes*, Göttingen, [13]1953, p. 366 ; Dodd, *op. cit.*, p. 54.

[6] Matthew Black, *An Aramaic Approach to the Gospels and Acts*, Oxford, [3]1967, pp. 101, 106, 125.

## I

Jn 13 : 21–30, as we now have it, has a definite setting in the Gospel. It follows the story of the Footwashing (Jn 13 : (2) 4–17), with its appended sayings (vv. 18–20), and precedes the discourses upon the theme of Jesus' " going away " (Jn 13 : 31 ff.). All of these in turn are enclosed in a wider framework, namely that of the Last Supper, which rightly begins at Jn 13 : 1 ff., with the phrase, " Before the Festival of the Passover ", which has been described as a kind of " headline " to the whole section.[7] Now in vv. 1–3, practically the only material which can be properly termed " narrative " is this headline, and also the note in v. 2, " and during (a) supper . . ." : the rest is very largely interpretative and reflects the style and interests of the author. It does, however, contain two elements perhaps echoing traditions akin to those found in other Gospels, *viz.*, the words in v. 1, " Jesus knowing that his hour had come . . ."—thoroughly Johannine, but cf. Mt 26 : 2 (Lk 22 : 14 ?)—and the statement telling that the devil had already decided to use Judas to have Jesus betrayed (cf. Lk 22 : 3—and of course, Jn 13 : 27a).[8] We cannot go into these points in detail here, but shall content ourselves with noting that the first reference in this section to the betrayal comes immediately after the phrase " during supper ". Now the word used here for " supper "—*δεῖπνον*—does not appear in the corresponding context in the Synoptic Gospels, but occurs at 1 Co 11 : 20 (" the Lord's Supper "). Again, when Judas does in fact leave the meal (Jn 13 : 30), we are told that " it was night " (*νύξ*), recalling the language of 1 Co 11 : 23, but *not* that of the Synoptic writers. These points are in themselves of no great weight, but they may nevertheless offer us a hint that the framework of the Johannine Supper sequence does not depend on the Synoptics, but if anything is nearer to the Eucharistic tradition consciously cited by Paul in 1 Co 11.[9] We may have cause to return to this later. Meantime we may note that the Johannine Supper sequence ends at Jn 17 : 26.

If we now look briefly at vv. 4–20, we find two further references to the betrayal : vv. 11 and 18 respectively. Of these, v. 11

[7] R. H. Lightfoot, *The Gospel of St. John*, Oxford, 1956, p. 262.

[8] Cf. the discussion in Dodd, *Hist. Trad.*, pp. 26 ff.

[9] See the discussion in Dodd, *Hist. Trad.*, p. 63 ; J. Jeremias, *The Eucharistic Words of Jesus*, ET, London, 1966, pp. 100 ff.

is clearly interpretative and seems due to the author : it strikingly recalls the language of Jn 6 : 64b, also an interpretation of a saying of Jesus. Note the way the words of Jesus are here quite consciously cited. Both sayings are seen as foreshadowing the betrayal.

V. 18 is more explicit : appeal is made here both to the words of Jesus (18a) and to the Old Testament (18b). One member of the group is unworthy, and his unworthiness is seen as " according to scripture ". However, the Old Testament passage concerned—Ps 40 (41) : 10—appears in a different form in Mk 14 : 18, as an explanatory addition to the " Word of Jesus " cited there. Now it is interesting that although both John and Mark refer to this same passage they not only diverge from one another in detail, but also from the LXX and the other Greek Old Testament versions known to us. Moreover, they have no parallel here in either Matthew or Luke. This is the more striking in the case of Matthew, where (Mt 26 : 21) the parallel with Mark is otherwise all but verbal. That is, the tradition of the application of Ps 40 (41) : 10 to the identity of the betrayer is common to Mark and John, and to them only. Even so, however, it is hard to argue for interdependence here, since not only do their versions of the Psalm differ, but they are in fact applied to different " Sayings of Jesus ". If the agreement is not fortuitous, nor due to a gloss on Mark,[10] which seems highly unlikely in view of the nature of the words concerned, its origin may well be traceable to a basic tradition of interpretation upon which both Mark and John have drawn. Perhaps we may note in passing that Ps 40 (41) was one of the Old Testament sections regarded by C. H. Dodd as a possible primary source for *testimonia* (esp. vv. 3b, 11).[11] That John leans towards the Hebrew text here, against the LXX, should not be overlooked.[12]

But there the verse has other features too. The use of the strange word τρώγω here points at once to the Bread of Life discourses of Jn 6, especially vv. 54, 56, 57, and 58. If we set these four in parallel with the citation found in Jn 13 : 18b, the resemblance is most compelling, and can hardly be accidental. It would seem more logical to argue that a divergent Old Testament

[10] V. Taylor, *op. cit.*, p. 540, mentions this possibility, citing evidence of v. 11. in support. But the reading of B sa bo seems ameliorative.

[11] *According to the Scriptures*, London, 1952, pp. 100, 108.

[12] E.g., John reads the singular " bread ", with the Hebrew, against the LXX. Cf. C. K. Barrett, *The Gospel according to St. John*, London, 1955, p. 371.

textual tradition has here influenced the language of Jn 6 : 54, 56, 57, 58, than that a deliberate Johannine usage in those verses has produced the aberration in the Old Testament citation. For after all, John cites the " Words of Jesus " underlying the passages from Jn 6 in an alternative form, using the ordinary verb φάγειν, in other verses in the very same chapter, e.g., Jn 6 : 51, 53. Now this may of course reflect the tradition found in Mt 26 : 27 (although not Mark, Luke or 1 Co 11) : but it may also echo the Old Testament citation in Jn 6 : 31 (Ps 77 (78) : 24; Ex 16 : 4, 13–15 ; cf. Jn 6 : 49). On this analysis it would seem reasonable to suppose that the form of the citations in question has been the determining factor in the wording of the associated " Sayings of Jesus ". P. Borgen would trace it to the " eucharistic traditions ", the word τρώγω having come from a peculiar translation of Ps 41 : 10.[13] There is, however, another point. Jn 6 closes with a " Word of Jesus " foreshadowing the betrayal, and expressed in language recalled in Jn 13 : 18a, *viz.*, " Did I not *choose* you Twelve ? Yet [14] one of you is a devil " (Jn 6 : 70). This statement is promptly interpreted in v. 71 as referring to Judas. (Note that the expression in Jn 6 : 71, " one of the Twelve ", may perhaps reflect the tradition of Mt 26 : 14, 47 ; Mk 14 : 20, 43, 10, and possibly Lk 22 : 3.[15]) That is to say, in both Jn 6 and 13, a eucharistic reference is closely related to a betrayal prophecy, and the same citation—Ps 40 (41) : 10—appears to have affected both sections. But nowhere is the connection between the Last Supper (or the Eucharist) and the betrayal more succinctly put than in 1 Co 11 : 23, where Paul explicitly refers to a tradition :

". . . the Lord Jesus Christ, on the night when he was betrayed, took bread. . . ."

The fact that this conjunction of ideas is found in both chs. 6 and 13 of John would seem to point to the " eucharistic tradition " as one of the formative factors in the shaping of these sections.

## II

The paragraph in Jn 13 : 21–30 itself is introduced with a linking formula found elsewhere in the Gospel, *viz.*, " having said

[13] *Bread from Heaven*, Leiden, 1965, p. 93.
[14] Treating the " and" as the Semitic adversative.
[15] Cf. especially Lk 22 : 3, and Jn 13 : 2, 27.

these things . . .",[16] apparently intended to tie it to the preceding section, more especially the sayings of Jesus in vv. 18–20. (But the Johannine tone of vv. 19–20 should not be overlooked.) The proper connection is thus probably with v. 18, which we have just discussed. This would make good sense here. We may leave on one side the question whether the words " Jesus was troubled in spirit ", derive from Ps 41 (42) : 7, and refer to the discussion of it elsewhere.[17] The key to the passage, however, would seem to be the saying of Jesus in v. 21b, introduced by what looks very like a set formula : " Jesus . . . testified and said . . ." [18] The saying is almost identical with that in Mk 14 : 18, except for the repetition of the " amen "—characteristic of John—and the absence of the allusion to Ps 40 (41) : 10, which John places a moment earlier in 13 : 18b, as we have already seen. Of course, it might be held that John is following Matthew here, not Mark, for Matthew also " omits " the allusion at this point (Mt 26 : 21b). The presence of the reference to Ps 40 (41) : 10 in both Mark and John, along with its absence from Matthew, may be held to tell against a too mechanical or simple theory of dependence. We may also note in passing the Semitism in the saying, " εἷς ἐξ ὑμῶν . . ." reflecting Aramaic *ḥaḏ minᵉhōn*.[19]

V. 22 is basically closer in thought to Luke (Lk 22 : 23) than to either Matthew or Mark (Mt 26 : 22 ; Mk 14 : 19). The disciples simply wonder who the villain can be. In Matthew and Mark they enquire, " Is it I ? " No clear verdict is possible here, and the general outline of the story—if a story it really is—runs broadly parallel to the Synoptic accounts. The asyndetic opening of the verse is not necessarily Semitic : it may well be a mark of the author's style (in the absence of other signs of Semitism in the verse).[20] The words " περὶ τίνος λέγει " would seem to be a bridging piece relating the saying of Jesus in v. 21b to *both* vv. 23–25, and v. 26. See especially v. 24b, " τίς . . . περὶ οὗ λέγει ". The " explicative " nature of it suggests the author's hand, but we cannot be sure.[21]

[16] E.g., Jn 7 : 9 ; 9 : 6 ; 11 : 43 ; 13 : 21 ; 18 : 1 ; cf. also 18 : 22, 38 ; 20 : 14, 20 ; 21 : 19 (*bis*). The form is also found in Luke in Lk 19 : 28 ; 23 : 46b (Lukan " additional saying "), 24 : 40 (all peculiar to Luke) ; cf. Ac 1 : 9 ; 19 : 41 ; 20 : 36.

[17] Dodd, *Hist. Trad.*, pp. 37–38, 53.

[18] Cf. also Ac 13 : 22 (Paul at Pisidian Antioch) ; Rev 22 : 20.

[19] Black, *op. cit.*, pp. 105–6.

[20] Cf. Black, *op. cit.*, p. 56.

[21] Cf. e.g., Jn 6 : 42, 52, etc. Or again, Jn 2 : 21.

Vv. 23–25, by way of contrast, constitute a closed whole and introduce material peculiar to John. V. 23 is the first reference in the Gospel to the so-called " Beloved Disciple ", and in a typically Johannine way provides us with an expression reappearing elsewhere in the book almost as a " definition " of the otherwise unnamed man.[22] Similarly, the words " *ἐν τῷ κόλπῳ τοῦ Ἰησοῦ, ὃν ἠγάπα ὁ Ἰησοῦς* " are re-phrased in v. 25, *ἐπὶ τὸ στῆθος τοῦ Ἰησοῦ* . . ., and recur in Jn 21 : 20 in an even fuller description or " definition " of the disciple. This " re-use " of material to form a " definition " or cross-reference is a striking feature of the Fourth Gospel.[23] The main question here, however, is whether vv. 23–25 originally formed part of the story, or whether they represent an independent tradition incorporated by the author (or his circle) at this point, or are in fact due directly to his own hand.

Now the apparent Semitism in v. 23, " one from his disciples " (literally),[24] is probably to be traced directly to the words of the saying of Jesus cited in v. 21, " one of (*lit.* from) you . . ." Likewise, the words of Peter, *εἰπὲ τίς ἐστιν περὶ οὗ λέγει* (v. 24) seem to recall v. 22, as may also be true of the Beloved Disciple's question (v. 25). The asyndetic opening of v. 23 may be no more than Johannine style,[25] similarly the use of the periphrastic imperfect there. None of these is in itself strong, although the presence of three " weak " Semitisms in one verse may seem to call for comment.[26] If we could only convince ourselves that v. 23 reflected a basic element of tradition, originally in Aramaic, we might be tempted to see in it yet another Semitism : a possible pun—

" in the bosom of Jesus (*b$^e$ḥubeh d$^e$yešûʿa*)
whom Jesus loved (*d$^e$ḥab$^e$beh yešûʿa*)

Note that the word-order in the Greek text would suit this well.[27] This cannot be pressed, but it is perhaps worth recording. If we look here for Synoptic parallels, we may observe the use of

[22] Jn 19 : 26 ; 21 : 7, 20 ; possibly 20 : 2.

[23] Other cases are those of Nicodemus (Jn 3 : 2 ; but cf. 7 : 50 and 19 : 39, where elements drawn from 3 : 2 reappear in a set form), Lazarus (Jn 11 : 1, 43 ; but cf. 12 : 1), and Cana (Jn 2 : 1 ff. ; but cf. 4 : 46). The list could be larger.

[24] Black, *op. cit.*, p. 106.

[25] *Ibid.*, p. 56.

[26] On the periphrastic imperfect, see Black, *op. cit.*, p. 130 ; M. Wilcox, *The Semitisms of Acts*, Oxford, 1965, pp. 123 ff.

[27] Similar examples from other parts of the Gospels are cited by Black, *op. cit.*, pp. 160–85. A problem is that the present verse (Jn 13 : 23) is narrative, not direct speech.

ἀνακεῖμαι in v. 23, as in Mk 14 : 18 (cf. also Mt 26 : 20), and that of ἀναπίπτω, v. 25, as in Lk 22 : 14. But it would seem rather optimistic to regard these small points as indicative of dependence of John upon Mark (or Matthew) and Luke. The case of ἀναπίπτω may rather be traced through Jn 13 : 12 (peculiar to John) to Jn 6 : 10, the Feeding-story, where it appears also in the Synoptic parallels.[28] We shall return to a discussion of these verses in a moment.

With v. 26 we are once again on firm ground. It is a saying of Jesus, introduced by the familiar " Jesus therefore answered ". Let us look at the saying first, and begin by noting that it contains a Semitism, the use of the resumptive pronoun following a relative pronoun.[29] If we now compare it with the parallel passages in Matthew and Mark (Luke omits), we find that it is Matthew, not Mark, who has a Semitism in the corresponding saying (Mt 26 : 23 ; cf. Mk 14 : 20) ; moreover, it is the similar " casus pendens "—" He who dipped . . ., he (this one) will betray me . . ." [30] But if this is so, it is hard to argue that the Matthaean passage is dependent upon the Markan, although they are obviously closely related. It would seem much more likely that Matthew, (Mark), and John here preserve traces of a common basic tradition, apparently with Semitic (Aramaic ?) roots.[31] On the other hand, v. 26 does show marks of the author's hand : the use of the finite verb ἀποκρίνεται instead of the participle preferred by the Synoptics, οὖν, and the favourite ἐκεῖνος, this last-named being embedded here in the actual " saying of Jesus " itself. Turning to the introductory words, comparison with Mt 26 : 23 and Mk 14 : 20—in so far as it is valid—points to a view similar to that which emerged from our consideration of the saying. The form in Jn 13 : 26 could not come directly from Mk 14 : 20, but it could be derived from Mt 26 : 23 ; nevertheless, Mt 26 : 23a could at least as well be derived from a conflation of Jn 13 : 26 and Mk 14 : 20, or the traditions underlying them.[32] Whatever else is true, John at least seems

[28] I.e., Mk 6 : 40 ; 8 : 6 ; Mt 15 : 35. It is noteworthy that it appears in *both* Markan feeding-stories.

[29] Black, *op. cit.*, p. 101.

[30] *Ibid.*, p. 53.

[31] Note that Matthew gives two related definitions of the betrayer : Mt 26 : 21 " one of you will betray me " ; v. 23, " He who dipped . . ., he will betray me ". Does this point to the existence of a set of " Betrayal-Sayings " ?

[32] Not that we are committed to any of these possibilities. The evidence is simply insufficient to be sure.

to have rewritten the actual saying of Jesus itself to suit its present context, but not so radically as to have erased all traces of its older (Semitic) form.

We should next take up a point we made earlier, namely, that the words of v. 26 not only answer the question of the Beloved Disciple in v. 25; they would fit the unspoken doubt of v. 22 every bit as well. But the sequence vv. 21, 22, 26 would correspond even more closely to that of Matthew and Mark. This fact might strengthen our suspicion that vv. 23–25 may well not have formed part of the material originally, but have been intruded into their present context (either from additional traditional material, or from the author's own hand) to explain or comment on v. 22. Similarly, it would help to account for two other features of the passage: (a) the reference to "*the* morsel" in vv. 26, 27 has been held to imply that the meal was a Passover one, whereas the wider context of Jn 13 : 1–30 suggests that it was not; [33] (b) the words, "the morsel", are introduced quite baldly, without a shred of explanation, as though the reader of the Gospel would know what was meant[34]—in fact, almost as though something had been omitted from the narrative. One is reminded of the way in which John refers to Mary Magdalene finding "the stone" rolled away from the tomb of Jesus (Jn 20 : 1): it is the first mention of the stone in his book, and the reader is presumed to know the details of the Burial-Story already—or has something been omitted? The presence of similar features in the Markan Passion-Story led Martin Dibelius to conclude that it was based on a much older form: that the primitive Passion-Narrative envisaged a different date for the Crucifixion (and so also, the Last Supper) from that in our Mark; [35] it was much briefer and was later filled out with other blocks of early tradition.[36] Can the same have happened in the Johannine account?

Let us by-pass v. 27 for the present, and look at vv. 28–29. These verses seem to take the line that the Passover was yet to come (so especially the comment about buying something needed for the festival).[37] Further, the words ascribed to Jesus by some

[33] Cf. Barrett, *op. cit.*, p. 373.

[34] A. Loisy, *Le quatrième évangile* . . ., Paris, [2]1921, pp. 396–97.

[35] "Das historische Problem der Leidensgeschichte", *ZNTW* 30 (1931), 193–201; esp. pp. 194 ff., etc.

[36] Dibelius, *loc. cit.*, pp. 194 ff.

[37] But this is disputed by Jeremias, *op. cit.*, pp. 53 ff.

of those present—" that he should give something to the poor "—would appear to be strongly reminiscent of Jn 12 : 5 or its Synoptic parallels.[38] It seems that we have yet another instance of the familiar Johannine habit of announcing a theme at one point, and then picking it up again at a later one. But the affinities between Jn 13 : 28–29 and 12 : 4–6 (indeed, vv. 1–6) are quite striking and can scarcely be due to chance : the saying about giving something to the poor, unspecific as to the speaker in the Synoptics, is attributed to Judas in John ; moreover it provides the (human) " motive " for the betrayal. In both places we find the words πτωχοῖς, παραδιδόναι, and γλωσσόκομον, the last confined in the New Testament to these two texts. Furthermore, R. Bultmann has drawn attention to the fact that if vv. 28–29 are omitted there is a smooth transition from v. 27 to v. 30. Moreover, vv. 28–29 state that *no one* heard what Jesus said, which would seem to complicate matters somewhat. He concluded that the Evangelist must have inserted it into his source.[39] Now, before we proceed, let us observe that there is no small resemblance between Jn 12 : 1–6 and Jn 13 : 23–25.[40] This might strengthen our impression that vv. 23–25 as they stand did not form part of the original form of the Betrayal-story. But of course, if we omit vv. 23–25 and 28–29 from Jn 13 : 21–30, the remainder conforms fairly closely to the outline as found in the Synoptics, especially Mark. Nevertheless it is very hard to argue for direct dependence of John on Mark here, as we have already seen. But both streams may go back to a common basic tradition. The presence of the term εὐθύς in v. 30 may point in the same direction.[41] However, at this point it should be observed that the language of v. 30a is even nearer to that of v. 26b, than it is to v. 27a.[42] This means that we must now turn back and examine v. 27.

V. 27 falls naturally into two parts, a " narrative " element (27a) καὶ μετὰ τὸ ψωμίον τότε εἰσῆλθεν εἰς ἐκεῖνον ὁ σατανᾶς, and a saying of Jesus, introduced by a simple formula : λέγει οὖν αὐτῷ Ἰησοῦς ὃ ποιεῖς ποίησον τάχιον.

Now the words after τότε in v. 27a have long been recognized as closely parallel to Lk 22 : 3, εἰσῆλθεν δὲ σατανᾶς εἰς Ἰούδαν

[38] Mk 14 : 5 ; Mt 26 : 9.
[39] *Das Evangelium des Johannes*, p. 366.
[40] Cf. Jn 12 : 2b and 13 : 23a.
[41] So Bultmann, *op. cit.*, p. 366, n. 6 ; but cf. Jn 13 : 32.
[42] Thus, 26b, βάψας οὖν τ. ψωμ. λαμβάνει, 30a, λαβὼν οὖν τ. ψωμ. κτλ.

τὸν καλούμενον Ἰσκαριώτην . . .[43] The " καλούμενον " is a Lukanism, and need not bother us.[44] Likewise, the ἐκεῖνον of Jn 13 : 27a is probably due to the Evangelist. Comparing the resulting statements, we may note that that of John is just a little less polished, and more Semitic in word-order than that of Luke, although we dare not stress this fact. Next, there is the well-known link between the two, *viz.*, the use in both of the otherwise non-Johannine term, " Satan " ; we should have expected the more usual word " devil " (e.g., Jn 13 : 2). The questions arise here : first, whether the words concerned are due to use of a source, and if so, what kind of source ; and secondly, why the Evangelist placed them here at all. Now dependence on Luke seems hard to defend (unless we have to do with assimilation, or a gloss), for the Johannine form is less polished than the Lukan : moreover, if John did in fact use our " Luke ", why did he follow it so closely here, while disregarding it elsewhere in the section ? But perhaps we should observe that the passage in Luke is peculiar to him, and recall that at quite a number of points John does seem to preserve a tradition akin to that of the Lukan special material. If there is dependence at all here, it would seem to be rather on a common basic element of tradition, prior to both Gospels.[45]

The other question is easier to approach. Jn 13 : 27a and Lk 22 : 3 alike seem designed to show that Judas' deed is no mere act of human malice, nor a case of dead men " telling no tales ", as Jn 12 : 4 might suggest. Rather his action is part of the Divine scheme of salvation : he acts not on his own account, but on that of Jesus' ultimate opponent.[46] Once again we are dealing with " explanation " on the part of the Evangelist, but here it seems to be founded on traditional material preserved for us elsewhere. Yet this interpretation is not wholly new : it is implicit in Mk 14 : 21 (Mt 26 : 24 ; cf. Lk 22 : 22), where we are told, " the Son of Man is going away (ὑπάγει), just as it stands written concerning him . . .". But what is meant here by " scripture " ? Certainly no passage suggests itself readily.[47]

[43] E.g., E. Nestle's *Novum Testamentum* gives it in the margin, etc.

[44] Cf. J. C. Hawkins, *Horae Synopticae*, Oxford, ²1909, pp. 19, 42.

[45] See the classical study by J. Schniewind, *Die Parallelperikopen bei Lukas und Johannes*, Leipzig, 1914, 2.Aufl., Darmstadt, 1958, esp. pp. 96 ff. E. Haenchen, *Der Weg Jesu*, Berlin, 1966, p. 477, n.1, regards 27a as a later addition but 27b as original.

[46] Cf. E. Fascher, " Judas ", *RGG*³ 3, pp. 965–66.

[47] Dn 7 : 13 has been suggested, but seems unconvincing. See Taylor, *op. cit.*, p. 542a.

Taylor rightly notes the use of *ὑπάγω* here as "typically Johannine", and preferable to Luke's "more prosaic" *πορεύεται*.[48] Whatever else, the saying of Jesus in Mk 14 : 21—whether genuine or not—implies that the "going away" of the Son of Man, interpreted a moment later as his "betrayal" (or "handing over"), takes place in accordance with Scripture—it is part of the Divine plan. But that does not acquit the betrayer. So far, then, basic agreement between all four evangelists.

Now some such saying would seem to underlie the section of John immediately following Jn 13 : 21–30, *viz.*, 13 : 31–35 ; 14 ; 16. Jn 13 : 36 ; 14 : 4, 5 ; 16 : 5, 7 suggest that its basic form was "I am going away" (*ἐγὼ ὑπάγω*). But if so, then perhaps both Mark and John are using the same saying, in two different forms. This would be the more striking if we were to accept G. Vermes' view of the expression "Son of Man" ; for then it would be possible to derive both forms from a single common Aramaic saying, the Markan version being a literal translation, the Johannine an idiomatic one.[49] In any event community of tradition would seem indicated.

But what of the expression, "*καθὼς γέγραπται* . . ." (Mk 14 : 21 ; but cf. also Jn 13 : 18 ; 17 : 12b) ? Two possibilities present themselves : either the reference is to an Old Testament passage not readily detectable in our Hebrew or Greek versions, or it may mean some other "writing", perhaps a collection of the "Words of Jesus".[50] In John, the occurrences of *ἐγὼ ὑπάγω* are introduced by words suggesting that we should regard it as a quotation.[51] Again, Jn 13 : 33—referring back to Jn 7 : 34—implies that the Supper was not the original setting of the saying. A similar case is Jn 15 : 20 (deliberately referring to Jn 13 : 16a), where the saying of Jesus is (a) introduced by a precise formula found elsewhere in the New Testament in a similar setting,[52] and (b) followed immediately by what amounts to a "pesher".

[48] Taylor, *op. cit.*, p. 542a. He rejects Bultmann's view that it is a secondary construction due to the Church (*History of the Synoptic Tradition*, ET, Oxford, 1963, p. 152).

[49] Appendix E, "The use of *br nš'*/*br nš* in Jewish Aramaic", to Black, *op. cit.*, pp. 310–28. Cf. also L. Vos, *The Synoptic Traditions in the Apocalypse*, Kampen, 1965, pp. 224, etc.

[50] Cf. E. D. Freed, *The Old Testament Quotations in the Gospel of John*, Leiden, 1965, pp. 119 ff., etc.

[51] Esp. 13 : 33.

[52] Cf. Ac 20 : 35 ; 11 : 16 ; Jn 2 : (19), 22, etc. Cf. O. Michel, *TWNT*, 4, pp. 678 ff.

Other cases might be cited. Again, Jn 16 : 4 echoes the formula, while in Jn 14 : 26 this " remembering " is seen as due to the action of the Holy Spirit. Finally, the sayings of Jesus concerned are not infrequently associated with Old Testament passages in such a way as to suggest that both the Scripture and the saying are virtually on the same level.[53] These facts taken together strengthen the probability that John may have used a primitive collection of such sayings, already regarded as almost " canonical ". Perhaps the same may be true also of Mk 14 : 21.[54] However this may be, John and Mark do seem to reflect a common element of tradition here.

Thus the " insertion " of Jn 13 : 27a, if such it is, seems to conform to a traditional explanation of the betrayal, as part of the Divine Scheme of salvation, as evidenced by its being foreshadowed in either the Old Testament or the words of Jesus, or both. The betrayal is thus to be seen as " *κατὰ τὰς γραφάς* ".[55]

On the other hand the actual " saying " recorded in v. 27b may well go back to an old tradition, although one suspects that it represents a variant stream from that found in the Synoptic gospels (where it is virtually without parallel).[56]

To summarize, then, we may observe that although there does not seem to be adequate evidence for positing a direct use of the Synoptics by John in Jn 13 : 21–30, yet if we omit vv. 23–25, 28–29, and possibly also 27a, the resultant text accords tolerably with the Synoptic scheme, especially that of Mark (and Matthew). It consists then almost entirely of sayings of Jesus related to the Betrayal theme, and in some of them we find Semitisms. Further, if we add to this the sayings of Jn 13 : 18 (which appears to link most directly on to v. 21), and 13 : 33, we can actually reconstruct an order akin to that in Mark :

| | |
|---|---|
| | Jn 13 : 18 (ref. Ps 40 (41) : 10) |
| Mk 14 : 18 ". . . one of you will betray me ", plus ref. Ps 40 (41) : 10. | Jn 13 : 21 ". . . one of you will betray me ". |

[53] This is especially true of Jn 2 : 19 (cf. v. 17=Ps 68(69) : 10), 22 and Jn 15 : 20 (cf. v. 25 ; Ps 68(69) : 5, etc.).

[54] V. Taylor, *op. cit.*, p. 541b, refers to the unusual presence of *μὲν . . . δὲ* in Mk 14 : 21, along with the use of *ὅτι* to introduce the words. This strangeness requires " either that *καὶ εἶπεν* has dropped out or that the passage is added from a saying-source ". We should agree with this view.

[55] Cf. 1 Co 15 : 3–4. Cf. Bultmann, *op. cit.*, p. 366 ; Haenchen, *op. cit.*, p. 477n.

[56] Unless we see some trace of it in Mt 26 : 25b, or Lk 22 : 23, *ὁ τοῦτο μέλλων πράσσειν*.

| | |
|---|---|
| Mk 14 : 20 (Mt 26 : 23) The Saying about dipping. | Jn 13 : 26 The Saying about the dipping of the " morsel ". |
| Mk 14 : 21 par : " The Son of Man is going ", as it is written of him, . . . | Jn 13 : (27a), 33 : ". . . as I said to the Jews, where *I am going*, . . .", etc. |

It seems hard to regard this as fortuitous. Rather it would appear that both John and Mark here reflect a similar (though not quite identical) basic tradition. Again, part at least of the purpose of the traditionists (or the evangelists ?) was to indicate that the betrayal was foreshadowed alike in Scripture and in the words of Jesus : like the other cardinal elements of the passion, it therefore took place " *κατὰ τὰς γραφάς* ", and so formed part of God's scheme of salvation. The presence of Semitisms and the use by both Mark and John of an Old Testament textual tradition at variance with the LXX, and other known Greek versions, but (in the case of John at any rate) akin to the Hebrew, point to an early date for the rise of this material. Additional support for this may be drawn from Jn 6.

In conclusion, we may note that Jn 13 : 21–30 appears to resolve into three main strata. These are the following :

(a) A basic framework, represented in vv. 21–30 only by the word *νύξ* (v. 30b), but to some extent reflected in the Betrayal theme itself, and in the general setting of the whole (at dinner, *δεῖπνον*). This would seem to be some such outline of the " eucharistic tradition " as is found in 1 Co 11 : 23 ff. Some further confirmation for this may be found in Jn 6, where we also have traces of a " eucharist-betrayal " pattern, followed in ch. 7, by the " going away " theme (7 : 34, etc.).

(b) A collection of sayings of Jesus, represented here by Jn 13 : (18), 21, 26 (27b ?), 33, etc.), woven about the betrayal theme (whether or not all of these sayings originally had such a setting), together with certain pieces of necessary connecting material (e.g., vv. 22 and 30). This collection conforms more or less to the Synoptic (especially, Markan) scheme, although the differences between them are such as to make the hypothesis of literary interdependence precarious. Its antiquity is indicated by the presence in it of Semitisms, and also by the use by both John and Mark of an Old Testament textual tradition varying from that of our known Greek translations, although nearer (in John's case) to the Hebrew. This application of Ps 40 (41) : 10 to the betrayal, would seem to be earlier than either John or

Mark—or indeed, their immediate traditions. The collection of sayings has presumably been inserted into the formal eucharistic tradition framework in order to comment upon or " interpret " the betrayal as having taken place according to Scripture and the word of Jesus.

(c) Other material, whether freely composed by the author, or drawn from oral tradition is not clear, although the latter would seem to have some evidence in its favour. It has some signs of an early date (perhaps Semitisms in v. 23 ?), and roughly covers vv. 23–25 (? 27a), and 28–29. It has been placed in its present context either by the author of the Fourth Gospel or by the traditionist(s) whom he represents in order to interpret or comment upon the Sayings-collection. The verses in question then are in the nature of " asides ".

The outcome of this study is twofold. First, it provides interesting confirmation for the general view suggested by Joachim Jeremias in his book, *The Eucharistic Words of Jesus*, where he dealt with the question of the rise of the Passion narratives from the basic tradition of 1 Co 15 : 3–4 ; the results of the present analysis would be to posit a similar development for the Betrayal story, within the actual eucharistic tradition itself (thus tying together interestingly the two Pauline traditional pieces in 1 Co 11 : 23–25 ; 15 : 3–4).[57] Secondly, it indicates that the relationship between the Fourth Gospel and the Synoptics is not likely to be treated adequately by a comparison of the texts as we have them, but only by an analysis which looks behind these texts to the basic traditional elements out of which they have evolved. Such conclusions as we may legitimately draw from the present study would suggest that the connection between John and the others is to be located well back in the primitive traditional material upon which each drew, rather than in actual literary interdependence. In this material two elements however were seen to be of paramount importance : (a) the basic " kerygmatic " or " credal " statements of the primitive Church (such as 1 Co 11 : 23–25 ; 15 : 3–4 ; etc.), and (b) collections of " Words of Jesus ".[58]

[57] *Op. cit.*, pp. 95–96. We should also mention again the view of Martin Dibelius, *op. cit.*, that behind the Markan Passion story there lay an older form.

[58] The use of such a collection or collections, possibly by both Matthew and Ignatius, has recently been shown probable by J. Smit-Sibinga, in " Ignatius and Matthew ", *NovT* 8 (1966), 263–83.

# II

## BEMERKUNGEN ZUM SCHLUSS DES MARKUSEVANGELIUMS

KURT ALAND

DIESE Betrachtung geht von der Voraussetzung aus, daß der sog. "lange" Markusschluß 16 : 9–20 eine sekundäre Hinzufügung zum ursprünglichen Text des Evangeliums bedeutet. Das braucht hier wohl nicht diskutiert zu werden, das Zeugnis der Handschriften ist ebenso eindeutig wie der innere Befund—schon die Benutzung einer modernen Synopse führt handgreiflich vor Augen, daß und wie sehr Mk 16 : 9–20 ein Mosaik aus den Auferstehungsberichten der anderen Evangelien darstellt.

Eine andere Frage ist es, ob die ursprüngliche Niederschrift des Markusevangeliums mit 16 : 8 endete und ob das Werk des Evangelisten nicht weiterführte. Man hat (vgl. z.B. die Diskussion zwischen Kenyon und Roberts) darüber nachgedacht, ob nicht das letzte Blatt mit dem ursprünglich auf 16 : 8 folgenden Text früh verloren gegangen sein könnte. Kenyon ging bei seiner These allerdings noch von der Voraussetzung aus, das Markusevangelium sei ursprünglich auf einer Papyrusrolle geschrieben gewesen. Ein Benutzer habe die Handschrift nach der Benutzung wieder zurückzurollen vergessen, d.h. sie mit dem Schluß nach außen liegen lassen. Dabei sei es zu der Beschädigung gekommen (*JTS* 40, 1939, 56–57). Roberts wies darauf hin, daß mit der Möglichkeit zu rechnen sei, daß das Markusevangelium von Anfang an nicht als Papyrusrolle, sondern als Kodex niedergeschrieben worden sei (ebda. 253–57). Er zieht dabei die Möglichkeit in Betracht: "the final leaf might easily have become detached" (S. 257), wenn er auch sehr skeptisch gegenüber der Möglichkeit ist, "whether bibliography can contribute much to the solution of this problem".

Roberts damalige Annahme, daß das Markusevangelium ursprünglich Kodex-Form besessen habe, ist nach dem (weithin auf ihn selbst zurückgehenden) Fortschritt unserer Kenntnisse inzwischen beinahe zur sicheren Voraussetzung geworden. So könnte man durchaus so operieren, daß man einen frühen Verlust der auf Mk 16 : 1–8 folgenden Verse durch einen Zufall behauptet. C. S. C. Williams z.B. (*Alterations to the Text of the Synoptic Gospels and Acts*, Oxford, 1951), der allerdings mehr der Theorie Kenyons von der Rolle zuneigt (S. 44), hält nicht nur das für möglich, sondern geht sogar so weit, eine absichtliche Abtrennung des letzten Blattes anzunehmen. Zwei Motive kommen nach seiner Meinung dafür in Betracht. Der ursprüngliche Markusschluß müsse entsprechend 14 : 28 und 16 : 7 die Erscheinungen des Auferstandenen in Galiläa beschrieben haben. Das habe im Widerspruch zu den Berichten der anderen Evangelien darüber gestanden, daß die Erscheinungen in Jerusalem stattgefunden hätten. Außerdem sei hier (wie 8 : 31 ; 9 : 31 ; 10 : 34) die Auferstehung *nach* drei Tagen beschrieben gewesen, nicht am dritten Tag wie in den anderen Evangelien. Deshalb habe man den ursprünglichen Schluß des Markusevangeliums unterdrückt. B. H. Streeters Argumente (*The Four Gospels*, London, 1927, S. 341) gegen eine beabsichtigte Unterdrückung der auf 16 : 8 folgenden Verse verlören ihre Gültigkeit " if we suppose that the autograph copy of Mark was mutilated not of course by a Council but by an individual who believed with St. Luke that the Apostles waited in Jerusalem for the Lord's Alter Ego or Spirit and who rashly assumed that if the Risen Lord appeared in Jerusalem, then He could not have appeared also to some disciples in Galilee and who perhaps was offended by the phrase ' after three days ' " (Williams, S. 45).

Soweit C. S. C. Williams, der hier als Sprecher für andere stehen mag. Natürlich besteht die Möglichkeit, daß das letzte Blatt eines Kodex verloren gehen bzw. absichtlich entfernt werden kann. Das hat allerdings, wenn es ohne Aufmerksamkeit zu erregen geschehen soll, zur Voraussetzung, daß das " Ur-Exemplar ", von dem die gesamte handschriftliche Überlieferung abhängt, in welcher das Markus-Evangelium mit 16 : 8 endet, auf dem vorletzten Blatt mit 16 : 8 schloß, und zwar so, daß die Seite mit ἐφοβοῦντο γάρ endete und diese Worte den Schluß der letzten Zeile bildeten. Nur dann konnte das Fehlen der Fortsetzung nicht auffallen und der spätere Abschreiber meinen, daß er ein vollständiges Exemplar des Evangeliums vor sich hatte.

Man wird dagegen einwenden, daß das sehr unwahrscheinlich, ja beinahe ausgeschlossen sei. Ein Zufall setzt mich jedoch in die Lage, den Beweis für diese Möglichkeit zu erbringen. Bei den Kollationen bisher nicht herangezogener Handschriften für das *Greek New Testament* (ed. K. Aland, M. Black, B. M. Metzger, A. Wikgren, Stuttgart, 1966) ergab sich nämlich, daß in der Minuskel 2386 (11. Jh., Pierpont Morgan Library 748) das Markusevangelium mit 16 : 8 schließt, und zwar genau am Ende des Verso von Blatt 92. Die Handschrift ist zweispaltig geschrieben, die letzte Zeile schließt: *ἐφοβοῦντο γάρ* + τ(ε)λ(ος), das nächste Blatt beginnt mit Lk 1 : 1.

Hier ist der Beleg dafür erbracht, daß eine Handschrift so enden kann, wie für die eben angeführte Hypothese erforderlich, nämlich daß Mk 16 : 8 so auf einer Seite auslaufen kann, daß man meint, den vollständigen Text des Evangeliums vor sich zu haben. Tatsächlich ist 2386 im *Greek New Testament* (S. 196) auch als Zeuge für den kurzen Markus-Schluß gebucht worden. Aber es handelte sich dabei um einen Irrtum, und insofern wird das Beispiel zur Fiktion. Denn eine Nachkontrolle der Kollationen (durch H. L. Heller und K. Junack) ergab, daß in 2386 nach dem mit Mk 16 : 1–8 endenden f. 92 ein weiteres Blatt fehlt. Die regelmäßig aus Quaternionen aufgebaute Handschrift beginnt f. 86 mit Lage 11. Diese Lage hat jedoch nur 7 Blatt. Daß sie ursprünglich 8 besaß, also nach f. 92 ein Blatt herausgerissen wurde, wird nicht nur dadurch bewiesen, daß f. 86, das Gegenblatt, locker im Bund sitzt und die Lagenmitte durch die Bindung zwischen dem 4. und 5. Blatt deutlich bezeichnet ist, sondern auch noch durch erhaltene (wenn auch geringe) Reste des fehlenden Blattes. Daß bei der Kollation 2386 als mit Mk 16 : 8 abschließend verzeichnet wurde, ist verständlich—so könnte es auch bei dem konjizierten "Ur-Exemplar" gewesen sein: der natürliche Abschluß der Rückseite des Blattes verleitete zu der Annahme, hier ende das Markus-Evangelium—während es in Wirklichkeit weiterging, so wie bei unserer Minuskel 2386.

Weshalb bei ihr das auf f. 92 folgende Blatt herausgerissen wurde, ist klar: ohne Zweifel stand auf dem Verso dieses Blattes eine ganzseitige Miniatur zum Lukasevangelium, sie erregte das Interesse eines "Sammlers" und fiel ihm zum Opfer. Was aber stand auf dem Recto? Natürlich kann man dafür plädieren, daß es leer war. Dagegen spricht jedoch die erhaltene Miniatur zum Johannesevangelium. Sie steht auf f. 150 v., die Vorderseite bietet den Schluß von Lk 24. So dürfte es auch bei dem f. 92 ursprünglich folgenden Blatt gewesen sein. Auf seinem Verso stand die Miniatur mit dem Bild des Lukas, auf seinem Recto der Schluß des Markusevangeliums, d.h. 16 : 9–20. f. 92 v. enthält Mk 15 : 45–16 : 8, d.h. etwa 26 Nestlezeilen, 16 : 9–20 entspricht genau diesem Umfang, nichts liegt näher als die Annahme, daß f. 92 r eben diese Verse enthalten hätte! Die Tatsache, daß nach f. 61 ebenfalls ein Blatt fehlt, das auf dem Verso die Miniatur zum Markusevangelium enthalten hat (es ist ebenfalls dem "Sammler" zum Opfer gefallen), und auf dem Recto offensichtlich leer war (f. 61 v bietet den Abschluß des Matthäusevangeliums, Kapitellisten aber hat die Handschrift offensichtlich nicht enthalten), bedeutet kein überzeugendes Gegenargument. Matthäus lief auf dem Verso von f. 61 aus, die Miniatur gehört ebenfalls aufs Verso, also hatte der Schreiber keine andere Möglichkeit, als das Recto des auf f. 61 folgenden Blattes leer zu lassen. Außerdem ist das "Telos" nach Mk 16 : 8 am Schluß von f. 92 v ein unwiderlegbarer Nachweis dafür, daß der Text weiterlief. Denn hätte 16 : 8 den Schluß des Evangeliums bedeutet, hätte der Schreiber hier (wie bei den anderen Evangelien) das Telos-Zeichen für die mit 16 : 8 endende Lesung nicht benötigt. Es beweist, daß noch eine weitere Lesung (eben 16 : 9–20) folgte.

So bleibt 2386 nur ein theoretisches Beispiel für den möglichen Ausfall eines ursprünglich auf 16 : 1–8 folgenden Textes. Es ist ja auch so, daß die Annahme der Abtrennung eines solchen auf Mk 16 : 1–8 folgenden "echten" Textes keinen eigentlichen "Sitz im Leben" hat. Der handschriftliche Befund läßt keine andere Annahme als die zu, daß das Markus-Evangelium von Anfang an mit dem kurzen Schluß zirkulierte, d.h. schon mit 16 : 8 endete, als es durch Kopien vom Urexemplar seine literarische Existenz begann. Nicht nur im griechischen Bereich (א, B, Clemens, Origenes, Euseb, Zeugnis des Hieronymus usw.), sondern auch in der syrischen (Sinai-Syrer!), armenischen, äthiopischen Überlieferung finden sich Zeugen, z.T. höchsten Ranges, dafür—eine Übereinstimmung, die nur unter der Voraussetzung der Ursprünglichkeit des kurzen Markusschlusses denkbar ist, es sei denn, daß jemand postulierte, der zufällige Verlust bzw. die bewußte Abtrennung sei schon beim Handexemplar des Verfassers geschehen, noch ehe die ersten Abschriften von ihm genommen wurden. Das erste ist von vornherein aufs höchste unwahrscheinlich, das zweite bedarf sehr viel stärkerer Begründung, als Williams und andere sie geben, zumal eine lange Reihe von sprachlichen, stilistischen und sachlichen Argumenten für die Ursprünglichkeit des gegenwärtigen Abschlusses sprechen; sie sind in der Literatur zum Thema bereits so oft erörtert worden, daß sie hier nicht wiederholt zu werden brauchen.

Doch nicht nur die Handschriften mit dem kurzen Markusschluß sind ein Beweis dafür, daß das Markusevangelium mit 16 : 8 endete, das gilt auch für die erdrückende Fülle der Handschriften mit dem langen Schluß[1], und nun ganz und gar für die Handschriften, die ihn mit textkritischen Zeichen oder Anmerkungen aufnehmen, ebenso wie für die, welche den kürzeren Markusschluß oder eine Kombination von kürzerem und langem Schluß bieten. Wir finden nirgendwo, sei es in der griechischen Textüberlieferung oder den Versionen oder bei den Kirchenvätern, eine andere Form des Markusschlusses als die fünf nachfolgenden:

(1) Mk 16 : 1–8.
(2) Mk 16 : 1–8 + 9–20 als fortlaufendem Text.
(3) Mk 16 : 1–8 + 9–20 mit textkritischen Zeichen oder entsprechenden Anmerkungen.
(4) Mk 16 : 1–8 + kürzerem Schluß.
(5) Mk 16 : 1–8 + Kombination von kürzerem und langem Schluß.

Nach allen Erfahrungen der Textkritik müßte sich, falls das Markusevangelium ursprünglich einen Text über 16 : 1–8 hinaus geboten hätte, irgendwo eine Spur davon finden (falls die Kürzung nicht schon im Urexemplar des Evangelisten stattgefunden hat, was so gut wie ausgeschlossen ist, s.o.). Das ist jedoch nicht der Fall. Alle Handschriften (f 1, 137, 138, 1110, 1210, 1215, 1216, 1217, 1221, 1241, 1582) welche durch Asterisci, Obelisci oder eine entsprechende ausdrückliche Anmerkung (das wesentliche Material dafür ist bei S. C. E. Legg, *Novum Testamentum Graece . . . Marcum*, Oxford, 1935) verzeichnet, aber auch schon bei Westcott-Hort, " Notes on Select Readings ", *The New Testament*, Cambridge, 1882, S. 28–57 und Th. Zahn, *Geschichte des neutestamentlichen Kanons* 2, S. 910–938, zu erkennen geben, daß sie vom Ende des Markusevangeliums bei 16 : 8 wissen, 16 : 9–20 aber um der herrschenden Tradition willen hinzufügen, sind als Zeugen der eindrucksvollen Gruppe anzuschließen, welche den Text mit

[1] Den im *Greek New Testament* S. 196 für den langen Schluß genannten Unzialen sind sämtliche anderen Markus-Unzialen hinzuzufügen, soweit sie nicht als Zeugen für den kürzeren oder den kurzen Schluß genannt sind.

16 : 8 abbricht. Die Handschriften mit dem langen Schluß ohne entsprechende Zusätze stehen in einer Überlieferung, welche diese Erinnerung nicht mehr besitzt (oder nicht mehr pflegen will). Nirgendwo aber verrät auch sie die Spur einer Kenntnis einer möglicherweise auf das " Urexemplar " zurückzugehenden anderen Fortsetzung von 16 : 1–8 (auf den Gedanken, 16 : 9–20 als genuine Fortsetzung von 16 : 1–8 zu bezeichnen, wird nach dem gegenwärtigen Stand der Diskussion, s.o., wohl niemand mehr kommen).

Am merkwürdigsten und am interessantesten von den oben genannten Gruppierungen sind vier und fünf, d.h. der sog. kürzere Markusschluß, wie ihn allein k und in Kombination mit dem längeren Markusschluß L, *Ψ*, 099, 0112, $274^{mg}$, 579 und *l* 1602 und die orientalischen Versionen bieten (der Name ist nicht ganz glücklich und auch nicht ganz logisch, denn wenn der kurze Markusschluß bis 16 : 8 geht, dann kann ein Abschluß des Evangeliums, der zu 16 : 8 noch etwas hinzufügt, nicht " kürzer " sein. Aber der Name hat sich nun einmal so eingebürgert). Der Bequemlichkeit halber nachfolgend der Text, die lateinische Form dabei von der griechischen (beides nach den Handschriftenphotos im Institut für neutestamentliche Textforschung) getrennt :[2]

*Πάντα δὲ τὰ παρηγγελμένα τοῖς περὶ τὸν Πέτρον συντόμως ἐξήγγειλαν. Μετὰ δὲ ταῦτα καὶ αὐτὸς ὁ Ἰησοῦς ἀπὸ ἀνατολῆς καὶ ἄχρι δύσεως ἐξαπέστειλεν δι' αὐτῶν τὸ ἱερὸν καὶ ἄφθαρτον κήρυγμα τῆς αἰωνίου σωτηρίας.*
L *Ψ* 099 (defect. : [*Πα*]*ν̣τ̣α̣ δε τα π*[*αρηγ*]*γελμεν*[*α τοι*]*ς περι τ*[*ο*]*ν* [*Πετ*]*ρ̣ο̣ν̣ συντομως . . .*) 0112 (defect. : [*Παντα . . . Μετα δε*] *ταυτα . . .*) $274^{mg}$. 579 *l* 1602

*Παντα* mit ausgerückter *Π*–Initiale L*Ψ* $099^{vid}$ *l*1602| [*Πα*]*ν̣τ̣α̣* 099| *παρηγγελμενα* mit ausgerückter *M*–Initiale 579 ; *π*[*αρηγ*]*γελμεν*[*α*] 099| [*τοι*]*ς* 099| *τον* : $274^{mg}$ ; *τ*[*ο*]*ν* 099|*Πετρον·* 579 ; *Πετρον.* *l* 1602 ; [*Πετ*]*ρ̣ο̣ν̣* 099| *συντομως.* *Ψ* | *εξηγγειλαν* : *Ψ* ; *εξηγγειλαν·* 099 (Zeile endet blind) 579 (*-γηλαν*) *l* 1602 ; *εξηγγειλαν.* $274^{mg}$ ; *εξηγγιλαν*† L| *Μετα* mit *M*–Initiale *Ψ* ; mit ausgerückter *M*–Initiale 099 *l* 1602| *δε* mit ausgerückter *Δ*–Initiale *Ψ* | *ταυτα.* *Ψ* | *αυτος*] *αυτοις* *l* 1602| *ο*]– *Ψ* 0112| *Ιησους*(*ι̅ς̅*)] *Ιησους,* L ; + *εφανη* *Ψ* ; + *εφανη·* *l* 1602 ; + *εφανη αυτοις* 099| *απ* 099. 579 *l* 1602| *ανατολης·* 579 ; *ανατολων.* $274^{mg}$ ; *ανατολης ηλιου* 099| *και*]– 0112| *μεχρι* *Ψ* | *δυσεως·* 579 ; *δυσεως.* $274^{mg}$| *εξαπεστειλεν.* $274^{mg}$ ; *εξαπεστιλεν* L| *κηρυγμα*† L ; *κηρυγμα.* $274^{mg}$ ; *κηρυμα* 579| *σωτηριας*† L ; *σωτηριας αμην* 0112 ; *σωτηριας* (*σ̅ρ̅ιας* + spatium $274^{mg}$) *αμην* : *Ψ* $274^{mg}$ *l* 1602 ; *σωτηριας αμην* 099 ; *σωτηριας·* *αμην*† 579

Omnia autem quaecumque praecepta erant et (eis ?) qui cum puero

[2] Den griechischen Text ohne die (variierenden) Einleitungsformeln, s. dazu die Übersicht S. 168.

(Petro ?) erant breviter exposuerunt. Post haec et ipse Iesus adparuit et (eis ?) ab orientem usque usque in orientem (occidentem !) misit per illos sanctam et incorruptam praedicationis* (praedicationem !) salutis aeternae. amen.

Zwar läge eine kritische Gesamtausgabe nahe, aber noch ist unsere Kenntnis der koptischen Überlieferung trotz des überaus verdienstvollen Aufsatzes von P. E. Kahle ("The End of St. Mark's Gospel. The Witness of the Coptic Versions", *JTS* n. s. 2, 1951, 49–57) unvollständig, für die der äthiopischen Überlieferung fehlen sogar noch alle Voraussetzungen. So sind in der vorstehenden Edition nur die Lesarten der griechischen Handschriften (L, *Ψ*, 099, 0112, 274$^{mg}$, 579 und *l* 1602) verzeichnet worden, der Text selbst wird nach Nestle[25] (=*Greek New Testament*) gegeben. Der Text von k (nach Jülicher/Matzkow, von H. Höfermann nach dem Original verglichen), ist ohne Zweifel an verschiedenen Stellen korrupt. Das gilt vor allem vom "et qui cum puero". Daß puero = Petro ist, liegt auf der Hand, aber erst wenn et in eis verbessert wird (= τοῖς περὶ τὸν Πέτρον in der griechischen Überlieferung) bekommt der Text einen Sinn. et = eis ist (vielleicht) auch in der Fortsetzung zu lesen: adparuit et ab orientem etc. Zwar ergibt er auch so einen Sinn, das et hat aber im griechischen Text keine Parallele; 099 dagegen liest nach Ἰησοῦς noch ἐφάνη αὐτοῖς (*Ψ l* 1601 nur ἐφάνη), so könnte adparuit eis die lateinische Entsprechung dazu sein. Puero und et sind leicht als Verlesungen zu erklären, wie k ja auch sonst an Irrtümern reich ist: doppeltes usque, orientem statt occidentem, praedicationis statt praedicationem.

k fügt den kürzeren Markusschluß direkt an V. 8 in den fortlaufenden Text ein. Zu diesem Zweck gestaltet er V. 8 um und liest: Illae autem, (cum del.) cum exirent a monumento, fugerunt, tenebat enim illas tremor et pavor propter timorem. Er läßt also (abgesehen von anderen kleineren Variationen, s. dazu Jülicher-Matzkow) im Gegensatz zur anderen altlateinischen Überlieferung das Parallelstück zu καὶ οὐδενὶ οὐδὲν εἶπαν aus. Der Grund dafür ist klar: der kürzere Markusschluß will sich sonst nicht recht anfügen lassen. Daß der Übergang auch so unbeholfen genug ist, hat ihn offensichtlich nicht gestört.

k ist, wie bekannt, die einzige Handschrift, welche den kürzeren Markusschluß allein bietet. Dazu kommt eine Reihe von (bisher allerdings nicht ausreichend untersuchten) äthio-

* am unteren Rande hinzugefügt, dicationis in ras., was vorher ?

pischen Handschriften (Legg spricht von 7). Alle anderen griechischen und koptischen Zeugen bieten ihn neben dem langen Schluß, allerdings auf eine Weise, die in Literatur und Kommentaren nicht selten unscharf oder gar falsch beschrieben wird. Die Ursache dafür ist in den Textausgaben selbst zu suchen. C. Tischendorf hatte in der ed. octava (*Novum Testamentum Graece*, 2 vol., Leipzig, [8]1869) noch die eigentliche Ausgabe (I, 403) mit 16 : 8 abgebrochen und in einer langen Anmerkung (I, 403–407) die Unechtheit von 16 : 9–20 begründet, um 16 : 9–20 dann anschließend an diese Anmerkung (I, 407–9) nach dem Textus receptus und Lachmann abzudrucken. Der kürzere Markusschluß war dabei im eigentlichen Text überhaupt nicht erschienen, sondern nur innerhalb der Argumentation der Anmerkung wiedergegeben worden. Westcott-Hort hatten dann nach Mk 16 : 1–8, wobei die Zeile mit Sternchen auslief, in Doppelklammern 16 : 9–20 und daran anschließend, wieder in Doppelklammern, den kürzeren Markusschluß gedruckt, und zwar mit der Überschrift : *ΑΛΛΩΣ*. Das hat sich seitdem praktisch durchgesetzt, Nestle verfuhr so, ihm folgten v. Soden, Vogels und das *Greek New Testament*. Souter ließ hinter 16 : 8 einen etwas vergrößerten Abstand, brachte 16 : 9–20 dann aber ohne Klammern und notierte den kürzeren Markusschluß lediglich im Apparat. Merk und Bover lassen 16 : 9–20 dagegen unmittelbar auf 16 : 8 folgen, der kürzere Markusschluß wird im Apparat zu 16 : 20 gegeben. Bei Bover geschieht das mit einer ganz mißverständlichen Angabe,[3] bei Merk mit einem Irrtum, der nun beinahe allen Ausgaben bis hin zu Nestle,[25] dem *Greek New Testament* (und meiner eigenen Synopse)[4] zu eigen ist. Hier heißt es nämlich überall, daß die Minuskel 274 den kürzeren Schluß nach 16 : 20 biete. Im *Greek New Testament* wird zusätzlich noch dasselbe für *l* 961 und *l* 1602 behauptet.

Die Anführung von *l* 961 im *Greek New Testament* muß auf einem Irrtum beruhen (sie ist anscheinend aus Merk übernommen[5]), denn soweit bekannt (Fotos sind mir im Augenblick leider nicht zugänglich) enthält es das letzte Kapitel des Markusevangeliums

[3] Das gilt auch für Vogels.

[4] Aber auch P. E. Kahle.

[5] Merk führt außerdem noch *l* 1566 als Zeugen an. Diese Angabe ist zu streichen ; *l* 1566 gehört zu *l* 1602, vgl. K. Aland, *Kurzgefaßte Liste*, Berlin, 1963. Wenn hier entgegen dem sonstigen Brauch die frühere Nummer gestrichen und die spätere beibehalten wurde, so deshalb, weil *l* 1602 den zweisprachigen Kern der Handschrift bot (82 Blatt), *l* 1566 nur einen kleinen Teil (5 Blatt ; die Doppelnummerierung geht auf ein Versehen von v. Dobschütz zurück).

überhaupt nicht. *l* 1602 ist eine griechisch-koptische Bilingue und wird bei Kahle (nach der Ausgabe von Heer) zutreffend beschrieben. Es entspricht dem Normaltyp, wie ihn L, Ψ und alle anderen griechischen Zeugen bieten, wovon gleich zu reden sein wird. Zur Minuskel 274 hatte Tischendorf bereits lakonisch bemerkt: "eadem (d.h. den kürzeren Markusschluß) $274^{mg}$ ad v. 7. litteris uncialibus adnotat". Legg verzeichnet 274 richtig.

Daß der Irrtum sich so verbreiten und bis heute erhalten konnte, ist nur aus der unbewußten Assoziation zu erklären, welche die Stellung des kürzeren Markusschlusses hinter 16 : 9–20 in den meisten der heute verbreiteten Ausgaben hervorrief (In $Nestle^{26}$ soll das geändert werden und der kürzere vor dem langen Markusschluß stehen). Die Situation in 274 ist ganz eindeutig. Zwar fährt der Text auf f. $104^r$ nach 16 : 8 (folgt +, Angabe des Lektionsschlusses für die 2.Heothina-Lektion = 16 : 1–8 sowie ein kurzer Zwischenraum) mit 16 : 9–20 fort. Dabei steht die erste Hälfte von V. 15 noch auf dem Recto, V. 15b–20 folgen auf dem Verso. Aber an den linken Rand der letzten Zeile von V. 8 (nicht V. 7, wie Tischendorf irrtümlich behauptet) ist von der Hand des ersten Schreibers ein Asteriscus gesetzt, und am unteren Rand von f. $104^r$ folgt dann in Majuskeln in 5 Zeilen der kürzere Markusschluß, wobei am Beginn jeder Zeile der Asteriscus noch einmal wiederholt wird, die Zugehörigkeit des ganzen zu (d.h. hinter) V. 8 dadurch noch einmal deutlich hervorhebend. f. $104^r$ hat zwar genauso 26 Zeilen wie die anderen Blätter, aber sie sind auf f. $104^r$ im Vergleich zu f. $103^v$ leicht zusammengedrängt, so daß für den Nachtrag von vornherein Platz bleibt und das Gleichgewicht der Seite nicht gestört wird.

274 stammt aus dem 10. Jahrhundert, das Bewußtsein, daß der kürzere Markusschluß hinter 16 : 8 und vor den langen Markusschluß gehörte, hat sich jedoch noch länger erhalten. Einziger Zeuge dafür ist bisher (von den im Institut für neutestamentliche Textforschung durchgeführten Kollationen ist möglicherweise neues Material zu erwarten, für den kurzen Markusschluß haben sie jedenfalls in 304, Paris Nationalbibl. Gr. 194, einen neuen Zeugen aus dem 12. Jahrhundert ergeben) die Minuskel 579 aus dem 13. Jahrhundert. Hier steht der kürzere Markusschluß auf f. $70^r$, unmittelbar an 16 : 8 anschließend. Nach *ἐφοβοῦντο γάρ* wird mit *τελος* das Ende der Lesung angegeben und ohne Zwischenraum oder irgendeine andere Hervorhebung im laufenden Text fortgefahren. Die Seite endet mit

dem letzten Wort des kürzeren Schlusses, + und αμην. Obwohl die Seite noch nicht ganz gefüllt ist, beginnt 16 : 9 (mit Initiale) erst auf dem Verso, dieses ganz füllend und wieder mit αμην schließend (aber ohne Sektionszahlen).

Von den vier Majuskeln, welche den kürzeren Markusschluß überliefern: 0112 (6./7. Jhdt.), 099 (7. Jhdt.), L (8. Jhdt.), Ψ (8./9. Jhdt.) verfährt Ψ so, daß der kürzere Schluß unmittelbar an 16 : 8 angeschlossen wird. 16 : 9–20 folgt auf ihn dann mit der einleitenden Bemerkung: εστιν δε και ταυτα φερομενα μετα το εφοβουντο γαρ. In 0112, 099 und L folgt der kurze Markusschluß ebenfalls auf 16 : 1–8, aber durch eine Zierlinie (o.ä.) abgetrennt (bei 0112 außerdem durch die subscriptio). In 0112 (wo der Anfang des kürzeren Schlusses fehlt, der lesbare Text beginnt mit ταυτα και αυτος)[6] folgt 16 : 9–20 mit derselben Einleitung wie bei Ψ unmittelbar, bei 099 (wo der kürzere Schluß anscheinend die Vorbemerkung hat[7]: εν τισιν αντιγραφων ταυτα φερεται) ist davor noch ein Zierstück eingeschoben, und setzt der lange Schluß mit einer Wiederholung von 8b ein, bei L wird der kürzere Schluß durch einen Zusatz eingeleitet: φερετε(αι) που και ταυτα, 16 : 9–20 folgt darauf mit derselben, aber in Zierlinien eingeschlossenen, Vorbemerkung wie bei Ψ.

Wenn wir *l* 1602 zum Schluß betrachten, dann haben wir in ihm den Typ der koptischen Überlieferung vor uns, soweit sie den kürzeren Markusschluß aufnimmt. Die Handschrift (Pierpont Morgan Library 615, Freiburg Univ. Bibliothek 615) ist wohl ins 7./8. Jahrhundert, evtl. etwas später, zu datieren. Für uns kommen die Folien 2–4 in Betracht (sämtlich in Freiburg). Auf f. 2$^{v}$ endet 16 : 8, und zwar so, daß noch eine Zeile freibleibt. Der Schreiber fährt auf f. 3$^{r}$ fort: εν αλλοις αντιγραφοις ουκ εγραφη ταυτα (in Auszeichnungsschrift) und schließt nach einer Zierlinie den kürzeren Schluß an. Wieder nach einer Zierlinie folgt: εστιν δε και ταυτα μεταφερομενα, worauf der lange Schluß, eingeleitet durch V. 8b, folgt. Der lange Schluß endet auf f. 4$^{r}$ Unmittelbar anschließend daran folgt dann (dem Aufbau der koptisch-griechischen Lektionare entsprechend) der koptische Text der Lektion, die 16 : 2–20 umfaßt. Auf f. 4$^{v}$ wird—das Koptische entspricht im Aufbau dem Griechischen—der kürzere

[6] Hier liegt die Ausgabe von Harris zu Grunde, die vorhandenen Fotos (zwei Folien der Hs. sind zusammengeklebt) erlauben nur eine begrenzte Kontrolle.

[7] Nach Horner von anderer Hand, auf dem Foto ist die einleitende Bemerkung nicht feststellbar.

Markusschluß folgendermaßen eingeleitet (Übersetzung nach Heer): In aliis exemplaribus haec inferuntur (müßte vielleicht heißen: addita sunt) adhuc, und der lange Markusschluß: Haec autem inferuntur (müßte vielleicht heißen: addita sunt) adhuc. Auffällig ist die Differenz zwischen den Einleitungstexten in der griechischen und der koptischen Überlieferung: im Koptischen stehen beide Schlüsse beinahe gleichwertig als verschiedene Nachträge nebeneinander (mit einer leichten Höherbewertung des kürzeren Schlusses), im Griechischen scheint der kürzere Schluß als Regel angesehen zu werden, so daß hervorgehoben wird, daß (manche) andere Handschriften ihn nicht haben, während der lange Schluß Ergänzungs- und Nachtragscharakter zu haben scheint.

Bereits aus dieser Übersicht, wenn sie auch nur in bezug auf die griechischen Zeugen vollständig ist (in bezug auf das Koptische ist noch manches, in bezug auf das Äthiopische noch so gut wie alles zu tun, ehe eine vollständige Übersicht möglich ist, s.o.), ergibt sich m.E. eine Reihe von Schlußfolgerungen:

(1) Die Entstehung des kürzeren Markusschlusses ist nur vorstellbar unter der Voraussetzung, daß das seinem Verfasser vorliegende Exemplar des Markusevangeliums mit 16:8 endete und ihm weder der lange Markusschluß noch eine andere Fortsetzung des Evangeliums bekannt war.

(2) Eigentlich schließt sich der kürzere Markusschluß an V. 8a an, er steht zu dem οὐδενὶ οὐδὲν εἶπαν im Widerspruch, weshalb k, der 16:8 und den kürzeren Schluß miteinander verbindet, V. 8 folgerichtig um diesen Satzteil kürzt.

(3) Deshalb, ebenso wegen seiner Kürze und Unbeholfenheit, weist der kürzere Schluß entweder auf eine frühe Entstehungszeit oder einen abgelegenen Entstehungsort—oder einen sehr ungewandten Verfasser hin. Er macht nicht den Eindruck einer Zusammenfassung von 16:9–20, sondern ist aus derselben Tendenz (Versuch der Abrundung eines als abrupt empfundenen Schlusses) in Zusammenfassung der Aussagen der anderen Evangelienschlüsse entstanden. So kann man ihn als primitive Parallelbildung zu 16:9–20 ansehen.

(4) Wenn er sich trotzdem in der griechischen Überlieferung bis ins 13. Jahrhundert erhalten und in der gesamten handschriftlichen Überlieferung eine Stellung vor dem langen Markusschluß behauptet hat, ergibt sich daraus eine starke Autorität. Sie ist in den Handschriften differenziert:

(a) Der lange Markusschluß wird überhaupt nicht zur Kenntnis genommen (oder ist nicht bekannt), der kürzere Schluß wird zum eigentlichen Abschluß des Evangeliums erhoben, und zwar unter Textänderung : k.

(b) Der kürzere Markusschluß wird direkt (ohne Änderung in V. 8) trotz des so entstehenden Widerspruchs an 16 : 1–8 angehängt (man hat das *οὐδενὶ οὐδὲν εἶπαν* offensichtlich nur als Schweigen gegenüber Außenstehenden interpretiert), so daß er den eigentlichen Abschluß des Evangeliums bildet : äthiopische Handschriften.

(c) Das Gleiche geschieht unter Zufügung von 16 : 9–20, wobei der lange Schluß Anhangscharakter erhält. Das ist bei 579 wie bei *Ψ* der Fall, wobei *Ψ* 16 : 9–20 durch seine einleitende Bemerkung sogar direkt zur Nebenüberlieferung erklärt.

(d) Dadurch, daß auch der kürzere Schluß eine einleitende Bemerkung erhält, rücken beide Schlüsse allmählich in ihrer Wertung nebeneinander : L.

(e) Der kürzere Schluß wird (unter Beibehaltung der beiden einleitenden Bemerkungen) von 16 : 1–8 immer stärker durch Zierlinien usw. abgetrennt : 0112 ; die Zusammengehörigkeit von 16 : 1–8 und 9–20 wird dadurch hervorgehoben, daß der lange Schluß V. 8b noch einmal aufnimmt : 099 (hier bekommt der kürzere Schluß außerdem eine einschränkende einleitende Bemerkung), *l* 1602, die koptische Überlieferung (s. Kahle).

Immer aber bleibt der kürzere Schluß in seiner ersten Position. Für das Stadium, in dem er aus den Handschriften verdrängt wird und der in den Handschriften des Abschnitts e) sich anbahnende organische Zusammenschluß von 16 : 1–8 und 16 : 9–20 durchgeführt wird, ist 274$^{\mathrm{mg}}$ bezeichnend : man ist sich noch bewußt, daß der kürzere Schluß zu 16 : 8 gehört, bringt das aber nur noch durch eine Zufügung am Rande zum Ausdruck. Schließlich wird an den kürzeren Schluß gar nicht mehr erinnert, er wird als überflüssig erachtet oder ist vergessen.

Die Versuchung ist nun nicht gering, auch die Handschriften in diesen Ablauf einzugliedern, welche den langen Schluß zwar an 16 : 8 anfügen, ihn aber durch textkritische Zeichen oder Bemerkungen als nicht überall überliefert und anerkannt charakterisieren. Man würde dann sagen, daß sich das zur selben Zeit wie die in Abschnitt e) charakterisierte Entwicklung vollzog oder im Anschluß daran. Das braucht aber keineswegs so geschehen zu sein. Vielmehr ist es ebenso gut möglich, daß der kürzere und der lange Schluß in völlig voneinander verschiedenen Bezirken entstanden. Unabhängig voneinander wurde Mk 16 : 8 durch eine Neubildung abgeschlossen; von dem Augenblick ab, wo sie aufeinander trafen, kam es erst zur Mischbildung, bis schließlich der lange Schluß siegte, was angesichts seines größeren Reichtums und seiner überlegenen Qualität unvermeidbar war. Problematisch bei dieser Annahme bleibt nur, daß bei allen Mischbildungen, die wir kennen, der kürzere Schluß die erste Stelle behauptet—und zwar gegen den Textzusammenhang (der lange Schluß fügt sich sehr viel besser an) und trotz der größeren Qualität seines Konkurrenten. Irgendetwas Besonderes muß dem kürzeren Schluß in den Augen derer, die ihn tradierten, angehangen haben.

Nun könnte jemand den gordischen Knoten dadurch gewaltsam lösen wollen, daß er behauptete, die uns bekannten Handschriften führten in die Irre. Denn sie seien sämtlich ägyptischen Ursprungs. Der kürzere Markusschluß nehme in ihnen nur deshalb eine so prominente Stelle ein, weil es sich bei ihm um eine ägyptische Lokaltradition handelte, welcher die Schreiber der von außerhalb Ägyptens kommenden Überlieferung des langen Schlusses den Vorzug gaben. Für eine solche These ließe sich anführen, daß L, Ψ, 099, 0112, 579 sämtlich bei v. Soden unter dem Sigel H laufen. Das Phänomen der koptischen Handschriften bzw. koptisch-griechischen Bilinguen könnte diese These verstärken. Aber—sie gehören eindeutig ans Ende der sachlichen Entwicklung (*l* 1602 gibt außerdem zu erkennen, daß der kürzere Schluß in der griechischen Tradition eine stärkere Stellung besitzt als in der koptischen), am Anfang steht (der Sache, wie dem Alter nach: 4./5. Jahrhundert!) eine altlateinische Handschrift, der Afrikaner k. 274 wird von Soden außerdem unter seine Gruppe $K^x$ gerechnet, gehört also sicher nicht in die ägyptische Überlieferung, die außerdem den langen Schluß schon verhältnismäßig früh bietet (vgl. die breite Unzialüberlieferung dafür). Außerdem ist der kürzere Schluß ja nicht nur im altlateinischen sondern auch im syrischen (Harclensis) und äthiopischen Sprachbereich bezeugt. Natürlich wird niemand mit Sicherheit sagen können, wo er sich zuerst bildete und ausbreitete. Aber die Wahrscheinlichkeit, daß das in Ägypten geschah, ist nicht sehr groß, vorausgesetzt, daß es vor 200 geschah. Denn damals lebte die ägyptische Kirche noch in der Isolierung (vgl. W. Bauer); als sie diese um 200 durchbrach, war der kürzere Schluß offensichtlich bereits Bestandteil des Markusevangeliums in mehreren Sprachbereichen.

Aber wann ist der kürzere Schluß entstanden? G. Hartmann (*Der Aufbau des Markusevangeliums*, Münster, 1936) antwortet darauf mit erstaunlicher Zuversicht: im Jahre 63. Damals trat nach Hartmann Markus seine Reise aus Rom nach Kleinasien an, dazu " passen Stimmung und Stil der kurz hingeworfenen zwei Sätze des k(ürzeren) S(chlusses) " (S. 256), nach seiner Rückkehr stellte Markus dann in größerer Ruhe den langen Schluß fertig (S. 255, ähnlich allerdings auch Streeter). Daß es so nicht gewesen ist, bedarf wohl keiner Darlegung. Aber wann ist der kürzere Schluß entstanden? Fragen wir die Kommentare, so erhalten wir, soweit sie überhaupt darauf eingehen, zwei Antworten: im 4. Jahrhundert (oder etwas früher: Wohlenberg[8]) Lohmeyer,[9] J. Weiss,[10] W. Grundmann,[11] Staab,[12] Dehn [13] und zwar in Ägypten, oder: ganz früh, vor dem 1. Klemensbrief (A. E. J. Rawlinson [14]), und zwar im Westen.[15]

[8] Zahns *Kommentar*, 1910, S. 390, so wie Zahns *Einleitung* ($^{3}$II, 233): " Der kürzere Text läßt sich zwar nicht höher als in das 4. Jahrh. herauf verfolgen, mag aber schon im 3. Jahrh. entstanden sein, und zwar wahrscheinlich in Ägypten, von wo er in einzelne Handschriften des altlateinischen Afrikas eindrang ". H. Branscomb (*Moffatt Commentary*), 1952, S. 314 drückt sich allgemein aus: " the ending was added after the Christian message had spread over a large part of the Roman world ".

[9] Meyers *Kommentar*, 14. Aufl. 1957, S. 364 ebenfalls etwas eingeschränkt: "scheint . . . aus Ägypten zu stammen und spätestens Anfang des 4. Jahrhunderts entstanden zu sein ". Eine Anmerkung ist hier allerdings nicht zu unterdrücken: Ich habe hier, wie früher in ähnlichen Zusammenhängen, darauf verzichtet, textkritische Irrtümer bei den ca. 40 von mir auf den Gegenstand dieser Studie hin durchgesehenen Kommentaren zu verzeichnen, bei Lohmeyer übersteigt die Zahl der Irrtümer das erlaubte Maß jedoch bei weitem: der Codex Bobbiensis (k) ist bei ihm h, L erscheint als *Γ* usw. usw.

[10] *Die Schriften des Neuen Testaments*, 2 vol., Göttingen, $^{3}$1917, I, 226: " der nach den ältesten handschriftlichen Zeugnissen im 4. Jahrhundert entstanden sein wird, und zwar wahrscheinlich in der ägyptischen Kirche ".

[11] *Das Evangelium nach Markus*, Theol. Handkommentar, Berlin, $^{3}$1962, S. 325: " Wahrscheinlich in Ägypten, weil in Texten aus und um Ägypten bezeugt, ist im vierten Jahrhundert dem Markus-Evangelium eine kürzere Schlußform zugefügt worden ".

[12] *Das Evangelium nach Markus* (Echter-Bibel), 1956, S. 98: " Ein Schreiber des 4. Jahrhunderts, der diesen letzteren (den langen) Mk-Schluß nicht kannte, wird die Worte an $16^{8}$ angefügt haben."

[13] *Der Gottessohn*, S. 254 " vermutlich erst aus dem 4. Jahrhundert, dessen Sprache er deutlich redet ".

[14] *St. Mark* (*Westminster Commentaries*), London, 1960, S. 248: " Like the

Bedauerlicherweise lassen uns die Kirchenväter bei unserer Frage im Stich. Mit ihrer Hilfe können wir lediglich den terminus ante quem für den langen Markusschluß feststellen. Das altbekannte Wort des Irenäus adv. haer. 3, 10, 6 (S. Chr. 34, 178):

In fine autem evangelii ait Marcus: Et quidem Dominus Jesus, posteaquam locutus est eis, receptus est in caelos et sedit ad dexteram Dei.

ist und bleibt das früheste sichere Zeugnis dafür. Das Diatessaron Tatians, das den langen Markusschluß gekannt zu haben scheint, gehört derselben Generation an wie Irenäus. Darüber hinaus führt möglicherweise noch Justin Ap. 45, 5 (Krüger 38 : 9 f.):

Τὸ οὖν εἰρημένον " Ῥάβδον δυνάμεως ἐξαποστελεῖ σοι ἐξ Ἰερουσαλήμ " προαγγελτικὸν τοῦ λόγου τοῦ ἰσχυροῦ, ὃν ἀπὸ Ἰερουσαλὴμ οἱ ἀπόστολοι αὐτοῦ ἐξελθόντες πανταχοῦ ἐκήρυξαν

und Hermas 102 : 2 (Sim. 9, 25, 2, Whittaker [2]95)

ἀπόστολοι καὶ διδάσκαλοι οἱ κηρύξαντες εἰς ὅλον τὸν κόσμον καὶ οἱ διδάξαντες σεμνῶς καὶ ἁγνῶς τὸν λόγον τοῦ κυρίου καὶ μηδὲν ὅλως νοσφισάμενοι . . .

Mit Irenäus sind wir vor 180, denn er hat den Markusschluß, über den er in adv. haer. berichtet, ja schon vorgefunden. Mit Justin und Hermas gelangten wir bis ±150, wenn man in beiden eine Bezugnahme auf den langen Markusschluß finden will, wobei Justin noch eher einen Hinweis bedeutet als Hermas. Im Petrusevangelium wie in der Epistula apostolorum scheinen ebenfalls Hinweise auf den langen Markusschluß zu finden sein:

Petrusevang. 59 (E. Klostermann, *Kleine Texte*, [2]1908, S. 7)

ἡμεῖς δὲ οἱ δώδεκα μαθηταὶ τοῦ κυρίου ἐκλαίομεν καὶ ἐλυπούμεθα, καὶ ἕκαστος λυπούμενος διὰ τὸ συμβὰν ἀπηλλάγη εἰς τὸν οἶκον αὐτοῦ.

Epistula apostolorum 2 (TU 43, 2 , 4 u. 7, hier die Übers. von S. 39)

(Und)es sind gegangen zu jenem Orte drei Frauen: Maria, die zu Martha Gehörige, und Maria Magdalena, und sie nahmen Salbe, um sie zu gießen auf seinen Leichnam, indem sie weinten und trauerten über das, was geschehen war . . . Wie sie aber trauerten und weinten, offenbarte sich der Herr ihnen . . .

---

longer ending, it was probably written at Rome. The phrase ' from the East as far as to the West ' is possibly echoed by Clement (*Ad Corinth.* v. 6), who wrote from Rome about A.D. 96."

[15] So auch C. E. B. Cranfield, *The Gospel according to St. Mark*, Cambridge, 1963, S. 476 (ohne Angabe der angenommenen Zeit): " apparently in the west ".

Die (wenn auch im Vokabular etwas abgewandelten) Aussage über das Weinen und Trauern (im Petrusevangelium der Apostel, in der Epistula apostolorum allerdings der Frauen) findet sich in den Evangelien singulär bei Markus, und zwar 16 : 10. So hätten wir hier evtl. einen Hinweis, der zeitlich noch über Justin hinausführt, gleichzeitig aber auch eine deutliche Abwehr der angesichts der eben zitierten Quellen möglichen Theorie, der lange Markusschluß sei im Westen entstanden. Das Petrus-Evangelium wie die Epistula apostolorum sind sicher nicht westlicher Herkunft; außerdem sollte die Bezeugung des langen Markusschlusses im Cureton-Syrer wie in der sonstigen orientalischen Textüberlieferung von vornherein von einer solchen These abhalten.

Eine eindeutige Antwort auf die Frage nach Alter und Herkunft des langen Markusschlusses hätten wir, wenn wir der von Conybeare zum ersten Mal bekanntgemachten Notiz der armenischen Handschrift E 222 trauen könnten. Hier heißt es zum langen Markusschluß in einer mit roter Tinte geschriebenen Überschrift: Ariston eritzu (= Αριστωνος του πρεσβυτερου). Aristion wird von Papias nach dem Bericht des Euseb (KG 3, 39, 7) als eine seiner Quellen genannt—womit wir etwa an die Zeit der Wende vom 1. zum 2. Jahrhundert gelangt wären (und in den Osten!). Aber man tut wohl gut, in jener armenischen Zuschreibung nicht mehr als eine aus Eusebs Bericht entsprossene, wenn auch interessante, Konjektur zu sehen. Lagrange, *Critique textuelle* 2, p. 369 bemerkt zu Conybeares Theorie mit Recht " L'identification ne repose cependant que sur une approximation ". Mit einiger Sicherheit wird man nicht mehr sagen können, als daß der lange Markusschluß (bestenfalls) bis in die 1. Hälfte des zweiten Jahrhunderts zurückzuverfolgen ist.

Die Ausbeute in bezug auf frühe Kirchenväterzitate aus dem langem Markusschluß ist also mager genug. In bezug auf den kürzeren Schluß ist sie praktisch gleich Null. Nun muß man allerdings zugeben: wenn schon der lange Markusschluß (wegen seiner Berührung mit den anderen Evangelienschlüssen) in den Kirchenväterzitaten äußerst mühsam zu identifizieren ist, so gilt das noch mehr für den kürzeren Schluß. Was ist aus ihm zitierbar? Was hier mit unbeholfenen Worten gesagt war, konnte jeder Kirchenvater mit eigenen Worten besser sagen. Irgendwelche Fakten, die sonst nicht in den Evangelien standen, waren hier ebenfalls nicht berichtet. G. Mink hat in langer Arbeit die Sammlungen des Instituts auf Zitate aus den Markusschlüssen durchgesehen (und ihnen eine ganze Reihe neuer hinzugefügt), ein Hinweis auf den kürzeren Schluß fand sich unter ihnen nicht.

Wenn Rawlinson (s.o.) in 1. Klem. 5 : 6 die Aussage über Paulus: κῆρυξ γενόμενος ἔν τε τῇ ἀνατολῇ καὶ ἐν τῇ δύσει das ἀπὸ ἀνατολῆς καὶ ἄχρι (μέχρι) δύσεως des kürzeren Markusschlusses finden will, so geht das doch wohl (selbst wenn man das Verhältnis umkehrt) zu weit, auch für den, der hier nicht—wie gelegentlich geschehen—einen bloßen Reflex der Septuaginta (Ps 112 : 3) findet.

Die einzige Formulierung im kürzeren Markusschluß, die einen Einsatz möglich zu machen scheint, ist die vom ἱερὸν καὶ ἄφθαρτον κήρυγμα τῆς αἰωνίου σωτηρίας. Aber hier versagen alle Hilfsmittel. Hebr. 5 : 9 nennt Christus (nach Jes. 45 : 17) αἴτιος σωτηρίας αἰωνίου. Κήρυγμα kommt in den Evangelien nur Matth. 12 : 41; Luk 11 : 32 vor, und zwar lediglich als κήρυγμα Ἰωνᾶ. Etwas häufiger findet es sich in den paulinischen Briefen (1. Kor. 1 : 21; 2 : 4; 15 : 14; Röm. 16 : 25; 2. Tim 4 : 17; Tit. 1 : 3), aber jedesmal ohne Prädikationen, die an den kürzeren Markusschluß erinnern könnten. Ganz ähnlich ist es bei den Apostolischen Vätern (Barn. 12 : 6; Herm. 69 : 2; 92 : 4; 93 : 5). Bei den Apologeten liegen die Dinge nicht viel anders, κήρυγμα begegnet ganz selten (3mal bei Justin, im Normalfall aber, ebenso wie das Verb, auf das Alte Testament bezogen, vgl. dazu K. Goldammer, " Der Kerygma-Begriff in der ältesten christlichen Literatur ", *ZNTW* 48, 1957, 77–101). Bei Clemens Alexandrinus wird der Gebrauch des Wortes häufiger. Stählins Register nennt 18 Stellen (ohne die Bezugnahme auf das κήρυγμα Πέτρου), aber wieder ohne eigentliche Parallele zu unserem Text. Wenn Polyaenus im 2. Jahrhundert (*Strat.* 4, 7, 6) vom κήρυγμα τῆς ἐλευθερίας spricht, so will uns diese heidnische Parallele auch nicht viel helfen.

Ganz ähnlich steht es mit dem ἄφθαρτος, das als Beiwort zum κήρυγμα gebraucht wird. Das Wort begegnet im Neuen Testament (neben dem siebenmal gebrauchten ἀφθαρσία) siebenmal: es wird von Gott, von der κληρονομία, der σπορά, der ἀγάπη usw. ausgesagt. Auch bei den Apostolischen Vätern begegnet es mehrfach (Barn. 16 : 9; 19 : 8; 2. Klem. 6 : 6; 7 : 3; Ignatius, Trall. 11 : 2; Röm. 7 : 3), aber wieder ohne einen Bezug, der uns weiterhülfe. Bei den Apologeten findet es sich 12mal, bei Clemens Alexandrinus verzeichnet es Stählin 14mal—immer ohne daß sich eine Parallele zu unserem Text ergäbe. Lampes *Patristic*

*Greek Lexicon* gibt gewiß nur eine begrenzte Auswahl, aber sie umfaßt immerhin 3 Spalten: eine Anwendung wie im kürzeren Markusschluß zeigt sie nicht, nicht einmal einen ähnlichen sachlichen Gebrauch. Unter κήρυγμα finden wir wenigstens einige Male das σωτήριον κήρυγμα (bei Euseb u.a.), aber auch das hilft uns nicht.

Methodius von Olympos (†311) hat G. Mink schließlich als den Schriftsteller aufgestöbert, der in seiner Aussage dem kürzeren Markusschluß am ähnlichsten komme. Sämtliche von ihm beigebrachten Belegstellen seien der Reihe nach zitiert:

Symp. 3, 8 (GCS 37 : 8 f.):

. . . βοηθοῦντες τῷ κηρύγματι πρὸς τὴν τῶν λοιπῶν σωτηρίαν.

Symp. 4, 4 (GCS 50 : 1–2):

. . . ὅτι τὸ εὐαγγέλιον ἱερὰν ᾠδὴν εἶναι καὶ ἀπόρρητον διδάσκουσιν, ἣν οἱ ἁμαρτάνοντες . . . τῷ πονηρῷ προσᾴδουσιν.

Symp. 10, 3 (GCS 125 : 9–11):

καὶ πρῶτον αὐτῷ τὸ κήρυγμα μετὰ τὴν παράβασιν πέμπεται τὸ διὰ Νῶε, ἵν' ἐὰν προσσχῇ κἂν τούτῳ σωθῆναι τῆς ἁμαρτίας ἰσχύσῃ, ἀνάπαυσεν ἐπαγγελόμενον . . .

de autex. 1, 2 (GCS 146 : 2–6):

θείας δέ τινος ἀπολαύειν φωνῆς εὔχομαι, ἧς κἂν πολλάκις ἀκούσω . . ., οὐκ ἀκολάστῳ <τινὶ> φωνῆς ἡδονῇ νενικημένος, ἀλλὰ θεῖα διδασκόμενος μυστήρια καὶ τὸ τέλος οὐ θάνατον, ἀλλ' αἰώνιον ἀπεκδεχόμενος σωτηρίαν.

de autex. 1, 6 (GCS 147 : 6–7):

θάνατον οὐκ ἔχει· σωτηρίας ἐστὶν διήγημα ἡ παρ' ἡμῖν ᾠδή.

de resurr. 2, 8, 8 (GCS 345 : 2–5):

" ὁ γὰρ νόμος τοῦ πνεύματος τῆς ζωῆς ", ὅ δή ἐστι τὸ εὐαγγέλιον . . . διὰ τοῦ κηρύγματος πρὸς ὑπακοὴν τεθεὶς καὶ ἄφεσιν ἁμαρτημάτων . . .

contra Porph. 5 (GCS 507 : 15 f.)[16]:

φαίνεται γοῦν οἰκεῖον μὲν ἀληθῶς ἀγαθὸν ἡ περὶ τὸ ἄφθαρτόν τε καὶ θεῖον ἐπιστροφὴ καὶ πίστις.

Aber auch bei wohlwollendem Bemühen ist hier keine wörtliche Parallele zu finden, welche in die Nähe des kürzeren Markusschlusses führte. Gewiß klingt das ἱερὸν καὶ ἄφθαρτον

[16] Zur Echtheit dieser Schrift vgl. jedoch Buchheit, *TU* 69, S. 120 ff.

κήρυγμα dem, der liturgische Formeln der Ostkirche im Ohr hat, unwillkürlich spät, aber erst einmal müssen Belege—und zwar spätestens aus dem 4. Jahrhundert—dafür gefunden werden. Spätestens aus dem 4. Jahrhundert aus zwei Gründen: Der Codex Bobbiensis ist zwar im 4./5. Jahrhundert geschrieben, aber er gibt ganz sicher—das zeigt schon seine Unbeholfenheit—eine sehr viel frühere Textvorlage wieder (vgl. S. 176).

Außerdem scheint, worauf schon Th. Zahn im Jahre 1892 hingewiesen hat (*Geschichte des neutestamentlichen Kanons* II, 2, S. 912 f.) der Codex Vaticanus den kürzeren Markusschluß zu kennen. Nach dem Schluß des Markusevangeliums in Spalte 3 von S. 1303 (Recto) läßt B nämlich (benutzt wird die neue Farbreproduktion, auf Anordnung Papst Pauls VI. hergestellt, Vatikanstadt 1965) eine Spalte frei, ein ganz singuläres Phänomen. Denn in der Handschrift folgt ein neues Buch dem vorangehenden sogleich in der nächsten Spalte, wobei gerade die Spalte 3 des Recto (beim Ende der vorangehenden Schrift in Spalte 2) nicht selten als Einsatz verwandt wird: S. 1277 des Markusevangeliums, S. 1399 des Johannesevangeliums, S. 1437 des 1. Johannesbriefes, S. 1443 des Judasbriefes (in Spalte 1 hatte der 3. Joh. begonnen, der mit Spalte 2 ausläuft), S. 1461 des 1. Korintherbriefes.

Dieses erstaunliche Faktum der freien Spalte nach dem Schluß des Markusevangeliums läßt sich nur so erklären, daß der Schreiber von einer Fortsetzung nach 16:8 wußte, über deren Aufnahme er sich bei der Niederschrift jedoch nicht endgültig klar war. Sie ist dann (auf Veranlassung des Leiters des Scriptoriums, oder dessen, für den die Handschrift bestimmt war, oder einer befragten kirchlichen Stelle) unterblieben. Dabei kann es sich nur um den kürzeren Markusschluß gehandelt haben. Spalte 1 von S. 1303 hat die regulären 42 Zeilen mit Mk 15:43 ἐλθὼν Ἰωσήφ bis 16:3 ἀποκυλίσει ἡ[μῖν, d.h. nicht ganz 19 Nestlezeilen, Mk 16:9–20 umfaßt dagegen 26 Nestlezeilen. Wenn Hartmann (S. 238) den langen Schluß trotzdem in Spalte 3 unterbringen möchte (in Spalte 2 seien ja noch 11 Zeilen frei, außerdem hätte der Schreiber in Spalte 3 durch "Zusammendrängen der Zeilen" mehr Platz erzielen können), so hat er sich den Codex Vaticanus nicht genau angesehen. Nirgendwo findet sich in der ganz sorgfältig geschriebenen Handschrift zum Schluß eines neutestamentlichen Buches eine solche Vermehrung der Zeilenzahl. Außerdem stehen die zusätzlichen 11 Zeilen nicht (oder bestenfalls 3–4) zur Verfügung, denn die subscriptio, die jetzt in Spalte 2 steht, braucht ja auch ihren Raum, und der ist jetzt schon für das Markusevangelium recht knapp bemessen.

Daß der Codex Bobbiensis trotz seiner Niederschrift im 4./5. Jahrhundert in sehr viel frühere Zeiten zurückreicht, ist eine Binsenweisheit (die meisten altlateinischen Handschriften sind sehr viel später als er geschrieben und werden von der Forschung dennoch bedenkenlos als Repräsentanten einer sehr frühen Zeit genommen). Auch eine andere Tatsache erzwingt diese Annahme, nämlich die enge Zusammengehörigkeit von k mit dem Bibeltext Cyprians (" So ist es evident, daß Cyprians Citate und die Hs k einen variantenlos identischen griechischen Text voraussetzen ", H. v. Soden, *Das lateinische NT*, 1909, S. 133).[17] Außerdem dürfte im Beginn des 3. Jahrhunderts der lange Markusschluß in Afrika durchaus bekannt gewesen sein, worauf Zitate z.B. bei Tertullian und anderen hinweisen, im 4./5. Jahrhundert ist er weithin anerkannt, wie die große Zahl (man kann beinahe sagen : die Fülle) der Zitate daraus und die Bezugnahme darauf bei Augustin beweisen. Daß der kürzere Schluß in k, und zwar unter Veränderung von 16 : 8, erst im 4./5. Jahrhundert eingefügt wurde, ist eine völlige Unmöglichkeit, bestenfalls kann das im Anfang des 3. Jahrhunderts geschehen sein, wo man noch annehmen kann, daß in Afrika die Zahl der Handschriften mit dem kurzen Schluß relativ groß war. Aller Wahrscheinlichkeit nach geht die Urform von k jedoch auf eine griechische Vorlage zurück—womit wir im 2. Jahrhundert angelangt wären.

Es gibt ja möglicherweise noch einen weiteren Hinweis auf die Existenz des kürzeren Markusschlusses in der altlateinischen Überlieferung. Der Codex Vercellensis (a) aus dem 4. Jh. bricht auf f. 632b mit Mk 15 : 5 (Pilatus autem) ab, f. 633 bringt von jüngerer Hand Mk 16 : 7 (ab : galileam)—20 im Vulgatatext. Nach Gasquet (Coll. Bibl. Lat. III, Codex Vercellensis pars II, Rom 1914, S. 241 Anm. a) haben die früheren Herausgeber, Bianchini und Irico, nun zwischen f. 632 und dem heutigen f. 633 noch Reste von vier Blättern festgestellt. C. H. Turner (*JTS* 29, 1927–28, 16–18) hat auf dieses merkwürdige Phänomen aufmerksam gemacht und es näher untersucht. Er geht dabei (mit Recht) von der Voraussetzung aus, daß die verlorenen Blätter

[17] Vgl. auch B. M. Metzgers (*The Text of the NT*, New York, 1964, S. 73) Hinweis auf Lowe : " According to E. A. Lowe k shows palaeographical marks of having been copied from a second-century papyrus ".

den altlateinischen Text enthielten, und daß das letzte Blatt mit Mk 16 : 7a praecedo vos schloß, so daß das zu ersetzende Blatt [18] mit galileam ibi eum videbitis sicut dicerat vobis o.ä. beginnen mußte.

Wenn diese Theorie zutrifft—und sie scheint stichhaltig—, ergibt sich in der Tat kein anderer Schluß, als Turner ihn zieht: "a in fact must have had either the Shorter Ending or none at all" (S. 18). Ja, man kann noch weiter gehen: f. 632b (a ist zweispaltig geschrieben) ist gut erhalten, die Spalte hat (wie 632a, die teilweise zerstört ist) 24 Zeilen mit im Durchschnitt 10 Buchstaben. Mk 16 : 7b ab galileam bis 16 : 8 würden nur 10 Zeilen ausmachen, also sehr wenig für ein Blatt, das bis zu 96 Zeilen enthalten kann, wenn es beidseitig beschrieben ist. Der lange Markusschluß ist hier nicht unterzubringen, wohl aber der kürzere Schluß, mit welchem die erste Seite fast gefüllt wurde, während die zweite leer blieb. Ein Abschluß mit Mk 16 : 8 würde ein merkwürdiges Bild ergeben haben, zu der hervorragend und mit aller Sorgfalt geschriebenen Handschrift ganz unpassend. Ist das alles aber so—wir dürfen den hypothetischen Charakter der Rekonstruktion nicht vergessen—,dann zeichnet sich neben dem altlateinischen afrikanischen auch ein europäischer Zeuge für den kürzeren Markusschluß mindestens als Möglichkeit ab, wodurch das Bild eine wesentliche Abrundung gewinnt.

Das zweite Jahrhundert hat als Entstehungszeit des kürzeren

[18] Turner zieht als Möglichkeit in Betracht, daß die Heraustrennung der 4 Blätter zusammen mit der Ergänzung geschah: "Perhaps the original intention was to preserve the first three, and bind them up again with the new fourth leaf: perhaps the instructions for removing the last leaf were misunderstood as being instructions for removing the last gathering" (S. 18). Diese Theorie scheint unnötig kompliziert. Es genügt völlig die Annahme, daß der Codex noch vollständig war, als die Ergänzung erfolgte, die ihren Grund entweder in der gewünschten Korrektur des Textes hatte (so daß man das 4. Blatt herausriß und ersetzte) oder einfach deshalb geschah, weil das letzte Blatt verloren gegangen war. Die Abtrennung der fehlenden drei Blätter mit Mark 15 : 5–16 : 7a erfolgte später zufällig und irregulär (nach der Vulgataergänzung)—wenn die Abtrennung planmäßig und ordnungsgemäß geschehen wäre, wäre sie sauber erfolgt und hätte nicht Blattreste hinterlassen. A. Gasquet (ed., *Codex Versellensis* . . ., Roma, 1914, S. I, XI f.) spricht die Vermutung aus, daß f. 633 zu der Zeit geschrieben wurde, als Berengar 887 den Codex binden ließ. Unter dieser Voraussetzung bleibt eigentlich keine andere Möglichkeit als die Annahme, daß die Handschrift damals entweder bis Mark 16: 7a (oder weiter) reichte: das letzte Blatt wurde ergänzt, weil es fehlte (das Wahrscheinlichere), oder es wurde ersetzt, damit der Text die gewohnte Form bot. Die fehlenden weiteren drei Blätter hat ein Sammler irgendwann in den rund 1000 Jahren danach herausgerissen, das letzte Blatt verschonte er, weil es in seinem Äußeren mit der schönen alten Majuskel nicht zu vergleichen war.

Markusschlusses ohnehin alle Wahrscheinlichkeit für sich. Hierfür spricht nicht nur die immer wieder bestätigte textkritische Erfahrung, daß alle wesentlichen Textänderungen im Normalfall ins 2. Jahrhundert zurückgehen (mit Ausnahme z.B. des aus eindeutigen dogmatischen Interessen später Zeit entstandenen Comma Joanneum (W. Thieles Versuch, es früher zu datieren—" Beobachtungen zum Comma Johanneum ", *ZNTW* 50, 1959, 61 ff.—scheint mir nicht geglückt). Sondern ich sehe auch keine andere Erklärung für das Faktum des kürzeren Markusschlusses. Spätestens um die Mitte des 2. Jahrhunderts ist der lange Markusschluß entstanden. Er hatte vor dem kürzeren alle Vorteile. Wohin er vordrang, mußte er eigentlich das Feld behaupten. Dennoch hält sich der kürzere Markusschluß bis ins 13. Jahrhundert (579), und zwar im unmittelbaren Anschluß an 16 : 8 und weist den langen Markusschluß in die zweite Position, wo er mit ihm zusammen überliefert wird, im griechischen wie im koptischen Bereich. Seine Primitivität ist nur aus seiner frühen Entstehung zu erklären. Dass sein Verfasser es unternahm, dem Markusevangelium einen über Vers 8 hinausführenden Abschluß zu geben, ist nur unter der Voraussetzung vorstellbar, daß er—und seine Umgebung—vom langen Markusschluß nichts wußten.

Will man den kürzeren Schluß in eine spätere Zeit datieren, muß man die These eines entlegenen Entstehungsortes oder eines außergewöhnlich unbegabten Verfassers zu Hilfe nehmen. Dabei bleibt aber die Frage unbeantwortet und unbeantwortbar, wie er sich eine solche Verbreitung und vor allem die Stellung vor dem langen Markusschluß erwerben konnte, während doch alle Logik danach drängte, ihn—wie die modernen Ausgaben das tun—hinter den langen Markusschluß als Anhang zu stellen. Er enthält keine dogmatische oder sonstige Aussage, die ihn der Kirche besonders wertvoll machen konnte. Seine Formulierungen stehen wie ein erratischer Block in der Aussage der christlichen Schriftsteller. Nirgendwo—ob früh oder spät—hat sich bisher seine Formulierung ἱερὸν καὶ ἄφθαρτον κήρυγμα τῆς αἰωνίου σωτηρίας wiederfinden lassen. Solange das nicht der Fall ist, scheint mir kein anderer Ausweg als die hier vorgeschlagene Auffassung zu bleiben. Über den Ort der Entstehung läßt sich nichts sagen, ich würde jedoch meinen, daß Ägypten ebensowenig in Betracht kommt wie der eigentliche Westen. Als frühestes Entstehungsdatum ist die Zeit der Apostolischen Väter in Betracht zu ziehen. Ebenso gut ist es aber möglich, daß er etwa gleichzeitig mit dem langen Markusschluß entstanden ist oder kurz danach, also um die Mitte des 2. Jahrhunderts.

Goldammer (S. 80) meint, um der " Epitheta aus der kultisch-mystischen Sphäre " willen, bei dem ἱερὸν καὶ ἄφθαρτον κήρυγμα des kürzeren Markusschlusses handle es sich "um eine in gnostisch-mythologischer Terminologie umschriebene Hypostasierung der Heilsbotschaft ". Wenn seine Auffassung richtig ist, die immerhin eine Erklärung für das auffällige Vokabular bietet, wäre sie ein deutlicher Hinweis auf die Entstehung des kürzeren Markusschlusses im 2. Jahrhundert. Eine andere Beobachtung ergibt jedoch vielleicht eine direkte Unterstützung der These von der frühen Entstehung des kürzeren Markusschlusses. Soweit ich sehe, existiert zu seiner Formulierung τοῖς περὶ τὸν Πέτρον eine eigentliche Parallele nur bei Ignatius. Dieser erzählt Smyrn. 3 : 2 : ὅτε (Jesus) πρὸς τοὺς περὶ Πέτρον ἦλθεν, ἔφη αὐτοῖς. Im Neuen Testament findet sich einige Male eine vergleichbare Ausdrucksweise: Lk 8 : 45 heißt es in einer Reihe von Handschriften εἶπεν ὁ Πέτρος (καὶ οἱ σὺν αὐτῷ) parallel zur Formulierung von 9 : 32 : ὁ δὲ Πέτρος καὶ οἱ σὺν αὐτῷ. Dazu kommen noch Apg. 2 : 14 : Πέτρος σὺν τοῖς ἕνδεκα und 5 : 29 : Πέτρος καὶ οἱ ἀπόστολοι. Das sind alle in Betracht kommenden Stellen des Neuen Testaments—und gleichzeitig der gesamten frühchristlichen Literatur. Sie stehen der Formulierung im kürzeren Markusschluß und bei Ignatius verhältnismäßig nahe, sind aber nicht damit zu identifizieren.

Daß der kürzere Markusschluß wie Ignatius mit denen περὶ (τὸν) Πέτρον die Apostel meint, steht außer Zweifel. Smyrn. 3 : 2 leitet mit dem ἔφη αὐτοῖς ein Jesuswort aus einer apokryphen Quelle ein, das aber ganz parallel dem von Lk 24 : 39 ist, also aus dem Bericht über eine Erscheinung vor den Aposteln stammt. Und wenn im kürzeren Markusschluß gesagt wird, die Frauen hätten τοῖς περὶ τὸν Πέτρον Bericht erstattet, so kann sich das nach den parallelen Aussagen Matth 28 : 8 und Lk 24 : 9 wieder nur auf die Apostel beziehen. Zu Beginn des 2. Jahrhunderts kann man von den Aposteln noch auf diese Weise reden, später ist das nicht mehr möglich. Jedenfalls habe ich in der Literatur des 2. Jahrhunderts keinen weiteren Beleg für diese Ausdrucksweise gefunden (vgl. dazu auch J. Wagemann, *Die Stellung des Apostels Paulus neben den Zwölf in den ersten zwei Jahrhunderten*, Giessen, 1926, dessen zusätzliche Durchsicht ebenfalls keinen Beleg ergab). Und später scheint mir eine solche Bezeichnung der "Zwölf" mehr und mehr ausgeschlossen, wird doch diese Bezeichnung zu einem die höchsten Wertmaßstäbe setzenden festen Begriff, der eine solche Beschreibung wie im kürzeren Markusschluß und bei Ignatius nicht mehr zuläßt.

Daß wir nur insgesamt 6 griechische Textzeugen für den kürzeren Markusschluß kennen, ist kein Gegenargument gegen seine frühe Entstehung. Man muß sich vielmehr wundern, daß es überhaupt so viele sind—vergessen wir nicht, daß der kurze Markusschluß bisher nur in 3, mit der neu entdeckten Minuskel 304 zusammen in 4 griechischen Textzeugen überliefert ist. Denn der lange Markusschluß hatte, sobald er erst einmal verbreitet wurde, gegenüber dem kurzen wie gegenüber dem kürzeren Markusschluß alle Wettbewerbsvorteile für sich. Endgültiges zum kürzeren Markusschluß wird sich verständlicherweise erst sagen lassen, wenn seine orientalische Überlieferung besser aufgearbeitet ist als heute, und wenn aus der Kirchenväterüberlieferung mehr Parallelen zu seinem Sprachgebrauch beigebracht werden können, als das bis jetzt der Fall ist—deshalb auch die zurückhaltende Formulierung des Titels dieser Studie. Sollte jedoch die Kirchenväterüberlieferung auch in Zukunft nicht wesentlich über den vorgetragenen Stand hinausgebracht werden können, würde das eine nachdrückliche Bekräftigung der hier eingenommenen Position bedeuten.

# GADARENES, GERASENES, GERGESENES AND THE "DIATESSARON" TRADITIONS *

TJ. BAARDA

How difficult must have been the task of scholars who tried to establish the "original" text of the Greek New Testament in Mt 8 : 28 ; Mk 5 : 1 ; Lk 8 : 26, 37. Which of the three names given in the title of this study ought to be read in each of these passages ? The answer is not unanimous, as one might wish. But the tendency of the research has pointed toward the result now found in the most recent edition of the New Testament, that of the joint Bible Societies, to which Professor Matthew Black has devoted so much of his attention and time.[1] In this edition we read all three names, i.e., *Gadarenes* in Matthew, *Gerasenes* in Mark, and *Gergesenes* in Luke.[2]

I am very glad that I can by-pass many difficulties in the complicated textual situation in each of the passages. I shall limit myself to a detail, namely, which of these names the composer of the Diatessaron chose for his harmonistic patchwork. I hope that some of the remarks on this theme will be of interest to those who work on the problems of the Greek text.

The first attempt to give a reconstruction of the harmony was made by Zahn, as early as 1881.[3] This scholar worked mainly on the base of Mar Ephraem's commentary on the Diatessaron, which has been preserved in an Armenian translation ($T^{E\text{-arm}}$). Zahn had access to that work through the medium of a Latin rendering by Moesinger, published only five years before.[4] It was this work that convinced Zahn, that *Gergesenes* was the reading of the Diatessaron. He maintained that view in later publications, even

* I am glad that the invitation to contribute to this volume puts me in a position to thank Professor Matthew Black for the really great time that we could spend in and around his St Mary's during the Candlemas term 1967, in which I taught less than I learned.

1 *The Greek New Testament*, edited by K. Aland, M. Black, B. M. Metzger, A. Wikgren, Stuttgart, 1966.

2 *Op. cit.*, p. 29 (B-decision) ; p. 137 (C-decision) ; pp. 238, 240 (D-decisions).

3 Th. Zahn, *Tatian's Diatessaron*, Leipzig, 1881 (for our passages, see p. 140).

4 (J. B. Aucher-) G. Moesinger, *Evangelii Concordantis expositio facta a. S. Ephraemo Doctore Syro*, Venice, 1876 (Zahn referred to pp. 74 f.).

as late as 1920 in his important excursus on the passage in his commentary on Luke.[5]

Meanwhile, in 1913 Von Soden published his large edition of the New Testament,[6] in which the Diatessaron was such an important factor. His " reconstruction " had quite a different starting-point from that of Zahn. His deep appreciation of the Arabic version of the Diatessaron ($T^{A}$), published shortly after Zahn's publication,[7] often made him differ from the latter's reconstruction. Therefore, he completely neglected the Ephraemic text and introduced the Arabic reading *Gadarenes* as that of the Diatessaron.

Who was right ? The cards seemed to favour Zahn. First, Zahn appeared to be right in assuming that the reading *Gergesenes* was in the Armenian text of Ephraem. Moesinger's text was not always equal to the textual use that Zahn made of it, but in this instance his form of the name turned out to be right. Moreover, the high esteem that Von Soden had shown towards the Arabic text met with severe criticism : one cannot wholly trust that version, and certainly not when, as in this case, it agrees with the Syriac Vulgate ($Sy^{p}$).

It is interesting to observe the solutions of subsequent editors of the Greek New Testament who included the Diatessaron testimony in their apparatus. Unfortunately Vogels [8] did not show his colours in any of our passages. Why did he leave out his hero Tatian in these cases ? Was he perhaps somewhat embarrassed by the fact that the Latin and Syriac sides so completely diverged, and that this did not accord with his strong conviction that all Syro-Latin variants were Tatianic ? [9] What should one do when they differed ? Souter [10] and Bover [11] also

[5] Th. Zahn, " Zum Text von Lc. 8, 26 u. 37 ", Excurs VII, in : *Das Evangelium des Lucas*, Leipzig, [4]1920, pp. 760–64, esp. 761 : " Die lateinische Bearbeitung . . . und das arabische Diatessaron . . . sind in solchen Dingen wertlos " ; p. 764 : ". . . nach dem Zeugnis Ephraïms, dem zu misstrauen kein Grund vorliegt . . .".

[6] H. von Soden, *Die Schriften des Neuen Testaments*, II, Göttingen, 1913 ; for the texts in question, see pp. 23, 141, 282, 284.

[7] A. Ciasca, *Tatiani Evangeliorum Harmoniae Arabice*, Rome, 1888 ; for the Arabic text see pp. 44, 46 (arab.), for the Latin translation (Hadarenorum), see pp. 20, 21.

[8] H. J. Vogels, *Novum Testamentum Graece et Latine*, I. Freiburg-Barcelone, [4]1955, pp. 24, 122, 212, 214 (apparatus not altered since first edition, 1920).

[9] Cf. H. J. Vogels, *Handbuch der neutestamentlichen Textkritik*, Münster, 1923, p. vii ; Re-edition : Bonn, [2]1955, p. vi, see also p. 150.

[10] A. Souter, *Novum Testamentum Graece*, Oxford, [2]1947 (1956), *in. loc.*

[11] J. M. Bover, *Novi Testamenti Biblia Graeca et Latina*, Madrid, [4]1959, pp. (23), 115, 200 f.

left out the Diatessaron as a witness in the cases at issue. Did they not wish to risk a decision ?

Merk [12] does, although things are not very clear in his apparatus. He tells us that the following Tatianic variations occur :

1. *Γεργεσηνῶν* in Ta$^{e}$ (Matthew) : i.e., Ephraemic Diat. Commentary.
2. *Γερασηνῶν* in Ta$^{v.n.}$ (Mark) : i.e., Venetian and Dutch Diat.
3. *Γαδαρηνῶν* in Ta (Mark, Luke) : i.e., the Diat. as such (?).

The dilemma between the solutions of Zahn and Von Soden has been replaced here by three possibilities. Which one is the original reading ? From the annotations it appears that Merk preferred *Γαδαρηνῶν* and that he, like Von Soden, took the Arabic Diatessaron as his starting-point.[13] But it is not as clear as one might wish. Why did he mention only " Ta$^{e}$ " in Matthew, while passing over in silence the presence there of his " Ta " of Mark and Luke ?

Unfortunately, the edition of the Bible Societies has not completely avoided the arbitrary method of Merk. It gives [14]

1. *Γαδαρηνῶν* : Diatessaron (Matthew ; Lk 8 : 37), Diatessaron$^{p}$ (Mark), Diatessaron$^{a}$ (Lk 8 : 26).
2. *Γεργεσηνῶν* : Diatessaron$^{e}$ (Matthew).

The reading *Γερασηνῶν* is not mentioned. Elsewhere, however, the Western harmonies are often introduced into the apparatus, even when they differ from what could be assumed to be the Diatessaron reading. The new edition apparently coined the reading *Gadarenes* as the Diatessaron's, but why did it do so ? Was it because the reading was in the Arabic and Persian harmonies ? The choice of the Von Soden-Merk-N.B.S. editions is most probably the right one, rather than Zahn's. But the editions leave us with not a few questions.

## I

### *The " Palestinian " Harmonization : Gergesenes*

The writer's study has convinced him that, in spite of Sy$^{s}$, the drastic assimilation to the reading *Gergesenes* in all the Gospel passages of several Oriental versions does not have its

[12] A. Merk, *Novum Testamentum Graece et Latine*, Roma, [8]1957, pp. 24, 126, 225.

[13] Merk, *op. cit.*, pp. 17*–18*.

[14] *Op. cit.*, pp. 29, 137, 238, 240.

source in a Syriac text. This cannot be argued here,[15] but we shall consider in detail the case of the Diatessaron, for which T. Zahn supported the reading " Gergeseni ".[16] Must we not ask whether behind the harmonizing reading of the Oriental versions is the Diatessaron, which left so many traces of its influence throughout the Eastern world ?

Zahn's reconstruction of the name in the Diatessaron depended on Moesinger's accurate rendering of the Armenian in ch. 6 (26, 27) where the name twice occurs in the form " Gergesenes " (*gergesaçik'n*).[17] In this passage Ephraem deals with the story of the " Gergesenes " at its proper place, i.e., where it stood in the Diatessaron. Meanwhile, he appears to refer to that narrative in more than one place in his commentary.[18] In two of these passages he mentions explicitly the name of the people, and both times we hear about *Gergesenes*.[19] The reading, therefore, seems to be certain for the Diatessaron that Mar Ephraem commented on. One could object that it would be strange that the Diatessaron should have a reading differing from the traditional text in Syria, but such a state of affairs is not without analogy.[20] Moreover, the reading *Gergesenes* in Sy$^s$ was still there to be reckoned with !

Fortunately, we stand on safer ground today to determine which name Ephraem read in his Diatessaron. In the newly discovered vellum manuscript Chester Beatty 709 published by L. Leloir a good deal of the Syriac text of Ephraem's commentary has been preserved. In the only place where it contains a reference to the narrative *and* to the name of the people (16 : 1)

[15] Originally the argument was given here, but due to the length of the article the editors asked me to abbreviate this section which dealt with the so-called *Palestinian* harmonization. I hope to publish it elsewhere.

[16] See above, note 3.

[17] G. Moesinger, *op. cit.*, pp. 75 f. ; L. Leloir, *Saint Éphrem, Commentaire de l'évangile concordant, version arménienne* (C.S.C.O., vol. 145, ARM.2), Louvain, 1954 (Latin translation), pp. 64–65 ; L. Leloir, *Éphrem de Nisibe, Commentaire de l'Evangile concordant ou Diatessaron* (S. Chr. 121), Paris, 1966, pp. 136 f. (§27 is not numbered there) ; the text is found in L. Leloir, *Commentaire de l'évangile concordant, version arménienne* (C.S.C.O., vol. 137, ARM. 1), Louvain, 1953, p. 86 : *ll.* 4.27.

[18] T$^E$-arm, ch. 4 : 7 ; 16 : 1 ; 16 : 6 ; 16 : 9 ; 20 : 10.

[19] T$^E$-arm, 4 : 7, Leloir, *op. cit.*, p. 50 : *ll.* 13–14 *gergesaçwoç*, " of the Gergesenes " ; 16 : 1, *op. cit.*, p. 221 : *l.* 11 : *gergesaçik'n*. The French translation of Leloir has *Gergéséniens* in the first place (p. 97) but *Géraséniens* in the second (p. 281). The latter name is given also in the rendering of 6 : 26 f. (pp. 136–37) !

[20] Cf. *NTS* 8 (1962), 287–300, esp. pp. 296 f.

it has the name *Gadarenes* [21] Unfortunately, Leloir did not help his readers as well as he might have, for he renders that Syriac name once with *Gergesaei*,[22] once with *Géraséniens*.[23] The first of these translations seems to have been the cause of the fact that the apparatus of *The Greek New Testament* did not distinguish between " $e^{arm}$ " and " $e^{syr}$ ".[24]

It is most probable that when the Syriac commentary of Ephraem was translated into Armenian (in the fifth century ?) the reading *Gergesenes* was already " in vogue " in Armenia. That is, it was dominant in the oldest stratum of textual tradition there. Immediately the question arises how this latter name became predominant. Was it perhaps due to the hypothetical Armenian Diatessaron of the fifth century [25] that this harmonization permeated subsequent Gospel translations in Armenia and Georgia ? But if this were the case, another question emerges : why did the early Armenian translator of the Syriac harmony substitute in the Armenian version *Gergesenes* for the Syriac *Gadarenes* ? Who was ultimately the authority behind this deliberate alteration ?

It was Origen. It was through his remarks on Jn 1 : 28 [26] that the reading *Gergesenes* got its huge spread. This famous scholar must have been responsible for the gradual suppression of the reading *Gerasenes* both in Mark (א* B D) and Luke ($P^{75}$ B D). For which scribe would dare resist the forceful arguments of Origen ? Was it not true that " in the Greek copies mistakes were made in many places with regard to the names " ? [27] For the famous scholar had given so many examples in favour of his statement. Could anyone deny the fact that " Gerasa did not border either on sea or lake " ? [28] And was he not justified in

[21] L. Leloir, *Saint Éphrem, Commentaire de l'Évangile Concordant, Texte Syriaque* (Chester Beatty Monographs, No. 8) Dublin, 1963, p. 164 : *l.* 4.

[22] Leloir, *op. cit.* (n. 20), p. 165.

[23] Leloir, *op. cit.* (French translation), p. 281.

[24] *Op. cit.*, p. 29 (Mt).

[25] For literature see *Vox Theologica* 32 (1962), 112, n. 5.

[26] A. E. Brooke, *The Commentary of Origen on S. John's Gospel I*, Cambridge, 1896, *loc. cit.* ; E. Preuschen, *Origenes Werke*, Leipzig, 1903, 4, pp. 149–57, esp. p. 150 : *ll.* 3–20.

[27] Brooke, *op. cit.*, p. 158 : *l.* 23 f. : τὸ μέντοι γε ἡμαρτῆσθαι ἐν τοῖς ἑλληνικοῖς ἀντιγράφοις τὰ περὶ τῶν ὀνομάτων πολλαχοῦ . . . It is tempting to think that it was better in the " versions ", but he evidently opposes the Greek manuscripts to the Hebrew original of the Old Testament with respect to the names, cf. p. 159 : *ll.* 11 ff.

[28] Brooke, *op. cit.*, p. 158 : *ll.* 28–29 : Γέρασα δὲ τῆς Ἀραβίας ἐστὶ πόλις οὔτε θάλασσαν οὔτε λίμνην πλησίον ἔχουσα.

saying that " the Evangelists, men who had a careful knowledge of the geography of Judea, would not have uttered a lie that is so evident and easy to refute " ? [29] How could anyone cling to a reading that is pure nonsense ? [30] It is evident that Origen had changed the older dilemma for copyists, namely " Gadarenes *or* Gerasenes ", into a new one : " Gergesenes *or* Gadarenes ".

The reading *Γεργεσηνῶν* was most probably a conjecture of Origen.[31] He did not find it in his manuscript, as in the case of Bethany-Bethabara (Jn 1 : 28),[32] but he apparently guessed it on account of what he discovered during his explorations in the Holy Land, " when he was on the spot to trace the foot-prints of Jesus and of his disciples and of the prophets ".[33] It is, therefore, not wholly excluded that the " sacred geography " of his time led Origen to identify the place where Jesus landed with a " town " or village Gergesa (*τὰ Γέργεσα*).[34] If there really ever was a " town " of that name it must have been totally unimportant, as it does not occur elsewhere in early descriptions of Palestine. Origen has connected his discovery with the Old Testament *Girgashites* (*Γεργεσαῖοι*), and this in its turn suggested the name *Γεργεσηνοί* to him [35] on account of the analogy with *Γαδαρηνῶν* and *Γερασηνῶν* which he found in his manuscripts. It is even possible that his identification started from an identification of the territory of the Old Testament *Girgashites*. With his eagerness to detect the real meaning of the words [36] he tried to discover what *Γεργεσαῖοι* could mean: *ἑρμηνεύεται δὲ ἡ Γέργεσα παροικία ἐκβεβληκότων,*

[29] Brooke, *op. cit.*, p. 158 : *ll.* 29–32 : *καὶ οὐκ ἂν οὕτως προφανὲς ψεῦδος καὶ εὐέλεγκτον οἱ εὐαγγελισταὶ εἰρήκεσαν, ἄνδρες ἐπιμελῶς γινώσκοντες τὰ περὶ τὴν 'Ιουδαίαν.*

[30] Even Zahn was impressed by the facts which Origen adduced, cf. *Das Evangelium des Matthäus*, Leipzig, Erlangen, [4]1922, p. 363 f. ; *Lukas*, pp. 763f. He also denies that *Gerasenes* could even have stood in any Gospel text.

[31] M.-J. Lagrange, " Origène, la critique textuelle et la tradition topographique ", *RB*, 1895, 512 ff. ; *Évangile selon Saint Marc*, Paris, [4]1929, pp. 132 ff. ; R. G. Clapp, *JBL* 26 (1908), 65 ff. (cf. F. C. Burkitt, *JBL* 27 (1909), 129 ff.). Even Th. Zahn, *NKZ* 13 (1902), 926, still thought of a conjecture of Origen, who did not know the name from any manuscript, but guessed what was present in a manuscript unknown to him.

[32] Brooke, *op. cit.*, p. 157 : *l.* 29–30 : *ὅτι μὲν σχεδὸν ἐν πᾶσι τοῖς ἀντιγράφοις κεῖται ταῦτα ἐν Βηθανίᾳ ἐγένετο· . . .*

[33] Brooke, *op. cit.*, p. 158 : *ll.* 2–3 : *γενόμενοι ἐν τοῖς τόποις ἐπὶ ἱστομίαν τῶν ἰχνῶν 'Ιησοῦ καὶ τῶν μαθητῶν αὐτοῦ καὶ τῶν προφητῶν.*

[34] So in his commentary, tome X : 12 (A. E. Brooke, *op. cit.*, p. 196 : *l.* 2).

[35] That he wishes to read *Γεργεσηνοί* (not *Γεργεσαῖοι*) appears from, t. X : 19 (Brooke, *op. cit.*, p. 205 : *l.* 6) : . . . *εἰς τὴν χώραν τῶν Γεργεσηνῶν.*

[36] Cf. t. VI, 41 (Brooke, *op. cit.*, p. 160 : *ll.* 1–2) : *καὶ οὐ καταφρονητέον τῶν ὀνομάτων, πραγμάτων σημαινομένων ἀπ' αὐτῶν χρησίμων τῇ τῶν τόπων ἑρμηνείᾳ.*

ἐπώνυμος οὖσα τάχα προφητικῶς οὗ περὶ τὸν σωτῆρα πεποιήκασι παρακαλέσαντες αὐτὸν μεταβῆναι ἐκ τῶν ὁρίων αὐτῶν οἱ τῶν χοίρων πολῖται.[37]

Gergesa means, according to Origen, " Settlement of those that have thrown out ". This is most interesting. Retranslated into Hebrew, one might find something like gūrgōrᵉšīm. Do we have here one of his famous mistranslations ? Or is it necessary to seek another explanation ? [38] Anyhow, things are far more complicated than often has been suggested. What was the " local tradition " that Origen became acquainted with ? Was there really a tradition of that kind *before* Origen ?

As proof for that view I doubt whether we can adduce either the reading *gergᵉsāyē* (or gergūsāye ?) of Sy$^{s}$ in Mark, as Burkitt did,[39] or the reading *gergᵉšē* (gergešāyē) of Sy$^{pal}$ in Matthew and Luke, as Zahn has done.[40] At this point we can only say a few words concerning the latter reading. It is striking enough that in Sy$^{pal}$ the Greek *Γεργεσαῖοι* of Dt 7 : 1 is rendered with *gergᵉšāē*.[41] Therefore, I should not like to think of a local tradition behind Sy$^{pal}$ in Mark and Luke, of which the translator had knowledge independently of Origen. His choice of the Old Testament name in these passages can best be explained as a textual decision on the ground of Origen's conjecture.

When I agree with those who favour a conjecture, I feel the more safe because Zahn's arguments against it have partly fallen away. His main argument was that the name was known before

[37] Brooke, *op. cit.*, p. 159 : *ll.* 7–11 ; the same explanation t. X : 12 (p. 196: *l.* 2–4).

[38] Of course, the retranslation is only partly successful. But one must have a word at the beginning with *gimĕl* and *rēš*, meaning παροικία ; *gēr* would be πάροικος. One might suggest *mgwr* or *mgwrh*, but this does not fit in with Origen's *Gergesa*. I venture upon the hypothetical *gwr* (cf. LXX : Ps 119 : 5). For *gwr* as place-name, see 2 K 9 : 27 ; cf. *gwr-bʿl*, 2 Ch 26 : 7. One cannot leave out παροικία, *contra* D. Völter, " Die Heilung des Besessenen, im Land der Gerasener oder Gadarener oder Gergesener ", *Nieuw Theologisch Tijdschrift* 9 (1920), 285–297. He only re-translates ἐκβεβληκότων into *gᵉrûšāh* = banishment. Völter thinks that the original name ought to be read Γεσουρηνῶν (which he identifies with the " Gesurites " and with the country " Gesūrā ", see p. 295) ; this was wrongly written as Γερουσηνῶν which was explained as coming from *grš*, " to send away, banish " ; this brings us to *grwšh* which was written as *grgšh* afterwards (cf. 293). For mistranslations of Origen, cf. F. C. Burkitt, *The Syriac Forms of New Testament Proper Names*, London, 1912, p. 13.

[39] F. C. Burkitt, *JBL* 27 (1909), 129 ; *Syriac Forms*, p. 10.

[40] Zahn, *Lukas*, p. 764.

[41] A. S. Lewis, *Codex Climaci Rescriptus* (Horae Semit. VIII), Cambridge, 1909, p. 12 (a lesson with Dt 6 : 21–7 : 6).

Origen, as it stood already in the Diatessaron and in the Syro-Sinaitic.[42] We have seen that the Diatessaron no longer supports the argument, and this diminishes the importance of Sy$^{s}$ a good deal.

Even if Origen was not the first to introduce the name *Gergesenes*, he does turn out to be the great promotor of that name, possibly through the channels of Caesarean manuscripts copied after his commentary had been written. His influence is perceptible in many manuscripts, but his best success is visible in the versions [42a] and Greek manuscripts [42b] to which we have called attention in this first section.

## II

### *The " Western " harmonization : Gerasenes*

It is most remarkable that, as far as we know, all Old Latin manuscripts have the same reading *Gerasenorum* in Matthew,[43] Mark [44] and Luke,[45] and that the Vulgate [46] does not give another name either. Of course, there are slight variations in spelling,[47] but they are merely variations of the same name. Since the earliest textual transmission, this seems to have been the unique form of the name in Latin-speaking areas. For, as a matter of fact, the Latin Fathers constantly use that name in their quotations. Unfortunately there are only a few testimonies from pre-Vulgate times, among which we count the testimony of Hilary.[48]

In his booklet, " On the Soul ", Tertullian already refers to the story with the name *Gerasene*. But this is not a compelling reason to suggest that this name was already universal in his time. For we are not sure that he paraphrases a Latin Gospel text when he writes : ". . . et septenarii numeri, ut in Magdalena,

[42] Zahn, *Lukas*, p. 764.

[42a] Geo.$^{Op.Tb}$, Arm., Arab., Ethiop., Boh., (Sy$^{pal}$). See above, note 15.

[42b] ℵ$^{corr}$, L, 1–118–131–209, 700, 1071. See above, note 15.

[43] a, aur, b, c, d, f, ff$^{1}$, g$^{1}$, h, k, l, q.

[44] aur, b, c, d, e, f, ff$^{2}$, i, l, q, r$^{1}$.

[45] a, aur, b, c, d, f, ff$^{2}$, l, q, r$^{1}$ (v. 26 : e).

[46] J. Wordsworth, H. J. White, *Novum Testamentum D.N. Jesu Christi Latine*, Oxford, 1889–98, pp. 70, 208, 359, 361.

[47] E.g., Gerasin., Gerasyn., Gerassen., Gyrasen., Geresen., Gerazin.

[48] Dr W. Thiele of the Vetus Latina Institute at Beuron kindly informed me of the scarce pre-Vulgate material : HIL Mt cap. 8 (915C) ; Mt 8 : 3 (959B) ; An sy 2 (332, 57) ; Am Lc 4 : 55 (126, 686) ; Ps 61 : 18 (389, 10).

et legionarii numeri, ut in Geraseno . . .".[49] Even if he did so, it would not be conclusive. The mention of *legionarii* evidently shows that he referred to the Marcan, or rather to the Lucan story. For both references may originate from Lk 8, resp. from Lk 8 : 3 and Lk 8 : 26 ff. Now, the occurrence of *Gerasenes* in Mark and Luke is not so strange, even apart from the Latin tradition.

More conclusive for the sole occurence of *Gerasenorum* in Latin-speaking areas seems to be the discussion of Augustine, in his work on " the Agreement of the Evangelists ".[50] There he comments in detail on the difference between the *two* demoniacs in Matthew and the *one* in Mark and Luke, but he passes over in complete silence the difference between Matthew, Mark or Luke with respect to the name of the people of the region. This confirms how deeply rooted the name *Gerasenes* was in early Latin tradition.

The same can be said of Jerome. In his short commentary on Matthew,[51] written two years before Augustine's work, he did not mention any difficulty with regard to the name of the people in Mt 8 : 28. He simply speaks of *Geraseni*. It is hard to believe that he would have neglected to display his scholarship in this case if he had known about the difficulty. This is the more remarkable because he had read Origen's exposition of Matthew. We may question, therefore, whether Zahn is right in assuming that Origen may have written in his commentary on Matthew a more detailed discussion of the name problem than he did in his explanation of Jn 1 : 28.[52] Does not Jerome's silence suggest that Origen may have discussed the question only in the latter place? Or had it been so long since Jerome had read Origen's commentary on Matthew, that he had forgotten the details?

However, Jerome could have known about the problem. For some years before he had published his Latin recension of Eusebius' *Onomasticon*, in which the Greek author had given some hints. For example, in the list of names in the Gospels the name *Gergesa* is explained as the place " where the Lord had healed the

[49] J. H. Waszink, *Tertullianus, De Anima*, Amsterdam, 1933, p. 98 (25 : 8).

[50] *S. A. Augustini Opera Omnia* III, P.L. 34, Paris, 1845, col. 1104.

[51] *S. E. Hieronymi Opera Omnia* VII, P.L. 21, Paris, 1845, col. 53.

[52] Another argument against the idea of Zahn is that the Catenae reproduce only Origen's comment on the Johannine passage.

demoniacs ".[53] At the end of the note on Gergesa reference is made to an earlier exposition,[54] to be found in his list on Deuteronomy. Under the lemma *Γέργασει* (Dt 7 : 1 !) this town was identified with *Gerasa,* while others said that it was *Gadara.*[55] Eusebius concludes with the statement that " also the Gospel made mention of the *Γερασσινῶν* ".[56] Both these entries could have taught Jerome that there was a problem. At first sight it seems that he really learned from them, for he renders the last phrase as follows : " sed et evangelium meminit *Gergessinorum* ".[57] He introduces a form of the name which did not stand in his Greek exemplar and which was foreign to himself. Did Jerome know of a name *Gergesenorum* ? It seems so, but this is merely on the surface. He must have wondered what the last phrase of Eusebius' text could mean. He was not aware of the problem that Eusebius must have learned from Origen ; therefore he accepted the first three names as scholarly identifications without suspecting any connection with the Gospels. He did not know that *Gergesenes* and *Gadarenes* were rivals of his own familiar *Gerasenes.* But then the note at the end became a riddle to him, especially the *καὶ.* He did not connect the Greek *Γερασσινῶν* either with the *Gerasa* of Eusebius' text or with the name *Gerasenes,* which he was used to. But he tried to find a connection between this phrase and the lemma at issue, and so he corrected the Greek name *Γερασσινῶν* into his Latin *Gergessinorum* (-ss-!), which was closer to *Γέργασει.* The problem that had puzzled Origen and Eusebius could not trouble a man like Jerome, who was acquainted with a uniform textual tradition.

How can this uniform tradition be explained ? One of the most debated questions with regard to the Old Latin versions is whether there was behind them a common " ancestor ".[58] One might suggest that the unique form *Gerasenes* in the Latin tradition is another piece of evidence favouring a positive answer. But even if this were true, there would remain *one* question :

[53] E. Klostermann, *Eusebius Werke III* : 1, *Onomastikon der biblischen Ortsnamen,* Leipzig, 1904, p. 74 : *ll.* 13 ff. The plural τοὺς δαιμονιῶντας seems to refer to Matthew. Does this mean that Eusebius had a Matthaean text with *Gergesenes* ?

[54] *Ibid.,* p. 74, *l.* 15.

[55] *Ibid.,* p. 64, *ll.* 1–4.

[56] *Μεμνῆται δὲ καὶ τὸ εὐαγγέλιον τῶν Γερασσινῶν.*

[57] E. Klostermann, *op. cit.,* p. 65, *ll.* 3–4.

[58] M.-J. Lagrange, *Critique Textuelle,* II, *La critique rationelle,* Paris, 1935, pp. 244 ff.

why did the man responsible for that earliest version choose the name *Gerasenes* for all the passages? He might have found that name in both Mark and Luke, but was it also in his Greek exemplar of Matthew? Or was it he who made the harmonization?

In this connection we must remember the hypothesis put forward by Vogels, namely that the (Old Latin) Diatessaron " was the first attempt to dress the Gospel in a Roman garment ".[59] If this is true, it would explain how the harmonization could pervade subsequent Latin versions.

Is it possible to detect which name stood in the Old Latin Diatessaron? The reading " in regione *Gerasenorum* " appears in the famous Latin harmony, codex Fuldensis ($T^{L(f)}$),[60] and in its allies, e.g. codex Sangallensis ($T^{L(g)}$);[61] but we know that they represent the post-Vulgate recension of the Latin harmony. The same is true for the old German harmony ($T^{Ahd}$) with its rendering " in lantscaf *Gerasenorum* ".[62] But shall we never get back of the time of the Vulgate supremacy? Scholars who defend the existence of the Old Latin Diatessaron always refer to the more recent medieval harmonies in vernacular languages. Even if there is something right in this approach, what do these younger harmonies contribute to our problem?

Let us begin with the so-called Pepysian harmony. It tells us the story of the " tweye fendes out of the graves, proude & wel stoute ",[63] but it forgets to name the people in whose land the story happened. And again we are disappointed when we read the Italian harmonies, the Tuscan and Venetian Diatessarons. Here the names have been corrupted into names more familiar to the average reader of the Gospels, Caesarea and Gennesareth: cf. T " en la contrada dey *Çasarei* "[64] and $T^{T}$ " nella contrada di

[59] H. J. Vogels, *Handbuch der neutestamentlichen Textkritik*, Münster, ²1955, p. 150.

[60] E. Ranke, *Codex Fuldensis*, Marburg-Leipzig, 1868, p. 58.

[61] E. Sievers, *Tatian Lateinisch und Altdeutsch*, Paderborn, ²1960, pp. 73 f.

[62] *Ibid.*

[63] Cf. M. Goates, *The Pepysian Gospel Harmony*, London, 1922, p. 21, *l.* 18. The narrative of Jesus and the demoniacs is referred to in the Heliand, I would think, in *ll.* 2268–2283; cf. O. Behaghel, *Heliand und Genesis*, Tübingen, ⁷1958, pp. 80 f. But no name of the people is given there! Nor could I find the name in Otfrid's Gospel Book. It may be useful to point to the West-Saxon Gospels, that read " on geraseniscra rice " (Mt), " rice Gerasenorum " (Mk), " gerasenorum rice " (Lk); cf. M. Grünberg, *The West-Saxon Gospels, A study of the Gospel of St Matthew with Text of the Four Gospels*, Amsterdam, 1967, pp. 60, 148, 180.

[64] V. Todesco, *Diatessaron Veneto*, Città del Vaticano, 1938, pp. 52 f. (ch. 48).

*Genesaret* ".[65] It is very probable that both names are merely corruptions of *Gerasenorum*.

This reading is also attested by the Dutch harmonies, which vary in their rendering. In the famous Liège manuscript we read, " in en lantschap dat ghenamt *van Gerasenen* " ($T^{N(1)}$).[66] This seems to be no more than an acute paraphrase of a text similar to that of the two other Dutch manuscripts which have " int lantscap *Gerasenorum* ".[67] The fruit that we shall gather from the " younger " harmonies is not as excellent as we had hoped for.

If we may draw a conclusion from these materials with regard to the pre-Vulgate Old Latin harmony, it would be that the Old Latin Diatessaron already had the reading *Gerasenorum*. One cannot say that the evidence is very convincing, but it may give us a hint. More than these vernacular harmonies, it is the massive and deeply rooted tradition with the name *Gerasenorum* in the whole Latin area that might recommend the hypothesis of such an early Latin Diatessaron underlying the whole Latin textual tradition in all three Gospel passages.

In their note on the Matthaean passage, Westcott and Hort have labelled the harmonization that we deal with here as a Western phenomenon : " The Western text simply assimilates all three variations by introducing *Γερασηνῶν* in Mt ".[68] However, it is clear that they understood this assimilation in a broader sense than we have used it, i.e., of the Latin texts. Westcott and Hort referred also to Syriac and Egyptian traditions, and above all to a possible Greek witness to this Western harmonization.

Was it really a Syriac phenomenon ? As a matter of fact, in the margin of the Harclean recension we read the name *geräsäyē*, but interestingly enough only in Matthew and Luke,[69] not in Mark ! Can we say, therefore, that a Syriac Gospel text ever had this harmonization, or had this reading at least in one or two

[65] M. Vatasso, A. Vaccari, *Il Diatessaron Toscano*, Città del Vaticano, 1938, p. 237 (ch. 54). As to the corruption in $T^T$ we may refer to the Slavonic version that has a similar reference to Genesaret in Lk 8 : 26, cf. V. Jagić, *Quattuor Evangeliorum Codex Glagoliticus*, Graz, 1954 (=Berlin, 1879) *in loco*.

[66] J. Bergsma, *De Levens van Jezus in het Nederlandsch*, Leyde, 1895–98, p. 65 (ch. 67).

[67] J. Bergsma, *op. cit.*, p. 64 (ch. 63).

[68] B. F. Westcott, F. J. A. Hort, *The New Testament in Greek*, Introduction, Appendix, London, ²1907 (repr.), " Notes on select readings ", p. 11.

[69] J. White, *Sacrorum Evangelorum Versio Syriaca Philoxeniana*, t. I, Oxford, 1778, pp. 35 (Mt), 318 (Lk, v. 26).

Gospels? I would not think so. Just as in the case of *Gargūsāyē*[69a] we have to think of marginal glosses made by a learned Syrian scholar following Greek manuscripts, or scholarly glosses in one of his Greek exemplars, or even Greek commentaries.

The Sahidic version of the Gospels presents us with the same phenomenon that we have found in the Latin sector. In each passage we read the name *gerazēnos*, though with slight variations.[70] When we leave out the Syriac "witness" and limit ourselves to the Latin and Sahidic versions, we cannot avoid asking whether the agreement between these distant versions presupposes a common source. Was there possibly a Greek text in the second century that may account for the same assimilation in the two versions? If this were the case, then the possibility of an early Latin Diatessaron would become rather uncertain.

Westcott and Hort, in their reference to a Greek witness for the reading *Gerasenes* in Matthew, must have thought of Codex Bezae. For this manuscript has more than once been adduced as a witness for that reading.[71] Unfortunately, D is not extant in Matthew (it lacks 8 : 20b–9 : 2a). Therefore, we cannot say anything certain about it.

The view that D had *Γερασηνῶν* in Matthew is based on the fact that the Latin counterpart d has *Gerasenorum*. It is true that D often agrees with d, but it must be added that D also differs from d in many places. And if D agrees with d, it is often because D has been influenced by its Latin side [72] or by Latin tradition as a whole; therefore, even if D had *Γερασηνῶν* in the

[69a] See above, note 15. Cf. Sy$^p$ Gen 10 : 16; 15 : 21; Dt 7 : 1.

[70] (G. Horner), *The Coptic Version of the New Testament in the Southern Dialect, otherwise called Sahidic and Thebaic*, Oxford, 1911, vol. I, p. 70 (Mt), p. 411 (Mk); vol. II, p. 152. 158 (Lk). The variants are *garazēnos, gerasēnos, kērasynos*. Ms. M of the Bohairic comes close to the reading of the Sahidic.

[71] Zahn, *Lukas*, p. 763; M.-J. Lagrange, *Saint Marc*, p. 132, etc.

[72] A fine example of correction due to d can be found in Jn 21 : 21 (see Table 4–5 in the *Einführung* of Nestle in the different editions). Here we read in the text of the Latin side

. . . Petrus dicit ad ihm . . .

The Greek side has this text:

. . . ο πετρος λεγει ἀὐτω Ιηῡ

This is not, as Von Soden suggests (*op. cit.*, p. 490, 3d app.) αυτω loco τω; but it is evident that the Greek exemplar of D had a different text from d, namely λεγει αυτω loco λεγει τῳ Ιησου, just as Sy$^s$ has (was it also in 248 of Tischendorf?). The scribe of D copied his Greek text, saw then that it differed from the Latin and escaped any difficulty by putting dots above the αυ and by adding the abbreviation Ιηῡ.

text of Matthew, we cannot be certain that it represented there an independent type of the Greek text of the second century!

I would think that another view is no less probable: that D differed from d in Matthew. In Mark (א* B D) and Luke (P[75] B D) it is D that goes side by side with B; is it strange to assume that D offered the same text as B in Matthew (א* B C* *Δ Θ* pc) as well? I would think that it is not. These two considerations make it impossible to consider D as a late representative of the hypothetical Greek "Western" source for the assimilated readings in both the Sahidic and Latin versions.

I would like to put forward another solution. The Sahidic and the Latin may represent two independent assimilations. The "ancestors" of both versions started from a Greek text of the B (-D ?)-type, in which the name *Gadarenes* occurred in Matthew, and the name *Gerasenes* in Mark and Luke. In Matthew they independently corrected the first name into the second. Why did they do so? Was it because they wished to have *one* place where Jesus had landed and preferred the testimony of two witnesses (Mark-Luke) to that of one (Matthew)? This is not impossible, but there may have been another reason. It is known that both in Alexandria and Rome the Gospel of Mark must have been received with great reverence.[73] Was this perhaps the factor by which the two early translators in Egypt and in the Latin-speaking area were guided in their independent assimilations?

If this is true, it is no longer necessary to think that the Latin Diatessaron, through its harmonistic choice for *Gerasenorum*, influenced later versions. It is possible that when the Old Latin Diatessaron came into existence there was no choice except the choice of *Gerasenorum*.

## III

### *The "Syriac" harmonization*: *Gadarenes*

Since Tischendorf and Tregelles, or rather since Westcott and Hort, the name *Gadarenes* has been widely accepted as the original reading of Matthew. The decision in favour of that name has been made on the basis of only a few uncials against the majority of (what we used to call) Caesarean and Byzantine

[73] Cf. for Alexandria Eus. 2, 16, 2. The newly discovered letter of Clement, to be published by Prof. Morton Smith, seems to imply a special reverence for Mark in circles within and outside the church of Alexandria.

manuscripts. It is remarkable that the Byzantine text and a part of the Caesarean family support the name *Gadarenes* in Mark and Luke, where modern editions prefer to read one of the other names, again on the basis of only a small group of textual witnesses. It was just the Byzantine testimony that made Westcott and Hort speak of a " Syrian " reading in these Gospels. But they did not think that the Byzantine recension had preserved the original " Syrian " colour : " the Syrian text in the earlier form represented by syr-vg inverts the Western process by reading *Γαδαρηνῶν* in all three places ".[74] The Greek text of Constantinople deviated from the original form by adopting in Matthew the Alexandrian text.

I am not inclined to accept their view with regard to the textual process that led to the Byzantine text. But they brought to our notice the third complete harmonization that we have to deal with, namely the reading *gāḏ^erāyē* as it is found in the Peshitta version [75] and in the Harclean recension.[76] I would like to speak of a peculiar *Syriac* harmonization, and not of a " *Syrian* " assimilation ; for I would like to avoid the supposition of a more or less official recension of the Greek text which had the same assimilation.

Of course, one cannot deny that at least one Greek cursive has this harmonization, namely *1010*. But this may have been a stray phenomenon which came into existence by a mere coincidence and not before the twelfth century. It has been suggested that a similar harmonization occurred in the uncial manuscript A.[77] Now, A is defective and, just as in the case of D, one can make it what one wishes. But it is highly improbable that A can be made a witness for the harmonization in all the passages. It is not difficult to see that, in Mark, and Lk 8 : 26, 37, A is in the company of *K Π 1009 1079 1195 1216 1230 1242 1546 2148 2174*, the Byzantine recension, and the Gothic version. Would A have left that company in Matthew where all these witnesses have the reading *Γεργεσηνῶν* ? Therefore, we may speak of a *Syriac* harmonization.

What is to be said about the date when this phenomenon appeared in Syria ? It is most probable that the agreement

[74] B. F. Westcott, F. J. A. Hort, *loc. cit.*

[75] P. E. Pusey, G. H. Gwilliam, *Tetraevangelium Sanctum*, Oxford, 1901, pp. 56, 222, 370.

[76] White, *op. cit.*, pp. 35, 180, 318 f.

[77] Cf. Th. Zahn, *Lukas*, p. 763.

between Sy$^{p}$ and Sy$^{h}$ points to a deeply rooted tradition in Syria, a tradition which was still unshaken in a much later time when the Syriac Gospels were translated into Arabic[78] and Persian.[79] The agreement between Sy$^{p}$ and Sy$^{h}$ is not merely an " accord des versions syriaques récentes ",[80] but rather presupposes a long tradition. It was a tradition that originated in the Syriac Diatessaron. Since Von Soden the Diatessaron has been adduced more than once as a witness to support the reading *Gadarenes*. This now appears to be wholly justified although not because it was the reading of the Arabic Diatessaron (*al-ḥadarāniyīna*)[81] or even of the Persian Harmony (*gadarānīyna*)[82]; for both could have been influenced by the Syriac Vulgate. The mere fact of the harmonization in Sy$^{p.h}$ would have been a strong argument in support of the conjecture that the Diatessaron contained the name *Gadarenes*! But it is the newly found text of Ephraem's commentary, to which we referred above, that gives us confidence to say that the Diatessaron contained this name.

It was the Diatessaron that introduced into Syria the name *Gadarenes* as the name of the people in the story of Jesus and the demoniac. This name became so entirely domesticated in Syriac-speaking regions that when subsequent versions of the Gospel (or rather of the separate Gospels) were made, it crept into all places where the story was told. The Old Syriac ancestor of the Peshitta may have contained the name in all the Gospels. The Old Syriac text represented by Sy$^{s}$, or merely this manuscript, may tell us that in the Western regions of Syria the influence of Greek texts and of scholarly opinions in Greek scriptoria was felt. But in the main stream of Syriac tradition the Diatessaron influence was unshaken, at least so far as it concerns the name *Gadarenes*!

[78] If we follow the text of the Arabic manuscripts used for the Bible Society edition.

[79] We may refer to B. Walton, *Biblia Sacra Polyglotta*, Graz, 1964 (1657), 5, pp. 37, 175, 294, 296; A. Whelocus, *Quattuor Evangeliorum D.N. Jesu Christi Versio Persica*, London, 1657, pp. 39, 176, 272 f. The names have different forms, e.g., gadarāniyīna (=arab ?), gadarāniyān, ğadrāanīyān, etc.

[80] M.-J. Lagrange, *loc. cit.*

[81] A. Ciasca, *op. cit.*, pp. 44, 46 (tr. 20, 21). A.-S. Marmardji, *Diatessaron de Tatien*, Beyrouth, 1935, pp. 106, 110. The names differ in form in the various manuscripts, e.g., al-ḥadarāniyīna (text in both editions); in the first passage ms. A: al-ḥandanāniyna (?); ms. E: al-ḥadarāniyna (?); in the second passage ms. B: al-hadārānīyina. Marmardji wishes to correct all names into al-ğadar-āniyīna.

[82] G. Messina, *Diatessaron Persiano*, Roma, 1951, pp. 184, 186 (2 : 60).

What was the reading of the Diatessaron? It was certainly not, I would say, the reading *Gergesenes*. If this name was ever read in the Armenian Diatessaron, which is not impossible, it offers an example of how the Diatessaron could easily conform to a new textual situation.[83] This may have been the case in the Latin Diatessaron as well. There the reading *Gerasenes* may have been accepted because there was already a complete harmonization to that name caused by a special reverence for the text of the Gospel of Mark or, if the Diatessaron was the first Latin Gospel, by the same reverence on the part of its translator.[84]

Was the original reading then the name found in the Syriac Diatessaron, i.e., *Gadarenes*? Or was there, as some scholars have argued, a Greek Diatessaron which afterwards was translated into Syriac? Let us start from the facts that we have in hand. There was a Syriac Diatessaron, and this Syriac Diatessaron presents us with the name *Gadarenes*.[85] From which Gospel did the composer of the Syriac harmony take this name? Was it from Matthew which so often seems to have been the guiding Gospel for the Syriac Diatessaron? If this was the case, then it is evident that the Syriac composer made use of a Matthaean text of the type ℵ-B-C-Δ-Θ which has now been accepted as the original text of Matthew.

83 [Arm. Diat. (?)→] Old Armenian Gospels→Armenian Vulgate→$T^{E\text{-}arm}$.

84 Vet. Lat.→$T^{L}$ (→$T^{L\ (f.g.\ etc)}$, $T^{N\ (l.s.h)}$ $T^{V\ (?)}$, $T^{T\ (?)}$), or $T^{L}$→Vet. Lat.

85 $T^{Sy}$ (→$T^{E\text{-}sy}$, $T^{A}$)→$Sy^{p\cdot h}$ (→Arab ?)→Pers (→P-H).

# SOME PROBLEMS IN NEW TESTAMENT TEXT AND LANGUAGE

George D. Kilpatrick

Principal Matthew Black has for many years associated the study of problems of text and of language in the New Testament to the advancement of our understanding of both. It is a great pleasure to submit the following notes in honour of his work.

## Mk 1 : 27 and Ac 17 : 19.

Mk 1 : 27 *τί ἐστιν τοῦτο ; διδαχὴ καινὴ κατ' ἐξουσίαν καὶ τοῖς πνευμασι κτλ.* is the reading of modern editions, but there are three noteworthy variants, if we disregard minor differences :

(1) *τί ἐστιν τοῦτο* is omitted by DW *pc L* b c d e ff² q r¹ *S* s Geo Eth Arm.

(2) *διδαχὴ . . . ἐξουσίαν*] *τίς ἡ διδαχὴ ἡ καινὴ αὕτη ὅτι* *C Γ Δ Π Σ Φ ω* and similarly A D W *L* Geo.

(3) Does *κατ' ἐξουσίαν* go with what precedes or with what follows ? On variant (2) it goes with what follows, but the reading of ℵ B can be taken either way.

In trying to decide on the text our starting point is the phrase *ἡ διδαχὴ ἡ καινὴ αὕτη* against *διδαχὴ καινή*. In my paper " The Greek New Testament of Today and the *Textus Receptus* " in the Macgregor memorial volume p. 194 I argued briefly that the longer text was unGreek, Semitic and original, and the shorter text was normal Greek and a correction. The word order of the longer text, article noun, article adjective, demonstrative, is unparalleled in ordinary Greek (see Gildersleeve's collections, *Syntax of Classical Greek* 2 (1915), 328 f.), but occurs in the Gospels and Acts :

Mt 27 : 24 *τοῦ αἵματος τοῦ δικαίου τούτου* ℵ L W *Γ Π Σ ω* (cf. A *Δ Φ* 064)

Mk 12 : 43 *ἡ χήρα ἡ πτωχὴ αὕτη* D *Θ Φ Ωp* 565 700 *al*
Lk 21 : 3 *ἡ χήρα ἡ πτωχὴ αὕτη* A W *Γ Δ Θ Ω*
Ac 2 : 40 *τῆς γενεᾶς τῆς πονηρᾶς ταύτης* contra D *pc L*

6 : 13 *τοῦ τόπου τοῦ ἁγίου τούτου* B C *al*
14 *Ἰησοῦς ὁ Ναζωραῖος οὗτος* contra *pc*
21 : 28 *τοῦ τόπου τοῦ ἁγίου τοῦτου* A C²

From the LXX the following instances may be cited:

Gn 41 : 35 *τῶν ἑπτὰ ἐτῶν τῶν ἐρχομένων τῶν καλῶν τούτων*
Nu 16 : 26 *τῶν ἀνθρώπων τῶν σκληρῶν τούτων*
Dt 1 : 19 ; 2 : 7 *τὴν ἔρημον τὴν μεγάλην καὶ τὴν φοβερὰν ἐκείνην*
28 : 58 *τὸ ὄνομα τὸ ἔντιμον καὶ τὸ θαυμαστὸν τοῦτο*
3 Reg 3 : 6 *τὸ ἔλεος τὸ μέγα τοῦτο*

Other examples may be found in Hatch and Redpath. This word order repeats the Hebrew idiom, cf. A. B. Davidson, *Hebrew Syntax*³, p. 45.

In Aramaic the placing of the demonstrative is much freer and we can for example find instances of the order, noun, demonstrative, adjective. This recurs in the New Testament for instance at Mt 12 : 45 ; Mk 8 : 38.

Granted that *τίς ἡ διδαχὴ ἡ καινὴ αὕτη* is original, we recover a contact with Ac 17 : 19 *τίς ἡ καινὴ αὕτη ἡ ὑπὸ σοῦ λαλουμένη διδαχή* ; earlier scholars who worked with the Textus Receptus had noticed the resemblance, but it was lost to sight when the א B text took its place.

How are we to interpret the similarity? First, Acts from time to time echoes Mark and Luke. The best known example is Lk 23 : 34/Ac 7 : 60, but the following echoes of Mark are relevant:

Ac 1 : 7/Mk 13 : 32 ; 2 : 38/1 : 4 ; 4 : 25/2 : 12 ; 5 : 15 f./6 : 55 ; 9 : 40/5 : 40 ; 13 : 25/1 : 7 ; cf. Lake and Cadbury (*BC* 4) on Ac 1 : 7 ; 12 : 4.

Secondly, as can be seen, Mk 1 : 27 TR is much closer to Ac 17 : 19 than Mk 1 : 27 WH, but it is difficult to regard Mk 1 : 27 TR as an assimilation of Mk 1 : 27 WH to Ac 17 : 19. Assimilation, for example, does not account for the trace of Semitic idiom in Mk 1 : 27 TR. The alternative is that Ac 17 : 19 echoes Mk 1 :27 TR and in the context of the Areopagus speech avoids the Semitic structure of Mark in doing so. We can accordingly regard Ac 17 : 19 as guaranteeing the originality of Mk 1 : 27 TR.

We notice that the reading of WH lacks *τίς* before *ἡ διδαχή* thus avoiding a second question. On the other hand D and others omit the first question. These two variants reduce the two questions to one though they do so in different ways. On the other hand double questions of this kind seem to be characteristic of Mark, cf. 1 : 24 ; 2 : 7 ; 2 : 8 f. ; 4 : 13, 21, 40 ; 6 : 2 ; 7 : 18 f., etc. They may be a particular form of Mark's use of duplicate expressions. Cf. C. H. Turner, *JTS* 28 (1926–27), 155 ; W. C. Allen, *The Gospel According to St. Matthew*, Edinburgh, 1907, p. xxiv.

Sometimes these double questions form part of a pattern : question, question, ὅτι (=because), as at 6 : 2 *v.l.* ; 7 : 18 f. ; or question, question, γάρ, as at 4 : 21 f.; 8 : 36 ff. But ὅτι (=because) seems not to have been liable to corrections such as are indicated in the round brackets at Mt 5 : 45 (ὅς, ὅστις) ; 14 : 5 (ἐπεὶ) ; 23 : 10 (γὰρ) ; Mk 8 : 24 (om.) ; Jn 1 : 16 (καὶ); 5 : 39 (om.) ; 12 : 39 (γὰρ), 41 (ὅτε); Ro 9 : 7 (ὅσοι); Gal 3 : 13 (γὰρ); Ja 1 : 23 (om.); Rev 18 : 23 (om.). We should perhaps restore ὅτι at Mk 6 : 2 ὅ. καὶ ; 8 : 3 ὅ. καί τινες ; 11 : 18 ὅ. πᾶς ; Lk 7 : 28 ὅ. ὁ μικρότερος ; 17 : 19 ὅ. ἡ; 18 : 32 ὅ. παραδοθήσεται ; 19 : 5 ὅ. σήμερον, 21 ὅ. ἐφοβούμην ; Jn 8 : 53 ὅ. ἀπέθανεν ; 13 : 29 ὅ. τό ; Ac 17 : 25 ὅ. αὐτός 1 P 5 : 8 ὅ. ὁ; Rev 22 : 10 ὅ. ὁ. At Mk 11 : 18; Lk 19 : 5, 21 ; Rev 22 : 10 γάρ is an alternative reading.

The substitution of γάρ for ὅτι would agree with certain tendencies of Greek style. Classical Greek has a number of connectives which cannot come first in a sentence. The language gradually got rid of these, δέ being the last to go, and often substituted connectives which regularly came at the beginning of their clauses, καί for δέ being an obvious example. ὅτι for γάρ would be another. Already in the New Testament particles such as τε, γάρ, οὖν show signs of going out of use. The reversion to a more classical style in the second century would account for the substitution of γάρ for ὅτι, but it would not account for the substitution of ἐπεί for ὅτι. This suggests that scribes had other objections to ὅτι.

The reading ὅτι settles the punctuation. κατ' ἐξουσίαν goes with what follows.

The text that we have preferred, variant (2), agrees with Marcan language and patterns of style. It restores the original of a Marcan echo in Acts. If the argument is right, then we have a clear instance where the TR and its allies have avoided corrections that have befallen the Alexandrian and the Western manuscripts. It is noteworthy that the instrument of correction on this showing has been omission, omission of τί ἐστι τοῦτο, reduction of τίς ἡ διδάχη ἡ καινὴ αὕτη to διδαχὴ καινή and omission of ὅτι. This bodes ill for the maxim *lectio brevior potior.*

## Mk 4 : 30, Is 40 : 18 and the Gospel of Thomas

Nestle and most modern editions following WH have at Mk 4 : 30 πῶς ὁμοιώσωμεν τὴν βασιλείαν τοῦ θεοῦ, ἢ ἐν τίνι αὐτὴν παραβολῇ θῶμεν ; Mark does not seem elsewhere to have a certain example of a pronoun thrust between a noun and a preceding adjective and such an order seems intrinsically unlikely if, as we would expect, the language here is at all influenced by Semitic idiom. So we are not surprised to discover that for αὐτὴν παραβολῇ θῶμεν A Π Υ Σ Φ Δ Θ ω read παραβολῇ παραβάλωμεν αὐτήν. Here the pronoun is in a much more natural place according to Hebrew or Aramaic usage and we have in παραβολῇ παραβάλωμεν a much less comfortable expression in Greek, cf. F. Blass-A. Debrunner-R. W. Funk, *A Greek Grammar,* Chicago, 1961, pp. 106b–107a. Scribes sometimes avoided the association of verb and cognate noun, e.g., Ac 4 : 17 (*v.l.*), 7 : 17 (*v.l.*).

One other restoration may be made. For τίνι the same witnesses read ποίᾳς. τίς is not elsewhere used as an adjective in Mark, but adjectival ποῖος recurs at Mk 11 : 28, 29, 33 ; 12 : 28. Why was τίνι substituted for ποίᾳ ?

This question leads to the second part of our enquiry. The text now runs :

πῶς ὁμοιώσωμεν τὴν βασιλείαν τοῦ θεοῦ,
ἢ ἐν ποίᾳ παραβολῇ παραβάλωμεν αὐτήν;

This is obviously an echo of Is 40 : 18

*w'l-my tḏmywn 'l*
*wmh-dmwṯ t'rḵw-lw*

" and to whom will you liken God
and what likeness will you compare to him ".

Mark however is independent of the LXX which runs :

τίνι ὡμοιώσατε κύριον
καί τίνι ὁμοιώματι ὡμοιώσατε αὐτόν

We may suspect that the LXX translates and Mark echoes a Hebrew text which differed in some points from the Hebrew we

have. The principal difference can be represented by capital letters, the nouns being italicized and the verbs in Roman capitals. The pattern is in Mark A *B* B
LXX A *A* A
Hebrew A *A* B

In principle the Dead Sea Isaiah supports the MT; Aquila seems to do the same.[1] The Targum might represent something of the order C *A* B but this is debatable. In any case the text of Mark that we propose clearly alludes to Isaiah and is independent of MT and LXX. A corruption is not likely to have this result.

We may now suggest an explanation of the reading τίνι for ποίᾳ in Mark. It can be an assimilation to the LXX. At this point A D Θ and the Syrian witnesses will have resisted assimilation, but in the next line they have succumbed to reading τίνι instead of πῶς which occurs in ℵ B C L W Δ f13 28 *al.*

We can now take our result further. Professor J. Jeremias (*The Parables of Jesus,* Rev. Ed., London, 1963, p. 146) quotes from the Gospel of Thomas 20 " The disciples said to Jesus: Tell us what the Kingdom of Heaven is like. He said to them: It is like a mustard-seed smaller than all seeds. But when it falls on the tilled earth, it produces a large branch and becomes shelter for the birds of heaven." This version lacks the allusion to Isaiah. We may ask ourselves which is likelier to be original, Mark or Thomas. Mark's allusion is independent of MT and LXX but reflects Semitic idiom. The implication is that it goes back at least to the Aramaic stage of the tradition of Jesus' sayings and intrinsically there is nothing to suggest that it is not original. We may infer that the Gospel of Thomas gives us a simplified form of Mark's story in this as it appears to do in other respects.

What began as an exercise in textual criticism has recovered an interesting allusion to the Old Testament and has provoked a contrast with the Gospel of Thomas.

After writing this I came across Professor H.-W. Bartsch's note, " Eine bisher übersehene Zitierung der LXX in Mark 4 : 30 ", *TZ* 15 (1959), 126–28. We agree in seeing in Mk 4 : 30 a reference to Is 40 : 18 though Dr Bartsch believes that the evangelist cites the LXX here. He has a number of interesting comments on the passage.

[1] Prof. J. A. Emerton points out to me that the Peshitta has A*A*A, the same pattern of rendering as the LXX.

## Luke 18 : 30

F. C. Burkitt in *The Gospel History and its Transmission* Edinburgh, [3]1911, p. 50, suggested that we ought to read ἑπταπλασίονα at Lk 18 : 30. Mk 10 : 30 has ἑκατονταπλασίονα and Mt 19 : 29 πολλαπλασίονα. While most witnesses at Luke have πολλαπλασίονα there are the following variants:

ἑπταπλασίονα D *L* a b c d e ff² i l q r¹˒ ² Cyp Amb Aug *S* h^mg Ephr.
ἑκατονταπλασίονα 472 1271 *S* c s.
We can explain πολλαπλασίονα and ἑκατονταπλασίονα in Luke as harmonizations to Matthew and Mark but why did the evangelist change Mark's ἑκατονταπλασίονα to ἑπταπλασίονα in the first place?

At several places in the Old Testament a sevenfold penalty is mentioned, but at:

Sir 32 : 13 (35 : 10) ὅτι κύριος ἀνταποδιδούς ἐστιν
καὶ ἑπταπλάσια (*l*—σίονα) ἀνταποδώσει σοι

there is a reference to the reward for the man who gives generously to God. Luke is steeped in the LXX and *BC* 2, p. 525, notes contacts with Sirach. Further examples are listed at *BC* 4, p. 397; cf. M. Wilcox, *The Semitisms of Acts*, Oxford, 1965, p. 78 n. 2. It is possible that a careful study would reveal more.

## Luke 20 : 1

We have been urged to read at Lk 20 : 1 not ἀρχιερεῖς, the reading of the modern editions, but ἱερεῖς which appears in the TR. Yet K. Aland's *Synopsis* (Stuttgart, 1964) and the Bible Societies' Greek Testament (ed. K. Aland, *et al.*, Stuttgart, 1966) still read ἀρχιερεῖς. Can we find any justification for this?

In the LXX outside 1–4 Maccabees ἀρχιερεύς occurs rarely, but in all its occurrences it is always in the singular. The reason for this is obvious: ἀρχιερεύς is high priest and there was only one high priest at a time. In Hebrews with one exception we find in agreement with this principle that ἀρχιερεύς occurs only in the singular. The exception is at 7 : 27 ὥσπερ οἱ ἀρχιερεῖς and 28 ὁ νόμος γὰρ ἀνθρωποὺς καθίστησιν ἀρχιερεῖς, if this is the right reading. Here the plural need not mean that there were more high priests than one at a time, but may refer to successive high priests.

Elsewhere we find the same practice. In the *Letter to Aristeas* the singular is always used of the Jewish high priest, the plural once of Egyptian high priests. Similarly in the *Testaments of the Twelve Patriarchs* the singular is the rule and the one plural *Levi* 8 : 17 if it is correct probably refers again to successive high priests.

In Josephus we have a development. The article in H. St. J. Thackeray's *Lexicon to Josephus*, 87b, runs as follows : " °(1) the Jewish *high-priest*, A. vi. 244, vii. 72–6 (interpolated into Bibl. narrative), 245, *B*. i. 152, &c. : pl. οἱ-εῖς including, besides the acting h. p., ex-high-priests and members of the privileged families from which the h. priests were drawn (Schürer), *A*. vii. 222 ff. (two, under David), xx. 207, &c. and freq. in *B*. e.g. εἶς τῶν-έων *B*. ii. 566, vii. 423, ὁ μετὰ 'Α. γεραίτατος τῶν -έων iv. 238, ἐκ τῶν -έων v. 527 : οἱ -εῖς ‖ ἡ βουλή ii. 331, 336 (+δυνατοί), ‖ οἱ γνώριμοι (τῶν Φαρισαίων) 318, 410 f., ‖ οἱ δυνατοί 301, 316, 411, 422, 428, ‖ ὁ βασιλεύς 342 : of a succession of h. priests *Ap*. i. 29 τοῖς -εῦσι κ. τοῖς προφήταις τοῦτο προστάξαντες (the keeping of records) ; (2) ὁ ἀ. the Roman *pontifex maximus*, *A*. xiv. 190 R-2R, xvi. 162 R, xix. 287 R (+μέγιστος)."

Schürer's discussion, *HJP*, ii., I, 274–277, fills this out. During the last century of the Temple there was the high priest in office, there were former high priests and there were men who were available. Of all these the term with its plural ἀρχιερεῖς, could be used. So we can distinguish two uses of the term in Josephus, for the high priest in office at the time and for this wider group who might be called high priests. J. Jeremias, *Jerusalem zur Zeit Jesu*, Gottingen, [3]1962, II B 33–40 suggests a somewhat different interpretation of the data but both he and Schürer recognize a double use of the term, first for the high priest and secondly for members of a wider priestly circle.

Similar is the usage in the Gospels and Acts. ἀρχιερεύς from time to time is used of the high priest then in office, at other times for a much larger group. This much is clear despite textual variation.

For there is textual variation not only at Lk 20 : 1. Much of it seems to occur where one of the variants is the plural of ἀρχιερεύς :

Mt 2 : 4 ἀρχιερεῖς ] ἱερεῖς *Δ* (sacerdotibus *k*)
21 : 45 " ] " 1093
26 : 59 οἱ δὲ ἀρχιερεῖς ] ὁ δὲ ἀρχιερεύς Or *L* a n Sa (1) Bo (1)
27 : 20 οἱ . . . ἀρχιερεῖς ] princeps . . . sacerdotum *L* f h g vg (A F *Y* *Σ* al) *S* π

The following Latin renderings avoid the plural ἀρχιερεῖς where the Greek has no variant :

Mt 16 : 21 sacerdotibus *e* Iren
20 : 18 " "
21 : 15 pharisaei vg (Q)
27 : 6 princeps autem sacerdotum *a* vg (H* or Q)
28 : 11 sacerdotibus *e*

In Mark the relevant Greek variants look like errors or stylistic changes :

Mk 8 : 31 καὶ τῶν ἀρχιερέων ] om 565 Just
11 : 18 οἱ ἀρχιερεῖς καὶ ] om M$^{mg}$ 122 252$^{mg}$ 506 517 713 1555 *l*48
27 οἱ ἀρχιερεῖς καὶ ] om 106
15 : 10 οἱ ἀρχιερεῖς ] om B f1$^{pt}$ 115 349 389 544 579 1200 1375 *l*10 *l*13 *l*47 *S* s Bo *H* a.i.n.
11 οἱ δὲ ἀρχιερεῖς ] οὗτοι δέ 118 209 G
οἵτινες καί *Θ* 565 700 Arm
om *l*47

The following Latin renderings may be noted :

Mk 11 : 27 sacerdotes *i*
14 : 53 sacerdotes *sur l q r*$^{1, 2}$ vg
15 : 11 scribae *aur c*
sacerdotes *k*
31 sacerdotes *k*

In Luke there are the following :

Lk 3 : 2 ἀρχιερέως ] ἀρχιερέων 13 174 346 543 788 826 983 1689 517 Thdt *L* (-b d r$^1$) Bo
9 : 22 καὶ ἀρχιερέων ] om 565
20 : 1 ἀρχιερέων ] ἱερέων *A Π* W *ω*
19 ἀρχιερεῖς ] φαρισαῖοι *O* (716)
22 : 66 ἀρχιερεῖς ] om V

In Latin we have:

Lk 19 : 47 princeps autem sacerdotum *c q* vg (B)
20 : 20 ἀποχωρήσαντες D ] + principes sacerdotum *c*
22 : 52 ἀρχιερεῖς . . . πρεσβυτέρους ] om *l*
23 : 10 (cf 13) sacerdotes *c* (10 vg (k))
24 : 20 sacerdotes *c e* Aug

In John:

7 : 32 οἱ ἀρχιερεῖς καὶ οἱ Φαρισαῖοι ] om 6053 118 209 Cat *L* b e
18 : 3 ἀρχιερέων ] ἀρχόντων 544
35 οἱ ἀρχιερεῖς ] ὁ ἀρχιερεύς ℵ *L* b e

and in Latin:

11 : 47 scribae *d*
19 : 6 princeps sacerdotum *b* : sacerd[otes] *a*
21 sacerdotes *e* : principes *b c q r* [1]

In Acts:

4 : 1 οἱ ἀρχιερεῖς B C Arm Eth ] οἱ ἱερεῖς cet.
5 : 24 ὁ ἀρχιερεύς 1891 *g*
19 : 14 ἀρχιερέως ] ἱερέως D *d g p* r S* π*
25 : 2 οἱ ἀρχιερεῖς ] ὁ ἀρχιερεύς H P S ω
26 : 10 ἀρχιερέων ] ἱερέων 1898

and in Latin:

4 : 1 sacerdotes *omnes*
23 princeps sacerdotum vg (F)
5 : 24 princeps sacerdotum *g*
pontifex sacerdotum Lucif
9 : 14, 21 sacerdotibus *h*
22 : 30 sacerdotes vg
23 : 14 sacerdotes *h*
principem sacerdotum *g p r*

Hebrews has been already discussed but we may notice:

7 : 27 ὁ ἀρχιερεύς *D**
28 ἱερεῖς D* I$^{vid}$ Ephr

and in Latin:

7 : 27 sacerdotes exc. *r* Aug
28 sacerdotes *omnes*

We should probably add for consideration:

Lk 23 : 23 αὐτῶν P[75] ℵ B L 0124 130 1241 *L* c d f Sa Bo[pt] ]
+ καὶ τῶν ἀρχιερέων *cet* (Eth) cf. καὶ τῶν ἀρχόντων 1253

Omission through ὁμ. is easy:

αυτΩΝΚΑΙΤωναρχιερεΩΝΚΑΙΠιλατος.

Our author is ready to lay the blame where he thinks it belongs, cf. *JTS* 43 (1941–42), 34–36, and has his own ways of doing this, cf. Ac 3 : 17.

Some of these variations, e.g., Lk 3 : 2; Ac 19 : 14, look like attempts to deal with local difficulties, but others cannot be so explained. They seem to be attempts to avoid a plural ἀρχιερεῖς. Thus the singular ἀρχιερεύς would be substituted at Mt 26 : 59; 27 : 6, 20; Lk 19 : 47; Jn 18 : 35; 19 : 6; Ac 4 : 23; 5 : 24; 23 : 14; 25 : 2; He 7 : 27; ἱερεῖς at Mt 2 : 4; 21 : 45; Lk 20 : 1; Ac 4 : 1; 19 : 14; 26 : 10; He 7 : 28; ἄρχοντες at Lk 23 : 23; Jn 18 : 3; Φαρισαῖοι at Mt 21 : 15; Lk 20 : 19, and perhaps *scribae* at Mk 15 : 11. The plural may have been avoided by omission at Mk 15 : 11; Lk 22 : 66; Jn 7 : 32.

In the Latin *sacerdotes* may often be a translator's device for avoiding the difficulty. Unless there is other evidence we need not infer a reading ἱερεῖς for each example of *sacerdotes*.

Two scholars have already discussed the reading at Lk 20 : 1, H. Greeven in *NTS* 6 (1960), 295 f. and B. M. Metzger, *The Text of the New Testament*, New York, 1964, pp. 238 f., and are agreed that ἱερεῖς is original. I regret that for once I have hesitations about this conclusion. Professor Greeven, whom Professor Metzger follows, argues that, as the parallels in Mark, Matthew have ἀρχιερεῖς and that this is the regular expression appearing in formula some 46 times in the Gospel and Acts, there would be a very strong tendency to correct an original ἱερεῖς to agree with ἀρχιερεῖς in the parallels and the formula elsewhere.

It is quite clear that when we examine the occurrences of such formula in the apparatus that harmonization does not take place. On the other hand why on this showing does the evangelist here substitute ἱερεῖς in this place for the ἀρχιερεῖς which comes in his source?

Professor Metzger has written "In the passage under consideration there is no discernible motive for altering 'chief priests' to 'priests'" (239), but I would suggest that a number of variations and renderings for ἀρχιερεῖς in the New Testament are explained if we infer that correctors sought from time to time to avoid this plural because like the LXX and Hebrews they took ἀρχιερεύς in the sense of " high priest " of which there could only be one at a time and not in the sense of " chief priest " of which there could be a number as we see in the Gospel, Acts and Josephus.

Professor Greeven has pointed out that in several passages ἱερεύς is changed by some manuscripts into ἀρχιερεύς and of his six examples Mk 1 : 44 ; 2 : 26 ; Lk 5 : 14 ; 17 : 14 should be accepted without question. Other examples may be found in apocryphal books. For example in the *Protevangelium Jacobi* ἀρχιερεύς regular has a variant ἱερεύς both in the singular and in the plural. On the other hand *Acta Philippi* 6 : 10 f. εἰ μή ὁ ἀρχιερεὺς τῶν Ἰουδαίων and 6 : 15 f. Ἀνανίᾳ τῷ μεγάλῳ ἀρχιερεῖ τῶν Ἰουδαίων suggest an awareness that strictly speaking there was only one Jewish high priest at a time. Professor Greeven is quite right. There was a tendency to introduce ἀρχιερεύς into passages where it had no place, but on the evidence here submitted the tendency to avoid the plural ἀρχιερεῖς may perhaps have gone further and deeper.

Professor Greeven's paper is full of instruction for us all and avoids the mistake sometimes still made of considering passages and readings in isolation. I may claim to follow in his footsteps at this point and rejoice that we are so agreed in principle. We are also both ready to go outside ℵ B in our search for the original text and, if he has done this at Lk 20 : 1, I have done so at Lk 23 : 23. The passages where the reading is at issue are Lk 20 : 1 ; 23 : 23 ; Ac 4 : 1 and it is good to know that we seek to decide them on their merits.

# A COMPARISON OF THE PALESTINIAN SYRIAC LECTIONARY AND THE GREEK GOSPEL LECTIONARY

Bruce M. Metzger

In view of Principal Black's long interest in the Palestinian Syriac version, demonstrated by the publication of more than one manuscript involving that version,[1] it will perhaps not be out of place in a volume of essays written in his honour to compare the Palestinian Syriac Lectionary and the Greek Gospel Lectionary. Prior to about a generation ago such a comparison would scarcely have been feasible. Now, however, thanks to the increase in our knowledge of the Greek Gospel Lectionary, owing largely to the pioneering work in this area sponsored at the University of Chicago by Ernest Cadman Colwell [2] and Allen Wikgren,[3] it has become possible to answer certain questions concerning the Palestinian Syriac Lectionary which previously were either disputed or not even clearly formulated.

The existence of an ancient vellum codex containing a Church Lesson book written in an Aramaic dialect has been known to the scholarly world since about the middle of the eighteenth century when a full description of it was published by two Maronite scholars, the cousins Assemani.[4] During the next generation a Danish scholar, J. G. C. Adler, having examined the manuscript

[1] E.g., " A Palestinian Syriac Palimpsest Leaf of Acts xxi (14–26) ", *BJRL* 23 (1939), 201–14, and *A Palestinian Syriac Horologion* (*Berlin MS. Or. Oct. 1019*), Cambridge, 1954.

[2] See Ernest Cadman Colwell and Donald W. Riddle, *Prolegomena to the Study of the Lectionary Text of the Gospels*, being vol. I of *Studies in the Lectionary Text of the Greek New Testament*, Chicago, 1933. Volume II comprises six separate monographs (for a summary of their contents, see Wikgren's article mentioned in the next footnote).

[3] For a survey of recent research on Greek lectionaries see Allen Wikgren's chapter entitled " Chicago Studies in the Greek Lectionary of the New Testament ", in *Biblical and Patristic Studies in Memory of Robert Pierce Casey*, ed. J. Neville Birdsall and Robert W. Thomson, Freiburg, 1963, pp. 96–121, to which can now be added the publication of two Princeton dissertations, one by Ray Harms on *The Matthean Weekday Lessons in the Greek Gospel Lectionary*, Chicago, 1966, and the other by Ronald E. Cocroft, *A Study of the Pauline Lessons in the Matthean Section of the Greek Lectionary*, Salt Lake City, 1968.

[4] S. E. Assemani and J. S. Assemani, *Bibliothecæ Apostolicæ Vaticanæ codicum manuscriptorum catalogus*, Partis Primae, tomus II, Rome, 1758, pp. 70–103.

in the Vatican Library, published an extract from the Gospel according to Matthew.[5]

It was not, however, until a century after the Assemanis had drawn attention to the manuscript that a full and sumptuous edition was published by Count Francesco Miniscalchi Erizzo.[6] On the basis of this publication two important investigations were made. Theodor Nöldeke prepared a useful treatise concerning the peculiar dialect in which it is written,[7] and Theodor Zahn discussed its textual characteristics with reference to its presumed historical background.[8] On the eve of the discovery of two other manuscripts, similar to the Vatican manuscript, there was published posthumously the work of the renowned Orientalist Paul de Lagarde, who had made a fresh collation of the document and rearranged the text of its pericopes in the order in which it is found in the four Gospels.[9]

In 1892 Mrs Agnes Smith Lewis came upon another manuscript of the Palestinian Syriac Lectionary in the Monastery of St Catherine on Mount Sinai, and the following year at the same place Rendel Harris found a third. These were published, with the one that had been previously edited, by Mrs Lewis and her twin sister, Mrs Margaret Dunlop Gibson.[10]

Within a short time numerous investigations of these three manuscripts, as well as of several others that preserve portions of the text of several books of the Old Testament and of the Acts and several epistles of the New Testament, were published.[11] It was the lament, however, of more than one investigator of the Palestinian Syriac Lectionary that so little information about Greek Lectionaries was available. Both Eberhard Nestle[12] and

[5] *Novi Testamenti versiones Syriacæ simplex, Philoxiana et Hierosolymitana*, Copenhagen, 1789, pp. 135–201.

[6] *Evangeliarium Hierosolymitanum ex codice Vaticano Palæstino deprompsit, edidit, Latine vertit, prolegomenis ac glossario adornavit*, 2 vols., Verona, 1861–64.

[7] " Beiträge zur Kenntniss der aramäischen Dialecte ", *Zeitschrift der deutschen morgenländischen Gesellschaft* 22 (1868), 443–527.

[8] *Forschungen zur Geschichte des neutestamentlichen Kanons und der altkirchlicher Literatur*, 1, Erlangen, 1881, pp. 329–50.

[9] *Bibliothecæ Syriacæ*, Göttingen, 1892, pp. 258–402.

[10] *The Palestinian Syriac Lectionary of the Gospels, re-edited from two Sinai Mss. and from P. de Lagarde's edition of the " Evangeliarium Hierosolymitanum "* by Agnes Smith Lewis and Margaret Dunlop Gibson, London, 1899.

[11] For a list of these publications up to 1903, with a Scriptural index of the text preserved, see Friedrich Schulthess, *Lexicon Syropalaestinum*, Berlin, 1903, pp. vii–xvi.

[12] *A Palestinian Syriac Lectionary containing Lessons from the Pentateuch,*

F. C. Burkitt [13] despaired of solving certain problems concerning the Syriac Lectionary until scholars knew more of the structure and range of variation in Byzantine church reading books. The present investigation, made in the light of recent studies of Greek Gospel lectionaries, assembles certain data which may be useful as prolegomena to a more extensive study of the structure of the Palestinian Syriac Lectionary. Before presenting these data, however, it will doubtless be useful to summarize certain basic information concerning the language of the Palestinian Syriac Lectionary, and concerning the date and nature of the Palestinian Syriac version.

The dates of the three manuscripts of the Palestinian Syriac Lectionary are known from colophons preserved in the documents. The Vatican codex was copied A.D. 1030, the other two A.D. 1104 and A.D. 1118. The three manuscripts, which are usually designated, respectively, codices A, B, and C, are noteworthy both for their text and their language.[14] The only claim of the latter to be Syriac rests upon the script in which it is written ; [15] the language is properly a western dialect of Aramaic.[16] Thus, instead of writing the third singular masculine of the imperfect tense with the prefix *nun*, as is customary in Syriac, Palestinian Syriac uses the prefix *yod*,[17] agreeing in this respect with the Aramaic of the Old Testament, the Targum of Onkelos, and the Jerusalem Talmud. Moreover, the third person singular suffix attached to plural nouns is commonly written in the Aramaic manner, *-oi* instead of *-ohi*, characteristic of Syriac, and the *status emphaticus* of masc. plural nouns ends in *-aia'* instead of the contracted form usual in Syriac, *ê'*. These features relating to accidence agree completely with Nöldeke's judgment regarding the vocabulary, to the effect that the dialect is much closer to Jewish Palestinian

---

*Job, Proverbs, Prophets, Acts, and Epistles*, ed. by A. S. Lewis, with Critical Notes by Eberhard Nestle (*Studia Sinaitica*, No. 6), London, 1897, p. lxxiv ; cf. also p. lxiv.

[13] " Christian Palestinian Literature ", *JTS* 2 (1904), 180 f.

[14] For a facsimile of a specimen folio from each manuscript, see W. H. P. Hatch, *An Album of Dated Syriac Manuscripts*, Boston, 1946, pp. 247 ff.

[15] It resembles the Syriac script known as Estrangela, except that the characters are much more square in their outline and the *dolath* is usually without its diacritical mark ; the letter *pe* has two forms for the sounds " ph " and " p ".

[16] Friedrich Schulthess, *Grammatik des christlich-palästinischen Aramäisch*, Tübingen, 1924, pp. 1 ff.

[17] Nöldeke can find but three examples in the whole lectionary (codex A) where the scribe inadvertantly used the *nun* (*op. cit.*, p. 698, n. 1).

Aramaic than to classical Syriac current at Edessa.[18] It is a concession, therefore, to the strength of traditional nomenclature to continue to refer to the document as the Palestinian *Syriac* Lectionary.

When the Palestinian Syriac version of the Bible was made is a moot question. Nöldeke placed its origin sometime between A.D. 300 and 600, preferring an earlier rather than a later date within that period.[19] Burkitt assigned it to the sixth century.[20] Lagrange [21] argued that sacred books existed in oral tradition among Palestinian Christians during the fourth century, and that in the fifth century these took on a literary form. Sometime after the beginning of the fifth century seems to be required in the light of comments made by St Egeria (Aetheria). During her pilgrimage to Palestine at the end of the fourth or the beginning of the fifth century [22] she found

> in ea provincia pars populi et graece et siriste novit, pars etiam alia per se graece, aliqua etiam pars tantum siriste, itaque, quoniam episcopus, licet siriste nouerit, tamen semper graece loquitur et nunquam siriste ; itaque ergo stat semper presbyter, qui, episcopo graece dicente, siriste interpretatur, ut omnes audiant, quae exponuntur. Lectiones etiam, quaecumque in ecclesia leguntur, quia necesse est graece legi, semper stat, qui siriste interpretatur propter populum, ut semper discant.[23]

In other words, it appears that a Greek-speaking bishop was accompanied by a presbyter, who translated the Scripture lessons as well as his sermon into Syriac (i.e. Aramaic) so that all could understand. This suggests, as Vööbus points out,[24] that the

[18] *Ibid.*, p. 513. For instance, the frequent occurrence of *iath* (some 600 times ; cf. Miniscalchi Erizzo's lexicon in *op. cit.*, vol. 2, p. 192, *s.v.*), often with pronominal suffixes, is a clear indication of affinity with the language of the Targums. See also Friedrich Schulthess, *op. cit.*, pp. 1 ff.

[19] *Op. cit.*, p. 525.

[20] *Op. cit.*, pp. 174–85.

[21] " L'Origine de la version syro-palestinienne des évangiles ", *RB* 34 (1925), 481–504, esp. 497.

[22] The dates are those of Berthold Altaner [and] Alfred Stuiber, *Patrologie*, Freiburg im Breisgau, 1966, p. 245.

[23] S. Silvia, *Peregrinatio*, 47.3 (*Corpus Scriptorum Ecclesiasticorum Latinorum*, 39, p. 99, lines 13–21).

[24] Arthur Vööbus, *Early Versions of the New Testament ; Manuscript Studies*, Stockholm, 1954, pp. 126 f.

Palestinian Syriac version did not exist at that time, but that the church provided an official to translate the Greek Scriptures orally.

The vocabulary of the Palestinian Syriac version exhibits many Graecisms. Thus, although the other Syriac versions commonly represent Ἰησοῦς by *yesû'*, the Palestinian Syriac version almost always transcribes it *yesûs*. Even in Mt 16 : 18 this version uses a transliteration of Πέτρος rather than the Semitic *Kepha* (as in the Curetonian [25] manuscript and the Peshitta), destroying thereby the significance of the play on words in the context. Other proper names [26] that it renders in a more or less Graecized form are :

| | | | |
|---|---|---|---|
| *ḥana's* | for | Ἄννας | instead of *ḥanān* |
| *yûḥanîs* | for | Ἰωάννης | instead of *yûḥanān* |
| *rûba'am* | for | Ῥοβοάμ | instead of *reḥabe'am* |
| *yehûdas* | for | Ἰούδας | instead of *yêhûdā'* |
| *simôn* | for | Σίμων | instead of *šem'ûn* |

Graecizing went so far even in common words that occasionally ordinary Syriac words are abandoned for Greek words in Syriac dress. A typical example is the foresaking of *kenšā'*, the customary word in the Peshitta for " crowd ", and the use of *'oklos* (plural *'oklosē'*), which is a transliteration of ὄχλος. It is superfluous to show in detail how frequently the Palestinian Syriac vocabulary reveals traces of the Greek from which it was translated ; Schwally lists about sixty words that are transliterated in the manner of ὄχλος.[27]

Not only do individual words reveal their Greek origin, but the connected text displays several instances of exceedingly mechanical translation. These involve the translation of passages in which the Greek text of the Gospels preserves a Semitic word or phrase with an appended Greek translation. For instance, in the

[25] The Sinaitic Syriac is not extant here.

[26] Unfortunately neither Schwen nor Burkitt includes evidence from the Palestinian Syriac version in their investigations concerning Syriac proper names (Paul Schwen, " Die syrische Wiedergabe der neutestamentlichen Eigennamen ", *ZATW* 31 [1911], 267–303 ; and F. C. Burkitt, *The Syriac Forms of New Testament Proper Names* [*Proceedings of the British Academy*, 5 ; London, 1912]).

[27] Friedrich Schwally, *Idioticon des christlich palästinischen Aramaeisch*, Giessen, 1893, " Die griechischen und lateinischen Lehnwörter ", pp. 103–13. On the presence of Greek words in Syriac, see Anton Schall, *Studien über Fremdwörter in Syrischen*, Darmstadt, 1960, and S. P. Brock, " Greek Words in the Syriac Gospels (*Vet* and *Pe*) ", *Muséon* 80 (1967), 389–426.

Marcan narrative of the deaf and dumb man, the Greek text has retained the Aramaic word that Jesus used, adding its meaning in Greek.[28] Here the Palestinian Syriac, oddly enough, renders the entire text: "And he said to him, 'Be thou opened', which is, 'Be thou opened'".[29]

The cry from the cross as Matthew reports it (Mt 27 : 46) is found twice in the Palestinian Syriac Lectionary;[30] in all three codices the second instance involves the curious pleonasm: "'My God, my God (*'Êlī, 'Êlī*), why hast thou forsaken me?' which is 'My God, my God (*'Êlohī, 'Êlohī*),[31] why hast thou forsaken me?'"

The first chapter of John provides three more examples of mechanical literalism. It is thought necessary to interpret the Semitic word "rabbi" (1 : 38), the title "Messiah" (1 : 41 (42)), and the name "Cephas" (1 : 42 (43)). The last mentioned passage presents a strange conglomeration: "And the Lord Jesus looked on him and said, 'Thou art Simon the son of Jona; thou shalt be called Kepha, which is being interpreted, Petros.'"

In the light of the foregoing data concerning aspects of the nature of the Palestinian Syriac version, we may now turn our attention to a comparison of the Greek and Syriac lectionary systems. The first thing that one observes is their striking similarity.[32] The section known as the synaxarion contains lessons from the Gospels for every day of the week during the first seven weeks beginning with Easter. After Pentecost it presents only the Saturday and Sunday lessons for the rest of the year, except during Holy Week, when it is complete (with two or three slight exceptions). The synaxarion closes with the eleven Gospels of the Resurrection. Not only is the order of the lessons exactly like that of most Greek lectionaries, but the choice and extent of the Scripture lessons in the synaxarion are, with a few slight variations not greater than those found among Greek lectionaries themselves, identical in the two systems.

[28] Mk 7 : 34 *Εφφαθα* [= *'eṯpeṯaḥ*], *ὅ ἐστιν, Διανοίχθητι.*

[29] The Sinaitic Syriac (Curetonian *hiat*), Peshitta, and Arabic Diatessaron omit the explanatory phrase; the Harclean retains it.

[30] On pp. 203 f. and 212 of Lewis and Gibson's edition; the edition of de Lagarde is defective in omitting to mention the second instance of the passage.

[31] The form *'Êlohī* reflects the tradition embodied in Mk 15 : 34.

[32] In order to simplify the presentation, the oldest of the three Palestinian Syriac Lectionary manuscripts, codex A from A.D. 1030, has been chosen for comparison with the data in Colwell and Riddle's *Prolegomena*. Occasional divergences in codices B and C will be cited below.

The menologia of Greek lectionaries are notoriously diverse.[33] In view of such differences, it would not be surprising if the Palestinian Syriac Lectionary should be found to disagree radically in the choice of saints who are to be honoured as well as in the choice of lessons which are to be read. It is remarkable, however, that 80 per cent of the number of saints commemorated in the Palestinian Syriac menologion find parallels in one or more of the four Greek lectionaries collated in Colwell and Riddle's *Prolegomena.* Furthermore, when the Syriac lectionary is compared with data from Greek lectionaries in C. R. Gregory's *Textkritik des Neuen Testamentes,* still further parallels are disclosed.[34] In other words, although the Palestinian Syriac menologion does not agree with any one Greek menologion, it does not deviate to a greater extent from the collective testimony of Greek menologia than do individual Greek lectionaries themselves.

The correspondence between the Palestinian Syriac and Greek lectionaries in the choice and extent of the several lessons is particularly noteworthy inasmuch as both the earlier and the later Syriac lectionary systems present very considerable divergences from this one. The earlier system is remarkable for the exceedingly long lessons assigned to be read.[35] The later system was constructed on principles other than those now under consideration, and agrees with the Greek only on the occasion of such high festivals as hardly admitted a choice in their selection.[36]

The coincidence in the selection, extent, and order of the lessons and the saints commemorated is paralleled by the general coincidence in the choice of opening formulas. The Palestinian Syriac Lectionary makes use of all six varieties of incipit which are found in Greek lectionaries.[37] Of the 166 pericopes of the

[33] Colwell remarks, " The devices of rhetoric are not sufficient for the task of emphasizing the extent, the bewildering extent, of these divergences in textual quality " (*Prolegomena*, p. 15).

[34] Of 245 lections commemorating saints which are found in the Palestinian Syriac Lectionary, all but 48 can be paralleled in Colwell and Riddle ; and of the 48, eleven more can be paralleled in Gregory.

[35] Cf. F. C. Burkitt, *The Early Syriac Lectionary System*, London, 1923, p. 21.

[36] F. H. Scrivener, " Lectionaries ", Smith and Cheetham's *Dictionary of Christian Antiquities*, 1880, 2, p. 959 ; cf. A. J. Maclean, *East Syrian Daily Offices*, London, 1894, pp. 264–90. For a list of liturgical manuscripts used by Melchites in the Syrio-Byzantine period (the tenth to seventeenth centuries), see Cyrille Charon, " Le Rite byzantine et la liturgie chrysostomienne dans les patriarcates melchites (Alexandrie-Antioch-Jerusalem) ", in *Chrysostomika ; studi e ricerche intorno a S. Giovanni Crisostomo . . .*, Rome, 1908, pp. 506–16.

[37] For the six Greek incipits, see Colwell and Riddle, *Prolegomena*, p. 84.

Syriac synaxarion in codex A, 89 pericopes open with the formula, "At that time" or "And at that time".[38] Greek lectionaries also prefer the incipit τῷ καιρῷ ἐκείνῳ. The other opening formulas occur in the Syriac synaxarion less frequently (as also is true concerning Greek lectionaries): "The Lord said to his disciples" occurs 16 times; "The Lord said to the Jews who came to him" occurs once; "The Lord said to the Jews who believed on him", twice; "The Lord said", 23 times; "The Lord spoke this parable", ten times. The total number of agreements with the usage exhibited by what may be called the standard Greek lectionary is 141, or about 85 per cent of the entire number of incipits in the synaxarion. In view of the existence of a certain amount of variation in the choice of incipit among Greek lectionaries, the coincidence of so many opening formulas in the Syriac with the prevailing usage in the Greek system is noteworthy.

There is here, however, a difference between the Syriac and the Greek lectionaries. In the former the incipits are joined to the pericopes in a much more mechanical way than is customary in the latter. Greek lectionaries introduce minor modifications in whatever expressions of time happen to occur in the opening sentence of the lesson. But in the Palestinian Syriac Lectionary the incipits are prefixed to the pericope with no attempt at smoothing the sense. Naturally the result is sometimes unsatisfactory; one finds, for example, such *gaucheries* as "And at that time; moreover on the last day of the feast . . .", "The Lord spoke to his disciples; the Lord spoke this parable . . .", "And at that time; and on the next day he stood . . .", "At that time; and after this he walked. . . ."

If one asks how the Palestinian Syriac Lectionary was produced, three possibilities can be suggested, depending upon whether it was made directly from a Greek base or a Syriac base. If it was made from a Greek base, (1) it may have been translated directly from a Greek lectionary, or (2) the pericopes may have been translated from a copy or copies of the con-

[38] In true Semitic style many instances of this incipit begin with "and", a feature which Miniscalchi Erizzo frequently overlooks in his Latin translation. It may be mentioned also that in the Palestinian Syriac Lectionary the incipit "And at that time" is a curious hybrid of one Syriac word and one Greek word, *w^ebaiteh kairôsā'*. In other Syriac lectionaries the same incipit is regularly expressed with Syriac words throughout, *b^ehau dên zabnā'* (cf. Adler, *op. cit.*, p. 147, n. 6).

secutive text of the Greek Gospels and these excerpts then arranged in accord with the structure of the Greek lectionary. If it was made from a Syriac base, (3) the pericopes were excerpted from one or more copies of a continuous text of the Palestinian Syriac version,[39] marked by severe Greek literalism, and then arranged in accord with the structure of the Greek lectionary. In evaluating these possibilities quite opposite opinions have been expressed. According to Gwilliam, " There is no proof that that Syro-Palestinian Lectionaries are translations from Greek Lectionaries ; and it may be regarded as certain that they were preceded by complete copies of the Gospel, the Acts, and the Pauline Epistles, and of part, if not the whole of the Old Testament ".[40] On the other hand, Nestle took the opposite view concerning both the portions preserved in the Old Testament Syriac Lectionary as well those in the Gospel Lectionary : " The Syriac text was not excerpted from a complete Syriac Bible Version, but each lesson was translated by itself out of the Greek [of the Septuagint and the New Testament]." [41]

Nestle's judgment was based upon his finding several textual variations between two lessons involving the same Scriptural passage. Following Nestle's methodology, the present writer made a comparison of 195 verses that occur in duplicate (or triplicate) passages in the Palestinian Syriac Lectionary ; as a result a total of 151 textual variations was disclosed. Many of these are merely orthographic, involving simply the presence or absence of *matres lectionis*, but almost 90 variations involve changes in word order, syntax, and vocabulary. The following are several typical examples :

(1) At the opening of pericope no. [CC] [42] Jn 8 : 1 in codex A reads '$^{a}$*ṯā yesûs* '$^{e}$*lā' ṭûrâ' d*$^{e}$*zayṯaia*'; at the conclusion of pericope no. XLVIII, this same verse in the same manuscript [43] reads *mārā' yesûs dī* '$^{e}$*zal lēh l*$^{e}$*ṭûrâ' d*$^{e}$*zayṯa*'.

[39] That a continuous text of the Gospels in Palestinian Syriac once existed is proved by the preservation of several fragmentary remains ; see F. C. Burkitt, *JTS* 2 (1900–01), 179 f.

[40] *The Palestinian Version of the Holy Scriptures ; Five More Fragments . . .* ed. by G. H. Gwilliam (*Anecdota Oxoniensia*, I, 5), Oxford, 1893, p. xix. The same opinion is expressed by Rubens Duval in *La littérature syriaque*, 3rd ed., Paris, 1907, p. 47.

[41] *A Palestinian Syriac Lectionary containing Lessons from the Pentateuch, Job, Proverbs, Prophets, Acts, and Epistles*, ed. by Agnes Smith Lewis, with Critical Notes by Eberhard Nestle (*Studia Sinaitica*, No. 6), London, 1897, p. lxxi ; cf. p. xvii.

[42] Lewis and Gibson's ed., p. 242.

[43] *Ibid.*, p. 59.

(2) In Jn 12 : 41 the verb εἶπεν is translated by *'ᵉmar* in pericope no. XXXIX (attested by all three manuscripts) [44] but by *mallel* in pericope no. CXLV (attested by all three manuscripts).[45]

(3) In pericopes no. XXXVIII and no. XXXIX,[46] at Jn 12 : 18, 30, 38, 39, the three manuscripts are unanimous in utilizing the preposition *ligᵉlal* (*'lig(e)lal*), while in pericope no. CXLV [47] all manuscripts concur in using *lᵉbarêl* to translate the same words in the same verses of John.

(4) In Jn 12 : 34 the first occurrence of ὁ υἱὸς τοῦ ἀνθρώπου is rendered in pericope no. XXXVIII by *bārēh dᵉgabrā'* in all three manuscripts.[48] In no. CXLV,[49] however, two of the three manuscripts (A and C) employ the parallel phrase *bārēh dᵉbār nāšā'*.

One must beware against reading more significance into this kind of evidence than it can legitimately bear. Without raising the question at this stage concerning the nature of the source (whether it was a continuous Gospel text or a lectionary text), perhaps the most that can fairly be deduced is that the translator happened to choose for separate pericopes involving the same Scriptural passage equivalent but not identical Syriac phrases to render what appears to have been the same Greek text.

If one now passes from a consideration of variant renderings (what Vogels called *Übersetzungsfarbe*) to an examination of textually important variant readings among the duplicated pericopes in the Syriac Lectionary, the range of the evidence is considerably broadened. First, however, it will be appropriate to ask where Codex A found the text of Jn 8 : 1–11, a passage which is assigned to be read on St Pelagia's day, October 8th.[50] Not only do the Old Syriac texts (represented in the Diatessaron, the Sinaitic Syriac, and the Curetonian Syriac), but even the manuscripts of the Peshitta [51] betray no knowledge of the passage. Since only four other Syriac manuscripts are known to have the passage,[52] codex A of the Palestinian Syriac Lectionary in all

44 *Ibid.*, p. 49. 45 *Ibid.*, p. 169. 46 *Ibid.*, pp. 47–49.
47 *Ibid.*, pp. 167–69. 48 *Ibid.*, p. 48. 49 *Ibid.*, p. 168.

50 Cf. A. P. Wikgren, " The Lectionary Text of the Pericope, John 8 : 1–11 ", *JBL* 53 (1934), 188–98. The pericope was always read on some saint's day in the menologion and never on the feast of Pentecost, when the liturgy of the synaxarion presents Jn 7 : 37–52 and 8 : 11, omitting the intervening verses (F. H. A. Scrivener, *A Plain Introduction to the Criticism of the New Testament*, London, ⁴1894, I, p. 81, n. 1).

51 P. E. Pusey and G. H. Gwilliam, edd., *Tetraeuangelium sanctum juxta simplicem Syrorum versionem . . .*, Oxford, 1901, p. 526 note.

52 In only one of these four Syriac manuscripts (codex Barsalibæi) is the pericope exhibited *in loco* as part of the Gospel ; in the others it stands apart

probability derived it, not from a Syriac source, but from a Greek source. The Greek source may well have been a Greek lectionary, for on October 8th most menologia commemorate St Pelagia with the text of Jn 8 : 1–11 (sometimes 8 : 3–11).

In view of the circumstance that a Greek lectionary, in presenting the same Gospel passage in two (or more) sections of the lectionary, will occassionally exhibit textual variations between the lections, the following examples in the Syriac Lectionary are instructive.

(1) In Jn 12 : 42 (41) the reading *ʿal deṭebēh* in all three manuscripts of pericope no. XXXIX [53] presupposes the ordinary Greek text *περὶ αὐτοῦ*, but in pericope no. CXLV [54] all three manuscripts present the reading *ʿal deṭebēh demārā' yesûs*, which presupposes *περὶ Ἰησοῦ*.[55]

(2) Mt 22 : 15 in pericope no. CXLIII [56] reads *ʿalau(i)* translating *κατ' αὐτοῦ* of C² *Δ Θ Σ* 33 118 209 Cop^bo Arm Geo Origen (*bis*), while the same verse in pericope no. LXXVII [57] reads *ʿal yesûs* (codices A and B ; codex C omits *yesûs*, but nevertheless does not attach a suffix to *ʿal*), translating *κατὰ τοῦ Ἰησοῦ* of C³ M 477 1093 1279 1473 1515 1579 and four Greek lectionaries, which begin a lesson at this verse.

(3) Jn 1 : 34 in pericope no. CLXXXIII [58] concludes with *bărēh delāhâ'* in accord with most Greek manuscripts, but pericope no. II [59] reads (with minor variations among the three manuscripts) *bārēh delāhâ' baḥîrêh*, partly in accord with ℵ* 77 218 Old Lat Old Syr (sin. et cur.).

(4) Perhaps item no. 2 in the former list should be reckoned likewise among Syriac readings that presuppose different Greek readings. There is at least one Greek lectionary, cited by Colwell in *Prolegomena*,[60] which at Jn 12 : 41 in the lection for the fourth

---

from any context. For a learned account not only of the four documents, but also of how the passage got into Brian Walton's *Polyglott* and thence into modern editions, see John Gwynn, " On a Syriac MS. belonging to the collection of Archbishop Ussher ", no. VIII of *The Transactions of the Royal Irish Academy*, vol. 27, *Polite Literature and Antiquities*, Dublin, 1886, pp. 269–316, esp. 288–92. Cf. also E. Nestle, " Syriac Versions ", *HDB*, 4, p. 649b.

[53] Lewis and Gibson's ed., p. 49.

[54] *Ibid.*, p. 169.

[55] The phrase *mārā' yesûs* is used idiomatically for *Ἰησοῦς* and does not necessarily presuppose [*ὁ*] *κύριος Ἰησοῦς*. For a discussion of this passage, as well as the following two passages, see Theodor Zahn, *op. cit.*, pp. 340 f.

[56] Lewis and Gibson's ed., p. 156.

[57] *Ibid.*, p. 87. [58] *Ibid.*, p. 226. [59] *Ibid.*, p. 4.

[60] Lectionary no. 1642.

day of the sixth week after Easter reads ἐλάλησεν, but which in the same passage for the morning service on the fourth day of Holy Week reads the usual εἶπεν.

Whether or not this last item is admitted to contribute to the argument, the other items offer textual phenomena that find their readiest explanation in the supposition that the Palestinian Syriac lectionary was translated from a Greek lectionary which presented the same passage in slightly different textual forms in different lections.

At this point, however, one must candidly call attention to evidence that seems to run counter to the hypothesis of direct translation from a Greek lectionary. There is no Greek lectionary known to the present writer which exhibits such clumsy sutures of incipit with the opening of the pericope as are present in the Palestinian Syriac Lectionary (see p. 216 above). Does the abrupt and occassionally nonsensical joining of incipit to the text without modifying the opening sentence to accommodate the formula indicate a rather mechanical process of fitting into the framework of a Greek lectionary the several pericopes extracted from a continuous Palestinian Syriac version already in existence ?

Likewise, the differences among the Palestinian Syriac lectionaries themselves present further complications. Since it is not likely that each of them was translated from a separate Greek lectionary (the many similarities in text among the three forbid such an assumption), an alternative theory seems to be preferable, namely that an original Palestinian Syriac text—whether derived from a Greek lectionary or from a continuous Greek text—was subsequently modified both in text and (to some extent) in lectionary framework.[61]

In conclusion, it will have been seen that more than one perplexing problem connected with the Palestinian Syriac Lectionary still remains to be solved. At the same time, however, the material presented above reinforces the view, previously held by several scholars on less secure grounds, that the structure of the Palestinian Syriac Lectionary was derived throughout from a typical Greek Gospel lectionary.

[61] Besides the slight differences among the three codices edited by Lewis and Gibson, attention should be directed also to a fragment in the British Museum of a Palestinian Syriac lectionary which, according to Land, differs slightly from the Vatican codex ; cf. J. P. N. Land, *Analecta Syriaca*, 4, *Otia Syriaca*, Leiden, 1875, pp. 202–4 ; cf. also Zahn, *op. cit.*, pp. 341 f.

# III

# THE BOOK OF DANIEL AND THE QUMRAN COMMUNITY

F. F. Bruce

Among publications which have influenced the direction of my thought in the field of Gospel studies a prominent place is occupied by the Inaugural Lecture which Matthew Black delivered in October 1952 as Professor of Biblical Criticism and Biblical Antiquities in the University of Edinburgh.[1] In relating the Son of man in the teaching of Jesus to the Servant of the Lord in the book of Isaiah, and both to the Messiah, he adduced in evidence various bodies of literature from the closing centuries B.C., including in particular the book of Daniel and the Qumran texts. The purpose of this contribution in honour of Principal Black is to consider some evidence which would place the book of Daniel and the Qumran texts within one stream of tradition.

When Jesus announces that the time has been fulfilled for the kingdom of God to draw near,[2] or speaks of the Son of man coming with the clouds of heaven; [3] when Paul reminds the Corinthian Christians that the saints will judge the world; [4] when John beholds the last imperial beast blaspheming God, persecuting the saints and exercising universal sway over the bodies and souls of men for forty-two months [5]—in these and many other New Testament passages we see how the visions of Daniel moulded early Christian thought and language. Their influence on general Jewish thought and action in the same period is equally well attested. If the leaders of the revolt against Rome in A.D. 66 were encouraged by an oracle found in their sacred writings to the effect that a man or men from Judaea would attain world dominion at that very time,[6] it is to the book of Daniel that we must look for the oracle, and more particularly to the angelic utterance about the seventy heptads; [7] nowhere else in the

[1] Published as " Servant of the Lord and Son of Man ", *SJT* 6 (1953), 1–11.

[2] Mk 1 : 15.

[3] Mk 13 : 26; 14 : 62.

[4] 1 Co 6 : 2.

[5] Rev 13 : 5–8.

[6] Josephus, *BJ* 6, 312; Tacitus, *Hist.* 5, 13; Suetonius, *Vespasian* 4.

[7] Dn 9 : 24–27.

Hebrew canon are such precise time-indications given with respect to the future.

But there are grounds for thinking that a century before the beginning of the Christian era at least one group of Jews—the men of Qumran—gave serious thought to the study and interpretation of the book of Daniel, and looked on their " Unique Teacher "[8] as successor-in-chief to the " man greatly beloved " who is the hero of that book.

## I

Among the biblical manuscripts found at Qumran are fragments representing seven copies of the book of Daniel. There are fragments of two copies from Cave 1 (1QDn[a], exhibiting Dn 1 : 10–17 and 2 : 2–6, and 1QDn[b], exhibiting Dn 3 : 22–30), of four copies from Cave 4 (one of which, 4QDn[a], has Dn 2 : 19–35 intact), and of one copy, written on papyrus, from Cave 6 (6QDn[a], exhibiting Dn 8 : 16–17, 20–21 ; 10 : 8–16 and 11 : 33–36, 38). One fragment from Cave 1 (1QDn[a]) preserves the transition from Hebrew to Aramaic in Dn 2 : 4 ; two fragments from Cave 4 (4QDn[a] and 4QDn[b]) preserve the transition from Aramaic to Hebrew in Dn 7 : 28–8 : 1. They shed no further light on the problem of the bilingual character of Daniel.[9]

The portion preserved in 1QDn[b] includes the place where the Septuagint incorporates the Prayer of Azariah and the Song of the Three Hebrews, but like the Massoretic text it lacks these additions. The variations between the text of the fragments from Cave 1 and the Massoretic text are insignificant ; the fragments from the other caves also resemble the Massoretic text, apart from a few variants related to the *Vorlage* of the Septuagint.[10]

[8] CD 20 : 1.

[9] For the Cave 1 fragments see D. Barthélemy, *Discoveries in the Judaean Desert* 1, Oxford, 1955, pp. 150–52 ; for the Cave 6 fragments see M. Baillet, J. T. Milik and R. de Vaux, *Discoveries in the Judaean Desert of Jordan* 3, Oxford, 1962, *Textes*, pp. 114–16. The Daniel fragments from Cave 4 have not yet been published, but see F. M. Cross, " Le travail d'édition des fragments manuscrits de Qumrān : La grotte 4 de Qumrān ", *RB* 63 (1956), 56–58 ; *The Ancient Library of Qumran and Modern Biblical Studies*, New York, 1958, p. 33. In the latter place Cross mentions that one of the copies of Daniel from Cave 4 is to be dated palaeographically to the late second century B.C.

[10] F. M. Cross, *RB* 63 (1956), 58 ; J. T. Milik, *Ten Years of Discovery in the Wilderness of Judaea*, London, 1959, p. 28.

The textual character of these fragments throws little light on the question whether the book of Daniel was acknowledged as canonical at Qumran. Neither can we come to any certain conclusion on this question from such premises as the fact that 1QDn[a] has columns of roughly equal height and breadth (whereas other biblical manuscripts from Cave 1 have columns whose height is twice their breadth), or the fact that the Daniel fragment from Cave 6 is written on papyrus (whereas most biblical manuscripts from Qumran are written on skin), and in a cursive hand.[11] Our judgment on the canonical status of Daniel in the Qumran community must be based on less external criteria.

## II

In addition to the canonical fragments, other compositions bearing some relation to the canonical book of Daniel have come to light.[12] Of these the most important is the *Prayer of Nabonidus* from Cave 4 (4QOrNab). The best preserved part of this manuscript runs thus :

> The words of the prayer which was prayed by Neboni, king of the l[and of] Babylon, [the great] king, [when he was smitten] with a sore inflammation in Teiman by the decree of G[od Most High]. [With a sore inflammation] I was smitten for seven years and I was removed far from [men]. But I [prayed to God Most High] and an exorcist pardoned my sins. He was [a man who was] a Jew from [the exiles in Babylon]. He said : Tell this in writing to give honour and pr[aise and glory] to the name of G[od Most High]. [And I wrote this :]
>
> I was smitten with a s[ore] inflammation in Teiman [by the decree] of God [Most High]. For seven years [I] prayed to the gods of silver and gold, [bronze and iron], wood and stone and clay, because [I thought] them to be gods . . .

Here the text breaks off ; presumably the king, finding the gods of Babylon powerless to heal him, was directed by the Jewish " exorcist " (Aram. *gāzēr*, as in Dn 2 : 27 ; 4 : 7 [MT 4 : 4] ; 5 : 7, 11) to address himself to the God of Israel, and so was cured. The

[11] D. Barthélemy, *Discoveries in the Judaean Desert* 1, pp. 150 f. ; see also F. M. Cross, " Qumran Cave I ", *JBL* 75 (1956), 122 f. (On p. 123 of that article Cross mentions a papyrus copy of Kings found in Cave 6 ; see M. Baillet and others, *Discoveries in the Judaean Desert of Jordan* 3, *Textes*, pp. 107–12.)

[12] J. T. Milik, " ' Prière de Nabonide ' et autres écrits d'un cycle de Daniel ", *RB* 63 (1956), 407–15 ; D. N. Freedman, " The Prayer of Nabonidus ", *BASOR* 145 (Feb. 1957), 31 f. ; W. Dommershausen, *Nabonid im Buche Daniel*, Mainz, 1964.

exorcist is not named in the extant part of the document ; it is a natural, but not a certain, assumption that he was Daniel. The king's name (Aram. *nbny*) is apparently an abridged form of Nabuna'id, last king of the Neo-Babylonian Empire (556–539 B.C.). The reference to " Teiman " no doubt reflects this king's association with Tema in North Arabia, where, according to his Harran inscription, he made his headquarters for ten years.[13] The fragment's contact with the book of Daniel lies mainly in its general tendency, and partly in the coincidence of the seven years of Nabuna'id's " sore inflammation " with the seven years of Nebuchadnezzar's boanthropy in Dn 4 : 25, 32 f. Long before the discovery of the *Prayer of Nabonidus* at Qumran it had been suggested—first of all, it appears, by H. Winckler in 1899 [14]—that the Nebuchadnezzar of Dn 2–5 is the historical Nabuna'id (*nbnd* having possibly become corrupted to *nbkd*, which was then regarded as an abbreviation of Nebuchadnezzar). Whether the *Prayer of Nabonidus* be taken as a confirmation of this suggestion or not, it is at least plain that the king whose seven years' madness and exile are narrated in Dn 4 was the father of Belshazzar, according to Dn 5 : 18–21.

From Cave 4 we also have fragments of three other Aramaic documents belonging to one or more Daniel cycles (4QpsDn[a.b.c.]). Although these fragments are hopelessly mutilated, it is evident that Daniel is represented as addressing the royal court. He appears to rehearse events from earlier biblical history as well as to foretell the future. One fragment mentions the Flood and the Tower of Babel ; another refers to the Egyptian oppression, the Exodus and the crossing of the Jordan. The Babylonian exile is described as the punishment for Israel's idolatry ; the " first kingdom " (cf. Dn 2 : 37, 38 ; 7 : 4) will exercise power for seventy years, until the end of Israel's oppression (cf. Jer 25 : 11, 12 ; 27 : 7 ; 29 : 10 ; Dn 9 : 2). A foreview is given of events of the Seleucid kingdom, in the course of which mention is made of a king named Balakros (the Macedonian equivalent of φαλακρός, " bald "), of which the better known form Balas is a hypocoristic. The foreview points on to the time of the end, when iniquity will be abolished and the saints will be exalted.

[13] C. J. Gadd, " The Harran Inscriptions of Nabonidus ", *Anatolian Studies* 8 (1958), 35–92, esp. 57–65, 79–89.

[14] H. Winckler, " Die Zeit der Herstellung Judas ", *Altorientalische Forschungen* 2 (1899), 210–27.

These tantalizing fragments indicate (as do the deutero-canonical additions to Daniel) that there was a wider cycle of Daniel stories than that preserved in the Hebrew Bible, and that this wider cycle continued to circulate, and possibly to grow, after the publication (according to Dn 12 : 4, 9, the " unsealing ") of the canonical book.[15] But the Daniel documents from Qumran tend rather to raise new questions than to answer old ones about the composition of the book of Daniel.

## III

In the Aramaic part of Daniel, the solution of various problems is recorded in terms of *rāz* " mystery ") and *pᵉšar* (" interpretation "). In Nebuchadnezzar's dreams *rāzīn* (" mysteries ") are communicated to him by God (Dn 2 : 18, etc. ; 4 : 9 [MT 4 : 6]), but they remain mysteries until their *pᵉšar* (" interpretation ") is communicated by God to Daniel (Dn 2 : 24, etc. ; 4 : 18 [MT 4 : 15], etc.). The communication of the *pᵉšar* is the revelation of the *rāz*, the solution of the mystery. Thus, when the " mystery " of the king's dream about the great image " was revealed to Daniel in a vision of the night " (Dn 2 : 19), Daniel was ready to " show the king the interpretation " (Dn 2 : 24). Thanks to this experience of Daniel's divinely imparted wisdom, Nebuchadnezzar summoned him after his later dream of the great tree, because, said he, " I know . . . that no mystery is difficult for you " (Dn 4 : 9 [MT 4 : 6]). Daniel accordingly took up the details of the dream one by one and said, " This is the interpretation, O king : It is a decree of the Most High, which has come upon my lord the king " (Dn 4 : 24 [MT 4 : 21]).

Similarly, the writing on the wall at Belshazzar's feast is an unsolved mystery (although the term *rāz* is not expressly used of it) until Daniel reads it off and declares " the interpretation (*pᵉšar*) of the matter " (Dn 5 : 26) ; and Daniel himself cannot understand his own dream of the four imperial beasts until at his request one of the angels standing in the presence of the Ancient of Days makes known to him " the interpretation (*pᵉšar*) of the things " (Dn 7 : 16) ; then all becomes plain.

Daniel's use of *pᵉšar* is reminiscent of the use of the Hebrew verb *pāṯar* and substantive *piṯrōn* in the similar stories of Joseph's

[15] Another element of a Daniel cycle appears to be alluded to in Josephus, *Ant.* 10, 264.

interpretation of the dreams of Pharaoh's servants and of Pharaoh himself in Gn 40 : 5 ff. The Hebrew substantive *pēšer* in Ec 8 : 1 (" who knows the *interpretation* of a thing ? ") is apparently a loanword from Aram. *p$^{e}$šar* ; and this is the word so distinctively used in the Qumran commentaries on biblical texts. A biblical text is like one of the dreams or the writing on the wall in the Aramaic part of Daniel ; it is a divine communication, but a communication that remains a mystery until the interpretation also is divinely communicated, and usually to someone other than the recipient of the original communication. The message of God, so to speak, is broken into two halves, the *rāz* and the *pēšer*, and either half is given to a different person, so that the message is not understood until the two halves are put together again (we may compare the root meaning of *σύμβολον* from *συν-βάλλειν*, " put together ").[16]

The person to whom, in Qumran belief, the *pēšer* of the prophetic oracles was pre-eminently granted was the Teacher of Righteousness. In particular, God made known to him the time at which the prophets' words would come to pass, for this knowledge had been withheld from the prophets themselves. For example, " God commanded Habakkuk to write the things that were coming upon the last generation, but the fulfilment of the epoch he did not make known to him. And as for the words, *so he may run who reads it*, their interpretation (*pēšer*) concerns the Teacher of Righteousness, to whom God made known all the mysteries (*rāzīm*) of the words of his servants the prophets " (1QpHab 7 : 1–5). This is in line with what is said of the faithful remnant at the beginning of the Zadokite *Admonition* : " God took note of their deeds, for they sought him with a perfect heart, and he raised up for them a Teacher of Righteousness to lead them in the way of his heart, that he might make known to the last generations what he was about to do to the last generation—the congregation of deceivers " (CD 1 : 10–12).

As in Dn 2 : 27 ff. the interpretation makes it plain that the mystery conveyed to Nebuchadnezzar in his dream portended what was going to happen " in the latter days ", so in the belief of the Qumran community the mysteries of God were conveyed to the prophets in order that the last generations might know what God was going to do to the last generation. And the fact that the

[16] Compare the unintelligibility of glossolalic utterances (" mysteries ") in 1 Co 14 : 2–5 unless an interpretation is provided.

interpretation of these mysteries was entrusted to the Teacher of Righteousness was a token that the generation of the end-time was on the point of appearing—if indeed it had not already appeared.

To this we have a close parallel in the New Testament. At the beginning of his ministry Jesus announces, in language which echoes Dn 7 : 22, that " the time is fulfilled, and the kingdom of God is at hand " (Mk 1 : 15), and later he congratulates his disciples because they see and hear things to which prophets and righteous men looked forward eagerly without witnessing them in their lifetime (Mt 13 : 16 f. ; Lk 10 : 23 f.). To them, he said, had been made known that mystery of the kingdom of God which remained a riddle to those outside (Mk 4 : 11). According to 1 P 1 : 5, 10–12, the " salvation ready to be revealed in the last time " was foretold by the prophets, but the date and other circumstances of its revelation were withheld from them ; they " searched and inquired about this salvation " in an endeavour to ascertain " what person or time was indicated by the Spirit of Christ within them when predicting the sufferings of Christ and the subsequent glory ". These predictions, it is implied, had relevance not to the prophets and their contemporaries so much as to Christians living in the first century A.D. But Christians living in the first century A.D. had no need to search and inquire, for they had been taught the interpretation of these predictions : " *This* is that which was spoken through the prophet " (Ac 2 : 16). The person was Jesus ; the time was now. Similarly, with regard to one specific aspect of the long foretold salvation, Paul is enabled by revelation to divulge a mystery which was hidden from ages and generations but has now been manifested to the people of God (Col 1 : 26 ; cf. Eph 3 : 2 ff.).

## IV

With this emphasis on the time at which the Hebrew prophecies were to be fulfilled we may compare a remark which Josephus makes about Daniel, that " he was not only wont to prophesy future things, as did the other prophets, but he also fixed the time at which these would come to pass " (*Ant.* 10, 267). This kind of insight is expressed in both the Hebrew and Aramaic parts of Daniel by the root *śkl* (among others) ; in the Hebrew part of the book it is expressed particularly by the Hiphʿil, used both transi-

tively and intransitively. Thus, when Gabriel is about to make the revelation of the seventy heptads to Daniel, he says, " I have now come out to cause you to be wise (*l^e haśkīl^e ḵā*) with understanding . . . Know therefore and become wise (*w^e ṯaśkēl*) that . . . there shall be seven heptads " (Dn 9 : 22, 25). In the same way the Hiph'il participle *maśkīl* is used in Daniel's last vision to denote those who impart to others the insight which they themselves possess into the time and character of the eschatological events : " none of the wicked shall understand, but the *maśkīlīm* shall understand " (Dn 12 : 10). These *maśkīlīm* have a part to play before the end-time comes ; when the minds of many are confused by the arguments and example of the apostates, " those who make the people wise (*maśkīlē 'am*) shall make many understand ", although their faithfulness means that they will be subject to the severest persecution during Antiochus's attempt to abolish the true worship of God : " they shall fall by sword and flame, by captivity and plunder, for some days " (Dn 11 : 33). Indeed, so subtle will be the temptation, so fierce the persecution, that even " some of the *maśkīlīm* shall fall ", but their defection serves but to refine the ranks of the faithful (Dn 11 : 35). And when at last the righteous triumph with Michael's help and the faithful departed are raised to everlasting life, " the *maśkīlīm* shall shine like the brightness of the firmament ; and those who turn many to righteousness, like the stars for ever and ever " (Dn 12 : 3).[17]

The Qumran community appears to have stood in the direct succession of those faithful *maśkīlīm*.[18] The root *śkl* is used in

[17] CD 3 : 10–19 indicates that the Qumran community started as a splinter group, the faithful remnant of an originally larger number of covenanters, many of whom proved disloyal. This chimes in with the statement that Daniel's *maśkīlīm* were purified and reduced in number by the defection of those whose loyalty proved unequal to the beguilement of flattery and the strain of persecution. The Qumran community evidently regarded the majority of the heirs of the earlier *ḥăsīḏīm* (those who became the party of the Pharisees) as unworthy of the covenant. A comparison of what is said in Dn 12 : 3 about the *maśkīlīm* with what is said about the 'Ebed Yahweh—that he will deal wisely (*yaśkīl*) and " make many to be accounted righteous " (Is 52 : 13 ; 53 : 11)—suggests that the *maśkīlīm* fulfil corporately the portrait of the 'Ebed Yahweh. The Qumran community probably thought of itself as fulfilling the propitiatory ministry of the 'Ebed Yahweh (1QS 5 : 6–7 ; 9 : 3–5 ; 1QSa 1 : 1–3) and the judicial ministry of the Son of man (1QpHab 5 : 3–6), although these two designations do not occur explicitly in the Qumran texts.

[18] It may also be asked whether the designation *ḳ^e ḏōšē 'elyōn* in CD 20 : 8 is the deliberate equivalent of the *ḳaddīšē 'elyōnīn* in Dn 7 : 18, 22, 25, 27, and whether the Qumran community regarded itself as constituting in this sense " the

the same way in the Qumran texts as in Daniel. For example, the *Rule of the Community* prescribes that the *maśkīl* (the " Instructor ") shall, among other duties, " teach true knowledge and righteous judgment to those who choose the Way, to direct each in knowledge according to his spirit and the ordering of the time, and so to instruct them (*lehaśkīlām*) in the marvellous and true mysteries (*berāzē pele' we'ĕmet*) among the men of the community that each may walk perfectly with his neighbour in all that is revealed to them " (1QS 9 : 17–19). The singer in the *Hymns of Thanksgiving* repeatedly praises God for giving him insight (*śekel*) to understand his marvels (1QH 11 : 27 f.) : " as for me ", he says, " as a *maśkīl* have I come to know thee, my God, through the spirit that thou hast given me, and by thy Holy Spirit I have faithfully listened to thy marvellous secret counsel " (1QH 12 : 11 f.). The *maśkīl* here, as in Daniel, is one who, having received from God understanding in his hidden purpose, is thus in a position to impart that understanding to others.

The *maśkīlīm* of Daniel, bearing the brunt of the persecution under Antiochus, looked for divine intervention to bring the persecution to an end. Their spiritual kinship was with those loyal souls who fled, early in the persecution, to dwell in the wilderness according to the law of God, and were slaughtered to a man because they would neither offer resistance to their enemies nor leave their caves on the sabbath day (1 Mac 2 : 29–38). Yet, while we admire their fidelity, we may wonder what would have been the outcome of the struggle if their policy had prevailed. The majority of the *ḥasīdīm* judged that the situation demanded common action with the Hasmonaean insurgents (1 Mac 2 : 42). To the *maśkīlīm* of Daniel, however, the Hasmonaean resistance was but " a little help " (Dn 11 : 34). Their expectation was that the persecution would increase in severity, that the king would go on acting according to his will and prospering, " till the indignation is accomplished ; for what is determined shall be done " (Dn 11 : 36). Then he would come to his end, with none to help him, whereas the archangel Michael would arise as the champion of the people of God. The distress would reach its climax ; there would be a time of trouble such as men had never known, but those

saints of the Most High ". Much depends on whether the designation in one or both places denotes men or angels ; for the latter interpretation see Chaim Rabin, *The Zadokite Documents*, Oxford, [2]1958, pp. 38 f. ; J. Barr, " Daniel ", in *Peake's Commentary on the Bible*, London, [2]1962, p. 598.

enrolled for life would endure to the end and be saved. Let Daniel seal up the record of his vision ; when the time of fulfilment came, it would be unsealed and vindicated as true.

## V

What happened we know. The " little help " provided by the Hasmonaeans proved greater than the *maśkīlīm* had expected. The abomination of desolation was removed, religious freedom was recovered, the daily sacrifice and other details of the temple worship were resumed. But the resurrection age did not dawn. Instead, the Hasmonaeans won political independence in addition to religious freedom, and established their dynasty of priest-kings. This new order gave little satisfaction to the puritan convictions of the *maśkīlīm* or to their legitimist espousal of the exclusive right of the house of Zadok to exercise the high priesthood in Israel. Whatever some enthusiastic adherents of the Hasmonaeans might think, the *maśkīlīm* could not see in their régime the establishment of everlasting righteousness which was to come, according to Daniel's third vision, at the expiry of seventy heptads " from the going forth of the word to restore and to build Jerusalem " (Dn 9 : 25).

The oracle of the seventy heptads is itself a reinterpretation of Jeremiah's prediction that seventy years would pass before the desolations of Jerusalem came to an end (Jer 25 : 12 ; 29 : 10) ; this reinterpretation is a sample of a line of biblical exegesis which we find variously reproduced in the Qumran texts and in the New Testament.[19] It may be regarded as a further indication of the affinity between Daniel and the Qumran community that the seventy heptads, on their usual interpretation, are bound up with the fortunes of the house of Zadok. The first seven heptads terminate with the installation of Jeshua as first Zadokite high priest in the post-exilic Temple ;[20] the sixty-two heptads that

[19] K. Elliger, *Studien zum Habakuk-Kommentar vom Toten Meer*, Tübingen, 1953, pp. 156 f. Another example is the reinterpretation of Balaam's ships from Kittim (Nu 24 : 24) in Dn 11 : 30, discussed below. We may compare the way in which the warning of Hab 1 : 5, " Look among the nations, and see . . ." (itself an echo of Is 29 : 14) is applied to the coming of the Kittim (Romans) by the Qumran commentator (1QpHab 2 : 12) and to the situation created by the apostolic preaching by Paul in Ac 13 : 41.

[20] Dn 9 : 25 (*māšīaḥ nāgīḏ*).

follow terminate with the deposition and assassination of the last legitimate Zadokite high priest, Onias III.[21] Both the restoration of the Zadokite priesthood after the exile and its cessation in the reign of Antiochus are viewed as fateful epochs.

With the postponement of the desired consummation the seventy heptads, or at least the seventieth heptad, had to be reinterpreted by Daniel's successors as he himself had recorded the reinterpretation of Jeremiah's seventy years. The history of the exegesis of the seventy heptads in Jewish and Christian circles is largely the history of this further reinterpretation. First the seventieth heptad was identified with the seven years' interregnum in the high-priesthood between Alcimus and Jonathan; [22] then the chronology of the post-exilic period was remodelled so as to make the last heptad begin with the accession of Alexander Jannaeus in 103 B.C.[23] But in the event Jannaeus's reign lasted much longer than seven years, and the seventieth heptad seems to have been stretched to cover the whole period of Hasmonaean rule.[24] Josephus and some parts of the New Testament attest a reinterpretation in which the oracle points to the events of A.D. 70.[25] The chronology of *Seder ʿOlam*, on which the traditional Jewish calendar is based, reckons the seventy heptads as extending from the destruction of the First Temple by the Babylonians to the destruction of the Second Temple by the Romans. Irenaeus and Hippolytus, making the first sixty-nine heptads end with the coming of Jesus as the Christ, envisage a gap between them and the seventieth heptad, which they

[21] Dn 9 : 26 (*yikkārēṯ māšîaḥ wᵉʾên lō*).

[22] This interpretation is reflected in Josephus, *Ant.* 20, 237.

[23] This interpretation is reflected in Josephus, *Ant.* 13, 301 and is responsible for the inflation by half a century of Josephus's chronology of the period between Cyrus and the Hasmonaeans. See also Eusebius, *Dem. Ev.* 8, 2.

[24] Test XII Levi 16 : 1–17 : 11.

[25] Josephus identified Vespasian with the coming prince of Dn 9 : 26 (*BJ* 6, 313), the cessation of sacrifice and offering with the discontinuance of the daily sacrifice on 17 Panemos, A.D. 70 (*BJ* 6, 94), and the crowning abomination with the victors' worship of their standards in the temple precincts (*BJ* 6, 316). Either this last event or Gaius's attempt to set up his image in the Jerusalem temple is the "abomination of desolation" of Mk 13 : 14 || Mt 24 : 15. The "forty-two months" during which the Gentiles will "trample over the holy city" (Rev 11 : 2)—concurrent, no doubt, with the period during which the two witnesses prophesy (Rev 11 : 3), the mother-church is sheltered in the wilderness (Rev 12 : 6, 14) and the beast from the abyss exercises authority (Rev 13 : 5)—represent a reinterpretation of the half week of Dn 9 : 27 (compare Dn 7 : 25; 12 : 7). Similarly the beast from the abyss itself (Rev 11 : 7; 13 : 1–8, etc.) represents a reinterpretation of the four beasts of Dn 7 : 3–8, more especially of the fourth.

interpret in terms of the rise and overthrow of Antichrist in the near future.[26]

What light do the Qumran texts cast on the interpretation of the seventy heptads? No direct answer to this question is available, but we may have pointers to an answer in the account of the Teacher of Righteousness in the Zadokite *Admonition*. Bewildered and unhappy at the untoward turn of events, unable to accept the Hasmonaean ascendancy as the fulfilment of God's purpose, the *maśkīlīm* greeted with thankful relief the appearance of the Teacher of Righteousness who explained the sacred scriptures to them and showed them the part they were to play in promoting the divine purpose revealed in those scriptures. The Zadokite writer dates the rise of this godly community 390 years after God had given his people into the hands of Nebuchadnezzar (CD 1 : 5 f.). For twenty years they groped for the right way until the Teacher of Righteousness was raised up as their guide (CD 1 : 9–11). The reference to 390 years is in all probability a reinterpretation of the 390 days during which Ezekiel was commanded to bear the iniquity of the house of Israel, each day representing a year (Ezk 4 : 4 f.). But the Zadokite writer seems to incorporate this figure into a more comprehensive scheme, based perhaps on Daniel's prophecy of the seventy heptads. If to the 390 years we add the 20 years of groping before the Teacher of Righteousness arose, together with the 40 years that were to elapse after the Teacher's death "until the consuming of all the men of war who returned with the Man of Falsehood" (CD 20 : 14 f.),[27] we have 450 years. But to these 450 years we have to add the unknown duration of the Teacher's ministry. Seeing we are in any case dealing with schematic numbers rather than with numbers which a chronologer could use, we may tentatively postulate the schematic period of 40 years for the Teacher's ministry, and this, added to the figures already specified, would provide a period of 490 years (seventy heptads) from the emergence of the godly community to the extirpation of evildoers. This reconstruction must remain entirely hypothetical unless and until more definite evidence

[26] Irenaeus, *Haer.* 5, 25, 4; Hippolytus, *Comm. on Daniel* 12–22; *Antichrist* 43.

[27] This language echoes Dt 2 : 14–16. Compare the forty years after which the wicked are to be no more (4QpPs37, fragment A, 2 : 6–8) and the forty years of eschatological warfare (1QM 2 : 6–14, thirty-five years of active engagement and five years of release).

comes to light, but in view of the many attempts made to interpret (or reinterpret) the seventy heptads during the last two centuries of the Second Commonwealth, it is antecedently probable that the Qumran community had its own interpretation, and that the Zadokite writer gives us an inkling of what it was.

## VI

In Daniel's last vision the career of Antiochus Epiphanes is outlined in recognizable conformity with what is otherwise known of him in Dn 11 : 21–35. What is known of his career after 165 B.C. bears no relation to the continuing forecast in vv. 40–45. Antiochus did not invade Egypt again, nor was it " between the sea and the glorious holy mountain " that he met his end. It is not surprising, therefore, that attempts were made (and in some quarters continue to be made) to interpret these verses of some other person or persons. Probably the earliest of such attempts is found in the Qumran *Rule of War*, parts of which may not ineptly be regarded as a sort of *midrash* on the end of Dn 11 and the beginning of Dn 12.

The eschatological warfare described in this document is to be waged in the first instance against the Kittim. Whether the Kittim of the *Rule of War* (and of the Qumran commentaries) are to be identified with the Seleucid forces or with the Romans is still a debated question, but the identification with the Romans is more probable. If we ask why the Romans should have been designated Kittim in the Qumran community, we need look no further for an answer than Dn 11 : 30, where the " ships of Kittim " that come against Antiochus are the Roman vessels that put Popilius Laenas and his companions ashore in Egypt in 168 B.C., with a message ordering Antiochus to return to his own territory forthwith.[28] If we ask further why the term Kittim is used for Romans in Dn 11 : 30, the answer may well be that this passage represents a reinterpretation of Balaam's oracle in Nu 24 : 24, according to which " ships shall come from Kittim and shall afflict Asshur and Eber ".[29]

The Roman occupation of Judaea seemed to the men of Qumran to provide a setting in which at last they might expect

[28] Polybius, *Hist.* 29, 27 ; Livy, *Hist.* 45, 12 ; Appian, *Syriakē* 66. In the earlier " Septuagint " version of Dn 11 : 30, Kittim is rendered by " Romans ".

[29] In the Targum of Onkelos, Kittim here is rendered by " Romans ".

the concluding scenes of Daniel's final vision to be enacted in real life. The plan of action was therefore drawn up for the time of trouble foretold in Dn 12 : 1. The sons of light were to take the field against the sons of darkness, the army of Belial, which consisted mainly of the " troops of the Kittim of Asshur "[30]—the Roman forces in the province of Syria. Among other contingents of the army of Belial are " the violators of the covenant " (a truly Danielic touch), and also the nations mentioned in Dn 11 : 41—Edom and Moab and the children of Ammon—together with Philistia. " The king (?) of the Kittim in Egypt "—i.e. the commander of the Roman forces in Egypt (a reference to the king of the south of Dn 11 : 40)—is to be attacked by the sons of light as he goes forth to do battle against the " kings[31] of the north " (1QM 1 : 1–4). The warfare will be long and fluctuating, and attended by unmatched tribulation for the recipients of God's redemption, but with heavenly aid redemption will be secured, and " iniquity shall be vanquished, leaving no remnant " (1QM 1 : 6).

With this eager expectation may be compared a passage from the fragmentary *Book of Mysteries* (1Q 27) where, after an enigmatic reference to the " mysteries of iniquity" (*rāzē peša'*),[32] it is further said of the ungodly:

> They knew not the mystery (*rāz*) that is to be and the former things they understood not; they knew not what was to come upon them nor could they save their life from the mystery that is to be. And this will be a sign for you that it is coming to pass: when the children of iniquity are shut up, evil will be banished from the presence of righteousness as darkness is banished before light; and as smoke disappears and is no more, so will evil disappear for ever, and righteousness will be revealed like the sun, the regulator of the world. Then all who hold back[33] the wonderful mysteries (*rāzē pele'*) shall be no more. Knowledge shall fill the world and there will be no more folly. The word shall assuredly come to pass; the oracle is true.[34]

---

[30] The archaic " Asshur " may be used here under the influence of Nu 24 : 24. (Kittim and Asshur are similarly brought together in 1QM 11 : 11–12, but here the Old Testament passage quoted is Is 31 : 8, which is echoed in Dn 8 : 25; 11 : 45.) Another of Balaam's oracles which played an important part in Qumran eschatology is the prediction of the " star out of Jacob " in Nu 24 : 17; see 1QM 11 : 4–6; 4Qtest 9–13; CD 7 : 19–21.

[31] The singular of Dn 11 : 40 (" the king of the north ") has been (no doubt de ignedly) altered to the plural.

[32] Compare the μυστήριον τῆς ἀνομίας of 2 Th 2 : 7.

[33] Compare the restrainer (τὸ κατέχον, ὁ κατέχων) of 2 Th 2 : 6 f.

[34] *Discoveries in the Judaean Desert* 1, Oxford, 1955, p. 103.

Against the background of the Qumran interpretation of the book of Daniel and other Hebrew scriptures we can understand better the New Testament exegesis and fulfilment of these writings —exegesis and fulfilment on which the personal impress of Jesus has been stamped as clearly as that of the Teacher of Righteousness has been stamped on the Qumran interpretation, and in which we are provided with the foundations of Christian theology.[35] The gist of this theology is that Jesus incarnates the figure of the " one that was to come ", by whatsoever designation this Coming One was called.

*Additional Note*: Since this article was written, the full surviving text of 4Qflorilegium has been published in J. M. Allegro and A. A. Anderson, *Discoveries in the Judaean Desert of Jordan* 5, Oxford 1968, pp. 53–57; it contains (2 : 3 f.) a quotation of Dn 12 : 10 and 11 : 32, said to be " written in the book of Daniel the prophet ". This expression (cf. Mt 24 : 15) should put an end to doubts about the canonical status of Daniel in the Qumran community (see p. 223 above).

[35] See C. H. Dodd, *According to the Scriptures*, London, 1952.

# *REPUDIUM* IN DEUTERONOMY

David Daube

Elsewhere I have drawn attention to the shame cultural element in Deuteronomy.[1] Deuteronomy contains the only law in the Pentateuch with a punishment consisting in public degradation: the *consors* who treacherously refuses to marry his childless brother's widow must suffer her in the presence of the elders to loose his shoe and spit in his face.[2] In Deuteronomy alone of all biblical codes we meet a form of statute which stresses the disgusting spectacle offered to God by a crime or its results: four statutes begin " If there be found ", meaning " If the observing eye of God comes upon this blemish ".[3] No provision outside Deuteronomy is directed against " hiding yourself ": you may not hide yourself from somebody else's animal which has wandered off, or indeed whenever you find anything he has lost; nor may you hide yourself from somebody else's animal which has fallen down.[4] These are warnings against abstention from service, so we must expect somewhat unusual phrasing; say, " thou shalt not fail ", " thou shalt not forsake ".[5] " Thou shalt not hide thyself " is very curious. The explanation lies in the emphasis on shame. You may not give in to the temptation to avoid the awkward sight, and in a manner which dispenses with straight, open refusal. To be ashamed involves unwillingness to see and unwillingness to be seen; sometimes one of the two feelings prevails, sometimes the other, occasionally both are strong. The Deuteronomic writer assumes, I guess, that in the situations he contemplates you will be embarrassed by the unseemly object and also try to escape

[1] With extensive documentation in *Law and Wisdom in the Bible*, Edinburgh Gifford Lectures 1963, Lecture 2 on Deuteronomy, as yet unpublished; singling out a particular point in " To be found doing wrong ", *Studi Volterra*, to appear in the near future.

[2] Dt 25 : 9. See my " Consortium in Hebrew and Roman Law ", *Juridical Review* 62 (1950), 77 ff.

[3] " A man that serveth other gods, the sun or moon ", Dt 17 : 2 f.; " A man slain, lying fallen in the field ", Dt 21 : 1; " A man lying with a woman married to a husband ", Dt 22 : 22; " A man stealing any of his brethren ", Dt 24 : 7.

[4] Dt 22 : 1, 3, 4.

[5] *Ḥāḏal*, *ʿāzab*.

without being noticed and possibly having to proffer excuses. It is this hiding yourself which he condemns.[6]

In a law relating to re-marriage of a divorcee,[7] divorce is represented in a way distinctly reflecting a preoccupation with shame. The law starts by putting the case of a wife who " finds no favour in the eyes " of her husband. To find favour in the beholder's eyes is the great aim in a setting where shame is a dominant consideration : it is the opposite of to incur disgrace. The point, however, is made even clearer, for the law goes on : " because he found some shaming thing in her ". This term, " shaming thing ", recurs only once in the Bible, in another law of Deuteronomy, insisting on the removal of uncleanness from the war camp. It ends up by reminding the people that " the Lord walketh in the midst of thy camp, and he shall see no shaming thing in thee and turn away from thee ".[8] The husband renounces the wife in whom he discovers such a thing. It is interesting that, in a subsequent portion of the law, where the lady's second marriage goes wrong, the law does not repeat this specifically Deuteronomic description of the situation but says " and the latter husband hate her ". The specific Deuteronomic elaboration is reserved for the opening of the statute where it is bound to be most conspicuous and impressive. " Hating " as the motive for divorce is common throughout the ancient East and indeed may be found in other biblical texts.[9]

Divorce belongs to, or approaches, the sexual area where shame plays a part even though it may not be of enormous importance in a culture generally. Anyhow it is remarkable that the Roman concept of *repudium* has definite affinity with Deuteronomy ; all

[6] Probably he has in mind chiefly the former side, unwillingness to see : Dt 22 : 1 and 4 speak of hiding yourself from the errant or broken down animals. I shall not here go into the various passages with " to hide yourself " (or related ones with " to hide your eyes "), except to remark that in Sir 38 : 16 the term surely has the kind of meaning just outlined : " Hide not thyself from a man when he is expiring ". The Greek translation turns this into an injunction against neglect of burial, and Box (CAP 1, p. 451) subscribes to it. But the shame tradition accounts far better for the Hebrew as it stands ; a dying man is most unpleasant to behold and, again, you will try to keep away without drawing attention to yourself.

[7] Dt 24 : 1 ff.

[8] Dt 23 : 15. The phrase is not found, for instance, in the comparable ordinance Nu 5 : 3.

[9] See R. Yaron, *The Law of the Aramaic Papyri*, Oxford, 1961, pp. 55, 101 f. In *Revue Internationale des Droits de l'Antiquité*, 3rd ser., 4, 1957, 127 f., Yaron rightly argues that the mention of a " shaming thing " in Dt 24 : 1 does not make it incumbent on a husband to show cause if he desires a divorce.

the more remarkable as any dependence one way or the other is out of the question. *Repudium* almost certainly derives from *pudet, pudor*: the Roman lexicographers are right for once,[10] and even if they were not the fact would remain that those who employed the word believed in the connection. The word signifies repulsion and/or revulsion on account of shame. Festus [11] quotes Verrius Flaccus (died 4 B.C.) as holding that *repudium* is so called *quod fit ob rem pudendam*. This is highly reminiscent of " he found some shaming thing in her ". He also quotes a line from Accius (born 170 B.C.), probably from his *Io*, in which a woman (Io) tells about herself: *repudio eiecta ab Argis iam dudum exsulo*—reminiscent of " he found some shaming thing in her and sends her out of his house ".

As is well known, *repudium* is normally conveyed through a messenger, not declared face to face. *Repudium remittere* is a frequent, almost technical, expression.[12] This is not surprising: shame is a huge obstacle to immediacy, you avert your face both when disgraced yourself and when upset by disgrace outside. To be sure, there are more grounds than this one for husband and wife not meeting at the moment of divorce; it is none the less significant that this feature should be implied by the term *repudium* rather than other terms for divorce. As for Deuteronomy, it is clear that the bill of divorcement was already in use at the time: the law here inspected takes it for granted that it is handed to the wife. The main reason for introducing the bill had no doubt been to enable a woman to prove that she was divorced.[13] However, a written document is slightly less direct than the spoken word, and the prominence the law under notice accords to the bill (it is mentioned in connection with both dismissals of the

[10] See A. Ernout and P. J. A. Meillet, *Dictionnaire étymologique de la langue latine*, 4th ed., Paris, 1959, 2, p. 571.

[11] 281.

[12] E.g., Plautus, *Aulularia* 799; and despite the humorous coating, the *repudium* is sent because the betrothed woman has a child from a third party. In 788 we find *repudium renuntiare*, but it is the messenger who does the *renuntiare*, at the principal's bidding. In *Persa* 384 a daughter reminds her scoundrelly father, who is about to dispose of her by a fake sale, that the *fama* of such a transaction involving her person will make any match with her *repudiosae*, liable to be cancelled by *repudium*. According to Nonius 383. 21, in Lucilius, Book 29, Sat. 3, one Albinus is represented as staying at home sorrowfully because his daughter has been sent a *repudium*.

[13] Prior to the bill there might be dire consequences if she or her family wrongly believed that divorce had taken place; see my " Error and Accident in the Bible ", *Revue Internationale des Droits de l'Antiquité* 2 (1949), 193 f., 210.

lady, by her first husband and her second) may again have to do with the concentration on the shame aspect. Certainly, in post-Deuteronomic development, transmission of the bill of divorcement by messenger became a very common practice: that much is evident from the space and position given it in Rabbinic discussion.[14]

[14] E.g., Mishnah Gittin 1. 1 ff.

# STUDIEN ZU JOSEPHUS

## Apokalyptische Heilsansagen im Bericht des Josephus (*BJ* 6, 290 f., 293–95) ; ihre Umdeutung bei Josephus.[1]

Otto Michel

## I

Die Gruppe verschiedenartiger " Erscheinungen " (τέρατα)—kosmischer Vorzeichen der kommenden Katastrophe—in *BJ* 6, 288–99 unterscheidet sich formal und inhaltlich von dem darauf folgenden Bericht über den Unglückspropheten *BJ* 6, 300–9, der ganz stark alttestamentlich gefärbt ist. Es liegt nahe, die erste Gruppe *BJ* 6, 288–99 als eine Anordnung von sieben Ereignissen anzusehen, die von Josephus übernommen oder geschaffen wurde. Doch ist damit noch kein Urteil über die Herkunft der einzelnen Traditionsstoffe gefällt.

Die Siebenzahl der von Josephus aufgeführten Prodigien entspricht dem rabbinischen Schema der Vierzahl in b. Joma 39b : " Unsere Meister lehrten : Vierzig Jahre lang vor der Zerstörung des Hauses kam das Los nicht in die Rechte, noch wurde der rotgefärbte Stoffstreifen weiss, noch brannte das westliche Licht, und es öffneten sich die Türen des Tempels von selbst. Bis Rabbi Jochanan, Zakkais Sohn, sie anfuhr und zu ihm sagte : Tempel, Tempel, warum erschreckst du dich selber ? Ich weiss von dir, dass dein Ende zukünftig Zerstörung sein wird, und schon Sacharja, Sohn Iddos, hat über dich verkündigt : Tue auf, Libanon, deine Tore, dass

[1] Die hier vorgelegte Untersuchung ist aus der jahrelangen Zusammenarbeit mit O. Bauernfeind und der Tübinger Josephusgemeinschaft entstanden. Über die hier angeschnittenen Probleme muss Band II 2 unserer Josephus Ausgabe Auskunft geben können.

Zur Literatur vgl. S.V. McCasland, " Portents in Josephus and in the Gospels ", *JBL* 51 (1932), 323–35 ; H. W. Montefiore, " Josephus and the New Testament ", *NovT* 4 (1960), 139–60 ; 307–18. Montefiore unternimmt den Versuch, zwischen den im NT berichteten Zeichen, die die Heilsgeschichte begleiten, und den von Josephus berichteten Manifestationen Gottes, die Vorzeichen der kommenden Katastrophe sind, einen sachlichen Zusammenhang herzustellen. Nach ihm wäre eine ursprünglich christliche Tradition von einer bei Josephus aufgenommenen jüdischen Umdeutung nachträglich auf die Zerstörung des Tempels übertragen worden.

Zum Ganzen vgl. auch O. Michel, " Spätjüdisches Prophetentum ", *Neutestamentliche Studien für R. Bultmann*, Berlin, [2]1957, pp. 60–67.

Feuer deine Zedern verzehre" (Sach. 11, 1 vgl. auch j Joma 43c). Diese vier Vorzeichen haben kultisch-priesterliches Gepräge und ereignen sich im Tempel; sie setzen voraus, dass bestimmte kultische Unregelmässigkeiten auf das Ende des Kultus hinweisen.

P. Billerbeck (*SBK* 1, p. 1046) entscheidet sich dafür, dass die Chronologie des Josephus, der die Unheilszeichen auf das Jahr 66 n. Chr. legt, gegenüber der rabbinischen Tradition, die an das 40. Jahr vor der Tempelzerstörung denkt, vorzuziehen ist. Gemeint sei ein Jahr des Unheils, auf das man schlechte Ereignisse konzentriert habe.[2]

Ein besonderes Problem ist der Sprachgebrauch von τέρας bei Josephus (*BJ* 6, 288; vgl. K. H. Rengstorf, TWNT 7, pp. 122–23). Es handelt sich um kosmische Machttaten und Kundgebungen, die mit einer Botschaft (κήρυγμα) verbunden sind. Es gehört ein ausserordentliches Mass der Verblendung dazu, diese Machttaten und Kundgebungen Gottes zu übersehen und zu überhören; aber das Volk ist durch Betrüger und falsche Propheten völlig verblendet worden. Abweichend von dieser Anklage in 6,288 erscheint die in 6,290 gegebene Unterscheidung zwischen einer möglichen günstigen Vorbedeutung eines Zeichens und einer von Schriftkundigen gegebenen richtigen, aber entgegengesetzten Erklärung. Die erfahrenen Schriftkundigen, die den Unerfahrenen entgegengesetzt sind, wissen sofort, dass es sich um die späteren Unglücksereignisse handelt. Dasselbe gilt auch für die plötzliche Öffnung der Tempeltore: Sie gilt den Unerfahrenen für eine ausnehmend günstige Machttat und Kundgebung Gottes (κάλλιστον τέρας): Gott selbst öffnet die Tür zu den Heilsgütern. Für die Einsichtigen dagegen liegt in diesem Geschehen der Hinweis darauf, dass Gott nunmehr den Schutz seines Heiligtums aufgebe, den Feinden zuliebe das Tor öffne, und dass es die Pflicht der Einsichtigen sei, das Zeichen der Verwüstung in den eigenen Kreisen offenbar zu machen (*BJ* 6, 295).

Zunächst sieht es so aus, als seien die Machttaten und Kundgebungen Gottes (τέρατα ἐναργῆ) unmittelbar einsichtig, und es sei lediglich der Verführung der Betrüger und Pseudopropheten zuzuschreiben, wenn das Volk nicht sieht und hört (*BJ* 6, 288)—bei zwei besonders gearteten Zeichen wird dagegen zwischen einer unverständigen und einer erfahrenen Schriftdeutung ausdrücklich unterschieden (*BJ* 6, 291, 295). Es ist die Aufgabe der Exegese, auf die Verschiedenheit in der exegetischen Konzeption aufmerksam zu machen.

Um zu einem richtigen Verständnis des ganzen Zusammenhangs zu kommen, muss man daran denken, dass die antizelotische Haltung des Josephus notwendig zu einer Polemik gegen die Apokalyptik führen musste, soweit sie sich mit dem zelotischen Streben verband. Selbst im Augenblick der höchsten Not war, wie *BJ* 6, 285 ausführlich erzählt, ein

[2] Das Fasten R. Zadoks, um die Zerstörung Jerusalems abzuwenden (b Git. 56a), ist mit dieser Zeit "40 Jahre" ebenfalls verbunden.

Pseudoprophet aufgetreten, der das Volk aufforderte, in den Tempelbezirk zu steigen und dort die Wundergaben der Rettung entgegenzunehmen (τὰ σημεῖα τῆς σωτηρίας). Der besonders hervorgehobene Begriff : " Wundergaben der Rettung " zeigt an, dass es sich um eine eschatologische Epiphanie handelt, also ein Eingreifen Gottes wunderbarer Art. Die Machthaber begünstigten, wie *BJ* 6, 286 ausdrücklich sagt, diese pseudoprophetische Heilsverkündigung.

Bei den durch *BJ* 6, 392 (epiphanes Unglücksgeschehen) getrennten Geschehnissen handelt es sich um *kultische Offenbarungen*, die auf die alttestamentlich-prophetische Weissagung zurückgehen :

*BJ* 6, 290 f. : das nächtliche Offenbarwerden der göttlichen Schechina, die Altar und Tempelhaus [3] um die 9. Stunde der Nacht umfliesst, ist die am Fest sich offenbarende Erfüllung von Jes. 60, 1–2 : " Steh auf : leuchte, denn es kommt dein Licht, und die Herrlichkeit des Ewigen bestrahlt dich. Denn siehe, Finsternis bedecket die Erde und Wolkendüster die Völker—doch dich wird der Ewige bestrahlen, und seine Herrlichkeit wird über dir erscheinen." Vgl. Apk.Joh. 21, 23 ff. in der christlichen Tradition : hier wird die prophetische Verheissung sogar noch gesteigert. Die himmlische Stadt wird ganz vom himmlischen Glanz erfüllt !

*BJ* 6, 293–95 dagegen nimmt den exegetischen Zusammenhang Jes. 60, 11 auf : " Deine Tore bleiben ständig geöffnet, bei Tag und bei Nacht unverschlossen, dass man zu dir bringe das Vermögen der Völker unter der Führung ihrer Könige ".

Dass die beiden " Heilszeichen ", die ursprünglich vom Offenbarwerden der Schechina im Tempel und von der Öffnung der Tore für die Schätze der Völker reden wollten, apokalyptisch einwandfrei gedeutet worden waren, setzt Josephus noch voraus ; für ihn sind aber die Vertreter der apokalyptischen Prophetie "*Unkundige* " und " *Unerfahrene* ". Josephus sagt nicht, dass erst durch die Katastrophe der Zerstörung des Tempels die " Einsichtigen " den wahren Sinn der " Unheilszeichen " verstanden haben, sondern dass sie in ihren Kreisen sofort die richtige Deutung verbreitet hätten (§295).[4] Diese Angabe ist glaubwürdig ; es muss in priesterlichen Kreisen beide Gruppen gegeben haben, die bei eintretenden " Unregelmässigkeiten " im Kultus

[3] Die Voranstellung des Altars vor dem Tempel könnte damit zusammenhängen, dass die Sicht der Erscheinung vom Osten erfolgt. Vgl. ausserdem die Parallele Tac. *Hist.* 5, 13 : subito nubium igne conlucere templum.

[4] Die Wendung ἀπέφαινον ἐν αὐτοῖς ist wohl in Sinn einer Diskussion unter einander zu verstehen.

sich auf die apokalyptische Heilstradition beriefen, oder aber in ihnen Warnungen Gottes an sein Volk sahen. Josephus schlägt sich auf die Seite derer, die halachisch normiert waren, ordnet aber die " Unheilszeichen " in einen grösseren kosmischen Zusammenhang ein.

Die halachische Tradition geht von den Unregelmässigkeiten im Kultus aus und sieht in ihnen eine ungünstige Vorbedeutung : man fürchtet das Ende des Tempels (vgl. Jochanan ben Zakkai, R. Zadok, der auf Grund der Öffnung der Tempeltore 40 Jahre gefastet hat). Die halachische Tradition setzt die Legitimität des Tempels und des Kultus voraus. Die apokalyptische Tradition erinnert an die prophetische Tradition und erwartet den Anbruch der Heilszeit. Hier ist die Frage der Legitimität von Tempel und Kultus nicht ohne Weiteres entschieden. Es ist durchaus möglich, dass das Erscheinen der Schechina eine Verwandlung und Verklärung von Tempel und Kultus andeuten kann. Die beiden Tempeltraditionen werden von Josephus auf die Passahzeit des Jahres 66 n. Chr. festgelegt, aber die Verschiedenheit der beiden Traditionen, die mit einander ringen, dürfte älter sein. Billerbeck (*SBK* 1, p. 1046) hat recht, wenn er der Chronologie des Josephus einen Vorzug gibt vor der ungefähren Angabe der rabbinischen Überlieferung. Falls die apokalyptischen Heilszeichen auf Passah 66 n. Chr. zu legen sind, dann muss ein konkreter Anlass für sie aus der damaligen Situation gefolgert werden. Ausserdem dürfte die Verschiedenheit in der Zeitangabe darauf hinweisen, dass die beiden Zeichen schon vor Josephus getrennt erzählt wurden (9. Stunde der Nacht = §290 ; 6. Stunde der Nacht = §293). Es ist nicht unmöglich, dass in einer ursprünglichen " Sammlung von Heilszeichen " (τὰ σημεῖα τῆς σωτηρίας) zunächst die Öffnung des Tempeltores, dann erst die Erscheinung der Schechina erzählt wurde.

Jedenfalls sollten die apokalyptischen Heilszeichen, die für Josephus zu Unheilszeichen geworden sind, nicht mit den umgebenden " prodigia " und " portenta " ohne Weiteres gleichgesetzt werden : sie entstammen noch der alten Auseinandersetzung zwischen den Gruppen der Zeit vor 70 n. Chr. Es ist durchaus möglich, dass die Siebenergruppe in *BJ* 6, 288–99 von Haus aus keine festgefügte Einheit war, sondern erst allmählich zu einem geschlossenen Komplex wurde. Gedacht ist bei Josephus an eine geschichtliche Abfolge von Machttaten und Kundgebungen Gottes, die auf die kommende Katastrophe ausgerichtet ist. Gott lässt sein Volk nicht im Unklaren über den eingeschlagenen Irrweg, sondern lässt durch die Zeichen seine Botschaften ergehen. Weder die messianischen " Wehen " der Endzeit noch auch die heidnische Vorstellung der " portenta " und " prodigia " können die Konzeption der josephinischen τέρατα verständlich machen, obwohl man immer wieder den Versuch gemacht hat, diese bekannten

Wege der Erklärung einzuschlagen. Gemeint ist doch wohl, dass eine geschichtstheologische Wende durch den Plan Gottes planmässig vorbereitet wird.

## II

Eine hermeneutische Schlussfolgerung aus diesem für Josephus wichtigen Fragekreis darf gezogen werden: Josephus hat entscheidende geschichtstheologische Konzeption aus seinem Verständnis priesterlich-kultischer Traditionen abgeleitet. Die Fixierung historischer Urkunden und Stammbäume liegt nach Jos. *c. Ap.* 1, 29 im Unterschied von den Fremdvölkern in den Händen der Hohenpriester und Propheten, die mit grösster Genauigkeit ihren Dienst verrichten. Wo die ältesten Zeiten beschrieben werden, tritt die göttliche Eingebung hinzu, die den Propheten Zuverlässiges mitteilt. *Für Josephus steht die prophetische Überlieferung im Schatten der priesterlichen.* Auch in der Situation der Hinwendung zu den Römern erinnert er sich an nächtliche Traumgesichte mit entsprechenden Weisungen Gottes (*BJ* 3, 351), an Traumdeutungen und Weissagungen heiliger Schriften, die ihm als Priester und Nachkommen von Priestern nicht unbekannt waren (*BJ* 3, 352). Als " Diener Gottes " geht er zu den Römern über (*BJ* 3, 354). *Hier liegt ein wichtiger Aufschluss über bestimmte hermeneutische Voraussetzungen des Josephus.*

A. Schlatter, *Die Theologie des Judentums nach dem Bericht des Josefus*, Gütersloh, 1932 bringt einen Versuch, Josephus aus dem Pharisäismus zu verstehen. " Er zeigt uns in griechisches Denken und griechische Rede gefassten Pharisäismus und führt uns damit zu derjenigen Bewegung im Judentum, die die Herrschaft über die ganze Judenschaft, auch über die in den griechischen Ländern angesiedelte, erlangt hat " (Vorwort S.V). Überprüft man diese These, dann stellen sich zum Mindesten im *Bellum* entscheidende Widerstände heraus: 1. Der Pharisäismus wird keineswegs unkritisch oder letztlich zustimmend dargestellt (z. B. *BJ* 1, 110–14, 571), 2. die hermeneutischen Voraussetzungen, mit denen Josephus arbeitet, sind nicht ohne Weiteres pharisäisch.

Die pharisäische Gruppe ist vorsichtig gegenüber der Obrigkeit (Ab. 1, 10); Josephus ist wie alles Priestertum bestrebt, in den Schatten der Obrigkeit zu treten und von ihr selbst wieder autorisiert zu werden. Die Erziehung, die Josephus nach seiner *Vita* empfangen hat, entspricht nicht der pharisäischen (Ab. 5, 24). Sicherlich sind pharisäische Elemente in seinem Denken verarbeitet, doch müssen sie näher bestimmt und abgegrenzt werden.

# DAʿAT AND GNOSIS IN INTERTESTAMENTAL LITERATURE

B. Reicke

THE following contribution to biblical philology sets out to show that the Judaism of the intertestamental period still represented characteristic Old Testament ideas of religious knowledge. We shall first deal with the most important Hebrew text of the intertestamental period, the Qumran Manual of Discipline, and then add some remarks on rabbinic texts and the Septuagint (including the Apocrypha). Philo and Josephus are not treated since they are representative of a more artificial and international literature.

## I

Old Testament scholars have pointed out the practical orientation characteristic of the Hebrew verb *yāḏaʿ* and related words.[1] When the Old Testament says that God "knows" somebody, it is a question of His interest, election, providential care (Gn 18 : 19 ; Ex 33 : 12 ; Jer 1 : 5 ; Nah 1 : 7). Accordingly, man's knowledge of God is often the same as confession and obedience (Ps 9 : 11 ; Is 1 : 3 ; Hos 4 : 1) and is especially characterized as fear of the Lord (e.g., Pr 1 : 7).[2] In postexilic Judaism some features were gradually brought into stronger relief, so as to give the whole idea a somewhat different shade. However, the general correspondence with Old Testament conceptions is striking. This should be a caution-sign to those who talk uncritically of a general Gnostic background of primitive Christianity.[3]

[1] Among several recent contributions, a few may be quoted here: G. J. Botterweck, *Gott erkennen* (1951) ; H. M. Féret, *Connaissance biblique de Dieu* (1956) ; H. Haag, *TZ* 16 (1960), 251–58. A brief summary is found in B. Reicke, "Erkenntnis", *Biblisch-historisches Handwörterbuch* 1 (1962), cols. 428–29.

[2] Reicke (n. 1), col. 428 ; "The Knowledge of the Suffering Servant", *ZATW* Beih. 105 (1967), 186–92.

[3] On the author of the Manual of Discipline we agree with M. Black's judgment (*The Scrolls and Christian Origins*, London, 1961, p. 134) : "In this respect [with regard to dualism] he stands in the Hebrew and Biblical, not the Greek tradition,

Among the specialists in knowledge referred to in the Old Testament, three groups still played rather predominant rôles in the intertestamental period: teachers of the law, apocalyptists, and wisdom teachers. To a certain extent the three groups coincided, two or three of them being often represented in the same writing. This coincidence was facilitated by the circumstance that nearly all guardians of divine knowledge presented themselves as teachers. In fact most of the creators of intertestamental literary productions appear as writing teachers who chose to disseminate their knowledge through books. Even if oral traditions as well as traditional themes are still discernible in these books, in their present form they were generally written and published as religious tracts to be read by the public in an actual situation. This makes their genesis somewhat different from the circumstances giving rise to the Old Testament. On the whole it may be stated that the intertestamental literature has a didactic character. Although the idea of divine knowledge was developed in a theoretical direction, the practical implications of the Old Testament root *yḏʿ* were still preserved to a considerable extent. We hope to make this evident in the following linguistic observations.

## II

The different meanings of the Hebrew root *yḏʿ* found in the intertestamental period may be illustrated (a) by one of the Dead Sea Scrolls, and (b) indirectly by some later Rabbinic writings.

(a) The so-called Manual of Discipline or 1QS, the Community Rule of Qumran, is the most instructive Hebrew text known to us from the intertestamental period not only because it describes the piety and structure of a Jewish community in detail but also because of its particular importance for the study of *yḏʿ*, *daʿaṯ* and similar terms. For in it these words are favourite expressions. The following collection of 1QS passages containing some form of *yḏʿ* represents a literary translation of the pertinent context (sometimes explained by a few bracketed words). Each passage is generally a paraphrase of the *specific meaning* which the words for

though in comparison with the New Testament his speculative interest is slightly more pronounced: but it is in no way comparable to the later speculations and mythological systems of Gnosticism."

" knowledge " must be supposed to have with regard to this very context. We italicize the relevant expression, in a few cases keeping the word " knowledge ", in most cases giving some explanatory synonym or paraphrase.[4]

1QS 1 : 11b–12a (concerning new members of the community) : They shall apply their whole *mind,* power and property to God's community. (It is not a question of their knowledge, but of their interest.)
1 : 12b : in order to purify their *mind* in the truth of God's commandments.
2 : 3 (part of the covenant benedictions) : May He enlighten thy heart with a living insight, and grace thee with eternal *obedience.* (Since 2 : 2 refers to perfect behaviour, " knowing " is here the same as observing, i.e., obeying the commandments.)
2 : 22 : so that every man in Israel shall *observe* his position in God's community.
2 : 26–3 : 1 (concerning an impenitent man) : His soul detests any censure implying *obedience* to righteous commandments.
3 : 2 : *mind* (as in 1 : 11b).
3 : 15 : From the God of *providence* (Hebrew *'ēl hadē'ôṯ,* reminding one of 1 S 2 : 3) do all present and future things come. (In 1 S 2 : 3, the expression means " the God of knowledge " ; the idea is that God knows all thoughts of man. But here the context refers to God as the one who determines all things : for God " knowing " is the same as doing.)
4 : 4 : a spirit of *prudence* in every practical pursuit.
4 : 6 : to conceal faithfully any secrets (of knowledge) which are *known* to one.
4 : 22 : in order to inform rightminded people about *obedience* to the Most High and wisdom as represented by the sons of heaven, and in order to instruct people who are correct in their behaviour.
4 : 25 : For God placed them (the spirits of truth and sin) side by side until the appointed time and the new creation, and He *determines* the effect of their influence during all periods.
4 : 26 : He bestowed them (the two spirits) on men so that they were *confronted with* good and evil. (*da'aṯ* is used in the primitive sense of contact, here implying a choice between good and evil.)
5 : 11 : They have not sought Him in His commandments in order to *discover* the hidden points in which they have gone astray.
5 : 19 : They are all vanity who do not *acknowledge* His covenant, and He will obliterate all who disdain His word.
6 : 9b–10a : so that everybody may convey his *opinion* to the council of the community.
6 : 24b–25a : everyone who lies about his property, and is personally *conscious* of this.
7 : 3 : the one who lies with a personal *intention.*

---

[4] Translators of Qumran texts generally render *da'aṯ* as " knowledge " or something similar, without concerning themselves with the different meaning that this modern conception has.

7 : 4 : the one who, without justification, reviles his neighbour with a personal *intention*.
7 : 5 : or practices deceit with a personal *intention*.
8 : 9 : in eternal *obedience* to the covenant of justice.
8 : 18 f. : He must not *have contact with* any of their assemblies until his actions have been cleansed from all wickedness, so that he walks in a correct way : then they shall let him enter the council.
9 : 17 : One has to prescribe true *obedience* (to the Law) and a righteous judgment to [5] those who choose the (right) way.
9 : 18 : One has to guide them in *obedience* (to the Law), and thus instruct them about wonderful and veritable secrets. (Cf. 9. 19 : so that they walk correctly, everybody toward his neighbour.)
10 : 9 : I will play (the harp) with *skill*.
10 : 12 : (I will call) the Most High an establisher of my good, a source of *knowledge*, and a fountain of holiness.
10 : 16 : I *realize* that in His hand lies the judgment of everything living.
10 : 24b : Vanities I will blot out from my lips, impurities and anomalies from the *consciousness* of my heart.
10 : 24c–25a : With judicious deliberation [6] I will announce *prudence* and with prudent discretion I will trace around it a solid boundary.
11 : 3 : And through His righteousness my sin is wiped out. For from the fountain of His *providence* He has revealed His light. (According to passages like Jer 1 : 5 ; Gal 4 : 9 God " knows " man in the sense of accepting, electing him ; see also 1QS 11 : 5 : from the fountain of His righteousness comes my justice, light comes into my heart from His wonderful mysteries.)
11 : 6 : (In the One who is for ever) my eye finds a judiciousness that is concealed from man, *providence* and wise planning beyond the capacity of men.
11 : 11 : According to His *providence* everything is done, and He establishes all existence according to His plan.
11 : 15b–16a : Praised be Thou, my God, who hast opened the heart of Thy servant for *obedience*. Lead in righteousness all his actions.
11 : 17c–18a : Without Thy consent nothing is done. Thou prescribest total *obedience*, and everything that happens takes place with Thy consent. (The usual translation, " thou hast taught all knowledge ", cannot be harmonized with the context, and no Gnostic ideal of metaphysical knowledge is found here.)

This list of 1QS passages is representative of several meanings that *da'aṯ* and related expressions also have in the Old Testament. A definite predilection for practical implications is observed. In some cases *da'aṯ* means just " knowledge " in a theoretical sense, and there we have not paraphrased the conception but simply retained the word " knowledge " or used some word of similar

[5] As in Gn 24 : 14, 44, the construction is here *hōkiaḥ l^e*, " assign ", " prescribe to ".

[6] The parallelism of 1QS 10 : 24c and 25a makes this rendering preferable to the one usually found : " in the council of insight ".

import. However, even in such cases the context indicates a tendency towards a practical way of thinking. And for the most part a practical meaning is directly to be observed which, in modern languages, is seldom expressed by " knowledge ", but rather by other words.

It may also be noticed that the Qumran Hymns of Thanksgiving, 1QH, contain numerous passages showing the same characteristics. The very first case will give an impression of this :

1QH 1 : 7 : And before Thou madest them, Thou hast *determined* all their actions. (What is meant is evidently God's providence.)

It is not possible to quote here the other instances found in 1QH. They are between two and three times as many as in 1QS, and the variety of meaning is of a corresponding extent.

(b) Some additional illustrations from rabbinic literature will show that in post-biblical Hebrew *yḏ'* still had a much wider, a more personal and practical meaning than our word " knowledge ". First there are some cases where *yḏ'* has the primitive meaning " to observe ", from which is derived the theoretical meaning " to understand " :

Kid. 81b : I did not *observe*, or *think of* it.
Zeb. 115b : When Abraham *understood*.
GnR 22 : Adam . . . *understood* what Eve had done to him.

Even within the theoretical sphere *yḏ'* shows an applicability which has no correspondence in our " knowledge ". Thus when the noun *da'aṯ* is used with a theoretical import, it is frequently a question of some Rabbi's " opinion " :

Sheb. 42a : According to *opinions* (i.e., according to the majority's opinion).
Sanh. 33a : Examination of an *opinion*.
j Keth. 2 : 26b : According to the *opinion* of the Rabbis.
*Ibid.* 6 : 30c, and j Yeb. 1 : 2b : Different *opinions* were ascribed to R. Johanan.
Pes. 2a *et pas.*, Sot. 45b *et pas.* : Now your *opinion* may be that . . .

Compare with this :

Hul. 90b : The *import* of a legal prescript.

When the emphasis is on the receptacle of the theoretical content, the meaning will be " mind, consciousness " : Sot. 45b : Might it come into our *mind* (instead of heart, as in 38b). A meaning which is closely related to this is " mind " or " heart " in the sense of "temper ", " character ":

Sanh. 100b–101a : The one whose *mind* (or heart) is agreeable . . . hard . . . broad.
j Hag. 2 : 7 f. : Their *mind* was not clean.
M. Kat. 17a : My *heart* is glad.
Git. 70b : A confused *mind*.

In such cases *daʿaṯ* can even mean " person " : CaR. 22d (4 : 8, §1) : The rotten *mind* (i.e., person) of Ahasverus. Bab.M. 11b : Another *mind* (i.e., person).

On the other hand there are also examples in rabbinic literature illustrative of the intimate, personal meanings of *yḏʿ* that are found in the Old Testament. For instance the meaning " to acknowledge " or " to accept " is represented by the adverb *bīḏūaʿ* which means " as is generally accepted " (R. Hash. 20b, etc.), and by the noun *yeḏīʿā* which means " acknowledgement " (Hor. 2a, j Sot. 1 : 16c, etc.).

Another characteristic meaning taken over from Old Testament traditions is " to elect " : Zeb. 115b : His sons were the *elect* of the Place. Finally the practical character of *yḏʿ* will be illustrated by the following example : Sanh. 25a–b : It depends on the *capacity* of the dove, etc.

These examples from rabbinic writings may be sufficient to indicate that *yḏʿ* preserved a great variety of meanings which generally corresponded to Old Testament modes of expression, and went far beyond modern conceptions of " knowledge ". They especially included personal and practical involvement.

## III

In the Septuagint including the Apocrypha, the nearest Greek equivalent of Hebrew *yāḏaʿ* is *gi(g)nōskō*.[7]

(a) In a concordance one will find *ginōskō* represented about 600 times by the canonical writings. Among these instances there are about 545 where the Greek verb corresponds to *yḏʿ* in the Qal (Gn 3 : 5, etc.), and about 20 where it corresponds to other verbal or nominal forms of the same radical (Gn 2 : 17 ; Ex 25 : 21 ; Lv 23 : 28, etc.). For the rest there are other words behind *ginōskō*, such as *'mr, bīn* or *mṣ'*. A causative verb corresponding

[7] R. Bultmann, γινώσκω : *TWNT* 1 (1933), 688–715, is still of great value.

to *ginōskō* is *gnōrizō* which is used for translating *yḏ'* when a causative meaning is implied (e.g., Ex 21 : 36 ; 1 K 6 : 2 ; in Pr 3 : 6 it corresponds to *yḏ'* in the Qal).

The noun *gnōsis* occurs upwards of 40 times in the canonical writings. In some cases it is uncertain which Hebrew word it serves to translate since the LXX did not use the Masoretic text in these passages. Otherwise *gnōsis* is the rendering of *da'aṯ* and *dē'ā* in 31 certain instances, and of *yḏ'* in 3. Although these Hebrew nouns are represented as many as 49 times in the Masoretic text, it can be stated that *gnōsis* is the general translation preferred by the LXX.

An equivalent of *ginōskō* is *oida* which has much the same meaning.[8] In the canonical writings it is used by the LXX about 200 times to render *yḏ'*. In about 25 cases it corresponds to other words, and a few others are uncertain. Possibly a slight difference can be inferred between *ginōskō* and *oida*. For the latter seems to incline to a theoretical meaning, and there are only a few cases with a practical implication. But the difference is actually very slight.

The two verbs occur alternatively in similar phrases and, to give a phrase more emphasis, they may even appear both at once with quite the same meaning. Compare this passage : 1 S 20 : 3 : γινώσκων οἶδεν ὁ πατήρ σου (*yāḏōa' yāḏa'*). On the whole it seems evident that *oida* is merely a synonym of *ginōskō*. And it can be added that *epiginōskō* and similar compounds also have much the same meaning.

Some examples may now illustrate to what extent the LXX, by *ginōskō*, etc., preserved the specific Old Testament meanings of *yḏ'*. The deutero-canonical Jewish-Hellenistic writings of the period also will be considered in this survey. Nothing peculiar is to be noticed when *ginōskō*, etc., corresponds to *yḏ'* in the sense of " experience ", " understanding ", " acquaintance ". Therefore, we shall concentrate upon cases where the verb has those meanings of " consideration " and personal " involvement " that were observed in the Hebrew texts of the intertestamental and post-biblical period. These cases are particularly interesting, for in several of them *ginōskō*, etc., is used although the Masoretic text does not contain any mention of *yḏ'*.

Not infrequently *ginōskō* means " to care for ", " to esteem ", or even " to elect ", as the following examples show :

[8] H. Seesemann, οἶδα : *TWNT* 5 (1954), 120.

Nu 16 : 5 : ἐπέσκεπται καὶ ἔγνω ὁ Θεὸς τοὺς ὄντας αὐτοῦ.
Hos 11 : 12 : νῦν ἔγνων αὐτοὺς ὁ Θεός, καὶ λαὸς ἅγιος κεκλήσεται (the Masoretic text is different here).
Wis 4 : 1 (concerning virtue) : καὶ παρὰ Θεῷ γινώσκεται καὶ παρὰ ἀνθρώποις.

These phrases imply that the active subject is superior in rank to the passive object. If the subject is inferior to the object, one obtains the meaning " to respect ", " to pay regard to ", " to believe " or " to obey ", for instance :

1 Ch 28 : 9 : γνῶθι τὸν Θεὸν τῶν πατέρων σου, καὶ δούλευε ἐν καρδίᾳ τελείᾳ.
Jth 8 : 20 : ἕτερον θεὸν οὐκ (ἐπ)έγνωμεν.
1 Mac 4 : 33 : οἱ εἰδότες τὸ ὄνομά σου.
Wis 5 : 7 : τὴν δὲ ὁδὸν Κυρίου οὐκ (ἐπ)έγνωμεν.
Wis 13 : 1 : οὐκ ἴσχυσαν εἰδέναι τὸν Ὄντα.
*Ibid.* : οὔτε . . . ἐπέγνωσαν (τὸν) Τεχνίτην.
Wis 15 : 2 : εἰδότες σου τὸ κράτος.
Bar 4 : 13 : δικαιώματα αὐτοῦ οὐκ ἔγνωσαν (compare Bar 3 : 20, 23, 31).

As was the case with *yḏʿ*, it is equally important to observe these personal, practical meanings of *ginōskō* and *oida*. One should, then, avoid a mechanical rendering of such phrases by " to know ", which implies theoretical conceptions alien to the context.

When *ginōskō* appears in the imperative, it often has a similar meaning : " consider ". Such imperatives are rather frequent in the LXX, and occur many times even when there is no corresponding *yḏʿ* in the Masoretic text. This further contributes to the observation that *ginōskō*, etc., was capable of implying a personal involvement. In the following examples the imperative of the verb has such a meaning and may be translated " consider ! ", " be aware ! " :

Gn 20 : 7 : γνῶθι ὅτι ἀποθανῇ.
Jg 4 : 9 (Deborah speaking) : πλὴν γίνωσκε ὅτι (in the Masoretic text " nevertheless ") οὐκ ἔσται.
Job 19 : 3 : γνῶτε μόνον (the Masoretic text is quite different) ὅτι ὁ Κύριος ἐποίησε (cf. 19 : 6).
Job 36 : 5 : γίνωσκε δὲ (in the Masoretic text " behold ") ὅτι ὁ Κύριος.
Is 44 : 20 : γνῶθι (reading *dᵉʿeh* instead of *roʿeh*) ὅτι σποδὸς ἡ καρδία αὐτῶν.
Is 47 : 10 : γνῶθι (not in the Masoretic text).
Is 51 : 12 : γνῶθι (not in the Masoretic text) τίς οὖσα ἐφοβήθης.
Sir 9 : 13 : ἐπίγνωθι ὅτι ἐν μέσῳ παγίδων διαβαίνεις.

The noun *gnōsis* may also correspond to an absolute *daʿaṯ* in the sense of " practiced knowledge " of God, man's " humble surrender ", " obedience " ; and there are even some instances where *gnōsis* is used in the same way without a corresponding *da'aṯ*. The compound *epignōsis* is nearly always used in this way. Compare the following examples :

Ps 98 (99) : 10 : *ὁ διδάσκων ἄνθρωπον γνῶσιν* (a humble mind).
Ps 118 (119) : 66 : *χρηστότητα καὶ παιδείαν καὶ γνῶσιν δίδαξόν με.*
Pr 2 : 5 f. : *τότε συνήσεις φόβον Κυρίου, καὶ ἐπίγνωσιν Θεοῦ εὑρήσεις, ὅτι . . . ἀπὸ προσώπου αὐτοῦ γνῶσις καὶ σύνεσις.*

Compare Pr 8 : 10, 12b ; 9 : 6 ; 16 : 8 (the last two instances differ from the Masoretic text), and furthermore :

Pr 19 : 23 : *φόβος Κυρίου εἰς ζωὴν ἀνδρί, ὁ δὲ ἄφοβος αὐλισθήσεται οὗ οὐκ ἐπισκοπεῖται γνῶσις* (the Masoretic text is different). Compare Pr 24 : 26 f. (30 : 3 f.).
2 Mac 9 : 11 : *ἤρξατο . . . εἰς ἐπίγνωσιν ἔρχεσθαι* (come to consideration) *θείᾳ μάστιγι.*
Wis 14 : 22 : *πλανᾶσθαι περὶ τὴν τοῦ Θεοῦ γνῶσιν* (the context proves that it is a question of the worship of God).

On the whole *gnōsis* is a favourite expression of the wisdom books, and these books are still more inclined to use *sophia*. The examples above may further show that in Proverbs *gnōsis* is combined with " the fear of God " where it is used to describe a humble state of mind. This is also true of Sirach and other later books. Although the word occurs in different contexts and sometimes has a more intellectual meaning, the emphasis is generally on prudence and humility. And it may be stated that this is the characteristic meaning of *gnōsis* in the wisdom literature. Prudence is meant to be not an innate faculty but a result of consideration in the face of God's majesty and power. It is not important to know many facts, but merely one fact : that God is the supreme master of the universe. This fact is not secret, but should be evident to everybody who does not prefer to be a fool. To have this insight means to have *gnōsis*, " prudence " (Pr 1 : 19, 21 : 13 f. ; etc.).

(b) In the wisdom apocrypha of the LXX these ideas are more often represented by another Greek word that requires a few concluding remarks. This is *sophia*, " wisdom ". A fundamental meaning of *sophia* is " skill ", " cleverness ". In earlier Greek it was often regarded as the virtue of politicians ; compare the Seven Sages of ancient Greece (Plat. *Prot.* 343a, Diog. L. 1, 40 ff., 108). This character of the word is also represented by the

Apocrypha of the Old Testament. It always refers to political cleverness in 1 Esdras and Judith. Otherwise *sophia* characterizes God's creative power (Sir 1 : 1 ff. ; Wis 7 : 7 ff. ; etc.). It is sometimes connected with obedience to the Law (Sir 1 : 36 ; 17 : 11 ff. ; Wis 6 : 17 f. ; etc.), and this occurs in an even more elaborate manner than in Proverbs. But it is still a question of the individual's behaviour in political respects and of how civil life is best conducted.

In particular it must be noticed that the religious and political virtue called *sophia* refers to the fear of God, i.e., humility and submission :

Sir 21 : 11 : ὁ φυλάσσων νόμον κατακρατεῖ τοῦ ἐννοήματος αὐτοῦ, καὶ συντέλεια τοῦ φόβου Κυρίου σοφία.
Sir 22 : 6 : παιδεία ἐν παντὶ καιρῷ σοφίας (" is always part of wisdom ").
Wis 1 : 4 : εἰς κακότεχνον ψυχὴν οὐκ εἰσελεύσεται σοφία.
Wis 1 : 6 : φιλάνθρωπον γὰρ πνεῦμα σοφία.

Thus, although *sophia* is often the same as worldly prudence, it has a religious and metaphysical background and is very much related to humility and submission. In fact *sophia* coincides with *gnōsis* which, in wisdom literature, is also the virtue of a humble and submissive heart.

Yet one should not altogether identify *gnōsis* and *sophia*. The words originally had different meanings, and this difference may always have been more or less felt. It is true that they are both used to portray a personal attitude. Nevertheless *gnōsis*, as it is connected with the verb *ginōskō,* is a relatively objective conception referring to a content of the mind. That is, it is something that is " known " or otherwise embraced by the consciousness. On the other hand, *sophia,* as it is connected with the adjective *sophos,* is a relatively subjective conception and represents a personal ability, an existing quality.[9] This is proved by the fact that with *gnōsis* one may find or postulate an objective genitive, which is impossible with *sophia.* Even in cases where *gnōsis* implies a pure attitude, it refers in the background to a knowledge or feeling of something. But one cannot speak of a *sophia* or wisdom of something. Hence it is obvious that *gnōsis* and *sophia* could never be complete synonyms, even if they do occur alternatively in several instances.

---

[9] Always a quality, never an activity, as pointed out by U. Wilckens, σοφία: *TWNT* 7 (1964), 467.

In the intertestamental writings *da'aṯ*, *gnōsis* and related words do not denote in any considerable degree the theoretical " knowledge " of established facts that is the ideal of modern science. They have more to do with personal contact and feeling, consideration and involvement. It would not be fair to explain this as evidence of a more primitive Oriental thinking which had to be surpassed later by Hellenistic rationalism. The correct explanation would refer rather to God's absolute sovereignty as the dominating idea of biblical traditions.[10]

[10] L. Coenen, " Erkenntnis, Erfahrung. Zur Verkündigung ", *Theologisches Begriffslexikon zum Neuen Testament*, I (1967), 255 ff.

# HE IS THE BREAD

## Targum Neofiti Exodus 16 : 15

GEZA VERMES

WITH his disinterment in 1956 of Codex Neofiti I from the depths of the Vatican Library, where it had lain falsely labelled as Targum Onkelos, A. Díez-Macho enriched Jewish studies with a document comparable in importance to the Qumran finds.[1] Although the *editio princeps* is still awaiting publication, preliminary study already indicates that we may expect an improvement almost beyond recognition of our present knowledge of early Jewish biblical exegesis.[2]

The purpose of this short paper is to draw attention to a curious text from this new Targum. It was recently brought to my attention by one of my research students, Rabbi Hiroshi Okamoto, who is in the process of writing a D.Phil. thesis on the entire Neofiti Exodus.

The passage in question reads :

*wyr'w wḥmwn bny yśr'l w'mryn gbr l'ḥwy mn' hw' 'rwm l' hww yd'yn*[3] *mšh w'mr mšh hw' lḥm' dy yhb yyy lkwn lmykl*

In the margin the following variant is appended :

*bmymr' dyyy lkwn.*

[1] *The recently discovered Palestinian Targum : its Antiquity and Relationship with the other Targums, Supplements to Vetus Testamentum* 7 (1960), 222–45. A specimen edition of Dt 1 was published by the same scholar under the title, *Biblia Polyglotta Matritensia*, Series IV, *Targum Palaestinense in Pentateuchum*, Madrid, 1965. See also M. Martin, *The Palaeographical Character of Codex Neofiti* 1, *Textus* 3 (1963), 1–35 ; G. E. Weil, *Le Codex Neofiti* 1, *Textus* 4 (1964) 225–29 ; R. Le Déaut, *Introduction à la littérature targumique*, 1ère partie, Rome, 1966, pp. 114–21.

[2] I have made extensive use of Neofiti in *Scripture and Tradition in Judaism*, Leiden, 1961 ; " The Targumic Versions of Genesis IV 3–16 ", *The Annual of Leeds University Oriental Society* 3 (1961–62), 81–114 ; *Haggadah in the Onkelos Targum*, *JSS* 8 (1963), 159–69. For detailed bibliographical references, see R. Le Déaut, *La nuit pascale. Essai sur la signification de la Pâque juive à partir du Targum d'Exode XII* 42, Rome, 1963. M. McNamara, *The New Testament and the Palestinian Targum to the Pentateuch*, Rome, 1966.

[3] One would normally expect *yt* before an accusative, although its absence is by no means unique.

Leaving the three crucial words in Aramaic, the verse may be translated :

The children of Israel saw and said to one another, *mn' hw'*, for they did not know Moses. And Moses said, *hw'* is the bread which the Lord has given you to eat.

The variant reads :

by the *Memra* (word) of the Lord for food.

This exegesis of the Exodus verse is unique, as will be seen from the following brief survey of the Masoretic Text and the ancient versions. The Hebrew original may be rendered as follows :

When the children of Israel saw it (the manna), they said to one another, What is it ? (*mn hw'*) For they did not know what it was (*mh hw'*). And Moses said to them, It is the bread which the Lord has given you to eat.

With the exception of the Onkelos and Pseudo-Jonathan Targums, the ancient translators of the Septuagint, Peshitta and Vulgate were satisfied with the popular etymology provided for the word "manna" (*mn hw'*=*mh hw'*, what is it?) and rendered the verse literally.

Pseudo-Jonathan safeguards the Hebrew play on words but adds a haggadah relating to the creation of the manna.[4]

*wḥmwn bny yšr'l whwwn tmhyn w'mryn 'ynš lḥbryh m'n hw' 'rwm l' yd'yn mh hw' w'mr mšh lhwn hw' lḥm' d'yṣṭn' lkwn mn šyrwy' bšmy mrwm' wkdyn yhbyn lkwn lmykl.*

The children of Israel saw and were astonished and said to one another, What is it ? For they did not know what it was. And Moses said to them, This is the bread which has been preserved for you from the beginning in the high heavens and is now given [5] to you to eat.

Onkelos, on the other hand, falls victim to his own scruples. He tries, as usual, to remain faithful to the original, and consequently omits all paraphrastic increment. At the same time, he is fully aware that *mān* in biblical Hebrew does not signify

[4] Manna is one of the ten marvellous things created by God on the eve of the first sabbath *byn hšmšwt* (during the twilight). Cf. Aboth 5 : 8 and the summary reference in Ps. Jonathan on Gn 2 : 2.

[5] Note the impersonal form of the verb. Instead of, " the Lord has given you " the text reads, " they give you ". Cf. the Neofiti marginal variant below.

" what ", and therefore renders it as *mannā'*, thus spoiling both the pun and the etymological intent.

They said to one another, This is manna. For they did not know what it was.

In clear contrast to all these versions, Neofiti must have understood *hw'* in *mn hw'* as a pronoun referring, not to an object but to a person. Otherwise the clause " for they did not know Moses " makes no sense. The Aramaic words *mn' hw'* are therefore to be translated, " Who is he ? " or more probably, " What is he ? ".[6] If this interpretation is correct,[7] then Moses's answer must be rendered :

He is the bread which the Lord has given you to eat.

Or, if the marginal variant is followed :

He is the bread given [8] to you by the word of the Lord for food.

In both replies, the essential assertion remains the same, namely, that the *lḥm'* or heavenly bread symbolizes Moses.

The various elements contained in this allegory appear, jointly or separately, in rabbinic as well as in Hellenistic sources (amongst which I count also the Fourth Gospel). As they have been subjected to repeated, though cursory, examination in a number of modern studies [9] and in commentaries on John,[10] I will restrict myself to a classification of the principal themes and to providing the reader with their textual basis.

[6] In Aramaic, *man* or *mā'n*=who ; *mānā'* or *mān*=what. Cf. J. Levy, *Chaldäisches Wörterbuch über die Targumim*, Leipzig, 1868, 2, p. 45.

[7] During a recent visit to Budapest, I had the privilege of discussing the present study with Prof. A. Scheiber who advanced two further possibilities. One is to alter *mšh* to *mšhw*. Against this it may be argued that this a purely conjectural emendation resulting in a *lectio facilior* and that the word is a Hebraism seldom appearing in Palestinian Aramaic. In the second hypothesis emphasis is to be laid on the fact that if the Israelites spoke to one another, this was because they did not know Moses. I do not think, however, that this explanation of the passage is easier to defend than the one put forward here.

[8] This text appears to demand a pᵉʿil participle *yᵉhiḇ* instead of the third person pᵉʿal *yᵉhaḇ*.

[9] Cf. *S̄BK*, 2, 482 ff. ; R. Meyer, *TWNT* 4, 466 ff. ; Peder Borgen, *Bread from Heaven*, Leiden, 1965 ; E. D. Freed, *Old Testament Quotations in the Gospel of John*, Leiden, 1965, pp. 11–16.

[10] See for instance the two authoritative works published in English : C. H. Dodd, *The Interpretation of the Fourth Gospel*, Cambridge, 1953, pp. 333 ff. ; C. K. Barrett, *The Gospel according to Saint John*, London, 1955, pp. 239 f.

# I

## Rabbinic Sources

Leaving aside the haggadah on the return of the manna in the messianic age, which does not directly concern the Neofiti exegesis,[11] the remaining two chief interpretative themes relate to Moses' part in procuring the heaven-sent food and the metaphorical identification of manna (and the well) with divine revelation expressed in the Torah.

(a) *Manna—merits of Moses*

According to the Exodus account, Israel received in the wilderness three gifts : the manna, the well, and a pillar of cloud to direct them by day and by night. To the question, on whose behalf these gifts were extended to the chosen people, Rabbi Yose b. Judah (a contemporary of the patriarch Judah in the late second century) declares in Tos. Sotah 11 : 10 :

Three good leaders arose for Israel, Moses, Aaron and Miriam, and through their merits three precious gifts were bestowed on Israel, the well, the pillar of cloud and the manna.

That the gifts are listed in reverse order to the " good leaders " through whose merits they were obtained, appears from *Mekhilta* on Ex 16 : 35 :

When Miriam died, the well ceased ; when Aaron died, the clouds of glory ceased ; when Moses died, the manna ceased.

A derivative tradition voiced by Rabbi Jose b. Judah, and before him by Rabbi Joshua b. Hananiah (late first century A.D.), and preserved in the above-quoted passages, associates with Moses not only the manna, but also the restoration of the two other heavenly presents.

When Miriam died, the well ceased, but returned through the merits of Moses and Aaron. When Aaron died, the cloud ceased, but both returned through the merits of Moses. When Moses died, all three ceased and did not return.

If the attribution to Joshua b. Hananiah is correct, the basic motif on which he presents a variation is bound to antedate the last decades of the first century A.D. Sceptics needing further

[11] Cf. *Mekhilta* on Ex 16 : 25 ; 2 Bar 29 : 8.

reassurance on the great antiquity of this haggadah can find it in Pseudo-Philo's *Liber Antiquitatum Biblicarum* (20 : 8) :

Et hec sunt tria que dedit Deus populo suo propter tres homines, id est, puteum aque mirre propter Mariam, et columnam nubis propter Aaron et manna propter Moysen. Et finitis his tribus ablata sunt hec tria ab eis.[12]

(b) *Manna-Torah*

Manna is one of several allegories designating the Law as heavenly, spiritual nourishment. The following striking parable by an anonymous exegete appears in *Mekhilta* on Ex 13 : 17 :

The Holy One, blessed be he, did not bring them by the direct way to the land of Israel, but by way of the wilderness. He said, If I bring Israel now to the Land, straightway one will attach himself to his field, the other to his vineyard, and they will neglect the Torah. But I will cause them to go about in the wilderness for forty years so that they may eat the manna and drink the water of the well, and the Torah will be assimilated into their bodies.

Also, the " food " offered by Wisdom in Pr 9 : 5 is interpreted by Rabbi Joshua b. Hananiah in GnR 70 : 5 :

The bread is the Torah, as it is written : Eat of my bread.

External corroboration of an early date comes, as will be seen presently, from Philo, and indirectly, apropos of the well, from the Qumran CD 6 : 4 :

The well is the Law.

In sum, rabbinic exegesis of Ex 16 : 15 manifests a distinctly allegorical tendency. Nevertheless, it does not settle satisfactorily the problem raised by Neofiti, the actual identification of Moses as the heavenly bread, since none of the texts provides an exact parallel. The one possible exception is Meg. 13a where, in a midrash on 1 Ch 4 : 18, Yered (he descends) is said to be Moses " because manna descended (*yrd*) in his days ".

## II

## Hellenistic Judaism

(a) *Josephus*

In the field of Hellenistic Jewish literature there is no trace of manna-Law symbolism. However, Josephus, *Ant.* 3, 26 incorporates two haggadic details not without importance to the

[12] See also *Jewish Antiquities* 3, 26 below.

present discussion: the manna descends in answer to Moses' prayer (ἀνέχοντος γὰρ Μωυσέος τὰς χεῖρας ἐπὶ ταῖς εὐχαῖς), and the dew which produces it first congeals about his hands. In other words, the heavenly food is not only obtained through Moses; he is also the first to receive it and subsequently to give it to the astonished Israelites who had imagined it to be snow (3, 27).

(b) *Philo*[13]

It is well known that in his allegorical teaching Philo equates manna, i.e., "the heavenly incorruptible food of the soul",[14] with "words (λόγοι) poured like rain from . . . heaven",[15] with the "word of God" (λόγος θεοῦ),[16] with God's "most generic word", i.e., the Logos which is "above all the world and is eldest and most all-embracing of all created things",[17] with the "saying of God and word of God", source of παιδεῖαι καὶ σοφίαι,[18] or simply with "the heavenly wisdom".[19] He deduces this doctrine of manna = Logos = wisdom = Torah by reading Ex 16:15 in combination with the beginning of 16:16:

So they (the Israelites) enquire, What is this . . . ? And they will be taught by the prophet that, This is the bread which the Lord has given them to eat. Tell me, then, what kind of bread is this? This saying, he says, which the Lord ordained.[20]

Who gives this bread of the soul? Philo asserts that it "is sent by God like snow . . . with none to share his work",[21] but with Josephus and the Rabbis he also attributes its descent to the intercession of Moses.

What he does not find in his own store, he asks for at the hands of God . . . and he opens his heavenly treasury and he sends his good things as he does the snow and rain . . . And it is his wont to bestow these gifts in answer to his suppliant Logos (τὸν ἱκέτην ἑαυτοῦ λόγον) . . . ; for it is said in another

[13] The main texts are examined in Peder Borgen's *Bread from Heaven*, subtitled "An exegetical study of the concept of Manna in the Gospel of John and the writings of Philo".

[14] *Quis rerum* 79; cf. *Leg. all.* 3, 162; *Mut.* 259; *Fuga* 137, etc.

[15] *Leg. all.* 3, 162. Cf. *Quis rerum* 79.

[16] *Leg. all.* 3, 169.

[17] *Ibid.*, 175.

[18] *Fuga* 137. "Both Logos and wisdom are used . . . in the sense of the Law of Moses" (H. A. Wolfson, *Philo*, vol. 1, Cambridge, Mass., 1962, p. 258).

[19] *Mut.* 259.

[20] *Fuga* 138. Cf. also 137 and *Leg. all.* 3, 173.

[21] *Mut.* 259.

place, when Moses had made supplication (Μωυσέος ἱκετεύσαντος), "I am gracious to them in accordance with thy word" (Nu 14 : 20).[22]

In this passage a new and particularly significant link appears in the chain of evidence leading to an elucidation of the Neofiti exegesis. The earlier quotations from Philo present manna as a symbol of the Logos; here, Moses is the ἱκέτης λόγος. A transposition of images such as this, illogical though it may seem, is perfectly normal in the allegorical process. Thus, playing no doubt on the interchangeability in the Bible of "Torah of God" and "Torah of Moses", Philo elsewhere describes the laws of Moses as "truly divine". But simultaneously he represents Moses as the incarnation of these laws, as one in whose soul the patterns of his Torah were imprinted.[23] He applies to Moses in an especially pregnant sense the saying, The king is a living law (νόμος ἔμψυχος).[24]

In brief, in rabbinic tradition Moses is associated with manna and Torah, and manna is accepted as an allegorical Torah. In Philo, manna is connected with Logos, wisdom and Torah, and Moses is presented as Logos and Torah incarnate. In Neofiti, all these trends meet, making it possible for Moses the Lawgiver to identify himself, in circumlocutional speech,[25] as the heavenly bread itself, a personification of the divine nourishment allotted by God to Israel.

*He is the bread which the Lord has given you to eat.*

## III

## The New Testament

As is scarcely necessary to remark, the most enlightening corroboration of the accuracy of the interpretation proposed here comes from the New Testament. According to Pauline and Johannine symbolism, the well and the manna are identified with

[22] *Migr.* 121 f. Although Moses is not mentioned in the first half of this passage, the reference to rain and snow appears to indicate that Philo has the manna episode in mind. It is the person of Moses, not his prayer, that is allegorically described as "the suppliant Logos" in the same way that, in *Migr.* 78, Aaron is entitled "the uttered Logos" (ὁ λόγος προφορικός).

[23] *Mos.* 2, 8–12. See E. R. Goodenough, *By Light, Light—The Mystic Gospel of Hellenistic Judaism*, New Haven, 1935, p. 89.

[24] *Mos.* 2, 3–4.

[25] "*He* is the bread." On circumlocutional speech, see my contribution, "The use of *br nš/br nš'* in Jewish Aramaic", in Matthew Black, *An Aramaic Approach to the Gospels and Acts*, Oxford, [3]1967, pp. 320–27.

the person of Jesus. The well, Paul writes, sprang from a "spiritual rock", ἡ πέτρα δὲ ἦν ὁ Χριστός.[26]

The manna allegory is even more sharply developed in the picture of Jesus as contrasted with Moses. In the discourse on the "bread of life" in the Fourth Gospel,[27] Jesus is ὁ ἄρτος τῆς ζωῆς [28]; ὁ ἄρτος ὁ καταβὰς ἐκ τοῦ οὐρανοῦ [29]; ὁ ἄρτος ὁ ζῶν ὁ ἐκ τοῦ οὐρανοῦ καταβάς.[30]

More noteworthy still, although most of the statements are expressed in the 'Εγώ εἰμι form, i.e., in the first person, v. 50 contains in Greek an almost exact rendering of Neofiti's *hw' lḥm'*:

οὗτός ἐστιν ὁ ἄρτος (ὁ ἐκ τοῦ οὐρανοῦ καταβαίνων)[31].

In conclusion, Neofiti Ex 16 : 15 provides a warning, insofar as it demonstrates that certain allegorical elements in Philo's thought are not necessarily Hellenistic, but may possess direct Palestinian antecedents.

In addition, it acts as yet one more pointer to the manner in which the authors of the New Testament took over in full Jewish haggadah and made use of it in the creation of the Johannine (and Pauline) theology.[32]

I have great pleasure in offering this study to Matthew Black on his sixtieth birthday with the traditional good wish:

עד מאה ועשרים

[26] 1 Co 10 : 4. [27] Jn 6 : 31 ff. [28] Jn 6 : 35, 48. [29] Jn 6 : 41.
[30] Jn 6 : 51.

[31] I have used the Fourth Gospel for the sake of its external evidence in establishing the meaning of the Neofiti Targum. It is for New Testament scholars to decide how far the new data may affect their understanding of the Johannine speech as a whole. They may also ask whether Jn 6 : 51 ff. is not a further midrash on Pr 9 : 5 : Come, eat of my bread and drink of the wine I have mixed. It should be borne in mind that the metaphor wine/blood (of the grape) is biblical (Gn 49 : 11, Dt 32 : 14) and that the noun *lḥwm* (bowels ?) which follows *dmym* (blood) in Zeph 1 : 17 was understood in antiquity (cf. LXX, Targum, Vulgate, ExR 42 : 4) to signify "body". A pun *lḥwm/lḥm* or *lḥm'* = *bśr* or *bśr'* would be quite natural in both Hebrew and Aramaic. In the Ex Rabbah passage the following comment is attached to Zephaniah's *lḥwmm*: *b'rby' ḳwryn lbsr' lḥm'*. In Arabia flesh is called *lhm'*. See also Sir 15 : 3; 24 : 19–21.

[32] Cf. my *Scripture and Tradition in Judaism*, Leiden, 1961, pp. 178–227; "The Targumic Versions of Genesis IV 3–16", *The Annual of Leeds University Oriental Society*, 3 (1961–62), 109 ff.

# THE NEW *PASSION OF JESUS* IN THE LIGHT OF THE NEW TESTAMENT AND APOCRYPHA *

R. McL. Wilson

The London *Times* for July 15, 1966,[1] announced the discovery of a manuscript the character of which was such as to lead its finders to call for " a scientific re-appraisal of the beginnings of Christianity in the light of the newly-discovered 1500-year-old texts of a Judaeo-Christian sect claiming descent from the disciples of Jesus himself ". Fresh light on the history of Christian origins is always welcome, and demands investigation; the sources of information at our disposal are by no means so extensive as might be wished. But on the other hand it is possible to over-estimate the significance of new material, to give such emphasis to the new, at the expense of the old, as to distort the picture. In the present case one scholar is reported to have claimed these texts as comparable in significance to the Dead Sea Scrolls ; and on the other hand it has been said : " It is difficult to assess the respective shares of the lecturer and the reporter in the exaggerated importance attributed to the texts. Newspapermen, who do not claim to be experts, could easily over-estimate the importance of such discoveries, and it is clear that many of the absurdities and confusions in the press accounts must be imputed to them." [2] Even so, it is to the credit of the scholars concerned in the original announcement that they have so presented the evidence that it is possible to draw other conclusions from the data which they have themselves supplied.[3]

The full text of the document, to my knowledge, is not yet available in edited form, but an " enlarged version " of the original lecture announcing the discovery, with extensive quotations in

* A paper read in its original form at the Fifth International Conference on Patristic Studies, Oxford, 1967.

[1] Also, e.g., in *Time* Magazine of the same date [R. A. Kraft, *JBL* 86 (1967), 329].

[2] S. M. Stern, *Encounter* (May 1967), p. 53.

[3] The present paper was drafted on the basis of the original press report, but has been revised and expanded to take account of the other literature listed.

English translation, has been published by Shlomo Pines.[4] The Arabic text of two passages relating to the Passion and a third containing texts on the descent of Jesus has been published by S. M. Stern.[5] The new texts are claimed by D. Flusser as an independent witness to the shorter "Eusebian" conclusion of the Gospel of Matthew.[6]

The texts are contained in a work by a tenth-century Moslem author, but Pines claims they are not of Moslem origin and could only derive from a Jewish-Christian community. The work in question falls into two distinct but interwoven parts, one of which was written by a Moslem author, the other not; and in most cases there are indications which provide sufficient ground for differentiating the Moslem additions from the texts in which they are interpolated. Thus far there appears to be agreement: Nikolainen, for example, agrees that "the main part of the polemic in this Arabic manuscript is of Jewish or Judaistic nature and not of an Islamic one".[7] Opinions differ however as to the character of this "Judaistic" material, for where Pines argues for Jewish-Christian documents dating from the fifth or sixth century Stern holds that the Moslem author was indebted to Christian converts to Islam for his information.[8] It is precisely this kind of uncertainty that prompts to caution: we do not know definitely the source from which the Moslem author derived his information, and even if Pines is correct there is a gap from the first century to the fifth, of which we know nothing and in which the texts might have been subjected to considerable adaptation.

To revert to the original press report, the grounds on which the claim is made for a "scientific re-appraisal" are three in number: (1) that the manuscript "portrays the first Christians in Jerusalem as synagogue-goers who regarded Jesus as a prophet but not

[4] "The Jewish Christians of the Early Centuries of Christianity according to a New Source", *Proc. Israel Academy of Sciences and Humanities*, Vol. 2, no. 13, Jerusalem, 1966 (reviewed by Kraft, *op. cit.*; see also A. T. Nikolainen, *NTS* 14 (1968), 287 ff.).

[5] *JTS* 18 (1967), 34 ff. (texts pp. 53 ff.; translations in the body of the article). A further article (*JTS* 19, 1968, 128 ff.) appeared after the present paper had gone to the press.

[6] *Annual of Swedish Theological Institute* 5 (1967), 110 ff.

[7] *NTS* 14 (1968), 287.

[8] *JTS* 18 (1967), 36. Later (p. 50) Stern writes: "'Abd al-Jabbār seems to have got hold, presumably in the book of some Muslim predecessor, of an apocryphal account of the passion, the ultimate provenance of which is unknown".

divine, and who observed Jewish law to the letter". (2) The texts "give an account of the Passion which strongly suggests that another Jew may have been singled out by Judas Iscariot, and crucified instead of Jesus". And (3) "they also report sayings by Jesus, some of which contradict those in the Scriptures".

## I

To take the last point first, two examples are given. One is the episode of Mk 2 : 23 ff. and parallels, in which the Pharisees protest against the disciples' action in plucking and eating corn from the fields on the Sabbath. Plucking corn, it is said, is "unequivocally prohibited by rabbinical law". The new text says: "Jesus walked through the sown land and his disciples became hungry and began to rub corn and to eat it." "Rubbing corn on the Sabbath", says the report, "was permitted by rabbis." [9] Three points may be noted: (a) Dt 23 : 25, often cited in the commentaries on the Marcan passage, permits plucking with the hand in a neighbour's field, as against reaping with a sickle, but says nothing about the Sabbath. Mishnah Shab. however (7 : 2) [10] lists 39 kinds of work which are prohibited on the Sabbath, including reaping, grinding and sifting. The Pharisees' complaint evidently rests upon a legalistic interpretation of this ruling, in which the plucking was construed as reaping and the rubbing as grinding. At all events there appears to be ground for questioning the statement as to what was allowed by the rabbis. (b) The alleged discrepancy lies in the omission by the new text of the reference to plucking. This however is surely implied in the context of the story: if Jesus "walked through the sown land", and his disciples "began to rub corn", the inference surely is that they first plucked it. In other words, we have not a discrepancy but an alternative or abbreviated form of the same story. (c) Perhaps more significant is the fact that the disciples are said to have *rubbed* the corn, for this detail is

[9] Pines (*op. cit.*, p. 63) refers to the Talmud (Shab. 128a), according to which "rubbing" may be permitted within certain limits on the Sabbath, but adds (a) that this opinion of the Sages is preceded by that of R. Yehudah, who also permitted plucking; (b) that both opinions refer to spices; and (c) that the Jewish Christians of the texts held that the action was legitimate, on grounds of necessity (see also *op. cit.*, p. 5).

[10] Cited in C. K. Barrett, *The New Testament Background : Selected Documents*, London, 1956, p. 154.

expressly mentioned by Luke alone. A single word is a precarious foundation on which to build, and it could be argued that the rubbing is implied in Mark and Matthew, but at least the point should prompt a closer inspection for traces of knowledge of Luke; for this would surely be remarkable in a document of Jewish-Christian origin. According to Irenaeus (1, 22 Harvey) the Ebionites used only the Gospel of Matthew. And if the sect was not Ebionite, what other Jewish-Christian groups are known to have survived, and what evidence have we for distinguishing them? Pines refers to the Nazarenes described by Epiphanius, but himself indicates the difficulty of distinguishing the two groups.[11] There are in fact two problems here: first the assessing of the reliability of Epiphanius' information, and second the recovery from his statements of adequate criteria for distinguishing one group from the other. Allowance must also be made for some measure of mutual influence and interpenetration, which only makes identification of the sect to which the texts belonged more difficult.

The second example quoted in the press report is the saying: "I shall not judge men or call them to account for their actions. He who sent me will do this." This, it is correctly stated, contradicts the saying in John (5 : 22): "For the Father judges no man but has committed all judgment to the son." Reference to Jn 12 : 47 ff. however presents a different picture. As Barrett says,[12] "In different passages in John it is said that Jesus acts as judge (5 : 22, 27; 8 : 16, 26) and that he does not judge (3 : 17; 8 : 15). It is hardly credible that John should have been unaware of this apparent contradiction, or that it should have been undesigned." To select one side or the other only may be to distort the picture. We need to know more about the context of the saying in the new text. Moreover if this saying is a conscious contradiction of John this might again have implications for any theory of Jewish-Christian origin, as it certainly would for Ebionite origin.

[11] *Op. cit.*, pp. 11 f. The combination of belief in Christ (though not his divinity) with insistence on observance of the Law " is used by Epiphanius as a definition of the sect which he calls *Nazōraioi*, and which, in his perhaps somewhat arbitrary terminology, is one of the two main Jewish Christian sects, the other being the Ebionites "; but on the following page Pines notes " these two denominations appear to designate one and the same sect ".

[12] *The Gospel according to St. John*, London, 1958, p. 361. Pines (*op. cit.*, p. 74) refers to Jn 3 : 17–18; 8 : 15–16 and 12 : 48–49 in a post-script to his lecture.

## II

As to the Passion Story, " two narratives of the Passion included in the manuscript are conflicting. One comes close to the version of John but differs in details." Of this no more is said, but once again similarity to John in a document identified as Jewish-Christian must give us pause. Are we to think of a document based on John's sources ? Or of one dependent on the Fourth Gospel itself ?

The other narrative is " vastly different from the account in the Gospels ", and it is on this that the finders concentrate their attention. Once again, however, a closer inspection must give rise to doubts. It begins with a complaint by a group of Jews [13] to Herod that Jesus " corrupted and led astray our brethren ". Brought before Herod, the prisoner denied that he was Christ, and Herod washed his hands of the matter, saying to the Jews : " I see you attribute to him sayings that were not his and you wrong him. There is a basin of water for me to wash my hands of this man's blood." This is reminiscent of Mt 27 : 24, with the substitution of Herod for Pilate, which in turn reflects the known tendency in the development of the Gospel tradition towards the exoneration of Pilate and the Romans from responsibility for the death of Jesus.

We are then told that Pilate asked for Jesus to be sent to him for a talk " as he had heard that he was an intelligent man ", but later sent him back to Herod. This recalls the episode related, significantly, by Luke alone (23 : 6–16), with the necessary reversal of the roles of Herod and Pilate. It may be noted here that in the Gospel of Peter [14] we read " But of the Jews none washed their hands, neither Herod nor any one of his judges. And as they would not wash, Pilate arose. And then Herod the king commanded that the Lord should be marched off . . ." On this Swete comments : " The object is to minimise the sin of the Procurator by laying the chief guilt at the door of Herod, the representative of the Jews ".[15] The new text apparently goes

[13] Cf. the complaint brought to Pilate in the *Acts of Pilate*, E. Hennecke-W. Schneemelcher, *New Testament Apocrypha*, ET London, 1963, 1, pp. 450 f.

[14] See Hennecke-Schneemelcher, *op. cit.*, p. 183. Possibly we should recall also the story quoted from Hegesippus by Eusebius (*HE* 3, 20) about the grand-children of Jude the brother of Jesus, who were brought before the emperor Domitian, but after examination were dismissed as people of no importance.

[15] *The Akhmim Fragment of the Apocryphal Gospel of Peter*, London, 1893, p. 1.

even further: Herod sends Jesus to prison for the night,[16] and the following day *the Jews* seize and torture him, finally crucifying him and piercing him with lances so that he should die quickly.[17] Here then Herod also is largely exonerated—he is responsible only for the imprisonment. This would represent a culmination of the process by which responsibility for the crucifixion was shifted from Pilate and the Romans to the Jewish people.

Mt. 27 : 24 belongs to Matthew's special material, Lk 23 : 6–16 to that of Luke. It is of course possible to argue that the author of the new Passion Story had access to the Evangelists' sources, but it is more probable, in view of the facts already stated, that he made use of our Gospels themselves. This in turn would entail a comparatively late date for his work, and this again must reduce the value of his narrative as an ostensibly historical account of the Passion.

The two points noted here are the comparative exoneration of Judas, who was amazed when told of the crucifixion, and the suggestion that another man was crucified instead of Jesus. The first of course runs counter to the usual assessment of Judas in Christian tradition, but it does not go the length of the Cainite heresy, according to which Judas alone possessed the true *gnosis*, and therefore accomplished "the mystery of the betrayal".[18] As to the second point, it is not stated in the passages quoted that another man was crucified in Jesus' stead, but only that Judas said the crucified man was innocent. Something has apparently been "read in" here, presumably by the Moslem author of the final work. Thus Pines writes: "On the whole, it seems likely that the Moslem author's thesis is a mere piece of Islamic apologetics".[19] Stern also notes: "We must distinguish between what the text says and the inferences made from it for the purposes of Muslim apologetics", and argues that we have

[16] This may have some relevance for the longer chronology of the Passion suggested by Mlle Jaubert (see most recently *NTS* 14 (1968) 145 ff.).

[17] Swete notes (*op. cit.*, p. 7): "The *crurifragium* was, it seems, employed in crucifixions among the Jews in order to comply with the law of Deut. xxi. Comp. John xix. 31, 32, where an exception is made only in the case of our Lord, because He was already dead". The natural interpretation of the passage in the Gospel of Peter (4) is however that the Jews were enraged at the malefactor who rebuked them, and in retaliation commanded that *his* legs should not be broken "that he might die in torment". The piercing with lances may recall Jn 21 : 34.

[18] A Gospel of Judas is mentioned by Irenaeus (1, 28, 9 Harvey), and the sect concerned is identified with the Cainites (see Puech in Hennecke-Schneemelcher, *op. cit.*, 1, pp. 313 f.).

[19] *Op. cit.*, p. 56.

here " not a primitive text but an elaboration representing the author's reflection on the story ".[20] The conclusion that somebody else was crucified instead of Jesus " fits very well the main trend of Islamic tradition ",[21] and in the following pages he gives a number of examples of such substitution theories, including one in which the victim was Judas. We may also recall Irenaeus' account of the system of Basilides, in which Simon of Cyrene takes the place of Jesus, and the Docetic theories which distinguished between the human Jesus and the divine Christ. The claim that the Jewish Christian texts employed by the Moslem author " give an account of the Passion which strongly suggests that another Jew may have been singled out by Judas Iscariot, and crucified instead of Jesus " is very far from well grounded. This is the interpretation read into the texts by the Moslem author.

## III

To sum up, Nikolainen accepts the Jewish or Judaistic rather than Islamic nature of the polemic in this manuscript, but adds that it is another question whether the manuscript increases our knowledge of the first beginnings and development of the Jerusalem Church itself and Christian history in New Testament times in general. " The text in its present form presupposes a close acquaintance with all our canonical gospels and is in this sense a very young source ".[22] Pines notes a " great familiarity with Christian literature " (p. 6), including not only the Gospels but Acts and the Pauline epistles. Furthermore there are references to the Empress Helena, to Constantine and Nicaea (p. 14) ; the arguments against the divinity of Christ are largely identical with those of the Arians (pp. 12 f.) ; there are references to Mani (pp. 66 ff.). A notable feature is that James is not prominent, while Peter is criticized. In this respect the texts differ from the Pseudo-Clementines (p. 62). On the other hand there are no references to the Moslem conquest, and in the light of all this Pines suggests a date in the fifth or sixth century (pp. 21, 32 ff.).

The survival of a Jewish-Christian group in Syria long after the Fall of Jerusalem is not in itself impossible. That a Moslem theologian should have used for his own purposes older documents

[20] *Op. cit.*, p. 44.

[21] *Ibid.*, p. 45. For Judas as the victim see pp. 47, 49. Perhaps we may recall also the story of Ananias in a Coptic fragment ascribed to the Gospel of Bartholomew (see Hennecke-Schneemelcher, *op. cit.*, 1, p. 505).

[22] *Op. cit.*, pp. 287 f.

of Jewish-Christian origin is again not impossible. But a theory which requires both of these to be not only possibilities but realities, and at one and the same time, places a certain strain upon the credulity. In conclusion, a few points may be listed which call for further examination :

(1) We have a gap of three centuries at least to fill—can we be sure that original documents were preserved and copied with complete fidelity throughout that period? Certainly some elements seem to present a primitive appearance ; the presentation of Jesus as a prophet, and not divine, could be the mark of a very early stage—but is it *necessarily* indicative of a primitive stage, before Christological development had taken place? Other features, such as the progressive exoneration of the Romans, seem to presuppose considerable development.

(2) There is polemical reference to Orthodox, Nestorians and Jacobites (Pines, p. 3)—what other contemporary influences have we to allow for at various stages? From the point of view of the New Testament and Christian origins, the fifth or sixth century is a comparatively late date, and it is legitimate to question the possibility of the survival of authentic original Jewish Christian traditions in pristine purity to this late stage.

(3) The texts are in Arabic, but are said to have a Syriac basis. The ultimate originals were presumably Aramaic or Hebrew—what allowance must be made for modification, possibly tendentious, at the stages of translation?

(4) What precisely is the nature of the source? Are we to think of a document, or of a compilation by the Moslem author from a variety of older sources? The occurrence of two accounts of the Passion suggests the latter—but this would mean that the separate parts of the manuscript would require to be treated each on its own merits ; the primitive character of one section would prove nothing for the material as a whole.

Finally (5) we have to account for the use in these Jewish Christian texts of material from the canonical (i.e., Gentile Christian) gospels, and for the affinities which these texts show with the apocryphal literature.

In short, the new discovery may be significant, within limits yet to be determined. It requires however a considerable amount of investigation for its proper evaluation, and should not prematurely be made the basis for far-reaching claims about its importance for the history of the Christian origins.

# TABULA GRATULANTIUM

Savas Agourides, Thessalonika
K. Aland, Münster
G. W. Anderson, Edinburgh
Hugh Anderson, Edinburgh
Sagasu Arai, Yokohama
Tj. Baarda, Amsterdam
J. A. Baird, Wooster
W. Barclay, Glasgow
R. S. Barbour, Edinburgh
Allan Barr, Edinburgh
C. K. Barrett, Durham
Markus Barth, Pittsburgh
J. Christiaan Beker, Princeton
Pierre Benoit, Jerusalem
Ernest Best, St Andrews
H. D. Betz, Claremont
J. Neville Birdsall, Birmingham
E. F. F. Bishop, Redhill, Surrey
E. C. Blackman, Toronto
Josef Blinzler, Passau, Bayern
P. Bonnard, Lausanne
G. H. Boobyer, Winscombe, Somerset
Peder Borgen, Bergen
M. Bouttier, Montpellier
François Bovon, Genève
John Bowman, Melbourne
S. G. F. Brandon, Manchester
William D. Bray, Nishinomiya, Japan
British and Foreign Bible Society, London
Raymond E. Brown, Baltimore
F. F. Bruce, Manchester
Rudolf Bultmann, Marburg
B. C. Butler, Ware
A. Cabaniss, Oxford, Miss.
Jean Carmignac, Paris
H. Chadwick, Oxford
J. J. Collins, Weston
C. Colpe, Göttingen
H. Conzelmann, Göttingen
B. Corsani, Roma
C. E. B. Cranfield, Durham
O. Cullmann, Basel
N. A. Dahl, New Haven
Frederick W. Danker, St Louis
D. Daube, Oxford
J. G. Davies, Birmingham
W. D. Davies, Durham, N.C.
M. de Jonge, Leiden
I. de la Potterie, Roma
G. Delling, Halle
Albert-Marie Denis, Louvain
Erich Dinkler, Heidelberg
C. H. Dodd, Oxford
Karl Paul Donfried, Northampton, Mass.
C. W. Dugmore, Puttenham, Surrey
Jacques Dupont, Brugge
E. Earle Ellis, New Brunswick
S. Ifor Enoch, Aberystwyth
Eldon J. Epp, Cleveland
C. F. Evans, London
Owen E. Evans, Manchester
W. R. Farmer, Dallas
Erich Fascher, Berlin
A. Feuillet, Paris
Floyd V. Filson, Chicago
Bonifatius Fischer, Beuron
Gottfried Fitzer, Vienna
Joseph A. Fitzmyer, Woodstock
W. F. Flemington, Cambridge
W. Foerster, Münster
Hermann Josef Frede, Tuttlingen
G. Friedrich, Kiel
G. W. S. Friedrichsen, Washington
Robert W. Funk, Nashville
A. George, Sainte Foy-lès-Lyon
B. Gerhardsson, Lund
A. S. Geyser, Johannesburg
Charles H. Giblin, New York
F. Wilbur Gingrich, Reading, Pa.
Mark E. Glasswell, Freetown, Sierra Leone
J. Gnilka, Münster
L. Goppelt, München
Erich Grässer, Herbede
E. M. B. Green, London
Heinrich Greeven, Bochum
D. R. Griffiths, Penarth
W. K. M. Grossouw, Nijmegen
W. Grundmann, Eisenach
D. Guthrie, London
D. Y. Hadidian, Pittsburgh
Ferdinand Hahn, Kiel

Frank Hambly, Adelaide
R. J. Hammer, Birmingham
Harald Hegermann, Leipzig
Uwe-Peter Heidingsfeld, Erlangen
Martin Hengel, Tübingen
A. S. Herbert, Birmingham
James D. Hester, Redlands
A. J. B. Higgins, Leeds
David Hill, Sheffield
Toshio Hironuma, Osaka
T. Holtz, Greifswald
M. D. Hooker, London
Claus-Hunno Hunzinger, Hamburg
John C. Hurd, Toronto
Annie Jaubert, Paris
S. Jellicoe, Lennoxville
J. Jeremias, Göttingen
A. R. Johnson, Wotton-under-Edge
J. L. Jones, Philadelphia
Jakob Jónsson, Reykjavik
Klaus Junack, Münster
L. E. Keck, Nashville
G. D. Kilpatrick, Oxford
H. P. Kingdon, Bristol
A. F. J. Klijn, Groningen
Hans Kosmala, Jerusalem
Robert A. Kraft, Roslyn
Edgar M. Krentz, St Louis
Georg Kretschmar, Hamburg
Gerhard Krodel, Philadelphia
Karl Gg. Kuhn, Heidelberg
Gerard J. Kuiper, Charlotte
W. G. Kümmel, Marburg
J. Kürzinger, Eichstätt
G. E. Ladd, Pasadena
G. W. H. Lampe, Ely
F. Lang, Tübingen
P.-E. Langevin, Montreal
A. R. C. Leaney, Nottingham
R. Leivestad, Aas
X. Léon-Dufour, Lyon
Barnabas Lindars, Cambridge
Gösta Lindeskog, Åbo
E. Lohse, Göttingen
George W. H. Loudon, Pencaitland
E. Lövestam, Lund
Robert W. Lyon, Wilmore
Stanislaus Lyonnet, Roma
Ulrich Luz, Männedorf
H. K. McArthur, Hartford
J. D. McCaughey, Melbourne
G. W. MacRae, Weston
John Marsh, Oxford
I. Howard Marshall, Aberdeen
R. P. Martin, Manchester
Carlo Martini, Roma
E. Massaux, Louvain
B. A. Mastin, Bangor
H. M. Matter, Hellevoetsluis
Chr. Maurer, Bern
Ulrich Mauser, Louisville
Goro Mayeda, Tokyo
J. S. Mbiti, Kampala
Helmut Merkel, Erlangen
B. M. Metzger, Princeton
Otto Michel, Tübingen
Paul S. Minear, New Haven
C. L. Mitton, Birmingham
H. R. Moehring, Providence
Ian A. Moir, Edinburgh
J. Molitor, Bamberg
H. W. Montefiore, Cambridge
M. J. Moreton, Exeter
R. C. Morgan, Lancaster
Leon Morris, Melbourne
C. F. D. Moule, Cambridge
H. K. Moulton, Bromley, Kent
Franz Mussner, Regensburg
Hideyasu Nakagawa, Hokkaido
William Neil, Nottingham
P. Nepper-Christensen, Gylling
E. Nestle, Ulm an der Donau
Eugene A. Nida, New York
D. E. Nineham, Cambridge
Bent Noack, Birkerød
H. Odeberg, Lund
G. Ogg, Anstruther-Easter
J. C. O'Neill, Cambridge
J. J. O'Rourke, Philadelphia
E. F. Osborn, Melbourne
H. P. Owen, London
P. Parker, New York
J. R. C. Perkin, Hamilton, Ont.
W. Pesch, Mainz
Peshitta Institute, Leiden
C. Stewart Petrie, Sydney
Josef Pfammatter, Chur
Clark H. Pinnock, New Orleans
Petr Pokorný, Praha
T. E. Pollard, Dunedin
Bo Reicke, Basel
J. Reiling, Bilthoven
K. H. Rengstorf, Münster
C. R. Renowden, Lampeter
J. Reumann, Philadelphia
J. R. Richards, Carmarthen
A. Richardson, York
H. Riesenfeld, Uppsala
B. Rigaux, Bruxelles
D. W. B. Robinson, Sydney

J. M. Robinson, Claremont
K. Romaniuk, Warszawa
W. Rordorf, Neuchâtel
Eugen Ruckstuhl, Lucerne
E. T. Ryder, Peterston-super-Ely
H. Sacon, Tokyo
H. A. E. Sawyerr, Freetown, Sierra Leone
M. H. Scharlemann, St Louis
R. Schippers, Amsterdam
H. Schlier, Bonn
J. Schmid, München
H. J. Schmitt, Strasbourg
R. Schnackenburg, Würzburg
Bernadin Schneider, Tokyo
Paul Schubert, New Haven
Siegfried Schulz Küsnacht
H. Schürmann, Erfurt
Benedikt Schwank, Beuron
E. Schweizer, Zürich
O. J. F. Seitz, Gambier
Seminar für Geschichte des Urchristentums, Erlangen
J. N. Sevenster, Amstelveen
Massey H. Shepherd, Berkeley
Markos A. Siotis, Athens
Stephen S. Smalley, Ibadan
Charles W. F. Smith, Cambridge, Mass.
D. M. Smith, Delaware, Ohio
T. C. Smith, Greenville, S.C.
Gustav Stählin, Mainz
David M. Stanley, Willowdale, Ont.
E. Stauffer, Erlangen
Ludwik Stefaniak, Kraków
Krister Stendahl, Lexington, Mass.
J. S. Stewart, Edinburgh
G. Strecker, Göttingen
A. Strobel, Neuendettelsau, Mainfranken
Peter Stuhlmacher, Erlangen
J. P. M. Sweet, Cambridge
Kenzo Tagawa, Tokyo
T. M. Taylor, New York
Walter Thiele, Sigmaringen
Margaret E. Thrall, Bangor
W. Trilling, Leipzig
Etienne Trocmé, Strasbourg
E. Ullendorff, London
B. van Elderen, Grand Rapids
A. Vanhoye, Roma
B. M. F. van Iersel, Nijmegen
W. C. van Unnik, Bilthoven
Geza Vermes, Oxford
Vetus Latina Institut, Beuron
Philipp Vielhauer, Bonn
J. J. Vincent, Rochdale
A. Voegtle, Freiburg im Breisgau
Günter Wagner, Zürich
David E. Wallace, Covina
Arthur Marcus Ward, Richmond, Surrey
R. A. Ward, St John, N. B.
Peter Weigandt, Nienberge, Westf.
G. A. Weir, Roslin
A. Wikgren, Chicago
Max Wilcox, Newcastle-upon-Tyne
A. N. Wilder, Cambridge, Mass.
R. R. Williams, Leicester
R. McL. Wilson, St Andrews
Wilhelm Wuellner, Berkeley
M. Zerwick, Roma

# INDEX OF AUTHORS

# INDEX OF REFERENCES

## *Old Testament*

# *New Testament*

## *Apocrypha and Pseudepigrapha*

# *Dead Sea Scrolls*

## *Mishnah and Babylonian Talmud*



## *Jesusalem Talmud*

## *Other Jewish Writings*



## *Ancient Christian Writings*